ARCHAEOLOGICAL INVESTIGATION

Martin Carver

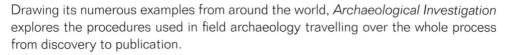

Drawing its numerous examples from around the world, *Archaeological Investigation* explores the procedures used in field archaeology travelling over the whole process from discovery to publication.

Divided into four parts, it argues for a set of principles in Part 1, describes work in the field in Part 2 and how to write up in Part 3. Part 4 describes the modern world in which all types of archaeologist operate, academic and professional. The central chapter 'Projects galore' takes the reader on a whirlwind tour through different kinds of investigation including in caves, gravel quarries, towns, historic buildings and underwater.

Archaeological Investigation intends to be a companion for a newcomer to professional archaeology – from a student introduction (Part 1), to first practical work (Part 2), to the first responsibilities for producing reports (Part 3), and in Part 4 to the tasks of project design and heritage curation that provide the meat and drink of the fully fledged professional.

The book also proposes new ways of doing things, tried out over the author's thirty years in the field and here brought together for the first time. This is no plodding manual but an inspiring, provocative, informative and entertaining book, urging that archaeological investigation is one of the most important things society does.

Martin Carver specialises in the archaeology of early Medieval Europe and field archaeology in all periods. He was a freelance archaeologist from 1972 until 1986, when he was appointed professor and head of department at the University of York. Since 2003 he has been editor of the journal *Antiquity*.

ARCHAEOLOGICAL INVESTIGATION

Martin Carver

Routledge
Taylor & Francis Group

LONDON AND NEW YORK

First published 2009
by Routledge
2 Park Square, Milton Park, Abingdon, Oxon, OX14 4RN

Simultaneously published in the USA and Canada
by Routledge
270 Madison Avenue, New York, NY 10016

Routledge is an imprint of the Taylor & Francis Group, an informa business

Typeset in Folio by
Keystroke, Tettenhall, Wolverhampton

Printed and bound in Great Britain by
MPG Books Group Ltd

British Library Cataloguing in Publication Data
A catalogue record for this book is available from the British Library

Library of Congress Cataloging in Publication Data
A catalog record for this book has been requested

ISBN 13: 978–0–415–48918–8 (hbk)
ISBN 13: 978–0–415–48919–5 (pbk)

To my friends pictured within.

TABLE OF CONTENTS

PART 2: IN THE FIELD   61

Here I review techniques and their applications for five principal types of field operation.

Chapter 4: Landscape survey   63

Chapter 5: Site survey   89

Chapter 6: Excavation   113

Chapter 7: Projects galore: Integrated Field Research   151

PART 3: WRITING UP   195

This shows how the records gathered in the field are studied and reported to researchers, to clients and to the public.

PART 4: DESIGN   333

*Armed with the basic methods of archaeological investigation, the reader is introduced to
the design process, and the context in which designs are prepared. Design feeds the research
community with new knowledge and supplies the conservation profession with new protected
resources. These interests constitute the main employment of archaeologists in the modern
world.*

LIST OF ILLUSTRATIONS

The following were reproduced with kind permission. While every effort has been made to trace copyright holders and obtain permission, this has not been possible in all cases. Any omissions brought to our attention will be remedied in future editions.

Colour plate section

Figures

Chapter 3

Chapter 4

Chapter 5

Chapter 6

Chapter 7

Chapter 8

Chapter 9

Chapter 12

Chapter 13

Chapter 14

Chapter 15

ACKNOWLEDGEMENTS

My first experience in excavation was at Winchester and on Chalton Down, places near my then home in England, and I am grateful to their directors Martin Biddle and Peter Addyman for their courteous initiation. I am also grateful to Peter Addyman for giving me my first chance as a supervisor, at Bishophill Senior in York, and to Rosemary Cramp for being my stimulating professor at Durham. I learnt a great deal from Philip Rahtz who remains for me one of the most successful excavators of the last hundred years; everything he did got finished and made sense – which must be almost unique.

For this book I have drawn inspiration from my team at BUFAU (now Birmingham Archaeology) – especially Liz Hooper, Annette Roe and Jenny Glazebrook; the Sutton Hoo team, especially Cathy Royle and Andy Copp; the Portmahomack team, especially my co-director Cecily Spall; from Field Archaeology Specialists staff, especially Justin Garner-Lahire, Cecily Spall and Nicky Toop; and my long-term field archaeology mentors and moderators, Phil Barker, Philip Rahtz, Catherine Hills, Sue Hirst and Helen Geake. In the York department of archaeology, Jane Grenville has been fun to work with, Steve Roskams has been fun to argue with and the students fun to teach, especially the MAs in Field Archaeology, Archaeology of Buildings, and Heritage Management. Madeleine Hummler has been my partner on projects in England, Scotland, France and Italy, tutor on numerous field schools, and the astute and good-natured assessor of theories and systems good, bad and crazy.

The published material has been gathered widely outside my own projects. I have drawn copiously on the authors published by *Antiquity*, and I am most grateful to them for giving permission to have many of their images reproduced. With a very few exceptions, other authors and publishers in the USA, Asia and Europe have also given me permission to use their work free of charge, with a generosity and charm that has been overwhelming.

Lastly thanks to Matthew Gibbons and Lalle Pursglove at Routledge, and to Jo Tozer in the *Antiquity* office for their help in bringing the book to the public.

Picture credits

Aarhus University Press Figs 10.13, 10.16

Academic Press Figs 11.7, 11.9

Acair Press Fig 12.11

Antiquity Publications Ltd CP 12, Figs 4.7, 4.8, 4.10, 4.11, 4.14, 5.5, 5.9, 5.10, 6.30, 9.18, 10.2, 10.11, 10.12, 10.17, 10.18, 10.19, 11.3

K. Alizadeh Fig 4.11

Sarah Allan and Yale University Press Figs 9.19, 10.3

Archaeological Data Service Fig 13.2

Arizona Archaeology Society Fig 1.4

Geoff Bailey Fig 7.2

A. A. Balkema Fig 7.11

Kurt Bänteli CP 11

Alex Bayliss Fig 11.3

Birlinn Fig 12.10

K. Borg Fig 7.9

Gian-Pietro Brogiolo CP 13, Figs 7.19, 12.7

Paolo Bruscasco Fig 10.18

Jon Cane Fig 12.8

Sue Colledge Fig 9.17

Robin Coningham Fig 4.14

Malcolm Cooper Fig 11.19

George Cowgill Fig 10.5

Gill Cruise and Richard Macphail Fig 9.12

Cultural Relics Press China CP 8, Fig 6.7

Andrew David Fig 5.10

B.J. Devereux Fig 4.10

Norman Hammond Fig 7.12

Editions de la Maison des Sciences de l'Homme Fig 7.22

Elsevier Figs 11.16–18

English Heritage Fig 4.13, 4.16, 7.20, 10.9, 11.12, 12.6

Madeleine Hummler Fig 5.13

FAS Ltd: CP 1, CP 5, CP6, CP15, Figs 4.1, 5.2, 5.12, 6.2, 6.5, 6.12, 6.13, 6.14, 6.15, 6.16, 6.23, 6.25, 6.26, 6.31, 6.32, 6.33, 7.1, 8.7, 9.1, 9.3, 9.6, 9.10, 9.20, 11.6, 11.20, 12.8, 13.5, 14.9

Antje Faustmann Fig 4.8

Helen Fenwick Fig 4.5

Andrew Fleming Fig 4.17

Glen Foard Fig 5.17

Framework Ltd. CP 14

David Frankel and Jennifer Webb CP 12

Vince Gaffney, CP 9

Attilio Galiberti Fig 6.2

Yosef Garfinkel Fig 6.30

Helen Geake and PAS Fig 4.4

HMSO Figs 7.4, 7.5

Ian Hodder and Macdonald Institute Figs 5.4, 9.22

Liz Hooper, Figs 1.10, 1.13, 1.14, 2.9, 6.1, 8.1

INRAP Fig 7.6

Irish Times Fig 14.6

Carl Knappett Fig 10.19

Jenny Glazebrook Fig 14.11

Jenny Glazebrook and East Anglian Archaeology Figs 4.19, 11.10

Claire Litt and Oxbow Books Fig 7.15

Vincent Lhomme Fig 10.2

Statens Historiska Museum, Stockholm Fig 10.4

Sofie Legrand Fig 10.11

Burghard Lohrum CP 11

Nigel Macbeth, Heritage photographer, (n.macb111@live.co.uk), CP 3, CP 4, CP 10, Figs 1.10, 2.8, 3.2, 3.9, 3.12, 3.13, 3.14, 6.11, 6.12, 6.13, 6.16, 6.17, 6.18, 6.19, 6.21, 6.23, 9.4, 9.5, 9.6, 13.6

William Marquardt Fig 7.3

Kaname Mayakawa Fig 6.28

Harold Mytum Fig 13.9

Royal Archaeological Institute Fig 12.2

Olivia Lelong Fig 12.3, 12.4, 14.8

Society for Medieval Archaeology Fig 8.8–20.

Stephen Mithen Fig 5.14

MoLAS Fig 7.21

Michael Müller-Wille Fig 6.6, 11.2

Bjorn Myrhe Fig 10.15

Alastair Northedge Fig 4.7

Mícheál O'Droma Fig 14.16

Joan Oates Fig 7.10

Laurent Olivier Fig 5.9,

Andrew Poulter Fig 5.15

Philip Rahtz Fig 1.1, 1.3, 2.1, 2.6, 12.12

Per Ramqvist Fig 6.22

RCAHMS: Fig 4.7, 5.3, 7.16

Andrew Reynolds Fig 4.3

Annette Roe Fig 6.17

Else Roesdahl Fig 7.7, 7.8

Steve Roskams Fig 6.10

Michael Schiffer Fig 6.8

Jean-Jacques Schwein Fig 14.12

Søren Sindbaek Fig 10.13

Anthony Snodgrass Fig 4.20

Society of Antiquaries of Scotland Fig 11.8

Lorraine Swann Fig 10.12

University of Texas Press Fig 7.23

Giuliano Volpe CP 7, Figs 7.13, 7.14

Wessex Archaeology Fig 5.18

Pascale Yvorra Fig 10.17

PREFACE

Before this book was a book, it was a course, and before it was a course, it was a procedure hammered out over three varied decades in the field, first in paid contract work and then in university research projects. During this time we tried everything, listened to the prehistorians and historians, the theorists and the public, kept the good and dumped the bad. It was an age of experiment and my hope is that its fruits – summarised here – will prove to be of some use to a broader constituency. I would not have this book considered prescriptive or dogmatic – I see it rather as a sketch of what worked.

I owe a great deal to the persons I have worked with as a commercial archaeologist particularly in Birmingham Archaeology and Field Archaeology Specialists Ltd, only a tithe of whom are listed. Like many others we learnt on the job and many of our systems subsequently became standardised – flattering, but not necessarily a good thing. As the reader will discover, I am a great believer in diversity and the appropriate approach. I was also stimulated by trying to teach the subject – sometimes to novices who had never before left home and sometimes to the already indoctrinated for whom there was only one way to do anything. The course, taught to field schools and to students doing archaeology at the University of York, included practical sessions that gave them a taste of survey, excavation, building recording, writing up, showing round visitors, supervising and mounting their own exhibitions. At the time of Lecture no. 1 most of them had never held a trowel; but nine weeks later they had lost much of their innocence and were ready for tougher stuff.

The book reflects the course. I start with familiar things and take a turn underground to introduce you to a sample of the hidden world of archaeological deposits and the names we give them. Then there is an account of principles, which should intersect usefully with any "history and principles" or "theory" courses (Part 1). Then we go in the field and find out what it's like out there (Part 2). As we come back indoors to do analysis and write up (Part 3) the tone gets more serious and the arguments more challenging. The last part (Part 4) deals with archaeology's most important professional activity, project design, and the social and economic theatre in which field archaeology happens. This theatre is also the one with the jobs, so it is a good place to end, and those who have read that far will be the ones who really want them.

In some ways this itinerary also reflects a life in archaeology. The Part 1 principles go with a first encounter with archaeology at university where you learn what the subject is trying to do. The Part 2 fieldwork goes with the first practical experience and one's first paid work as an archaeological labourer. Writing up (Part 3) is the concomitant of gaining a position of responsibility – such as recorder, surveyor, supervisor or director. And the preparation of the first project design (Part 4) is a sign you have arrived in the profession, whether as an academic or a commercial archaeologist.

At the end of each chapter I have placed a *Briefing*, a mixture between a tutorial and "further reading", intended as a rough guide to the rich hunting grounds of contemporary archaeological literature. This literature is voluminous and widely dispersed, and it is not obvious where to find the most useful matters relating to field archaeology. Those who are web-friendly will find another way of following the trail: we have a *Companion website* with more sources and examples. Archaeology is a visual subject and we like to see what things look like in the ground. In the pages that follow, the publishers have been generous with pictures, but on the website you will find many more.

This book is a primer, intended to start off a new generation. But my hope is that all kinds of reader will find it useful, particularly those for whom archaeology is a recreation or who deal with archaeologists in their own professional lives. Archaeology interacts with many other public activities – planning, politics, environmental science, tourism – whose practitioners may wonder what makes us tick and why we need our say. It is not that easy to know: the field archaeologist is a field marshal when designing a project, an explorer when surveying the land, a skilled labourer when digging a site, a naturalist when recording its phenomena, a scientist when analysing the results and a creative artist when painting pictures of the past. Not all of us can be all of these, all of the time. So we work in a team, and the team is famously varied, egalitarian and stimulating. And this book too addresses the heterogeneous company that sits around the campfire: the school leavers, undergraduates in anthropology, archaeology and history, anyone new to the subject (but who needs to use it) – and, best and basic, those archaeological academics and professionals not yet wholly set in their ways.

Martin Carver
Ellerton, 31 March 2009

PART 1
PRINCIPLES

A prodigious variety

Selinunte, Sicily, on a hot, hot day. A Greek temple composed of enormous blocks stands four-square on its columns. Just beside it – an untidy heap of large chunks of blinding white limestone cut into smooth geometric shapes that fit exactly to each other, face to face. There are no layers of soil: the area resembles the untidy playroom of a giant child. This is the fate of some famous architecture: it partly fell, or was demolished, dispersed and then tidied up, leaving the fragments broken and scattered or gathered into piles. And they are still there (FIG 1.1).

After a short journey north across the Tyrrhenian Sea, we arrive at Vesuvius, the volcano which erupted in AD79, burying the Roman towns of Pompeii and Herculaneum (FIG 1.2). Modern-day Ercolano is a mass of apartments stacked on

FIGURES 1.1 Temple into heap: limestone structures at Selinunte, Sicily (P.A. Rahtz and author).

FIGURE 1.2 The Roman town of Herculaneum, buried by volcanic eruption in AD79; and above it the modern town of Ercolano (author).

top of each other with the washing hanging out, overlooking streets full of cars hooting at dodging pedestrians. Ancient Herculaneum lies underneath it, with orderly straight thoroughfares and stepping stones which wagons could trundle over and people could cross. Herculaneum was overwhelmed by volcanic lava one afternoon, while its neighbour, Pompeii, was buried in ash raining from above followed by the white hot avalanche of a pyroclastic surge. Although many people got away, taking their most precious things with them, others were caught and carbonised, together with dogs, vineyards and gardens. Over these cities, the volcanic deposit lies some 10m deep. Excavated for more than two hundred years, archaeologists find mortared brick walls, the orange tiles of collapsed roofs, mosaic pavements rippled by the earth tremors that accompanied the eruption, and the occasional sad charred hollow of a human.

Further north still we can see numerous other kinds of building in the process of finishing their days. A farm shed in Herefordshire, Britain, made from a framework of stout timbers has been patched with planks and corrugated iron (FIG 1.3). After a long and neglected old age, its time is near: the timbers are rotting at the foot and lurch to one side, spilling the tiles off the roof. Soon the shed will turn into a shallow heap; the timbers will be eaten up by bugs and the iron sheets disappear into a rusty powder. What remains on the surface will be cleared away, leaving beneath it a curious imprint in the earth: long dark random stripes of rotten wood with broken sherds of tile and orange patches of decayed iron.

FIGURE 1.3 Timber-frame barn, on the way out, near Bromyard, Herefordshire (photo: P.A. Rahtz).

While the building totters, various agents like to help it on its way: people can always spot a ruin and love to fiddle with it. An Anglo-Saxon church that was falling down at Moreton on the Hill in Norfolk provided an intriguing stage set for these final years of a redundant building. Ivy and creeper encircled its round tower, slowly pulling it down by inserting tendrils and gouging out the soft mortar. Rats and mice widened every hole. Birds flew in and out of the roof-space and nested there. Inside, the ceiling was splitting and dropping down on the floor in slabs of plaster. The first plants were gaining a purchase in the cracks in the floor and in the wet patch inside the baptismal font. And someone had been attracted to this deserted romantic hideaway – possibly the homeless, but more likely the very young: no-one can modify a space as thoroughly as children building a den. Here they had pushed the pews against the north wall and lifted the font cover with its big iron spike and placed it at the east end where the altar was. Then they placed the chairs around the spike in a semi-circle. This is not how a church was used of course, and if the picture froze like this and sank back in this configuration into the earth, future archaeologists would deduce that they had found the ritual centre of a coven of spike worshippers.

Some human sites, each with its own contemporary drama, leave next to nothing on the ground. FIGURE 1.4 shows an example from Mexico, a photograph taken in 1886 of one of Geronimo's last camps before his surrender at Los Embudos. This *wickiup*

FIGURES 1.4 Geronimo's wickiup (a), and prehistoric stances left by shelters of the kind in the same terrain (b) (Arizona Historical Society).

was a shelter formed among rocky boulders out of branches and cloth. When such places are later dispersed by wind and scavengers there is nothing much left but a little oval clearing among the stones – or, if it got burnt down, a round patch of ash and partly burnt wood, like a bonfire, miles from anywhere. These ephemeral traces provide a poignant analogue for many millions of barely detectable dwellings built in the course of eventful lives throughout prehistory.

What archaeologists encounter in the ground is the end product of stories like this, stories of loss, decay and abandon. We will meet many examples in this book, but the colour plates offer a taster of their prodigious variety. Underneath the topsoil of a ploughed field, the doings of earlier people show as sets of spots and stripes (Colour Plate 1a). In well-frequented places, the debris builds up and lies deep, layer on layer (Colour Plate 1b). Modern instruments, like aerial cameras or radar, can sometimes sense these things before you see them (Colour Plate 2), but they become clearer when the soil comes off. Underground, while most structures are wispy traces, others are still robust – with mortared walls and mosaic floors (Colour Plate 7). Like buildings, our mortal remains also survive in very variable forms (Colour Plates 6a–c). Some, like the inhabitants of Pompeii, are now just a void in the baked volcanic ash. In the bog bodies of northern Europe acid has eaten out all the bones, but the flesh is preserved, tanned like a great leather bag. In Egypt and Mongolia, bodies were wrapped up in cloth by their burial parties, and survive as mummies, fibrous and desiccated. For people buried on chalky soils, the flesh quickly goes, but the bones survive clean and sharp – a white skeleton. On sandy acid soils, the bones disappear but the flesh may leave its signature on the grave floor – a stain or a rounded sand-shape. The ingenuity of the modern excavator can conjure up a striking image from the most ephemeral of traces: as an example I show a leather chariot in a Chinese tomb, evoked in three dimensions from the surviving film of paint that once covered the now vanished timbers (Colour Plates 8a–c).

Archaeological investigation starts here, with the pieces of the past, life's *disjecta membra*, the stuff. This is what we study. Making sense of this structured dirt, this materiality, is what gives us our mission, and our first task is to appreciate why we have what we have. All these cultural remains belong to people who deserve a history, but they do not equally leave us one. Some build to last, others build for the moment. Some seek immortality by wrapping up mummies and placing them in enormous tombs, others throw bodies deliberately or carelessly into bogs, or into holes in the ground. Other people die in accidents, never to be found or commemorated. Some take a lot of trouble to defeat time, and others do not. The survival of things is also clearly dependent on the type of soil in which things are buried. Chalk – well-drained and alkaline – is kind to bone; sand, well-drained and acid, is not. Anaerobic conditions, i.e. deposits that exclude air, like a bog, inhibit microbes so that organic materials are preserved. But the acid still dissolves the minerals, like the calcium salts of which bone is made. Under the ground, things are never alone for long. Humic soil is a mass of busy micro-organisms, digesting everything. Worms swallow the soil and spit it out, over and over again. Their tireless mixing raises the ground surface, until it climbs over the great flat stones of megaliths, buries Roman mosaics, creeps up the sides of stone crosses and over the steps of medieval churches. Beetles, rats and dogs like to dig and rummage in bodies. Pillagers dig them up to take the grave goods. Farmers plough the graves, rubbing down the first 25cm and mixing it up with the ploughsoil. Even when archaeological sites are deserted, they do not entirely die. They have a long and varied afterlife in which plants, animals and humans – archaeologists eventually among them – will intervene.

Methods of study

The archaeologist Michael Schiffer has made a comprehensive study of the factors that affect the creation of sites, factors which he called "Site Formation Processes", dividing them into natural and cultural agents, and distinguishing between the "systemic context"–the site when occupied, and the "archaeological context" – the site when buried and then rediscovered by us. The archaeological task is to use the one to read the other and deduce how the "transforms" occurred. It is handy to have a list of the factors that do the transforming (FIG 1.5) and to imagine the various stages that the site passes through as it gets buried (FIG 1.6). Here I propose five stages for this hypothetical journey: (1) before anything happens, (2) during occupation, (3) at abandonment, (4) when the site gets buried, and (5) after that. This model is not so much a straight transformation from one state to another, as a continuous itinerary of decay, suffered by all sites everywhere, in which at a given moment archaeologists may intervene with their trowels and shovels. This "intervention" may occur at any stage: we meet the oldest sites when they are well buried; but more recent sites may be examined just after they are abandoned, and some operations, like the recording of lived-in buildings, are carried out while the patient, so to speak, is still conscious. After a site has been visited by an archaeologist, it continues to deteriorate towards an ultimate state of nothing, unless actively prevented – the task of conservation. Every site in the world is therefore on the move to oblivion, fast or slow dependent on the measures we are able to apply. This management of our archaeological resources is the largest single activity in the archaeology business, and provides the context in which we all work. But we are not quite ready to talk about that yet (see Chapter 15).

It is worth trying to understand how sites are transformed, so as to understand more surely what we find, and the study can be approached in a number of ways. As a result of being enticed by research or forced by rescue work into many strange places, archaeologists can now call on a large body of *empirical knowledge* (FIG 1.7). We know that sites perched on top of rocky places suffer greatly from weather and subsequent visitors, both conquerors and climbers; the deposits leave little imprint on the rock and much of the useful material has been chucked down the slope. River

Pre-deposition

SUBSOIL:	pH – porosity
TOPOGRAPHY:	strata traps
CULTURE:	stone/ceramic vs. timber/leather

Post-deposition

NATURAL ATTRITION:	bacterial – chemical – vegetation – burrowing animals – frost – flood
HUMAN ATTRITION:	curate behaviour – vandalism – stone robbing – cultivation – digging (all kinds including archaeology)

FIGURE 1.5 Factors that affect the formation of archaeological deposits.

Stage	Factor	Properties	Affecting
Stage I: **Before deposition**	**Topography, subsoil**	Steepness and shape of slope, pH, porosity	Depth of deposit Preservation
Stage II: **During occupation**	**Culture**	Structures Burials	Preservation Visibility of behaviour
Stage III **At abandonment**	**Curation, recycling, scavenging, weathering**	Removal, dispersal, erosion	Reduction of diagnostic assemblage Visibility of features
Stage IV **The site gets buried**	**Sediment transport, humus, dumping**	Glacial wash, alluvium	Burial, addition, displacement or removal of layers
Stage V: **After burial**	**Biochemical degradation**	Differentially, of organic and inorganic materials	Preservation of materials
	Deflation	Uncovers a site through wind action	Displacement or removal of layers
	Tree-roots and plant roots	Dislodge walls and alter deposits	Reduced understanding of features
	Burrowing animals	Make tunnels through deposits	Reduced understanding of features
	Ploughing	Scrambles strata, pulls artefacts and biota to the surface	Destruction or reduced understanding of features
	Digging	Cuts into strata, redeposits finds	Destruction or reduced understanding of features
	Looting	Damages features and removes finds	Destruction or reduced understanding of features
	Archaeological excavation	Removes, but records strata and finds	Destruction, but increased understanding of features

FIGURE 1.6 What happens to history: the decay and dispersal of human settlements.

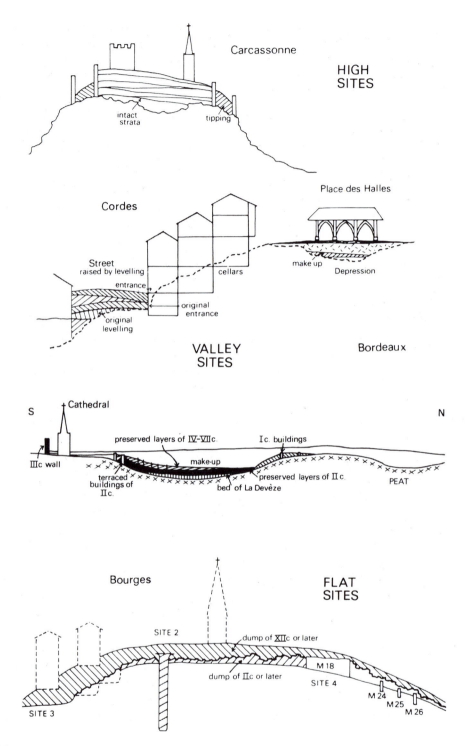

FIGURE 1.7 Trapping strata: some French examples (drawn by Liz Hooper).

valleys, by contrast, build up deposits, although they partly flush them out again. Rivers running through towns have often been subsequently canalised (to prevent the flooding), so their earlier deposits remain in situ, sealed in damp and often anaerobic conditions on old river banks. This has produced the set of northern European early town sites with famously rich organic preservation – Dublin on the River Liffey, York on the Ouse, Bergen on a Norwegian fjord, Bordeaux on the Garonne – the 'organic crescent'.

In general, European successive urban occupants have not been kind to each other, undertaking periodic demolition and levelling on a massive scale. Those who lived lightly, in timber, leather and cloth, like the people of the British Dark Ages, get sandwiched between the stone, concrete and brick constructions of the Roman and Medieval periods. The redevelopment of towns is nothing new. The later city dwellers love to dig out the remains of the earlier, levelling and terracing and recycling the building materials. Archaeologically speaking, long-lived towns are turbulent and noisy and hard to read. On the other hand, if these sequences can be resolved and decoded they are historically precious, being full of incident.

Sites can also build up deep deposits quickly on the flat, particularly when people build in mud brick as in western Asia (FIG 1.8). Every few decades the mud-brick houses crumble beyond repair or need replacing anyway, and a new building is placed on the broken clay platform of the old. So the settlement rises, and over thousands of years of occupation can become a veritable hill – locally a *tell* (Arabic), a *tepe* (Iranian) or a *höyük* (Turkish). These busy sites with their long sequences and depths of 30m and more, are the jewels of the Neolithic and Bronze Age in Turkey, Iraq and Syria, the lands of ancient Mesopotamia. They are rich in artefacts, but seeing and defining the buildings is no doddle: the edges of the bricks have to be distinguished from the mass of dry mud that contains them (FIG 1.9).

To these observations drawn from each others' experience we can add other kinds of study that draw on analogies from modern life, like the fate of a church and a barn that we just saw in England. This *ethnoarchaeology* occurs all around us. In communities that preserve traditional practices, we can see people digging cesspits, burning manure or spreading pottery (with their organic refuse) on the fields. The occupants of every type of site start forming its deposits while they are still there. Few sites are built once and abandoned once. They go on being built and abandoned piecemeal, and the inhabitants, depending on their predilections, dig holes for food waste or pile it into middens and allow the dogs to scatter it, one year's rubbish giving way to the next until the origins of a place have all but disappeared; and this is happening in a living place. New people occupying an old site often begin by helping themselves to the reusable debris left behind by their predecessors, demolishing sheds and digging out redundant walls to obtain building materials. Cemeteries are used for centuries, gradually changing their layout as new people die and earlier people are forgotten. So grave cuts grave, and old bones end up in the backfill of the newly dead. Many of these things can be seen in action today, the world over.

FIGURE 1.8 Archaeological strata viewed from the side. Director Mihriban Özbaşaran shows visitors the 30m section through the tell at Aşıkli höyük, Turkey, 10,000–3000BC, with a sequence of houses with hearths, built one over the other at the same place (centre top of image) (author).

FIGURE 1.9 Mud brick coursing of a building on the tell at Aşıkli höyük, Turkey (author).

A third way of studying formation processes is to set up an *experiment* and see if you can reproduce the observed effect: erect a timber building – and then burn it down to see how much ash and charcoal is produced and where it lies. Puzzled by the "sandmen" at Sutton Hoo (see Colour Plate 6), we buried meat, bread, wood, cloth and goose feathers in a hole, and dug them up again seven years later to see how rapidly they disappeared in the sandy soil. The answer was "fast": the meat had turned into black clay and the bread into brown silt. We also built a burial mound of the local soil and sand, to see how it fast it eroded and flattened. The answer was, it didn't. After construction, the mound and its ditch quickly stabilised with wild plants, and none of its make up eroded into the ditch, even under heavy rain. This helped with the interpretation of the two main ancient fills found in the excavated barrow ditches: they could not be the result of "erosion"; the lower layer had arrived during construction of the mound and the upper layer during subsequent ploughing (FIG 1.10).

A fourth package of investigation on the formation of strata uses *analytical approaches* and is focused on the minute remains of decayed organic materials and the crumbs of earlier soils. *Microstratigraphy* identifies fragments of artefacts and bone, stalks and leaves and other organic matter under the microscope. *Micromorphology* takes a slice of soil and soaks it in resin and bakes it solid, so its structure can be microscopically inspected. Not only do both these techniques identify the small scraps of material that are present, but also they use them to write a history of the deposit: how a forest had been cleared away, how a soil went sour, how bracken and heath must have been gathered, how something made of lead – a pipe or a coffin – was present at one time, leaving insoluble lead salts in the soil. Puzzling deposits known as *dark earth* occur in European towns in the post-Roman period (and intermittently after that). Confronting this problem, soil expert Richard Macphail has

FIGURES 1.10 Site formation experiment: a reconstructed burial mound at Sutton Hoo freshly made (a); and (b) the "stone roll" of an ancient mound seen in section (N. Macbeth).

shown that they are formed by combinations of hearths, ash, imported soils and cultivation.

Of course all this detective work doesn't just give us a soil history, it gives us some real history as well. The trick is to translate the fragments in the analytical samples into human events, and for this purpose modern comparisons can be useful. Starting from a modern site (we will already know a certain amount about it), we can analyse the soils for their minute contents: seeds, insects, chemical properties. These are the "decay products" of activities that have become invisible, but in this case we have some idea what they decayed from. Researcher Helen Smith plotted the organic and mineral decay products in an abandoned farmstead in the western isles of Scotland, finding that different farm areas – cattle sheds, middens, grain dryer, kail yards and gardens left different "signatures" in the form of mollusca, phytoliths, acidity and magnetic susceptibility (see Chapter 9 for more). Thus, in theory, one could make and interpret a chemical map of an area where there was absolutely nothing left to see. This is where the future is leading: not just more careful definition and recording of what we can see, but methods of enhancement which will help us to detect and map what is no longer there. The new science of proteomics is discovering how to detect proteins and DNA that remain in the soil, providing almost invisible evidence of the humans, animals and plants that once passed that way (Chapter 9 has more).

Now we can give an answer to the question: how do archaeological sites get buried? Some don't: you can still walk into Greek temples (as at Selinunte) or walk along the via Appia in Rome. Those that do may be overwhelmed by volcanic eruption or a flood which buried them many metres deep. Others simply bury themselves: people spread their rubbish and building debris about, and each generation digs itself into the leavings of the one before. When people dig pits and fill them up again, there is always soil left over, and the net effect is to make the ground level rise. In a graveyard, worms and people steadily raise the ground surface so that it seems that the graves of our ancestors lie ever lower as the centuries pass. Archaeological sites are alive; they are forever being modified, above ground by wind and weather, and below ground by air and water and a thousand different organisms which rot the works of humans and transport the pieces up and down. When we arrive to write our history we intervene in an earthy story that is still happening.

Defining archaeological strata

So two histories lie behind the deposits that archaeologists find: the history of the ancient people we seek, and the history of the deposit, our unedited documents. Seen from the top, the deposit is like a map in which events cut into each other (FIG 1.11; Colour Plate 1a); from the side it looks like a stack of papers, flat, tilted or crumpled (FIG 1.8; Colour Plate 1b). Archaeological deposits are often compared with geological deposits because of how they look like from the side, but there the resemblance ends. In geology, a number of layers of rock form on top of each other, like the layers of dead shellfish at the sea bottom. Subsequently heaved up, sheared off or eroded – all by natural processes – they present a fossil system, the generality or uniformity of which can be recognised from place to place. But archaeological strata are actually not like that. A small proportion are naturally formed, but the vast majority are dumped by people, who are anything but natural or uniform in their actions. They dig holes, make heaps, put up buildings, knock them down, set fire to them, throw bones about and then pick up all their belongings and march off to build a new site somewhere else. Rocks don't do this. A series of roads or floors renewed in the same place may occasionally make horizontal layers, like the layers of a cake (or like geological strata). But generally archaeological strata are very much more turbulent, still in a state of formation, and the key targets of recognition are not the layers, such as they are, but the anomalies that lie in them and under them.

The difference is the difference between natural and human phenomena: there is a finite number of chemical elements, minerals and geological formations, and a consistency in their behaviour; but human expressions are limitless – the number of types

FIGURE 1.11 Archaeological strata viewed from the top: a ditch, cutting plough marks, which cut the sandy white subsoil (FAS Ltd).

of archaeological strata and the way they relate to each other in the ground is as numerous as all the sentences that humans could ever utter in any language. There is also a marked difference between the dynamic of geology – very slow and a long time ago – and the more restless formation of archaeological sites, especially those of the last 10,000 years. These continue to change during our lifetimes, such that the archaeologists of one generation may really see something different to their predecessors on the same site.

Archaeological sites consist of dirt generated from the bedrock beneath, plus whatever the inhabitants have chosen to import from elsewhere. The older a site is, the cleaner, the more "natural" it tends to look. In the Palaeolithic, there is much rejoicing at finding a flint tool or a bone among the crusty clean sand. By the 20th century the sites are full of bottles, tin cans and eventually plastic. We loosely describe the material that we dig up as "dirt" (US), "earth" (UK), "soil" or "spoil". The first two words are general and conversational; but the second two have more specific meanings: *spoil* is what's left over after digging – the bit you don't keep: *soils* are naturally formed deposits influenced by the vegetation they carry, and as such have a science of their own – soil science. Humans can be involved in the soil-forming process, by cultivating the ground or abandoning it; but the main business is performed by roots, animals, worms, bacteria and chemistry, and is exceedingly complex.

Soil scientists map their world in horizons (FIG 1.12). The "R" horizon is the bedrock, with its weathered surface, C. Above this is the subsoil, a mixture of material weathered from below and leached from above, the B horizons. The A horizons above this are the soils proper. To the untutored archaeologist these look like earth, darker above and lighter below, with the "natural" at the bottom (i.e. the C horizon). But soil

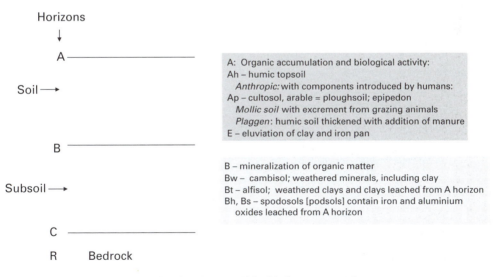

FIGURE 1.12 Soil horizons (after Goldberg and MacPhail 2006, 48–67).

scientists analyse these deposits, using (for example) "weight after ignition" which measures how much organic material it contains, and micromorphology, in which the contents and their structure are sampled and viewed under the microscope (more in Chapter 9). These methods reveal particular events: that the soil once supported a forest, that it was pasture, that it has been cultivated, that it was over-farmed and became a spodosol, white and infertile. They also emphasise an important message: some deposits are still "alive": they can change their character underground. Archaeologists and soil scientists make common cause at a "buried soil", e.g. a cultivated soil captured under a burial mound.

A more difficult question concerns the myriad other types of archaeological deposit: how useful is soil science for them? "Increasingly" is the answer. But in the meantime, while soil scientists would like us to be more scientific with our descriptions and analyses, archaeologists, aware of the variety of deposits and their highly artificial character, are not sure where this will lead. Defining every archaeological deposit with scientific precision will generate a great deal of data; but not yet a great deal of meaning.

The variation in strata is not only found from place to place, but within the same place. FIG 1.13 sketches something of the typical character of the archaeological deposits

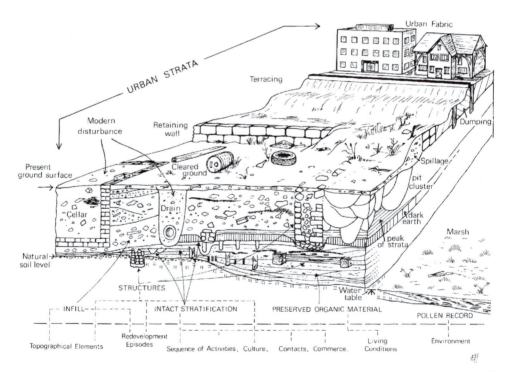

FIGURE 1.13 A slice of urban strata (drawn by Liz Hooper).

under a town, and their different historical assets. Organic preservation is encouraged by waterlogging, so that wood and plants survive at the lowest parts, beneath the water table. As living intensifies, people dig more and more pits, churning up the previous layers and making them hard to read. Major development means deep foundations, cutting away everything down to the natural subsoil on which they need to rest. Above ground, parts of early buildings may survive embedded in later ones. Each period of time is different in the way it appears and the way it looks now, and the sequence in which one period gave way to the next has to be disentangled one from the other. It is not just a matter of depth, with the oldest at the bottom and the most recent at the top. A deposit is like a big artefact carrying its history enmeshed within it. It cannot just be dug; it must be carefully dissected. The natural deposits (a marsh for example) contain pollen that reports on the environment. The deposits laid down by humans should report on buildings, on the pottery used, on the animals exploited (from the bones), and by extension on the crafts practised and the standard of living of the craftsmen. The rewards of turning mud and stones into stories are very great, but the story is only as good as its vocabulary. What kind of a language can we use to describe and discuss such a garrulous hotch-potch of material?

Archaeological vocabulary

Geology and soil science are useful friends, but neither offers archaeology an intellectual home. They expect uniformities that we cannot deliver, a consistency of meaning that is not our forte. We are too bound into the vagaries of human behaviour and individuality; our raw material rarely repeats, and the differences are as intriguing as the similarities. On the other hand, undisciplined descriptions and flights of fancy are no use either; these won't convince historians or allow other archaeologists to know what we saw. We have to invent our own language for the deposit, working painstakingly through its local vocabulary and grammar.

This archaeological language is in widespread use but has no dictionary; newcomers find it baffling and practitioners manage to confuse each other by using the same word to mean different things, or worse, by assuming they know the meaning without waiting for the definition. The world is a big place, and archaeological language is very varied. The best default is to use the language you know, define its meaning and hope that it will turn out to be useful to readers. My Glossary at the end of this book contains terms that I have used or heard of for 30 years in western Europe, and what I take them to mean. Now I need to define the key terms we will need for the argument that follows.

Let's start by defining the smallest thing we can see – a grain of sand, a fragment of charcoal, which I call a *component*. We continue by grouping components together in families that appear homogenous or related, and I call these *contexts*. They come in many shapes and sizes – lying flat like a mosaic floor, dished down into a pit, a vertical dark shaft showing where a post once was, a pile of stones, a rusty smear, a human skeleton, a row of tiles. All these are contexts. They are different on every site, and on any single site they rarely look the same. Deciding that a bunch of mud and stones makes a context is not just the result of observation or recognition, it is an act of definition. As well as defining the shape of a context, we try to discover exactly what it is made of, its components – and what put it there, its formation process. Contexts also contain components that you can't see, chemical compounds for instance; when detected these are assigned to the context they were found in. Of the visible components, the parts you keep are collectively "the finds" or "the objects" or "the assemblage"; they include things made by humans (*artefacts*) and things that are made naturally (bones, seeds – collectively here *biota*).

Every context has interfaces with other contexts, horizontal, vertical, sloping, merging, and these show that some succeeded each other, while others are contemporary. Although archaeological and geological formation processes are different, our common roots in the 19th century have led to the adoption of geological terms which we still use: *stratification* for the physical pile of strata and *stratigraphy* for the act of working out (and drawing up) what we believe the sequence was. The word *strata* is sometimes applied to the contexts themselves. *Contexts* are supposed to represent events of some kind, like dumping a spade full of earth, events which occurred together or followed each other. And we can use their assemblage or their stratigraphic relationships, and usually both working together, to put them into a sequence. This provides the basic story of what happened on a site (more on this in Chapter 11).

The vast majority of archaeological contexts were laid down as a result of human actions: grave-digging, pit-digging or wall-building for example, and these human activities represent the key episodes in the story we are trying to write. One action generates many contexts (the grave, the body, the fill), so the human action we seek to define is a property underlying a *set of contexts*. Some groups of contexts which belong together spatially also have this other property which can be interpreted in human terms and must be captured too: the grave-ness of a grave, the wall-ness of a wall, the pit-ness of a pit. Many terms are used for these groups of contexts – I use the term *feature*; other readers may have already encountered terms such as groups and blocks, which can refer to the same thing. The trick is to have a term which is suitably neutral, since in many cases we will know that humans did something, but we won't yet know what.

Examples of features are illustrated in FIG 1.14. Each feature is a family of contexts: the edge of a pit and the fill of a pit; the edge of a post-hole, the ghost of the post, its packing; the shaft of a well, and its lining and the silt, broken crockery and dead cat that lie at the bottom. Each of these things has its own record too, so that our ideas are built up in tiers like a language – letters, words, sentences, phrases and ideas. Many features are dug in, like pits and foundations – but not all. Some rise above the surface – prominently, like ruins, or slightly, like heaps of midden. Some

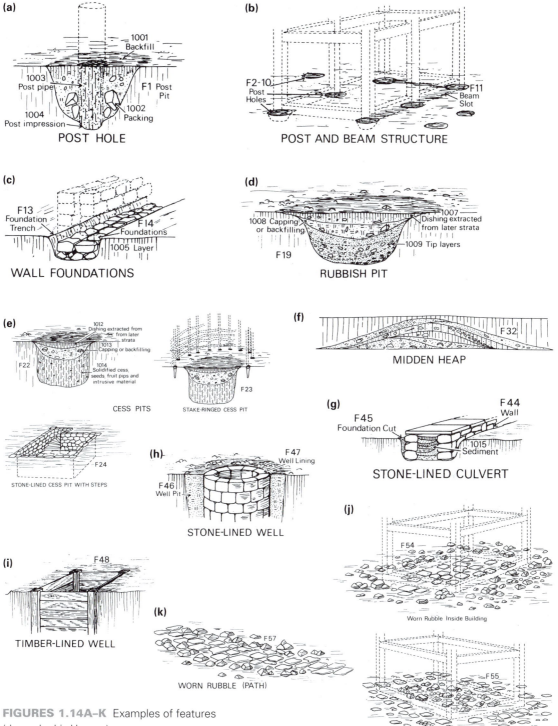

(a) 1001 Backfill · 1003 Post pipe · F1 Post Pit · 1004 Post impression · 1002 Packing · **POST HOLE**

(b) F2-10 Post Holes · F11 Beam Slot · **POST AND BEAM STRUCTURE**

(c) F13 Foundation Trench · F14 Foundations · 1005 Layer · **WALL FOUNDATIONS**

(d) 1008 Capping or backfilling · 1007 Dishing extracted from later strata · 1009 Tip layers · F19 · **RUBBISH PIT**

(e) 1012 Dishing extracted from from later strata · 1013 Capping or backfilling · F22 · 1014 Solidified cess, seeds, fruit pips and intrusive material · **CESS PITS** · F23 · **STAKE-RINGED CESS PIT** · F24 · **STONE-LINED CESS PIT WITH STEPS**

(f) F32 · **MIDDEN HEAP**

(g) F45 Foundation Cut · F44 Wall · 1015 Sediment · **STONE-LINED CULVERT**

(h) F47 Well Lining · F46 Well Pit · **STONE-LINED WELL**

(i) F48 · **TIMBER-LINED WELL**

(j) F54 · Worn Rubble Inside Building · F55 · Worn Rubble Outside Building

(k) F57 · **WORN RUBBLE (PATH)**

FIGURES 1.14A–K Examples of features (drawn by Liz Hooper).

are identified from the merest traces like the remains of Geronimo's wickiup – arrangements of stones, imprints in the rubble.

The process of grouping stratigraphic units into sets can be taken further. Features may also be defined into sets – a row of posts, for example, may be interpreted as a fence. This set of features may be further defined as a *structure*. And a set of structures, related in space and time, make a settlement; and a set of settlements can be defined as a landscape – and so on (more of this in Chapter 10). There is nothing to stop us making as many concepts as we may find helpful, because these are not facts, but acts of definition carried out by an archaeologist with his or her nose to the ground. They are designed to help make the underground world comprehensible, starting with the unambiguous (a grain of sand) and building up using defined contexts, features and structures, each tier with increasing amounts of interpretation. We will need to revisit these ideas when we see how excavations are recorded (in Chapter 6, pp. 139–41).

Conclusion

Any attempt to define a framework for our subject must start with these remains of the buried past, the stuff. Fragments of ruined buildings, cracked flints, broken pots and layers of clay, sand or peat are what field investigators set out to decode. This detritus is our raw material, and its study is what makes us different from historians and anthropologists. We can borrow their agenda and theories and political positioning all we wish, but in the end the job is to interpret the past's physical remains. All method and theory spring from this challenge: translating mud and stones into people and their histories.

There are two principal messages to take forward for the argument that follows: first, that archaeological sites are astonishingly varied, from period to period and from place to place in the world. Some are rich and robust, others ephemeral and elusive; but all the people who lived in them equally deserve a history – and it is the archaeologists' job to give them one. This brings us to the second message: that once we know what we might be missing, it is our task to find out how to make it visible. In other words, success in archaeological investigation depends both on what has survived and what we do to it. It should be, or will become, fairly obvious that there cannot be, must not be, any standard way of doing fieldwork. If we are to get the most information out of what lies in the ground we must imagine what we cannot see, as well as noting what we can. Imagination, intuition and observation then join forces.

Briefing

The way that **archaeological deposits** relate to their landscape (or "sites to their setting") was explored in Vita-Finzi's 1978 classic. Since then the study of **formation processes** (how archaeological sites, deposits and strata form) has expanded at both the macro and micro scale, led by Schiffer 1987. Large-scale overviews about how sites relate to their environment can be found under the heading **geoarchaeology**, with recent monographs by Barham and Macphail 1995, Rapp and Hill 1998, French 2003 and Goldberg and Macphail 2006. The entertaining Gregory Retallack 2001 shows how **soils** form, are classified and what organisms do to them, although you have to wait until Chapter 21 for the arrival of humans. He even shows us soils on other planets, where archaeologists have yet to venture. Special studies of the more famous **organisms** that like to rework deposits are Darwin 1888, Atkinson 1957, 1985 and Gresham 1961 (earthworms), Davies 1959 (termites) and Shafer et al 1997 (clams). For the decay processes of the human body (aka **taphonomy**), see Henderson 1987 (and other papers in Boddington et al 1987), Millard 2001, Nicholson 2001, and Haglund and Sorg 2002.

Methods of study

Schiffer's "processes" (1987) collects several projects, empirical, ethnographic, experimental and analytical and has inspired new ones. Many outdoor archaeologists feel that **empirical** studies (i.e. the lessons of experience) are the only reliable way to understand strata formation; see for example Wood and Johnson 1982 (natural agents in disturbance), Scholfield 1991 (artefact scatters on open land), Bell et al 1992 (erosion of sites) and for urban deposits, M. Carver 1983b, 1987, 1993 ('organic crescent') and Kenward and Hall 2000. For examples of **ethnographic** studies of deposit formation, Cameron and Tomkin 1993, David and Kramer 2001, Eidt 1984, Rothschild et al 1993, Seymour 2009. Renowned British subjects of the **experimental** method are the earthworks constructed in the 1960s and still going strong: Evans and Limbrey 1974, Bell et al 1996. **Analytical** approaches are preferred by soil scientists: Barham and Macphail 1995, French 2003 and Courty, Goldberg and Macphail 1990, and Goldberg and Macphail 2006. Other promising avenues in the study of how archaeological deposits form are **geochemistry**, Whitmer et al 1989, Gilbertson et al 1996, Banerjee 2008, **microstratigraphy**, Matthews et al 1994, Matthews et al 1997 and **micromorphology:** Kubiena 1953 (to whom we owe the kubiena box, see Chapter 9), Matthews et al 1994, 1996, French 2003; Courty, Goldberg and Macphail 1990, and Goldberg and Macphail 2006. The mysterious urban **dark earth** has been decoded by Richard Macphail (Macphail 1994, Macphail et al 2003, Goldberg and Macphail 2006, 271 and passim), making good use of micromorphology.

Defining archaeological strata; **stratification**, Lyell 1830–33 (the basis for geology), Harris 1989 and Roskams 2001, Chapters 9 and 13 adapt the geological idea for archaeology. *Archaeological vocabulary* is mostly passed on by word of mouth, not necessarily with the virtue of consistency. The **feature** has had a long and continuous history in US archaeology (see Hester et al 1997, 120 for modern definitions). The **context** was defined in York in 1972, and refined in London (MOLAS 1994, Roskams 2001). For earlier championing of the **multi-conceptual** systems used in this book, see M. Carver 1979b, 1999a.

2 APPROACHES

What do we want from fieldwork?

Into the underground world of archaeological strata have plunged a variety of diggers, some of them burglars, some adventurers, some historians and some never quite sure which they were. A proper account of this experimental prelude belongs in another book, and we will start here at the point where investigators first revealed their archaeological intentions, by publishing them as such. Early archaeological excavators did a lot of damage, but they were clumsy rather than villainous: they emptied tombs and cut trenches across Roman camps in the hope of retrieving objects or cutting themselves a slice of history; they drove into the ground nose-first in a procedure best described by the fine Australian word *fossicking* (FIG 2.1) – rummaging and

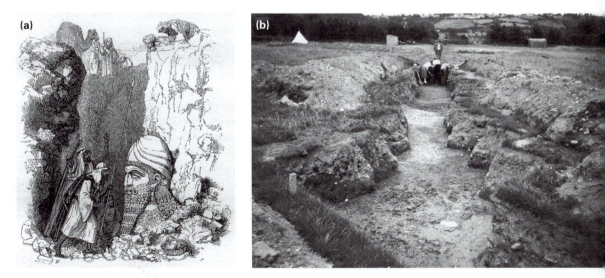

FIGURE 2.1 Approaches 1: Fossicking. (a) "Discovery of the giant head" at Nimrud, Iraq, 1840s (Layard 1854, I, 66) and (b) speculative trenching at Caerleon, Wales in the 1950s (P.A. Rahtz).

gouging in the hope of seeing something. Austen Layard, who trenched Nineveh (or what he thought was Nineveh) and Heinrich Schliemann who trenched Troy (or what he thought was Troy) meant well. They knew, as all have since, that the purpose of field archaeology is to learn about the past, to learn about people, their experiences on earth, their behaviour, their beliefs, their diet, their politics, the plains and forests and wild life where they lived and the other peoples that they attempted to control. The objective is to open windows on to empires and self-proclaimed greatness, and onto hovels, cruelty and unremarked misery. We go out in pursuit of a million stories and/or the grand process of time. All fieldworkers probably agree, very generally, about this objective; but how to achieve it is a different question.

Leaving behind the perpetrators of plunder or the wiggly trench (FIG 2.1), British archaeologists like to claim General Pitt Rivers as the instigator of systematic excavation, and praise his apparently objective stance (FIG 2.2). One quote characterises the principle: "Every detail should be recorded, in a manner most conducive of

FIGURE 2.2 Record vs. inquiry: (a) Pitt Rivers and (b) Petrie.

FIGURE 2.3
The forest and the trees,
A.V. Kidder.

reference. . . it ought to be the chief object of an excavator to reduce his personal equation to a minimum." This well-intentioned call for detachment and precision has been taken some way beyond its meaning – as if "every detail" was there for the finding, rather than caused by the methods of the General himself. Like other excavators, Pitt Rivers was simply recording the results of what he chose to reveal. Better heralds of modernity were Flinders Petrie (FIG 2.2) and Alfred Kidder (FIG 2.3) who both recognised that the real relationship between the archaeologists and their material was a creative one: "A man does not find anything he does not look for," remarked Petrie, with disturbing insight; and Kidder described the dilemma inside every digger's head, as he seeks to navigate between the thicket of detail and the primrose path of conjecture. It is a battle between looking without properly seeing, and seeing without properly looking.

Empirical to reflexive: five approaches

Since there are potentially as many approaches to archaeological investigation as there are archaeologists, it will be simplest to parade my own perceptions to show how I have arrived at the one about to be recommended and described in this book, which is of course also a prisoner of its own time. Leaving aside the fossicker as Approach no.1, I offer five others: the historical, the empirical, the processual, the reflexive and the evaluative. Each has had its own book, and some several, so I will offer the slenderest of summaries before leaving you at the mercy of Approach no. 6 (which is mine).

I use the term *empirical* to mean "knowledge based on experience", which in field archaeology maps onto the idea of digging without asking questions, in order "to see what's there". Phil Barker, arch-exponent of empirical field archaeology, decided that asking what was there, or what had happened there, was the only valid question one may ask of a site (FIG 2.4). He hated all the trenches that other archaeologists had cut across Roman Wroxeter in pursuit of their pet theories. Why have a pet theory at all? For him the archaeological site was like a series of newspapers or carpets laid over each other, and cutting slices through them would show you nothing but disconnected shreds. He advocated large areas (*area excavation*) and the detailed digging of everything (*total excavation*), even parts that were not thought significant to any research programme – because they might be one day. He claimed success at Wroxeter by mapping the imprint of a large vanished timber-built settlement of the 5th century settlement, otherwise invisible, on top of the ruins of the Roman baths basilica. He could also claim success in rescue work. Early commercial archaeologists

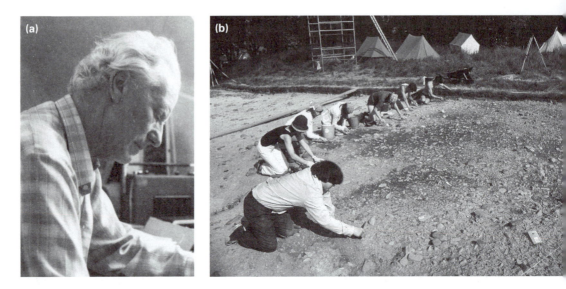

FIGURE 2.4 Approaches 2: the empirical (a) P.A. Barker and (b) excavations at Hen Domen, Wales in the 1970s.

liked his approach: it implied that "everything" that was to be destroyed should be recorded. And it implied that it was to be dug and recorded with great precision: small-scale, messy archaeology was next to useless. He set standards: archaeology must be very neat, immaculately clean, precisely defined and recorded in detail. Nothing else will do, and for those of us who learnt our trade in the late 20th century there can be no going back on this principle. Barker was an art teacher before he became an archaeologist, and his approach was to conjure a picture out of a sea of stony rubble by brushing and trowelling it – like a painter with a brush and a palette knife. And as in an old oil painting, picture lay over picture in his mind, offering a sequence of scenes frozen in time.

Look in contrast at the approach known as the *processual* (FIG 2.5). Here the goal is to use field archaeology to reveal patterns of behaviour, as in a social science. The main instrument used by social scientists is the questionnaire – get enough of them filled in, review the collected data statistically – and eureka! you discover that a significant number of retired colonels live in Bagshot. Applied to field archaeology, the questionnaire becomes a *sample*: the earth is a fossilised map of behaviours and social systems and we can get an insight into how they work using small pits and trenches, windows into the system. These windows, also known as "samples" can be *bore-holes*, e.g. small round holes drilled into a peat bog to record the sequence of plants; or *quadrats*, measuring 1×1m, spread at equal or at random intervals over the land; or *transects*, narrow strips, metres or kilometres long, laid across the landscape. These sample areas may be applied both to digging and surface collection. The chronicles of behaviour and the changing systems revealed by this method of

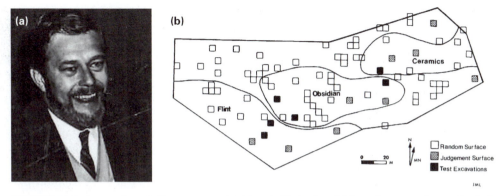

FIGURE 2.5 Approaches 3: the processual (a) Lewis Binford and (b) random sampling at Çayönü, Turkey, 1960s (Redman 1987).

inquiry are designed to lead to the determination of processes, processes governing social systems and the way they change – thus *processualism*. Lewis Binford, who promoted this ambitious procedure, felt that it would only work with careful design: frame a question, work out how to address it by cutting sample trenches, collect the data, analyse it to seek patterns, and then explain the patterns. Then a new system (a model) could be proposed, which should result in better defined patterns – but these need to be tested and so we start again. He felt that the samples should be placed at random, to give every aspect of the past an equal chance to be found. So, while a total excavation looks like one big carpet of rubble and soil, a sample excavation looks like a field full of randomly distributed pits, with a little heap of earth beside each one.

This approach has had lasting success, particularly in the USA, where it has been deployed both for research – interrogating a piece of landscape to see who was doing what, when – and in rescuing strata that is to be destroyed, by first sampling it to get an overall impression of its exploitation through time. It is perhaps worth noting that research questions and commercial mitigation in the USA often involve very large tracts of countryside, which was in the past relatively sparsely occupied. It is also worth noting that Native American sites do not necessarily show up well on the surface. Thus taking samples at intervals is a sensible way of mapping what there was, without the great expense of walking or digging every square metre. In Europe where there are Iron Age and Roman sites every hundred metres, not to mention thousands of Medieval ditches and houses, a random trench will nearly always hit something: for the last 6,000 years at least people seem to have been active everywhere.

Perhaps for this reason European archaeology has traditionally been concerned with the creation of history and prehistory. The sense of the past as a series of events – a *historical* approach – is very strong, and can be contrasted with the sense of the past as behaviour and process – an anthropological approach. History also has its agenda (to find out what happened and why), and archaeologists have put their shoulder to the wheel often by targeting sites that are already known to history – sites like Troy, Knossos, the Roman forum, the Tower of London. Mortimer Wheeler, a strong advocate of the historical utility of digging, targeted Roman towns like Verulamium, and Iron Age forts that had been overrun by the Romans like Maiden Castle and Stanwick (FIG 2.6). Because he needed a story, he liked a sequence best, and deduced it from looking at vertical slices cut through strata. If an earthwork had a single function – like the rampart of a hill-fort – then the sequence could be sampled with a trench cut through it at right angles. If he wanted to view the sequence within a settlement, his excavation area was large and rectangular and subdivided into boxes of equal size. Each box was excavated, and the earth wall (a baulk) between them carried, in its beautifully cleaned vertical surface, a record of all the layers that he had cut through. These *sections* were so many windows on the stratified deposit as a whole. Each one, reconciled with the others, provided an overall sequence ideal for story-telling. When he reached the bottom, the baulks would be demolished and he viewed the foundations of buildings in open area. Wheeler also thought that field archaeologists should carefully design their excavations: "Have a plan." A framework was needed to ask the right questions, and without questions, there could be no answers.

Astute readers will have noticed that I have not introduced my protagonists in chronological order, and my excuse is that none of these approaches, or the fieldwork procedures they espouse, has actually gone away. If they know about each other (and they often don't), field archaeologists may react to one another, especially when an approach becomes too dogmatic. Ian Hodder, exponent of my Approach no. 5, certainly reacted to empiricism, realising that Barker's total excavation, or the version of it then prevalent in British urban archaeology, had become obsessed by its own

FIGURE 2.6 Approaches 4: the historical (a) Mortimer Wheeler with Barry Cunliffe and (b) box excavation in progress at Maiden Castle Dorset, UK, 1930s (P.A. Rahtz; Wheeler 1954).

FIGURE 2.7 Approaches 5: the reflexive (a) Ian Hodder and (b) excavations in progress at Çatalhöyük in 2008 (author).

supposed objectivity (FIG 2.7). He wanted to see more interpretation on site, "at the trowel's edge". He also doubted that humans conformed to social systems and wrote a series of books explaining that people use symbolic language to signal their intentions, and that some parts of the material record were richer in personal expression than in social and economic facts. There was no single system or history, nor was there one system or history to find. An excavation resulted, or should result, in many answers, and not just the result the director hoped for. And what was true for the people in the past may be true for us too – so that each of us tends to bring a personal equation to the business – whether "reduced to a minimum" or not.

The style of excavation developed at Çatalhöyük (a *tell* site in Turkey) was especially interesting in matters of interpretation and in the sharing of ideas. It is proclaimed as "multi-vocal", taking many different opinions and interpretations into account, and "reflexive", asking people why they thought what they thought. On the ground it looks like an area excavation, but with a lot more monitoring by notebooks and video cameras than the conventional commercial area excavations were accustomed to employ. But conversely there was no designed and timetabled programme – the programme is agreed and revised and updated annually by a broad group of experts in discourse with each other.

Evaluative archaeology

By presenting these approaches in this anachronistic order I hope to offer you this idea – that all of them are good in their different ways. Each approach has its own emphasis, although exponents did not always appreciate that their "innovations" were widely practised already. Although the evaluative approach was first developed in the 1970s, it can be seen in retrospect to be a combination of the other approaches, with added ethics. Field archaeologists famously are always telling each other how things should be done, but rather more rarely admit what they themselves actually did, and with that, what they did wrong, what did not work, what they did not understand. If they did, an awful lot of bubbles would burst. So assuming there is really a large measure of underlying agreement, where do the differences in emphasis come from?

A first influential factor is clearly the type of *terrain*: an extensive, sparsely occupied prairie demands a different approach to a town site, or a deeply stratified tell. A second factor evidently is the social and economic situation in which the work takes place. A large area excavation in which the surface is lovingly trowelled requires a great deal of willing labour. Where there is no cheap or volunteer labour available, the rationale for this kind of excavation mysteriously diminishes. If the work is research and carried out by students, then these will want to cut their teeth on inter-pretation: they want to dig their own trench, or fill in their own recording sheet. As the world changes, from a colonial to an anti-colonial posture, from a dirigiste to a consensual mood, so does field archaeology, from an official expedition in pursuit of new history, to a more multi-vocal and reflexive programme, and many histories. One notices too that the approach to fieldwork changes depending on whether there are no research questions, just anthropological or environmental questions, or just historical questions.

It could therefore be that none of these approaches is entirely right or entirely wrong, they are simply addressing different kinds of questions, in different types of terrain and in different social contexts. Is there, then, room for random sampling and open area excavation in the same discipline? Of course there is – why not? – provided all can be seen as part of one intellectual toolbox, and none is ever allowed to become an inflexible dogma. It all depends what you are trying to do. The key to good field archaeology is not being trendy, or being orthodox, but in being appropriate.

The point of departure for my approach (no. 6) is really the comment with which I closed the first chapter: the results of fieldwork are determined by what can be seen and what measures we take to see it. As soon as a fieldworker decides that there is only one way of walking a field, cutting up strata or recording it, the options are reduced and the inquiry suffers. Empiricism, processualism, historicity, reflexivity all have obvious good points and we should note them. Furthermore there will be plenty more theoretical platforms and ideas in field archaeology in the future. The task I have set myself is not to replace these approaches (although I'll criticise them) but to argue for a framework in which any approach can be applied. I would want to design a railway train, not determining which conversations are permissible in its carriages.

If the type of terrain and the research questions between them determine what we want to know and what measures will be needed to investigate them, the social context, the least well-developed of the three factors just mentioned, is becoming equally determinant. One component of the social context needs to be mentioned now, namely ethics. Not that the other five approaches (or four of them) are unaware of ethics, but the terms of reference of ethics has broadened in the 21st century, and is likely to stay broad into the foreseeable future. Over the past few decades, and particularly since the world was first seen from space, researchers of all kinds have been aware of the shared values of our environmental and cultural assets; shared, not just in the sense of shared between people alive today, but deserving to be shared by the future population – those not yet born. This has changed the ethical stance for field archaeologists in two ways. First, as is well known, most countries in the world try to protect their archaeological sites, or, if they must be destroyed to make way for new development, take measures to record them. Second, less widely appreciated, is that the digging of all sites by researchers is, or should be, subject to ethical restraint. It would be wrong today to allow a large excavation at Wroxeter or Çatalhöyük simply because an archaeological "theory" or "method" demanded it. For the same reason, a proposal to excavate a prominent site would need to be scrutinised by anyone who could possibly have an interest in the outcome. In other words a modern project does not just need a design: that design must be published before work starts, and not just because this results in a better managed programme, but for ethical reasons. By the same reasoning the *project design* itself must contain a programme of short- and long-term conservation as well as programme of research. This gives a different spin to the idea of "multi-vocality"; the voices should not be confined to those working on the site or living near it; others living in faraway countries may consider themselves as stakeholders and should be informed through prior publication of the proposals. In this way we can address our obligations to the unborn.

This enlarges the field archaeologist's appreciation of the social context in which they work. We shall revisit the matter again in Chapter 14, but it needs to be mentioned here because, the *evaluative* approach, Approach no. 6 (FIG 2.8), is firmly embedded in its constraints. The consequence is that archaeological project design is mandatory, and not, or not just, for intellectual but for ethical reasons. Archaeological investigation is not a form of detached blue skies research, it is research about dead people in partnership with live people. This means that researchers, as well as rescue archaeologists, are bound by a contract with society, which means in turn that the same framework and its procedure apply to both. Maybe this ethical constraint will fall away one day – and perhaps more quickly than I think. But if it does, it will mean that archaeology, and our duty to our own descendants, will no longer have the value we give them today.

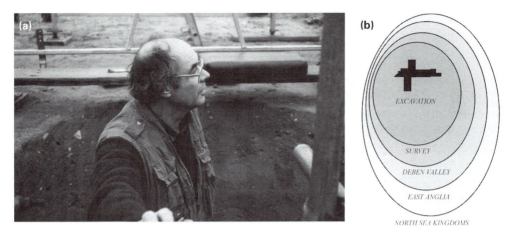

FIGURE 2.8 Approaches 6: the evaluative (a) the author and (b) extract from Sutton Hoo design (see Chapter 3) (N. Macbeth).

It might be worth briefly comparing the two most recent approaches, the reflexive and the evaluative, because they are both "in the frame" in our time. First there are strong areas of agreement. The reflexive approach, which is largely owed to the thinking of Ian Hodder, has alerted the archaeological community to important realities of the archaeological process: we are not just recording and analysing strata, we are reading and interpreting it. Furthermore, since interpretation has a personal element, it is important to involve a wide range of opinion, both expert and intuitive, in the inquiry on site. This is common ground.

It also ought to mean that the programme of an excavation is determined through continuous discourse, rather than laid down at the beginning. But I have difficulty with this last part, because it means that the stakeholder base for the discussion becomes too narrow: we also have to protect the interests of the unborn, and the only way to do that (since they are not here) is to get a broad consensus on what is planned and then stick to it. The way to compose a complete programme in advance is to study the ground, the research problems it can address and its social context from all angles as part of an initial *evaluation* stage. It is axiomatic that the project that is incorporated into such a plan must have a conservation programme as well as a research programme: deciding what to keep as well as what to disturb by investigation. It is also axiomatic that the combined project design is offered to the widest possible constituency before any work begins; in other words that it is published. With this degree of consultancy one can be reasonably confident that the interests of the research community and of those outside it have been served with due diligence.

There are other consequences in the evaluative approach. Since it is a research inquiry bound up in a social contract, its length in time will be related to the rhythm of society and its thinking. It is this same thinking that determines the emphasis of what we call archaeological theory. On the whole this evolves every six years or so, and it is rarely more than ten years before one suite of ideas begins to displace another. This means that an archaeological project is not only appropriate to its place, but to its time; the goals of a project cannot be expected to stay valid for an indefinite period.

The implication is that we need a framework that allows the research question, the terrain on offer and the social context to be matched in the case of every expedition. They will not stay matched for subsequent expeditions. We need to do it afresh each time: what we want to know, what is available for study, and the social constraints, at such and such a place, now. Matching these three factors is a *design* process. I call my approach "evaluative" because it asks us to match *values* at every stage: research value, social value and the value of surviving strata. A project happens when the values are in balance.

Field Research Procedure

The evaluative approach, like the processual, demands that archaeological investigation is conducted in stages, each stage being determined by the information gathered in the one before. In my scheme, procedure in the field, *Field Research Procedure* (FRP for short) is divided into six stages, each stage being defined not by its technique, but by its purpose (FIG 2.9). In *Stage 1*, reconnaissance, the terrain is

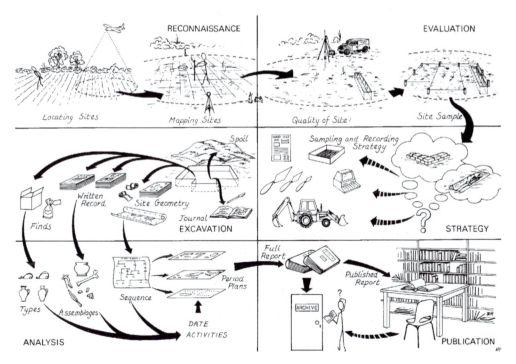

FIGURE 2.9 Field Research Procedure: a framework (drawn by E. Hooper).

reviewed without any particular aim in mind, except finding sites and other traces of the past and mapping them. In *Stage 2*, preparatory to an investigation, a piece of land is evaluated, i.e. it is assigned a current value in terms of what has survived there and what questions it can answer. This information, together with a study of the social context of the land in question, is fed into *Stage 3*, the project design ('strategy' in FIG 2.9). The task of this stage is to produce a research programme and a conservation programme, and let others see and comment on them before they are implemented. You might say that this is normal business or experimental procedure. And if you did, I would agree with you.

This design may never be implemented, or maybe only its conservation programme will be adopted. But assuming we have the go-ahead for both programmes, *Stage 4* (implementation) sees us in the field, carrying out the agreed programme to the letter. Is this too rigid? Supposing something juicy comes up? I am not saying it can never be varied, but it does mean breaking a social contract; so in the case of major change I would advocate another round of consultation. The point of sticking to the plan is that the plan determined which data were to be collected in the field, and which analyses were to follow. So a change of plan risks making orphans of the new or the previous data. I can hear the protests of certain university-based researchers, who have always preferred making up the programme as they go along, but I must urge them to accept that those days are gone. These sites are not ours to play with as we wish – we are ethically constrained. But how can we possibly know what to do in advance? How will we know what we will find, before we find it? That is the role of Stage 2, the evaluation (more of which in Chapter 14).

The records made in the field will include "data" in the sense of preconceived questions about the components of contexts, written down on proformae; they will also include much interpretation – some of it formalised (feature records) and some free style – in notebooks, diaries and video film. At the end of the fieldwork programme all this harvest is gathered in and the records are organised, curated and analysed. This is the task of *Stage 5*, analysis. Out of this stage will come a synthesis, a story, as well as an orderly archive of records for the future. Now we are ready to address our public; scholarly, expert, professional and popular. All are owed an explanation of what we have been up to on their behalf, and we may give it to them in the form of books, articles, displays and films *(Stage 6*, publication).

It will be appreciated that some design is incorporated in each of these stages: reconnaissance needs a design, so does evaluation, so does analysis – also known as a "post-excavation programme" and so does publication, given the large number of different clients that we should or could be serving. But project design at Stage 3 has its own stage for a particular reason. It is at this moment that the future of a site is decided. If Stage 4 (implementation) goes ahead, it will change its character and its assets for ever. Reconnaissance and evaluation, analysis and publication are, or are intended to be, non-destructive; these do not rock a site to its foundations as field investigation does. So Stage 3 is the key stage and must be given time and space to happen. Many things follow from this. The procedure must pause at this point, and widespread consultation is necessary. In field expeditions that are mainly research, the project will always require two separate funding grants – the first to carry out reconnaissance and evaluation and design, and the second, after an interval, to implement field investigation. It is wise to have a lengthy pause between them. In rescue or resource management projects, this often happens already since it under- pins the ideas of "impact assessment" and planning permission that many countries have in place (more in Chapter 14).

It also follows that, whether they realise it or not, archaeologists in the field are always engaged in one or other of these stages. Each stage can be recognised not by what archaeologists are doing, i.e. walking or digging, nor by what equipment they are using. These may give a clue, but the real signal lies in the purpose of the fieldwork, its goal, what the archaeologists are trying to achieve. If they are already engaged in implementation, then they should be able to produce a design from the back pocket, with a set area, programme and timescale. If they cannot, the chances are that, however the business might be dressed up, what they are doing is really just recon- naissance.

The way Field Research Procedure works can be most easily inspected and examined by means of an example, and that is what I propose for Chapter 3. Sutton Hoo is convenient because it had a beginning and an end, so passed through all the stages. Of course it does not represent everything we would like it to. It was not a town and was not a rescue site. But it was from my experience of rescuing sites in towns that the evaluative approach and Field Research Procedure developed, so it works there too. Does it provide a robust and flexible framework for use in any project? I think so, but that is for you to judge.

Briefing

What we want from fieldwork and how we get it is broadly the subject of **archae- ological theory**; useful introductions to the debates of the past 30 years will be found in Hodder 1992, Thomas 1998, Johnson 1999 and Trigger 2007; of the two most approachable, Thomas (American) tends to support the processual and Johnson (English) the post-processual stance (but so much the better). There is a nice outline of theory as it has related to fieldwork in the first part of Lucas 2001. The best **his- tory of fieldwork**, Fagan 1996, is not a history at all, but better than that – it is a compendium of excavators' tales told in their own words. Willey and Sabloff 1974 is a fine history of early approaches in the USA. Sharer and Ashmore 1979, Thomas 1998 and Bahn and Renfrew 2008 try to do it all. For reviews of scientific techniques: Mannoni and Molinari 1990 and Brothwell and Pollard 2001 are compendious and valuable works of reference.

For the **classics** of field method, begin with Jefferson (in Fagan 1996, 383–6) and others worth revisiting are Layard 1854 (for its unabashed pillaging), Schliemann 1880 (for its confidence) Pitt Rivers 1886–90 (for its command; the quote "every detail" is in 1987, xvii), Petrie 1904 (for its humanity, ethics and modernity of approach; the quote is on page 1), Koldewey 1914 (for an early big set-piece excavation), Kidder 1962 [1924] (for its inquiry-driven common sense), Hatt 1938, Steensberg 1940 (for open area), Atkinson 1946 (digging at Stonehenge), Crawford 1953 (champion of survey), Willey 1953 (structured research by survey) and Wheeler 1954 (for its zest). Current manuals of field archaeology with particular national themes are Connah 1983 (Australia), Joukousky 1980 (USA, but especially working overseas), Dillon 1989 (USA), Hester et al 1997 (the classic for USA), Dever and Lance 1982 (Israel), Gersbach 1989 (Germany).

Five approaches to fieldwork

The **empirical:** Barker 1977, 1993 (the initial), Roskams 2001 (the latest); **processual:** Binford 1972, 1983, 1989 (the original), Flannery 1972 (the most entertaining), Redman 1973, 1986, 1987, Mueller 1975, Cherry et al 1978, Hester et al 1997 (current in USA), Orton 2000 (current in UK); **historical:** Petrie 1904; Wheeler 1954; **reflexive:** Chadwick 1997, Hassan 1997, Hodder 1997, 1999, 2005, 2006; **evaluative:** M. Carver 1983a, 1989, 1990, 1996, 1999a, 2003.

Field Research Procedure: see next chapter.

3 FIELD RESEARCH PROCEDURE: A FRAMEWORK

A value-led project: the Sutton Hoo burial ground

Sutton Hoo was first investigated in the late 16th century. We don't know why, but we can take a shrewd guess. The site consists of a cluster of burial mounds (FIG 3.1) and the 16th-century archaeologists drove a vertical shaft into the middle of each one. They must have had a rich haul: where the burial chamber lay under the centre of a mound, later archaeologists found it empty apart from scraps of iron, bronze

FIGURE 3.1 Aerial photograph of the Sutton Hoo mounds (C. Hoppitt).

and gold. A second campaign took place in 1860, and these excavators drove an east–west trench through at least six mounds. In two cases, they cut steps down one end, while the other end was used as a barrow run. So here the objective was probably to examine the burial rite. If they were after treasure, they were disappointed – someone else had got there first. Apart from a newspaper cutting, this expedition was also unrecorded. The third campaign of 1938–9 was paid for by the new landowner and hit the jackpot. The team drove trenches through four mounds, finding three of them already looted. The fourth, the celebrated Mound 1, had been missed by the previous campaigns, because the chamber lay off centre and in the bottom of a large ship some 10m down. So the Sutton Hoo treasure was unearthed from the furnished chamber of an East Anglian aristocrat of the 7th century AD, a treasure donated by the landowner (whose property it was under English law) to the British Museum. The museum itself mounted a fourth campaign in 1965–71 to complete the total excavation of Mound 1 and to look for the prehistoric settlement that was thought to precede the early medieval mounds. In 1975–83, the museum in the person of Rupert Bruce–Mitford published three big volumes on the ship burial, at which point a new project was proposed. The first four investigations present us with a potted history of excavation: and this methodological evolution was to continue (FIG 3.2).

FIGURE 3.2 Excavators in Mound 2 in 1988, showing the rediscovered traces of earlier excavation campaigns (N. Macbeth).

The fifth expedition, which began in 1983, was intended to answer the question: why did the Anglo-Saxons bury someone in a chamber in a ship in the early 7th century? The discovery, with its beautiful artefacts, was not enough. Intellectual satisfaction lay in putting it into history: Why that? Why there? Why then? Recognising that they could not specify exactly what was to be done, the sponsoring Trust (formed by the British Museum, the Society of Antiquaries and the BBC) took a crucial decision, the implications of which have yet to be fully realised by our broader profession. They neither commissioned the new work, nor did they choose a director off the shelf: they opened the opportunity to a *design competition*, and advertised it in the *London Gazette*. This was an extremely unusual procedure, which announced that an archaeological research project was, like a public sculpture or a new symphony, to be seen as a creative endeavour.

Stage 1: Reconnaissance

My application, successful as it happens, represented a chance to try out Field Research Procedure on a rural research project, as opposed to the urban rescue scene that had given it birth. My governing Trust was surprised to be asked for three years to prepare a Project Design, and I was even more surprised to get it. The previous expeditions of looters, antiquaries, landowners and academics could count as Sutton Hoo's reconnaissance phase, within which we could also include the decades of information collected by East Anglian archaeologists. This was legitimate. In most countries in the world, archaeological reconnaissance is more or less continuous, its findings from the air or on the ground, of traces of sites or artefacts turned up by the plough, listed and described in central archives. Not complete, of course, but an expression of what there was, or what we know of it to date: this is the reconnaissance mission (FIG 3.3). In this case we already had, for example, a map of all Anglo-Saxon cemeteries, and a good idea where the early kingdom of East Anglia might be (not a million miles from the present region of the same name). So after a little preliminary mapping we could begin at Stage 2.

Stage 2: Evaluation

Having three years to evaluate a site and its surroundings was an outstanding opportunity. It ought to be routine of course, but even now it seldom is. There were three kinds of information to collect, the first being the character of the site and deposits: How extensive was the early Medieval cemetery? How extensive was the prehistoric settlement? How far had each survived? The site was divided into *zones* (FIG 3.4) and these questions were addressed in them by different kinds of site survey. First was the surface collection of pottery and flint in Zones D, E, F and G – fields and a plot of phosphate concentrations (to map the prehistoric settlements).

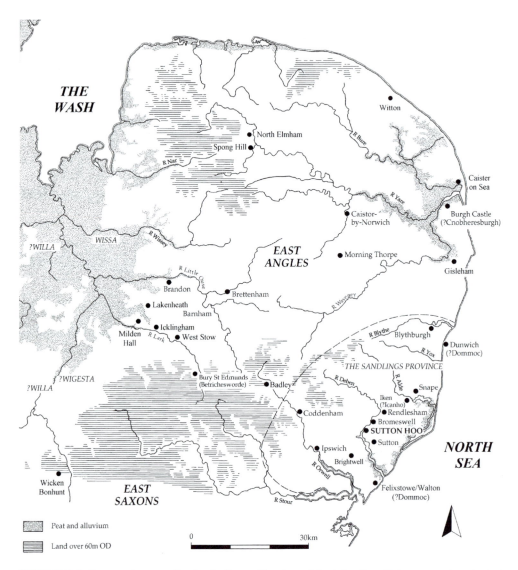

FIGURE 3.3 Reconnaissance: the Anglo-Saxon Kingdom of East Anglia with known archaeological sites.

Second was the mound cemetery (Zone A), now finely mown and relieved of rabbits and bracken – a map of the flowers and geophysical surveys to record the early ditches and re-excavation of recent holes: robber trenches in the mounds, an anti-glider ditch dug in WW2 and a 1950s farmer's silage pit. Emptying some of these gave us a sideways view from which to assess the quality of the strata. Later we stripped off the turf and looked at the bared surface of the sandy soil to gain a preview of what was to come, but without damaging it further. The result was a map of the early Medieval cemetery superimposed on the prehistoric settlements (the *site extent*:

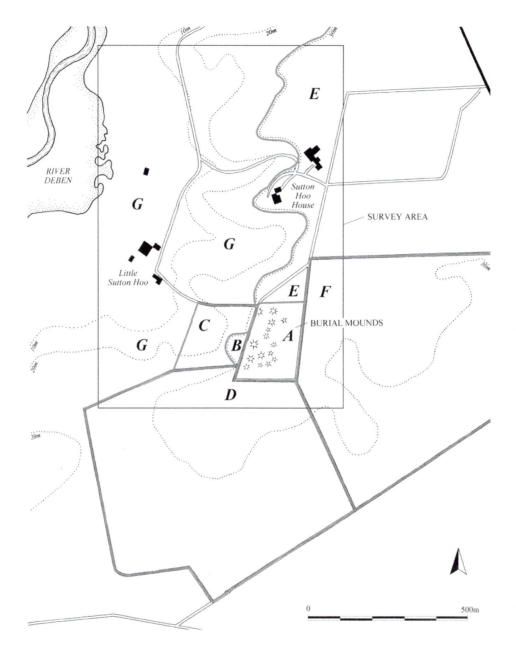

FIGURE 3.4 Evaluation: zones demarcated for remote mapping

FIG 3.5) and another map showing the depth of strata and how damaged they were (the *deposit model*: FIG 3.6). These would provide the basis for the excavation design.

The second task was to list what everyone wanted to know – so we could choose research questions appropriate to what was on offer on the ground (FIGS 3.7, 3.8).

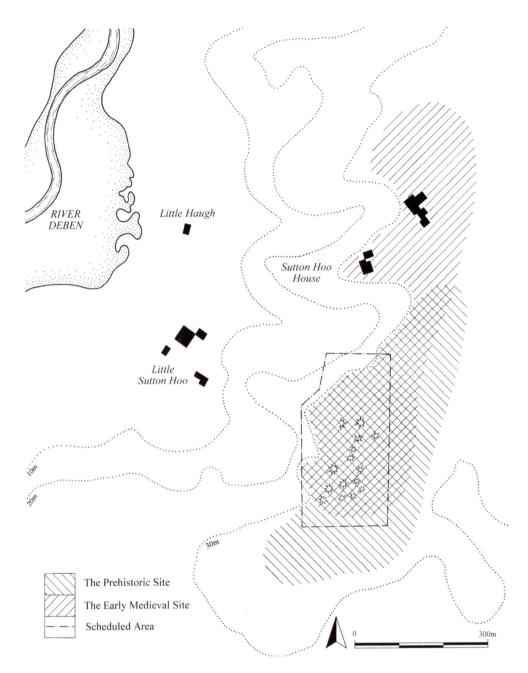

RIVER
DEBEN

Little Haugh

Sutton Hoo
House

Little
Sutton Hoo

10m

20m

30m

The Prehistoric Site

The Early Medieval Site

Scheduled Area

0   300m

FIGURE 3.5 Evaluation: likely limits of prehistoric and early medieval settlement.

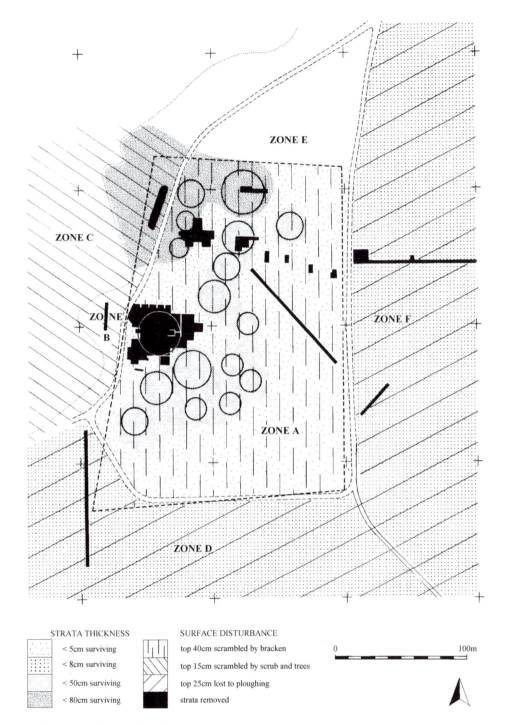

ZONE E

ZONE C

ZONE B

ZONE F

ZONE A

ZONE D

STRATA THICKNESS
- ⬚ < 5cm surviving
- ⬚ < 8cm surviving
- ⬚ < 50cm surviving
- ⬚ < 80cm surviving

SURFACE DISTURBANCE
- ‖ top 40cm scrambled by bracken
- ⧄ top 15cm scrambled by scrub and trees
- ▨ top 25cm lost to ploughing
- ■ strata removed

0 ———————————— 100m

FIGURE 3.6 Evaluation: deposit model. This shows the depth of strata that remained and the degree to which it had been disturbed.

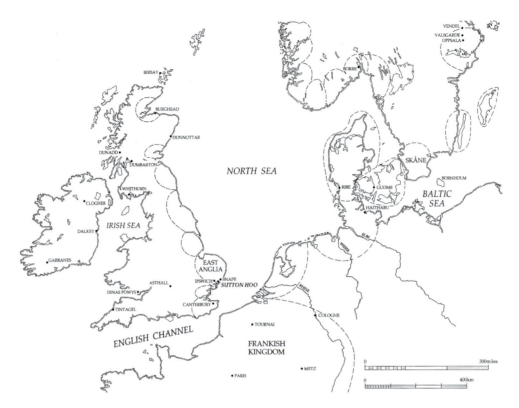

FIGURE 3.7 Research framework: kingdoms of the North Sea. This picture of newly formed polities around the coasts of the North Sea provided the principal context for research at Sutton Hoo. When were these kingdoms created, and how? What was the nature of their politics and their relations with each other?

This was done by putting forward some preliminary lists of ideas, and then holding a series of consultations, in the form of research seminars, to chew them over. These seminars showed that there was little curiosity about the prehistoric sites, even among prehistorians. For the early medieval cemetery the main demand was sequence: the sequence of burial rites. There was some optimism that we could use this sequence to throw light on the period at which the kingdom of East Anglia was formed and converted to Christianity – matters that are referred to, somewhat obscurely, in the exiguous contemporary documents. Many participants agreed that the project should not focus only on the site of Sutton Hoo. If it was to have a context, then broader inquiries would be needed: the settlement sequence in the Deben Valley where Sutton Hoo stood, and at a coarser focus, burial practices in East Anglia and in the lands that bordered the North Sea.

The third task, which I termed the "ethical stance", generated a certain amount of grumbling in the ranks of the sponsors (FIG 3.9). Top rank researchers were expected to be bold and carry all before them, rather than consult with the lower orders. But

FIGURE 3.8
Research agenda.

SUTTON HOO RESEARCH DESIGN

Fieldwork	Objective	Outcome
Excavation in sample area	Sequence of use Burial rites employed	Changing ideology and allegiance of the East Angles
Survey in site area	Map of prehistoric settlement and early medieval burials outside the excavation sample	Enhanced excavation sample
Survey in Deben Valley area	Map of sites from prehistoric to medieval	Changing land use and settlement hierarchies
Survey in other sample areas in East Anglia (The East Anglian Kingdom Survey)	Map of settlement at the time of Sutton Hoo	Definition of the kingdom Changing social structures
Comparative Studies	Liaison with other kingdom-finders	A European process

times were changing; if we had as yet no East Anglian aborigines to placate, the principles established in Australia and the USA were good ones and should be applied: look to the interests of the stakeholders – the project is for them too. Sutton Hoo already had an enormous public constituency at home and abroad, but there were four communities that needed to be directly engaged: academic, professional, treasure-hunters and locals. To serve the academic sector, we held seminars as already mentioned and appointed a research committee. But the academic community was not re-assured and wondered out loud whether the project was necessary at all, when they were so many other more important tasks in hand, like rescuing thousands of threatened sites elsewhere. The East Anglian professionals naturally had strong views here, since they felt we were on their territory. To show that I was willing to be judged, I held a public meeting in London, to which the nation's Medieval archaeologists were invited, and there unveiled our plans.

Involvement reduced hostility, and this was also the case with two other prominent groups. The metal-detectorists, represented by the journal *Treasure Hunting Monthly* had come out strongly against the project, which they found to be elitist – in other words, we were accused of keeping all the excitement of discovery to ourselves. They were mollified with a letter to the editor sketching the proposed design and its rationale. The site was full of shrapnel and bullets from WW2; only certain tasks were suitable for a metal detector and we had our own. An editorial in *THM* accepted this argument and we had no difficulties with treasure-hunters for the next ten years.

FIGURE 3.9 Sutton Hoo – the social context. Local residents, treasure hunters, historians, anthropologists, prehistorians, environmentalists, archaeologists and visitors from every nation (N. Macbeth).

The last community was probably the most important – those who lived locally and exercised their dogs on the mounds. These people of Woodbridge and the surrounding villages claimed a perceived and abstract ownership of the site. Together we formed the Sutton Hoo Society – and their role became the hosting of visitors and the giving of tours, a role exercised to this very day. Oh – and I nearly forgot, there was the landowner of course. She had no real interest in the mounds or the outcome of the excavation: but she owned all the land they stood in, and in England that matters. What price a little friendship offered regularly as a few hours of companionship? A very little. What rewards? Inestimable. There is much more to this story, but hopefully I have said enough to show that a field archaeology project is not something that happens in a vacuum. We do not stay in a library like a historian, we are not confined to a laboratory like a chemist – we work in the open air, where everyone else, rich or poor, knowledgeable or not, feels they have an equal right to be.

Stage 3: Project Design

The materials for constructing the project design were now largely gathered in, and we set about composing its two parts: the research programme and the conservation programme. Although it had generated little enthusiasm, I felt that the prehistoric site should be included, and I included it. I am glad we did: the significance of prehistoric monuments for early medieval cemeteries has steadily grown. The early medieval part of the site was more clearly our target, but how much of it to dig, and where? To

understand the sequence of burial rites at Sutton Hoo we would need to dig them up and put them in order. My rivals in the design competition had proposed a Barkerian "total excavation" of the whole site since only in that way could all the different burial rites be recovered. Any partial excavation or sample would only provide half an answer.

However I had barred myself from this prescription, because it was unethical. To dig the whole monument away and leave nothing for the future was the height of arrogance, and would not please the unborn. If our research questions required the excavation of all the mounds, they were the wrong questions and we should think again. Our solution was to lay a transect 30m across the mound cemetery from east to west and another from north to south (FIG 3.10). One or other of these transects

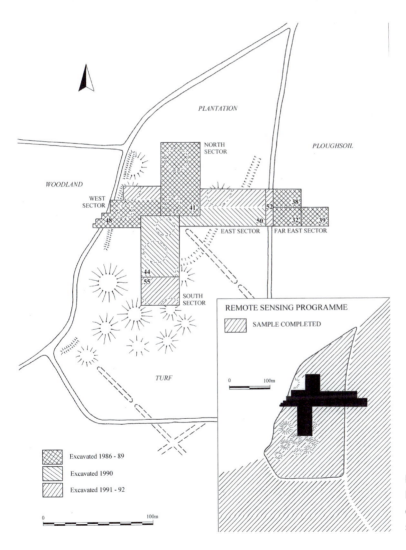

FIGURE 3.10
Design for excavation and site survey.

should catch the axis of growth and let us see how the burial rites were changing through time. The area was continuous since we knew little about what was happening between the mounds. The total area to be excavated was 1 hectare, about a quarter of the known extent of the mound cemetery: quite extravagant, but I mitigated its effect by placing it over that part which was already most disturbed by previous excavation (the north end). Coincidentally, the prehistoric site was best preserved and had been best defined in this same area. It was particularly well preserved, naturally enough, under the early medieval mounds. The estimated time needed to excavate this area was five years, just long enough to achieve this large sample, but not so long that the design, and the ideas on which it was based would become intellectually obsolete.

Outside the Sutton Hoo site there were three levels of survey proposed (FIG 3.10; 3.11): the first over the unexcavated part of the site where intensive geophysical and

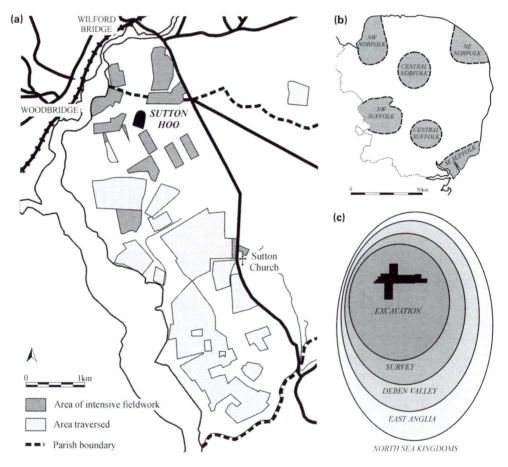

FIGURE 3.11 Survey Design: (a) local (the Deben Valley); (b) regional (East Anglia); (c) the nested overall design.

other surveys would be applied. This included a little patch of casual early medieval finds 300m to the north, implying another cemetery. Excavation there would have to wait until an opportunity arose (it did). Second, in the Deben Valley, a surface-collecting survey was to be carried out on every field to which we could again access. The Suffolk Archaeological Unit's John Newman was to map the settlement pattern from prehistoric to late Medieval times, and compare its story with five other parts of East Anglia (FIG 3.11). The 7th century proved to be a time of fundamental settlement shift.

The research design therefore took the form of a set of concentric areas around the Sutton Hoo sites, in which the range of questions at the centre were intensive, and further afield became increasingly extensive and more general (FIG 3.11c). You can't dig everything, ethically you mustn't, but a nested design goes a long way to being the next best thing.

The conservation programme began with measures for the protection of the site while we were digging it: site guards, regular mowing to keep down the bracken, game-keepers and gas to keep down the rabbits. There was also a design for public access (FIG 3.12–14) – first for our visitors who were managed by agreement with the landowners. Then there were TV crews whose agenda had to be reconciled with ours, and whose programmes would increase the visitor numbers, so they would need managing more. There were schools, enactment societies, royalty, book clubs and lots of parties – all to be fitted in, and both socially pleasurable and building up long term support for the protection of the site. In the long term, I felt it desirable that the site, in private hands since time immemorial, should move into public ownership for its own wellbeing and its public access. This too eventually came to pass. The National Trust now owns Sutton Hoo; the mounds are well-kept and surrounded by a rabbit-proof fence.

FIGURE 3.12 (a) Visitors gather on Mound 1. (b) Mound reconstructed for site display (N. Macbeth).

(a) Model for Presentation of Sutton Hoo

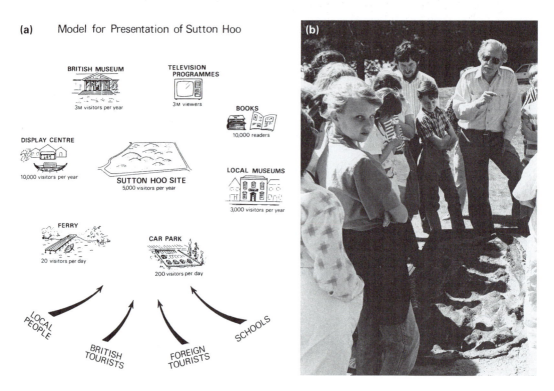

BRITISH MUSEUM
3M visitors per year

TELEVISION PROGRAMMES
3M viewers

BOOKS
10,000 readers

DISPLAY CENTRE
10,000 visitors per year

SUTTON HOO SITE
5,000 visitors per year

LOCAL MUSEUMS
3,000 visitors per year

FERRY
20 visitors per day

CAR PARK
200 visitors per day

LOCAL PEOPLE

BRITISH TOURISTS

FOREIGN TOURISTS

SCHOOLS

FIGURE 3.13 (a) Design for public access; (b) day out for school children (N. Macbeth).

The Sutton Hoo project began in 1983 and three years later the Project Design was published. We had no internet in those days, so it came out in hard copy and may not have reached everyone it should. But the intention was there. As a result, objections still on the table were withdrawn, we received our permit (Scheduled Monument Consent) and began work. The workforce was part professional, part volunteer: there were students, people on job creation schemes, full-time archaeologists on holiday and guest diggers from other countries. We lived together and worked together, so that conversations, exchanges and ideas drove each day.

Stage 4: Implementation

The excavation and survey programme followed the design published in 1986 and was completed in 1992 (FIG 3.15). The excavations stuck to the area proposed – we had to; it was our "social contract". We dug no more, but did dig slightly less: Mound 7 was not removed, and the area opened was fully mapped but not fully excavated. This was because as time went on we learnt the vocabulary of the sandy site, and could decide to leave in the ground what we already recognised and understood – for example, tree-pits where trees had stood and later fallen over: digging more would

FIGURE 3.14 A busy open day at Sutton Hoo. Visitors from archaeology societies mingle with members of the public and a film crew as excavators (in the foreground) try to keep their concentration (N. Macbeth).

FIGURE 3.15 Excavation complete (J. Garner-Lahire).

not tell us more. We had no more questions for them that we yet knew how to ask. This selectivity is of course only the privilege of a site which, after excavation, is to be thoroughly conserved. Its future conservation was embedded in the design. If the site was to be built on when we had finished with it, then the design would have been different.

The excavation itself was conducted with different techniques and at different levels of precision depending on the target (Chapter 6 for more). After the turf was removed, the exposed surface was surveyed and the pottery sherds and flints were plotted. Then the crust was removed with shovels, and cleaned with trowels, lightly sprayed and cleaned again, until a sharp variegated surface showed: the upper limit of the undisturbed archaeology. In this surface many were anomalies, dark and light patches and strips, the remains of the prehistoric settlement and the graves cut into it a thousand years later. The graves, in which every tiny detail was required by the Project Design, were dug with spatula and spoon. Those beneath Mound 17 were miraculously intact, with a horse in one and a young warrior in the other. The grave goods, which included a sword, shield, bucket and the horse's harness were lifted with the aid of fibreglass and polystyrene jackets for close scrutiny in the British Museum (see also Chapter 6 and 9). The chamber under Mound 2, pillaged on three previous occasions, was explored with delicate instruments and lights and then mapped chemically with 640 samples taken from its base (see Chapter 6).

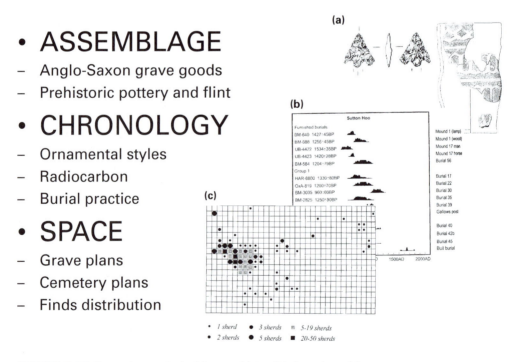

- ## ASSEMBLAGE
  - Anglo-Saxon grave goods
  - Prehistoric pottery and flint

- ## CHRONOLOGY
  - Ornamental styles
  - Radiocarbon
  - Burial practice

- ## SPACE
  - Grave plans
  - Cemetery plans
  - Finds distribution

FIGURE 3.16 Excavatory analysis: (a) assemblage; (b) chronology; (c) space.

So the excavation was conducted at a series of different levels or gears, the research targets matched by methods which in turn aimed at what we ought to be able to see, not just what we already knew how to see. These *"Recovery Levels"* developed for rescue sites form one of modern excavation's key principles (see Chapter 6 for more).

Each wing of the main excavation area was given an intervention number, and so were the site surveys. Starting from the earliest operations we knew about, there were 56 interventions at Sutton Hoo up to 1992. Our own, from 1983, generated 21 crates of field records and 54 boxes of objects. Inside the crates were site journals, context cards, feature cards, maps, plans, sections, photographs, videos and inventories; and inside the boxes were more boxes containing prehistoric pottery and flint, animal bone, human bone and the special assemblages of metal artefacts from the princely burials. All this formed the raw material for the analysis stage (FIG 3.16).

Stage 5: Analysis

The first task was to make sure we had listed everything and that it was in good condition. The archive was composed, and checked, and the vulnerable finds sent to the museum for conservation. Then we had to take stock. How far had the excavation design succeeded? Had it produced what we hoped? Not exactly, since nearly all the mounds had already been well fossicked by folk whose motives were not strictly archaeological. What had we got that we did not expect? A horse and rider grave – intact – and 39 execution victims, people who had been bundled untidily into their graves. And four phases of prehistoric settlement and a large tonnage of prehistoric pottery and flint. To serve the analysis stage, the Project Design, made in the light of what we knew then, would have to be revisited in the light of what we knew now.

The new programme divided up the tasks into four: study of the *assemblage* (the artefacts and biological samples), study of *chronology* (the stratigraphy and radiocarbon dating) and study of the use of *space* (the plans of graves and the development of the cemetery). These three inquiries converged on task no. 4: the *synthesis* – what had happened where and when. In some ways this is the most exhilarating part of any project. For some people the high-thrill moment is stripping off the topsoil with a bulldozer; for others it's the pale glint of a metal edge in the base of a grave. For me it's the laying out of hundreds of folders, drawings and photographs on a big table and dreaming of the book we are going to make from them.

If you are lucky (and we were) the analysis team will be the same people that worked on the site and saw the stuff come out of the ground. So work could start straight away in the hands of different experts: Madeleine Hummler on the prehistoric assemblages, Angela Evans on the early medieval material, Charly French on the soils. Their conclusions on the dates could begin to feed into task 2, chronology. Other team members were completing the stratigraphic analysis of mounds and chambers, and maps of the distribution of objects – these too could feed into the chronology. In other

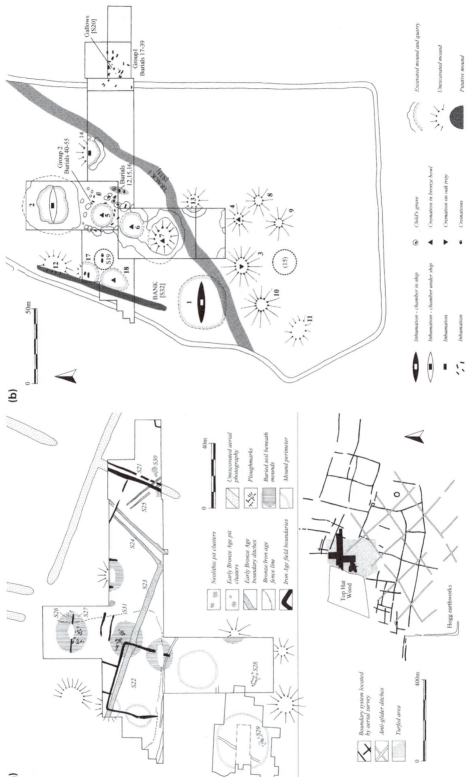

FIGURE 3.17 Synthesis: (a) prehistoric; (b) historic.

words, the three tasks, assemblage, chronology and spatial analysis, and the people engaged in them, were in dialogue with each other, and from this dialogue emerged the synthesis (FIG 3.17). This exercise took the form of identifying events from the late Neolithic to the 20th century, presented in words, maps and in pictures. The significance of all these events, and particularly those of Sutton Hoo's moment of glory (the 7th century) was studied in its local, regional and international context. Writing up, like digging, is therefore better with its own design. It then has a nice clear programme to follow, one with a beginning, a middle and an end. With this to hand, the report writes itself.

Stage 6: Publication

The end of a field project, in every sense, its terminus and its purpose, is publication. Publication how, and for whom? Yes, this needed a design too, because there were many interested parties to whom we owed a story: the Trustees who commissioned us, the Anglo-Saxon academics who expected fresh dispatches from the front line of the early Middle ages, the prehistorians who would get a long sequence, the visitors over the previous years who wanted a book for Christmas, and the visitors over the years to come who wanted something to see. In Chapter 13 we shall define eight kinds of publication – and we could offer most of them at Sutton Hoo (FIG 3.18). There was an online archive, a colourful site guide, a TV series, a popular account (1998) and eventually a big slab of a research report (2005). And facilities were prepared for visitors old and young to visit the site after we had gone, as they had during the digging. On site, the mounds were returned to their former shape, with the exception of Mound 2, which was reconstructed to its calculated 7th century height. The National Trust, new owners of the site, built a marvellous visitor centre, opened by Seamus Heaney. So the story is on the bookshelves, and told in the visitor display. As for the rest, it lies under the mounds in the undug site, safe we hope for the future; an early English archive to be accessed sparingly when new historical questions become both irresistible and answerable.

Reflection

Critics might complain that the circumstances of this project were exceptional and so was the funding; so what we did here has no great bearing on the real world. There are plenty of good criticisms to be made of Sutton Hoo, but this is not one of them. It is true that the site was already well known, but that made for more management rather than an easy ride, and the funding was a good deal less than an urban rescue project of similar size. For the purposes of this book and this chapter, I want to focus only on the procedure and its rationale – because I want to convince you that they are transferable – that they apply to every kind of project, and do so helpfully. The

FIGURE 3.18 Publication: (a) archive; (b) field reports online; (c) annual report to sponsors; (d) research report (e) popular book; (f) site guide; (g) site presentation; (h) newspaper report.

principle that a project should be staged is surely not controversial, and similar staged approaches have been successfully developed and widely practiced, for example in the USA. Before each stage there is a moment of decision: What next? That decision is based on what we know so far and on the predicted outcome to follow. These are decisions based on estimates of value – and not just value to the excavation team but to a much broader constituency. The decisions themselves are incorporated into a design, a design which consists of programmes. The most important of these design stages is the one that takes place before an excavation, since excavation means destruction for at least part of our cultural asset. A part of the cultural asset is to be expended to make history. This needs special thought.

Field Research Procedure is thus an *evaluative* procedure. It is not prescriptive, in that it does not require you to confine yourself to a particular form of recording (like context plans) or analysis (like the stratification diagram). It all depends on what you have got. At every stage we are assessing and matching questions to materials and methods to questions. The only principle is the framework, and that of announcing what you are going to do before you do it – and then sticking to it.

Let's ask again: Is this too rigid? Supposing a great discovery comes to light that seduces you into digging a new area or digging in a different way? Of course this happens, but the value-led principle is that you estimate the outcome, consult widely and agree the programme and implement it. At this point you have entered into a social contract, and this includes the obligation not to destroy what you failed to publicly justify in advance. A new project is of course always a possibility, and the surprising discoveries of the first project will serve the evaluation of the second.

Does it work in rescue? It was made for rescue. The sequence of review, evaluation, decision and contract, aligns with that of the business world. It is this down-to-earth, grown-up approach that has allowed archaeology membership of the professions that plan our future. In Chapter 14 we shall see how similar systems have developed for the purpose of managing the cultural heritage in the USA (CRM) and the UK (MAP and MORPHE) and briefly review the pros and cons of each.

With a framework for archaeological investigation in the knapsack, it is time to venture out in the field. The three main types of fieldwork – landscape survey, site survey and excavation – form the subject of the next three chapters (Chapters 4–6). In each case the techniques are reviewed and then I offer some applications. Although these equate roughly to reconnaissance, evaluation and implementation, the match is not perfect: these days all three field methods are applied at each stage of Field Research Procedure. Landscape survey is used in both reconnaissance and implementation, site survey features in evaluation projects and implementation. Excavation in some form may be used in reconnaissance, evaluation and implementation. Chapter 7 is intended to show such integrated packages in action – and to show how greatly fieldwork varies with the objectives of the archaeologists, and even more so with the terrain in which they work.

The subsequent five chapters are about writing up: designing the analytical programme (Chapter 8), assemblage (Chapter 9), spatial analysis (Chapter 10) chronology (Chapter 11), and synthesis (Chapter 12). Chapter 13 reviews the end product, publication. Project design comes at the end (Chapter 14), because it is the hardest and it presupposes that the designer knows how all the other parts work. To put together a Project Design you need to know something about field methods (Part 2) and analysis and publication (Part 3). The last chapter (Chapter 15) describes the professional scene today, the social situation and the actors who commission archaeology and allow archaeologists to be paid for doing what they like best. Logically, the book could have started here, since this is the profession in which everyone works, from the newest archaeological labourer to the loftiest academic. But, like project design, it is hard to discuss in the abstract. Good heritage management needs a familiarity with the strong smell of freshly turned earth.

Briefing

"Field Research Procedure" (FRP) as presented here was first developed during the 1970s, mainly on rescue sites in the British West Midlands (M.Carver 1978, 1987, 1990, 1999a, 2003) and tuned up on two large research projects (M. Carver 2005, 2008). FRP is designed for application in both the research and CRM sectors. Although focused on fieldwork, it aligns with staged project design as promoted by Binford's research design (1972), Clarke's recycled feedback and disciplined procedure (1968), and Redman's intra-site field strategies (e.g. 1987) as well as with the idea of the hermeneutic circle as promoted by Hodder (e.g. 1999). Moreover in the realm of fieldwork all these approaches whether processual or post-processual have more in common with each other than their champions care to admit. For comparison between FRP and other routines of staged archaeological investigation (mainly employed in the commercial sector in UK, USA, Australia), see Chapter 14. The Sutton Hoo project is described in summary in Carver 1998 and in detail in M. Carver 2005, especially Chapters 2 (Project Design) and 3 (Fieldwork and analysis). Hummler 2005 for the prehistory.

PART 2
IN THE FIELD

4 LANDSCAPE SURVEY

First day in the field

Eight people bump along a track in a minibus, and arrive at a farm gate with fields beyond. This is Fred Taylor's farm at Middlethorpe, where we are to look for the remains of sites of all periods, and hope to confirm earlier rumours of a Neolithic settlement. Access is limited: Mr Taylor's permission was obtained to walk over the fields planted with potatoes, but not the others. Even on the potato fields we must be careful to walk between the ridges and not trample the sprouting tops. It is a hot day in the plain of York.

Our group consists of new volunteers from the local archaeology society and university, and we all have different backgrounds and skills. Some sound rather confident while others are worried they will not recognise anything at all. Project director Kurt explains what to look for, and shows us some examples in a box: Neolithic, Iron Age and Roman pottery, tobacco pipe stems, burnt bone, and a barbed and tanged arrowhead made of flint. He gives us the pink flags we will carry and which we will put in the ground to mark a find. An area about 200m long has been marked out, with ten "lanes", each 5m wide parallel with the potato ridges. The lane is marked every 50m with a yellow flag, so we will know how far we have gone. It will be easy to stay on course: we just have to walk along a row between the potato tufts and look left and right.

The six of us line up each opposite a potato alley like swimmers waiting for the off. The ground looks decidedly dusty, and is peppered with little bits of white stone. Are these something or nothing? Nothing, I decide. Then we start. After 20m Heather has run out of flags and I have yet to put in a single one. Kurt wisely brings us all back, and has a look at the flagged objects. We are slightly relieved to see most of them chucked away, but Heather has a nice potsherd and we all admire it. Then we are off again, with a bit more confidence, starting to see things and flag them. At the end of the 200m transect we stop, change places and walk each other's lanes back again the other way. This raises morale because we see what others saw – and what they missed – creating general

This first day in the field was spent *field-walking* or collecting artefacts from the surface of a ploughed field (FIG 4.1). We might have spent it looking for earthworks or mapping field boundaries, for the sort of traces we are after show here and there as ruins or humps and bumps or as rubbish scattered on the surface (FIG 4.2). To use a famous phrase, the landscape is a palimpsest – that is, as in a well-lived life, everything that has happened to it is etched upon its face to various degrees. If we

FIGURE 4.1 Field-walking. Surface collection on an English spring day (Yorkshire) (FAS Ltd).

FIGURE 4.2 Out and about in Highland Scotland: traces of Bronze Age to Medieval stone buildings on the surface in Strathnaver, Sutherland (author).

can disentangle the thousands of markings, like a wall which carries generations of graffiti, then we should be able to read its story. We are not just finding sites, not even just making a map – we are compiling a sequence in time. The rewards of exploring landscapes are as uplifting as those of excavation: "Landscapes viewed from afar have a timeless quality that is soothing to the human spirit," wrote Gregory Retallack in 2001. Landscape survey gets you out and about in many lands, in fair weather and foul. There is no better way to acquaint yourself with the territory on which ancient people moved and lived than clambering about it or flying over it yourself. But it requires a certain dedication, like fishing: patience, cunning, focus and an unflagging sense of expectation.

Techniques

The techniques of landscape survey come in three main packages: Looking at maps: *cartography*; Looking at the surface of the ground: *surface inspection;* and Looking from the air: *aerial photography*. A few brief words about each, and then we will look at some applications.

All fieldwork starts indoors, with maps and archives which hold whatever information has been previously collected. Countries that have 19th century and earlier maps are

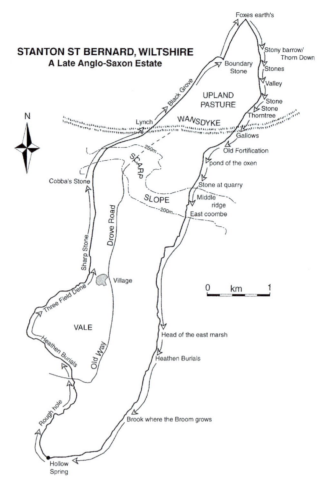

FIGURE 4.3 Mapping a 10th century estate from field names in England (Reynolds 1999, 82).

STANTON ST BERNARD, WILTSHIRE
A Late Anglo-Saxon Estate

Foxes earth's

Stony barrow/
Thorn Down

Boundary Stone

Stones

Black Grove

Valley

UPLAND PASTURE

Stone
Stone
Thorntree

N

Lynch

WANSDYKE

Gallows

250m

Old Fortification

pond of the oxen

SCARP

Stone at quarry

Cobba's Stone

SLOPE

Middle ridge

200m

East coombe

Sharp Stone

Drove Road

0   km   1

Village

Three Field Dene

Head of the east marsh

VALE

Heathen Burials

Old Way

Heathen Burials

Rough hole

Brook where the Broom grows

Hollow Spring

truly fortunate since these carry the lie of the land before the industrial revolution changed everything. Long-lived place names signal users of a particular language and therefore the settlements of the people who spoke it. The patterns can be on a big scale – in the UK names beginning in *pit-* (Pitlochry) show the land of the Picts, and those ending in -ing (Reading), the lands of the early English. On a smaller scale, names or early descriptions may survive, showing estate boundaries or tracks (FIG 4.3).

Monuments of a particular type are thought to mark out cultural territories, and so do coins, brooches and stocking hooks dropped by folk working or making merry in the fields. Every year brings a new harvest of these "casual finds". In the case of the English *Portable Antiquities Scheme* the harvest is prodigious, for these antiquities are the objects found by metal detectorists, hitherto collected in secret but now, by voluntary agreement, declared to local archaeologists who record and locate them. So every year we know more about the flotsam and jetsam of the land, and we have the makings of a map of ancient settlement before we even go outside (FIG 4.4).

(a)

	Metal Detecting		Chance Find whilst Metal Detecting		Field-walking		Other Chance find/Gardening		Controlled Archaeological Investigation		Building/ Agricultural Work		Total
North West	578	(84.38)	96	(14.02)	2	(0.29)	7	(1.02)	2	(0.29)	0	(0)	685
North East	223	(22.71)	29	(2.95)	1	(0.1)	729	(74.24)	0	(0)	0	(0)	982
Yorkshire & the Humber	2,121	(78.44)	122	(4.51)	355	(13.13)	13	(0.48)	93	(3.44)	0	(0)	2,704
West Midlands	1,993	(59.85)	780	(23.42)	500	(15.02)	51	(1.53)	1	(0.03)	5	(0.15)	3,330
East Midlands	8,274	(90.27)	389	(4.25)	233	(2.54)	254	(2.77)	14	(0.15)	2	(0.02)	9,166
East	8,736	(69.37)	324	(2.57)	2,366	(18.79)	80	(0.65)	10	(0.08)	1,078	(8.56)	12,584
South West	2,817	(48.84)	810	(14.04)	1,838	(31.87)	274	(4.75)	7	(0.12)	22	(0.38)	5,768
South East & London	9,859	(72.88)	1,028	(7.6)	1,377	(10.18)	934	(6.91)	19	(0.14)	310	(2.29)	13,527
Wales	580	(6.85)	135	(1.59)	7,702	(90.9)	49	(0.58)	0	(0)	7	(0.08)	8,473
Other	107	(95.54)	1	(0.89)	2	(1.79)	1	(0.89)	0	(0)	1	(0.89)	112
Total	35,288		3,714		14,376		2,392		146		1,425		57,341
	(61.54)		(6.48)		(25.07)		(4.17)		(0.25)		(2.49)		

North West · North East · Yorkshire & the Humber

West Midlands · East Midlands · East

South West · South East & London · Wales

Other · Total

Metal Detecting
Chance Find whilst Metal Detecting
Field-walking
Other Chance Find/Gardening
Controlled Archaeological Investigation
Building/Agricultural Work

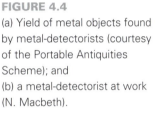

FIGURE 4.4

(a) Yield of metal objects found by metal-detectorists (courtesy of the Portable Antiquities Scheme); and

(b) a metal-detectorist at work (N. Macbeth).

Landscape surveyors enthuse about shallow earth banks and ribbons of stones, since these may be all the traces that former burial mounds, settlements and field boundaries leave. There may not be much in the way of finds. The stones and banks ("surface features") are located in short runs and may only make sense when drawn together on a map (FIG 4.5). Making measured plans and locating them on a map has become much easier since the arrival of digital survey instruments, which measure distance by laser and are located by satellite. At the time of writing, the queen of the surveyors' toolkit is the TST (total station theodolite), which plots points in three dimensions using a built-in laser range-finder and digital store (p. 129). One person holds the detail pole (or "prism") and places it on point after point on the earthwork or ribbon of stones – all morning. The other operates the theodolite and presses the button which records the co-ordinates for each point. And so on to the next hill, and the next. At the end of the day, the points are plotted on a map, where they trace the

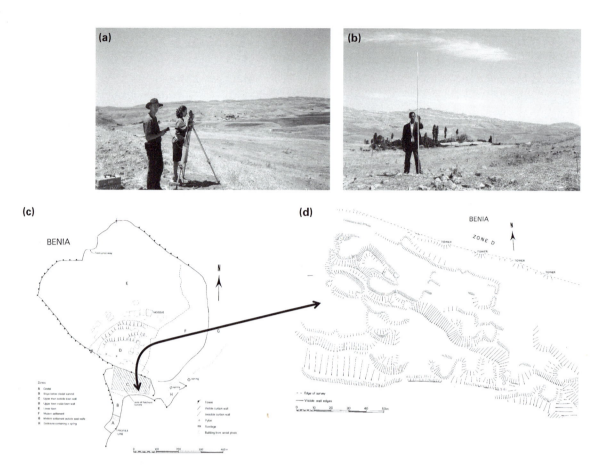

FIGURES 4.5 Mapping an earthwork, on the *haut plateau* at Benia, Atlas mountains, Algeria in 1993. (a) Theodolite; (b) staff; (c) plan of site; (d) hachure plan of Area C (author).

lines of the earthworks or stone dykes of field boundaries. The new series of TSTs features an instrument that automatically finds the detail pole on its own; only one professional field worker is needed, the one holding the pole – thus lowering the cost of the survey, an important matter in the commercial sector. To find out where you are on the ground (even without a map) you can use a GPS (global positioning system), which plots points on the ground by referring to a satellite passing overhead. It also only needs one person. The hand-held instruments can find a point with ever increasing precision, good enough for landscape survey and the static/rover GPS will plot to the nearest centimetre (see Chapter 5, FIG 5.5). To draw up the map from digital points you can use CAD (computed aided design) and store them as a stack of related maps in a GIS (geographic information system). So the current answer to the question "How do I map that earthwork?" is likely to be "Locate with your GPS, survey with your TST, draw up with your CAD and store in a GIS." If you do not have access to any of these desirable gismos, then the old ways must be used: discover your own position using a map and compass, and plot the surface features with measuring tapes at right angles to each other.

Lowland terrain is attractive to cultivation, and given the hunger of the human race, a great deal of the planet has now been ploughed for cereals. Provided the ancient people had a few imperishable artefacts, preferably flint or pottery, archaeologists can find them by walking the surface of ploughed fields – *field-walking* – in the manner described at the start of this chapter. Artefacts on the surface of the ploughsoil show up differently in different conditions: best in light soil and after rain (FIG 4.6). The scatters may represent sites that have been demolished, the artefacts usually coming from midden heaps that have been flattened. So, a concentration of pottery or flint can be read as "a site" and given a number in the archive. But some peoples used midden to fertilise their own fields, spreading the pottery and the cabbage stalks together. In this case the artefacts represent the ancient fields rather than the ancient settlement (see Witton, later). All the artefacts are therefore plotted, and only when that is done is it (usually) possible to distinguish a settlement site from the back-ground noise – the dark matter of ancient use. Other approaches qualify the pattern by using geochemical methods to detect ancient manuring (p. 93).

In other kinds of cultivation – olive groves and vineyards, for example – the surface is much less "talkative" and seems blank. Here artefacts must be coaxed to the surface with a shovel, dug in and turning over a sod every few paces – *shovel testing*. The more encumbered the land with vegetation, the more difficult surface collection becomes: difficult to see the surface and difficult to move over it. Thus where ancient people lived in lands that are now forest or jungle it is very hard to find them.

Salvation comes, partly at least, from the air. In archaeology, by a curious paradox, things that are hard to see close up are easier to see from further away. Thinking of the surface of the land as an oil painting, peering closely at it presents you with an

Factor	Good	Poor	Enhancement
Culture	Primarily users of pottery and flint	Primarily users of metal, wood, leather, bone	Metal detector surveys
Soil	Light, alkaline, ploughed	Heavy, acidic, overgrown	Shovel testing, test-pits
Weather	After rain; dry and dusty	Wet and muddy	
Crew	Familiar with artefacts, well motivated, professional	Random group	
Speed	Systematic and steady	Fast and uneven	Use staged programme

FIGURE 4.6 Factors affecting successful field-walking.

incoherent sea of choppy paints, which on standing back forms a clearer image. Standing back from the land or looking at it from high up gives a similar advantage. *Aerial survey* is now the most powerful method of finding new sites and checking the survival of those previously found. From about 500m up the landscape is laid out like a counterpane, the natural formations of rivers and hills marked by the regularities of human management over the centuries: field boundaries which are interrupted by later roads; the curve of an amphitheatre or a Roman street plan still visible in a modern town; seen from above, the geometric shapes of the Nasca lines in Peru, so clear from above that they gave rise to talk of aliens from outer space.

These anomalies may be found in *vertical air photographs*, so that there are large air force reconnaissance archives taken in the course of recent wars which may well be worth a search (FIG 4.7a). Aerial archaeologists prefer *oblique photographs* which put their sites into a more artistic, human context (FIG 4.7b). Shallow earthworks are more easily seen by viewing them in glancing sunlight or with a light covering of snow; the shadows heighten the lines and make them more visible. Sites that are completely buried may also show up from the air; they cause patterns in the vegetation – a cereal crop is particularly susceptible, growing tall and darker over buried ditches and shorter and lighter over stone or brick walls. Cropmarks show best when there is a marked moisture deficit (caused by a drought for example). Then they may even show on

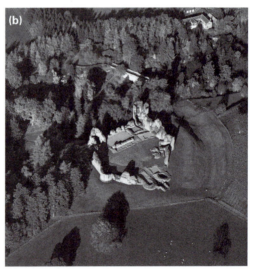

FIGURE 4.7 (a) Vertical air photograph of the early Islamic town of Samarra, Iraq (courtesy of Alastair Northedge) and (b) Kildrummy Castle in a slanting light (Crown copyright RCAHMS).

FIGURE 4.8 (a) Ways of getting aloft: using a paramotor in Armenia and (b) view from the paramotor Rog Palmer).

grass (parchmarks), and they can be enhanced by using different film – such as infrared (Colour Plate 2). Traditionally, aerial archaeologists like to fly in a slow-cruising light aircraft, of a type that can tilt on its side and circle back to get a closer look at something; but there is a widening repertoire of increasingly adventurous lightweight platforms (FIG 4.8). The searcher after cropmarks and earthworks has good days and bad days: cropmarks show well when the ground is dry and the crops grow better over buried ditches, and wither over buried walls (FIG 4.9).

Very shallow earthworks can be recorded nowadays with lidar (Light Detection and Ranging), which does not photograph the land's surface, but surveys it directly with a laser range finder and a GPS. The survey is so precise that it can detect regularities

FIGURE 4.9 Best conditions for finds and photographing sites from the air.

Factor	Good	Poor	Enhancement
Soil	Sand, chalk, light, well drained	Clays	Thermal imaging, exuberance
Crop	Cereals, grasses	Root crops, vines, orchards	Infrared
Relative humidity	Dry, high moisture deficit		
Surface cover	Open	Built-up, forested	Thermal imaging
Even light	Good for cropmarks	Poor for earthworks	
Slanting light, snow	Good for earthworks	Poor for cropmarks	
Air traffic	Light	Heavy, military of civil flight paths	Fly on holidays

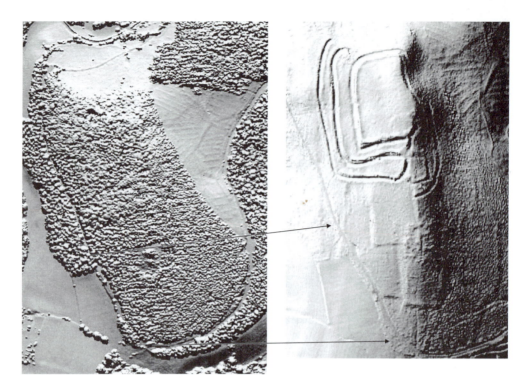

FIGURE 4.10 Lidar sees beneath the trees (B. Devereux).

of a few centimetres above the background. Moreover it works in thick vegetation too: the laser detects the tops of the trees, but penetrates them and hits the ground underneath a few nanoseconds later. A computer program "subtracts" the digital model of the canopy, leaving the digital model of the ground beneath. This is very good news for archaeological surveyors of forested landscapes (FIG 4.10).

Flying higher up, new views of the archaeology of the earth have been collected everywhere by *satellite*. Not all of their findings are available, since the information tends to be treated with some military sensitivity. But the Corona series, taken in the 1960s, has now been declassified and is accessible to all for a modest fee (FIG 4.11). These satellites, which circled the earth many thousands of times looking for missile silos and launch sites, have also found ancient roads and canals and can see something as small as a burial mound. The picture they give is what the world looked like many decades ago – but that is pretty useful: since then new towns and new agriculture have rubbed out many of the ancient features which now lie buried. But at least we know where they were.

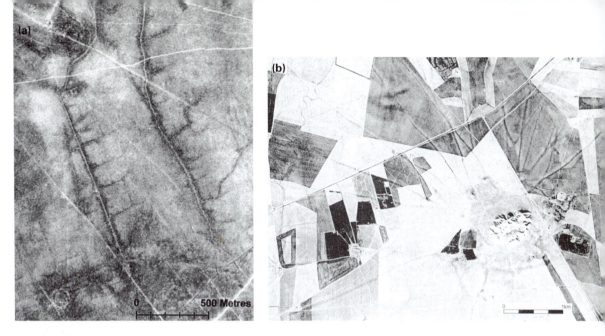

FIGURE 4.11 Corona declassified spy satellite pictures from 1950–70: (a) irrigation in NW Iran (Alizadeh and Ur 2007); (b) trackways around Tell Brak, Syria (Ur 2003).

Applications

The landscape surveyor's toolbox thus contains mapped placenames, surface features and artefact scatters seen on the ground and anomalies spotted from aeroplanes and satellites (FIG 4.12). Now let's examine what we currently do with them. I have divided the types of landscape survey into three, defined by their purpose: *Exploratory survey*, used in reconnaissance, just to see what there is; *evaluation survey*, used in evaluation, to assess visibility; and *research surveys*, designed to collect specific information.

All three applications are used in research projects, that is, projects driven by research questions and funded by research councils or other sponsors. All three applications are also used in rescue projects – that is projects designed to explore rapidly a piece of land about to be affected by a major change such as the construction of a railway line or motorway. In modern parlance, these may be termed "mitigation" surveys in that they mitigate, or compensate for, the inevitable damage to the landscape's archaeology (Chapter 14). In Britain, archaeologists and archaeological managers now talk about the legacy of the landscape as the *historic environment*, and the accumulated information about it as the *historic environment record* (HER). Landscape survey is therefore dedicated to mapping, conserving, researching and mitigating damage to the historic environment.

Exploratory survey takes place whenever an archaeologist looks out of an aeroplane window or picks up a strap-end by chance from the plough. These sightings contribute

Landscape survey

FIGURE 4.12 Techniques and applications for landscape survey

Techniques

- FROM MAPS
- Placenames

- FROM THE AIR
- Aerial survey
- Satellite

- ON THE GROUND
- Surface collection/mapping
- Shovel testing

Applications
- *Reconnaissance*: finding sites (all periods = inventory survey)
- *Evaluation*: Potential for finding sites
- *Field Research*: settlement patterns (selected periods)

to the permanent ongoing reconnaissance of the past. More systematic exploratory surveys are designed to map thoroughly a specific area of land, and follow a formal programme. These might be termed *Inventory Surveys*, since their aim is to record everything that can still be seen. This type of survey has long been the brief of the Royal Commissions on Ancient and Historical Monuments in the British Isles, which have produced some splendid examples of the genre. Early surveys used aerial photography and then checked what they saw by walking on the ground, designating each set of features as a "site" and giving it a number. With improving technology, the features may be mapped to their actual extent (FIG 4.13 shows an extract from an Inventory Survey of Bodmin Moor). Electronic recording of digital data means that very detailed ancient landscapes can be stored and studied at any scale you choose.

It will often happen that research or rescue projects need reconnaissance of vast tracts of land that were not densely occupied: here *sampling strategies* are widely applied. They use the principle of "windows" that are small (10 × 10m) and may be round, square or rectangular (FIG 4.14). The way they are distributed over the land depends on the terrain, the culture and what is already known about them. For real *terra incognita*, the samples may be numerous and randomly distributed (*random samples*); for better known lands, the samples may be evenly spaced (*systematic*) and applied in zones. Commercial archaeologists in the UK are inclined to use long transects ("line surveys") spaced at regular intervals.

Sampling surveys are ideal for reconnaissance projects; they cannot claim to give an inventory (samplers call inventory surveys "total coverage"). Nor are they so useful for research surveys, at least not in land that has been densely occupied, since so much will be missed. They represent a useful preliminary – a true reconnaissance. In

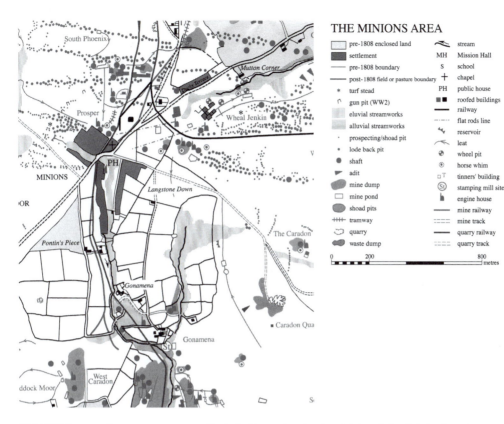

THE MINIONS AREA

☐	pre-1808 enclosed land	≈	stream
▨	settlement	MH	Mission Hall
—	pre-1808 boundary	S	school
—	post-1808 field or pasture boundary	+	chapel
∗	turf stead	PH	public house
∩	gun pit (WW2)	■■	roofed buildings
	eluvial streamworks	—	railway
	alluvial streamworks	----	flat rods line
·	prospecting/shoad pit		reservoir
•	lode back pit	↖	leat
●	shaft	⊘	wheel pit
►	adit	⊙	horse whim
	mine dump	☐T	tinners' building
☐	mine pond	Ⓢ	stamping mill site
	shoad pits	▮	engine house
┼┼┼┼	tramway	—	mine railway
◠	quarry	====	mine track
	waste dump	—	quarry railway
		====	quarry track

0   200   800
                                        metres

FIGURES 4.13 Inventory survey on Bodmin Moor showing key (right) (© English Heritage).

practice, there are few places on earth that are still totally unmapped, so there will normally be prior information of some kind. *Adaptive sampling* takes account of what we already know, targeting the location and intensity of surface collection to build on previous models or fill in gaps. In this respect sampling is moving closer to the idea of value-led survey, of which more later.

The face of the landscape is itself dynamic, changing its character with advancing age and with the time of year. So, even an inventory survey, however well planned, is still only a snapshot of what could be briefly seen then. *Site-formation surveys* are intended to assess and investigate the current performance of different archaeological methods of survey in different types of terrain. As an obvious example, aerial mapping of cropmarks will work most effectively on arable fields in late summer. Surface finds might be visible, but they may not exactly reflect the location of settlement: thanks to recent ploughing, the soil may have moved down the slopes into the flood plain, taking the surface finds with it. The help of geographers, environmentalists and soil scientists is welcome here, since they are concerned with soil and vegetation histories, not just the plains and forest as they are today, so can offer guidance on the way the soil has moved about and what the surface patterns might represent.

Historic Landscape Characterisation (HLC) is a neat modern technique for compiling the historic uses of a landscape, an exercise that finds use in both research and management of landscapes (FIG 4.15). The surface presented to us contains many clues about its use in the past: place names imply where woods once were and the boundaries of arable land can be tracked back many centuries and sometimes over millennia. These names and boundaries can be combined with the locations of known archaeological sites, so as to give layered maps. Place these layers on a GIS (Geographical Information System) and you have a powerful instrument for examining the landscape character and its potential for new exploration. The coincidences are very noticeable and show where people have returned over and over to access the benefits of pasture, arable, timber or water. At the same time sparsely occupied areas show up, inviting intensive survey on the ground or from the air to confirm they really were unoccupied. HLC is for landscapes what deposit mapping is for sites (Chapter 5

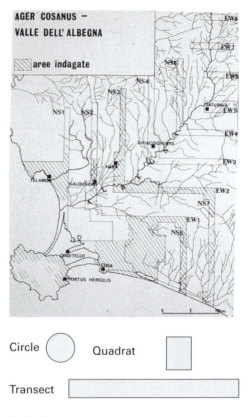

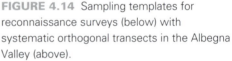

FIGURE 4.14 Sampling templates for reconnaissance surveys (below) with systematic orthogonal transects in the Albegna Valley (above).

has more information). The GIS of a Historic Landscape Characterisation provides a map with time depth, acting both as a synthesis of the story so far, and as a blueprint for future work.

That future work is likely to include the intensive survey of land which will be changed by new construction. For example, the construction of a motorway involves a corridor of land 300m wide and many kilometres long. In commercial projects, work usually begins indoors with maps and records, leading to proposals for survey in the field which in turn lead on to more intensive survey and excavation in advance of destruction (see Chapter 14 for more). These *mitigation surveys* follow what is essentially a value-led procedure, if only because large sums of money are involved. The first task (desktop assessment) is to collect what we know from earlier records and reconnaissance surveys, and then to try and assess what we cannot see (evaluation phase). A comprehensive survey or package of surveys would then be designed to try and fill all the gaps – effectively an inventory survey of the affected corridor. This

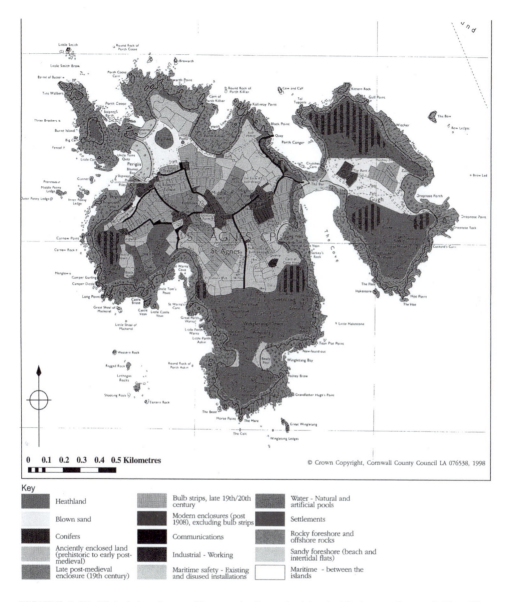

Key

Heathland		Bulb strips, late 19th/20th century		Water - Natural and artificial pools
Blown sand		Modern enclosures (post 1908), excluding bulb strips		Settlements
Conifers		Communications		Rocky foreshore and offshore rocks
Anciently enclosed land (prehistoric to early post-medieval)		Industrial - Working		Sandy foreshore (beach and intertidal flats)
Late post-medieval enclosure (19th century)		Maritime safety - Existing and disused installations		Maritime - between the islands

FIGURE 4.15 Historic Landscape Characterisation – the island of St Agnes, Cornwall. The different shades represent different types of land use (Crown copyright Cornwall County Council).

is a very frequent application of landscape survey used in developing nations busy creating new towns and an extensive infrastructure. The survey is intended to identify sensitive areas – for example, peat bogs containing well-preserved prehistoric trackways or part of a known Medieval village – and the archaeologists draw up a list of sites to be avoided or to be investigated further before the road is built (see Chapter 14 for an example).

Landscape survey is also the principal instrument of the academic archaeologist, for exploring new territory or interrogating well-known lands with specific questions for purposes of *research*. These questions have to be matched, as always, to what is available. On Dartmoor, Andrew Fleming had mainly ribbons of stones ("reaves") to work from (FIG 4.16). By mapping them all, from the air and on the ground, he could

FIGURE 4.16 Andrew Fleming's research survey of Dartmoor Reaves: (a) aerial photo of Horridge Common; (b) map of reaves (stony banks) on Eastern Dartmoor; and (c) interpretation of territories (A. Fleming).

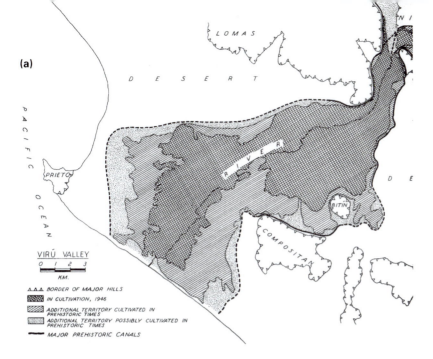

(a)

VIRÚ VALLEY

0 1 2 3
KM.

▲▲▲ BORDER OF MAJOR HILLS

▨▨ IN CULTIVATION, 1946

▨▨ ADDITIONAL TERRITORY CULTIVATED IN
PREHISTORIC TIMES

▨▨ ADDITIONAL TERRITORY POSSIBLY CULTIVATED IN
PREHISTORIC TIMES

▬▬▬ MAJOR PREHISTORIC CANALS

FIGURE 4.17 Willey in the Virú: (a) the survey area; (b) Willey's jeep; (c) key used on survey plans; (d) synthesis, suggested community patterns for the Puerto Moorin period; and (e) plan of a site (V-81) (G. Willey).

(b)

(c)

▨ STONE WALL,
IRREGULAR BOULDERS,
"DOUBLE-FACING".

▨ UNUSUALLY WIDE OR MASSIVE
STONE MASONRY WALL WITH
ABUNDANT RUBBLE FILL.

▥ ADOBE WALL OF SMALL
RECTANGULAR ADOBES.

▥ ADOBE WALL OF CONICAL
OR BALL-SHAPED ADOBES.

▯ WALL OF TAPIA
ADOBE SECTIONS.

▮ SINGLE ROW OF STONES.

▨ INDICATES
RAISED PLATFORM.

▨ INDICATES TWO LEVELS OF
RAISED PLATFORMS WITH
SOLID BLACK THE HIGHER.

▦ SOLID ADOBE PLATFORM OF
RECTANGULAR ADOBES.

⊏⊐ DOORWAYS.

〰 INDICATES ELEVATION
IN TOPOGRAPHY WITHIN
CONTOUR LINES.

°°° OLD EXCAVATIONS
USUALLY IN A CEMETERY.

▌▌ DRAINAGE OR WASH AND
DIRECTION OF FLOW.

⬮ LARGE BOULDERS.

⬬ HEDGE LINE,
TREES, MONTE.

═══ CANAL OR ROAD,
AS INDICATED.

----- INDICATES PRESUMED,
DOUBTFUL, OR APPROXIMATE
CONTINUATION, AS OF A
WALL OR CANAL.

(d)

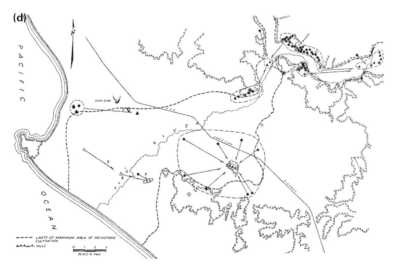

----- LIMITS OF MAXIMUM AREA OF PREHISTORIC
CULTIVATION

▲▲▲ HILLS

0 1 2
SCALE IN KMS.

(e)

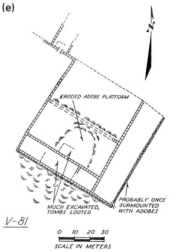

ERODED ADOBE PLATFORM

PROBABLY ONCE
SURMOUNTED
WITH ADOBES

MUCH EXCAVATED,
TOMBS LOOTED

V-81

0 10 20 30
SCALE IN METERS

see that they formed sets of field boundaries, each set put in place at the same time. The sequence, where one set gave way to another, could be determined by excavating the point where the banks of two systems crossed, to see which came first.

Early surveys developed by Alfred Kidder in Arizona and Gordon Willey in the Virú Valley of Peru made use both of ruins and pottery on the surface (FIG 4.17). First an excavation was necessary to put the pottery – then little known – into its chronological order using a stratified sequence. Then, armed with this typology, surveyors covered the land, plotting the occurrence, on the surface, of pottery of each type. The resulting maps showed by means of earlier and later pottery where the earlier and the later people had been living. Willey's survey area included a large number of still visible earthworks, buildings and tombs, which he grouped into types of monument. His maps showed where people had settled in each century, which types of sites they used and what types of land they exploited; but he took the analysis still further – asking what were the relative sizes of settlements and how did they relate to each other? This in turn suggested social and economic changes experienced by the peoples of the valley. This level of sophistication is possible when the landscape is rich in visible remains, but even then the picture is only partial, as Willey was the first to recognise. The pottery on the surface is only the pottery that has been disturbed, usually the latest occupation; an earlier settlement may still lie hidden.

Research surveys may also be used to provide a context for a major site – an exploration of its *hinterland* and an understanding of how town and country depended, each upon the other. The city of Anuradhapura has been the subject of large scale excavation by Robin Coningham with an international team who have traced its development from an Iron Age village to its famous days as the capital of Sri Lanka (from 500BC to AD1000). In 2004 the team initiated an exploration of the surrounding countryside using topographical inspection and surface collection (FIG 4.18). The town lies on the Malwatu River – an obvious attractor of settlement – so its banks were systematically searched for signs of ancient sites. In addition, a circle of 50km radius was measured from the citadel at Anuradhapura and the team investigated this search area using 24 transects positioned randomly, each 20km long. Within these transects, fieldwalkers recorded every type of site, ancient and modern, that they could see, and amongst them were able to distinguish those belonging to the medieval period. They counted 398 ceramic scatters, 68 monastic sites, 73 other sites with stone pillars and walls, 61 sites with slag, 11 possible megalithic tombs, 5 stone bridges and 56 water-management features. The ceramic sites were ranked by area, from over 250m across to those that measured only a few metres, while the presence or absence of fragments of luxury goods gave another indication of wealth. Monastic sites were identified from finds of Buddhist sculpture, *stupas* or inscriptions.

Some of the vegetation in the region such as forests and elephant grass can be difficult to get through or form a line and were hiding the sites, while in paddy fields 90% of the surface was underwater. On the other hand, in villages, parkland and ploughed fields, survey teams could form a line 10m apart and more easily spot

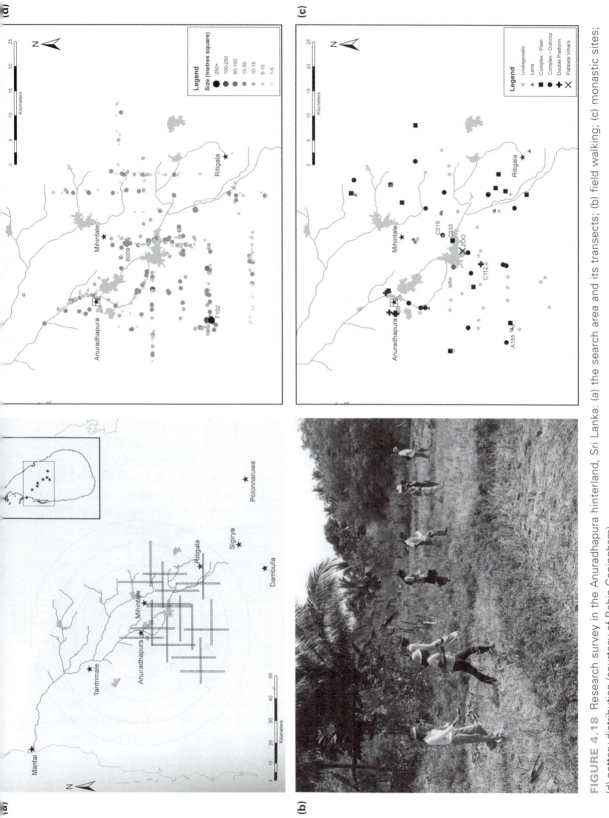

FIGURE 4.18 Research survey in the Anuradhapura hinterland, Sri Lanka: (a) the search area and its transects; (b) field walking; (c) monastic sites; (d) pottery distribution (courtesy of Robin Coningham).

pottery on the ground. The different types of terrain were also mapped so that the bias of the results due to varied conditions could be assessed. Although documents had predicted a marked hierarchy of sites, the survey found that the key settlement type outside ancient Anuradhapura was the Buddhist monastery. This led Coningham to propose a "theocratic landscape" in which monks played a major role in managing resources using a network of monasteries in touch with each other. This survey showed that, however large an excavation, its story cannot be complete without some knowledge of the contemporary environment – this gives it a context.

As noted above, one problem with pottery plotting is that ancient peoples dumped it on the fields with the midden intended as fertiliser. Archaeologists in Norfolk, England have addressed this by distinguishing pottery that marked a settlement from pottery that had been spread on the fields. In the parish of Witton, Keith Wade's point of departure was the collection of ceramics gathered by a farmer/landowner (also an enthusiastic archaeologist) who had been retrieving material off his fields for 25 years (FIG 4.19). Dating to the first millennium AD, some of the pottery looked freshly broken, while other sherds were small with abraded edges (rubbed smooth by being tossed about). Plotted out on the map, the more freshly broken sherds clustered together and so probably represented the sites of ancient settlements, while the abraded sherds ought to represent their ploughed fields. By plotting the dated pottery, a landscape could be seen to develop: in the 5th to 6th centuries a number of small villages, coalescing into a single large village in the 7th which endured to the 10th century and later. Meanwhile, the land under arable serving these settlements doubled in extent every 150 years.

In the Mediterranean, the problem can be the same, but the amount of pottery tends to be enormous. It is here that research procedures are being developed that can perhaps be more clearly seen as staged and value led. On Cyprus, for example, Michael Given and Bernard Knapp decided to investigate the homelands of the early copper extractors (who gave the island its name), focusing on the north side of the Troodos mountains where the copper is. They mapped the present topography and deduced where soils had been denuded or accumulated – and mapped the current distribution of plant types, noting where there were plants growing which were averse to copper. Then they interviewed local residents to learn what memories survived, either about how the land had been used in recent times or how it was supposed to connect to prehistory. This information in effect constituted an evaluation that could be fed into the design phase. The fieldwork programme mainly applied surface inspection and collection, using transects laid out 500m apart, each measuring 50m wide and not more than 100m long, and then walked at 5m intervals. Artefacts were counted and selectively retrieved, using the criterion of first difference, i.e. the first pottery sherd was joined only by examples that differed from it. This empirical stage revealed areas where ceramics or flint were plentiful or unusual and these were designated SIAs (or special interest areas), typically 500m across. These were then investigated more intensively: either by total coverage (a "block survey") or with

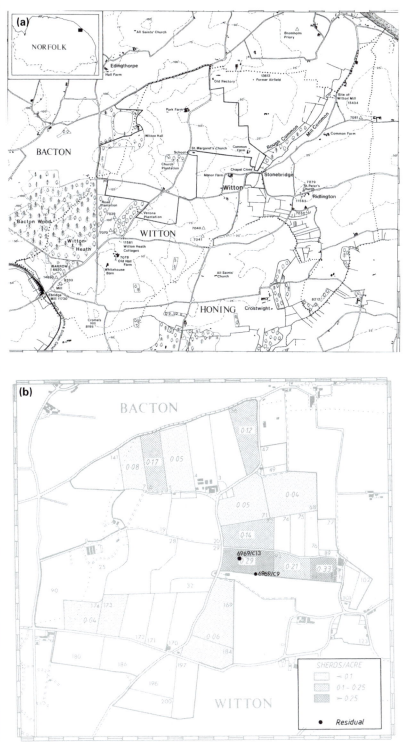

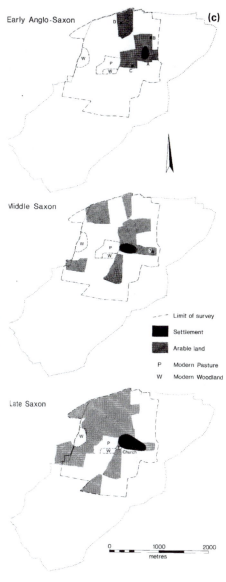

FIGURE 4.19 Twenty-five years'
field-walking on farmland at Witton, Norfolk:
(a) map of the search area; (b) densities
of surface pottery in the Middle-Saxon
period; and (c) interpretation: evolution of
settlement, AD500–1100 (East Anglian
Archaeology).

samples laid out along cruciform axes. These in turn revealed POSIs (or places of special interest), which were subsequently designated as sites or (where there was evidence for upstanding structures) as a settlement. Notebooks were used to encourage fieldworkers to comment on the conditions and the countryside, the work and each other. The results from surface inspection and aerial photography were entered into a GIS. Over five years the survey team members walked 6.54km² – i.e. 10% of the area of interest. They identified 11 SIAs and 142 POSIs, counted 87,600 sherds of pottery and 8,111 pieces of tile, 29,235 sherds of pottery and 2,846 lithics. The patterns of this material mapped the movement of quarries, ore extraction and settlements of different dates and sizes through time and gave an indication of the social structure at each prehistoric period.

In pursuit of settlement patterns in Archaic and Classical Boeotia, Greece, Anthony Snodgrass and John Bintliff also used a staged procedure, where one survey builds on the one before (FIG 4.20). They first covered their search area rapidly, not picking anything up but just counting the number of pieces of amphorae and tiles on the surface using a clickometer – (the little hand-held counter used to count tins on supermarket shelves). This "click survey" gave them an initial map of the density of

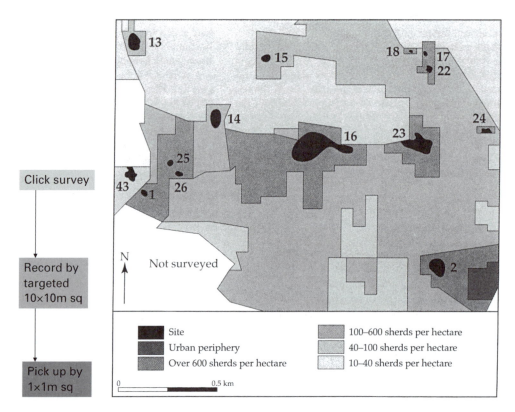

FIGURE 4.20 Value-led research survey – Boeotia, Greece (courtesy of Anthony Snodgrass).

surface material. The denser areas could then be targeted by more intensive survey, still not picking up, but by recording the content of surface assemblages in 10×10m squares. This revealed settlement concentrations which could be surveyed more intensively still – this time picking up datable sherds in 1×1m squares. The pattern produced was vivid and subtle: settlement areas, areas of middens surrounding them, and areas of cultivation beyond that.

These research surveys were not only executed in stages, but were value-led – in that the assessment of the results from each stage allowed the next stage to be programmed. Thus even where no excavation is intended, a survey project can benefit from the idea of following a staged procedure, i.e. reconnaissance – evaluation – design – research. Of these, the reconnaissance stage is already well developed, since this is what most inventory and mitigation surveys are, while a few surveys intended as research are actually addressing reconnaissance targets (mapping where the visible things are). More evaluation exercises are needed to discover why we can see what we can see, and so design the research to map the people we are looking for, not just the surfaces that are left to us. This objective is likely to benefit from more evaluation-investigations into how artefact distributions form and become skewed through later disturbance. Where this can be done, the design of a research survey will include a number of different instruments targeted at different zones. Landscape archaeology used for research or mitigation should therefore pass through evaluation and design stages before it begins. In evaluation, the full toolkit may be deployed: inspection of satellite records, followed by HLC, with assessments of visibility to aerial photography and surface collection. Specific questions are then posed and a specific set of areas (a template) laid on the map to answer them.

Mitigation surveys are usually targeted at what can be seen, either from the air or on the ground, and although they may be more intensive than partial these days, will often limit themselves to the question "What is there?" in the manner of an inventory survey. This is understandable given the pressure of time and money, and is certainly better than nothing. However, you will have noticed that the research surveyor coaxes information from the land using a staged approach, revisiting it several times with different techniques applied in different conditions. Threatened landscapes too deserve the increased understanding that results from the value-led approach, and should at least pass through the reconnaissance, evaluation, design and research stages. This is not as impractical (or expensive) as it might appear to developers, and is being increasingly adopted (see Chapter 14 for more). Perhaps the most significant difference for future surveyors, whether involved in mitigation or research, is that they will expect to survey an area of interest several times, each stage gradually raising the visibility of the unseen until it reaches the limits possible today.

In sum . . .

According to the European Landscape Convention, a landscape is "an area, as perceived by people, whose character is the result of the action and interaction of natural and/or human factors". The archaeological survey of a landscape is designed to bring to light its current historical value, making use of maps, archives, surface inspection, aerial and satellite photography to define historical character, zones and sites. Much landscape survey is dedicated to the reconnaissance stage – exploring new territory or compiling comprehensive inventories of everything that shows, often in advance of disturbance by modern building programmes. Deployed in the evaluation stage, landscape survey aims at understanding the formation process and the relative visibility of different periods on the surface. In research, a project design harnesses all the techniques at different scales and templates to address economic and social questions by mapping the changing patterns of settlement and land use. But the most widespread application of landscape survey is in mitigation, where a wide tract of land is to be erased or disturbed for the purposes of modern life. In this case, the aim is both to gather as much information as possible and to make sense of it – a terrific challenge, needing systematic application of the reconnaissance, evaluation, design and research stages.

"There is . . . a vast amount to be done by mere field-work without excavation at all. This sort of field-work is hardly practiced at all outside Britain and a few countries of North-western Europe." So said O. G. S. Crawford, editor of *Antiquity* in 1951. Landscape survey is now the most widely practiced form of archaeological fieldwork the world over: Crawford would be pleased. It is also one of the most exciting, in which geography, environment and archaeology combine to explore the unknown world in deep time.

Briefing

History and principles

Survey enthusiasts seem to write a great deal more than excavators – so there is a great deal to read. Crawford 1951, 1953 was an early advocate, but the classic survey projects are Kidder 1962 (south-west USA, 1920s) and Willey 1953 (Peru, 1940s). The tradition has continued in different parts of the world with (for example) Flannery 1976 (Mexico), McAdams 1981 (Iraq), Ammerman 1981, 1985 (Italy), Blanton et al 1982, Kowaleski et al 1989 (Mexico), G. Barker 1991, 1995 (Italy), Alcock et al 1994 (Greece), Pasquinucci and Trément 2000 (Mediterranean), Ogleby 1994 (Papua New Guinea), Underhill et al. 2002 (China), Coningham et al 2007 (Sri Lanka). Interesting modern UK examples are Powlesland et al 1997 (Vale of Pickering), and Edmonds and McElearney 1999 (Gardom's Edge). For discussions of principles see

Redman and Watson 1970, Redman 1987, Billman and Feinman 1999, Alcock and Cherry 1996, Ashmore and Knapp 1999. For how-to-do-it text books see MacManamon 1984, Hester et al 1997, Wilkinson 2001, Collins et al 2003 and *techniques*, below. **Ideas of landscape:** Tilley 1994 for its emotional aspects; Layton and Ucko 1999 for a great collection of studies; E. Carver and Lelong 2004 for landscapes as cultural assets. Retallack 2001 (ix) for the quote about landscape's timeless quality, and CoE 2000 (article 1) for the European Landscape Convention definition.

Techniques

For the state of the art one can do no better than to find the latest publication of the Royal Commission of Ancient and Historical Monuments of Scotland. At the time of writing this was their 2007 *In the shadow of Bennachie*, exemplary for its documentary and surface survey, and the book itself shows the quality of photography and mapping that archaeology deserves but rarely gets. The best introduction to **archives and map sources** is to go to the record office and start exploring with the help of the curators. Older overviews are Crawford 1953, C. Taylor 1974, Rogers and Rowley 1974 with Rippon 2004 as a neat modern manual; examples of **place-name studies** are Gelling 1988 (UK), Julyan 1996 (New Mexico). For an account of the **portable antiquities scheme** see Bland 2005; a report of the harvest of declared finds comes out every year, e.g. British Museum 2008.

The best exponents of **topographic survey** are the Royal Commissions of Scotland and England (the latter now closed down), but they have yet to issue a manual. Howard 2007 covers principles and techniques of **mapping land**, including the use of TST, GPS, CAD and GIS; Leach 1994 shows how to record *without* electronic equipment, i.e. with tape and theodolite. Carver and Souidi 1996 for FIG 4.5. For **GPS**, Bunting and Summers 2002 and Fitts 2005, while Fenwick 2004 gives a nice application for mapping roads in ancient Egypt (see Chapter 5). **GIS** is introduced in Kvamme 1989, Lock and Stančič 1990, and see Chapter 10. **Recording artefact scatters ("plowzone archaeology")** is the main subject of Banning 2002, and there are numerous accounts of experiences on different terrains, e.g. Ammerman 1985, Gaffney et al 1991, Francovich and Patterson 2000 (Mediterranean), Plog et al 1982, Odell and Cowan 1987, Dunnell 1990, Shott 1995 (USA), Fanning and Holdaway 2004 (Australia), Gardin 2000 (Asia), Haselgrove et al 1985, Kuna 1998 (Central Europe), Ogleby 1994 (forest), Scholfield 1991 (UK), Steinberg 1996 (Denmark), Underhill et al 2002 (China). Butler et al 1979 for no-collection strategy. **Shovel testing** is used on unploughed land, e.g. vineyards, Hodges 1993; and see Bloemker and Oakley 1999, Krakker et al 1983, Shott 1985, 1989; Howell 1993 for use of augers to obtain ceramic samples. Pasquinucci and Trément 2000 has examples of surface survey applied to sites in the Mediterranean area.

Aerial survey: reviews of the art by Crawford 1929, Palmer 1984, Edis et al 1989, Bewley 1993, Bewley et al 2005; Gould 1995a. Faustmann and Palmer 2005 for the use of a paramotor. For putting the cropmarks on a map: Wilson 1982, Gould 1995b, Haigh 1991, Haigh and Ipson 1994, but the photos can usually be rectified and plotted digitally for you now. **Lidar** was introduced in Bewley et al 2005 with Devereux et al 2005 (seeing beneath the trees), Challis et al 2008 for HER applications. Use of a **satellite** platform and **corona**, C. Cox 1992 (UK), Gheyle et al 2004 (Turkmenistan), Philip et al 2002, Ur 2003 (Syria), Hritz and Wilkinson 2006 (radar), Casana and Cothren 2008 (3-D imaging), Beck et al 2007, Sherratt 2004 (spotting tells from space). Pasquinucci and Trément 2000 has a section on aerial survey in the Mediterranean area.

Applications

Good examples of **inventory surveys** are RCAHMS 1993 (Strath of Kildonan), Johnson and Rose 1994, Herring et al 2008 (Bodmin); for a fine example from Ireland, O'Sullivan and Sheehan 1996. For discussion of its US equivalent, **full coverage survey**, see Cowgill et al 1990, Fish and Kowalewski 1990; Thomas 1998 (125–6, 138), Gardin 2000 (302). For survey by **sampling**, Redman and Watson 1970, Flannery 1976, Plog et al 1982, Redman 1987, Thomas 1998 (106–13) (Reese River), Hester et al 1997 (21–37). For **adaptive sampling**, Thompson 1996, Orton 2000. **Evaluation and site formation surveys** examine the territory for its formation processes and for what you can't see, focusing especially on the significance of pottery scatters: Rick 1976, Boismier 1997, Bollong 1994, Gaffney et al 1991, Palmer and Cox 1993, Terranato and Ammerman 1996, Yorston et al 1990. **HLC (Historic Landscape Characterisation)** was introduced in Cornwall by Herring 1998 and Turner 2006 uses it for research in the same area. Rippon 2004 for HLC as a management tool, especially Meare, Somerset (132–42). Two good examples of **mitigation surveys** for road schemes (out of many thousands unpublished) are Artz et al 1998 (USA) and NRA 2005 (Ireland). The selected examples of **research surveys** were: Fleming 1988, updated 2008 (Dartmoor, UK); Willey 1953, 1999 (Virú valley, Peru); Lawson 1983 (Witton, Norfolk, UK); Coningham et al 2007 (hinterland survey in Sri Lanka); Given and Knapp 2003 (staged survey in Cyprus); Alcock et al 1994; Bintliff and Snodgrass 1988a, b; Snodgrass 1990 (value-led research survey in Greece).

5 SITE SURVEY

Looking at sites

"Site" is one of those words archaeologists like to argue about. For some a site is a real place in the past where people lived or buried their dead. For others, that is potentially true of everywhere and a "site" is simply the place where archaeologists are working at the moment. Thus, when a cluster of pottery in a field is said to be a "site", the implication is that this cluster marks the location of an ancient village. But when archaeologists say "When you are next in town come and visit my site" they mean "the place I am working", as in a building site. Just to be annoying, in this chapter I am using the word in a third sense – that is, "an area of ground in need of investigation". It may well turn into a site in the sense of ancient site, and I will probably be working there, but at different parts on different days.

Site survey is simply landscape survey on a smaller scale: the area is smaller but the focus is finer. Site survey sports a terrific set of techniques, and they are increasing in number all the time. What connects them is that they find, or "sense", archaeological features, but do not damage them. They can probe beneath the surface, so they are "invasive", but they leave everything intact (or intend to), so they are non-destructive. Science is doing for site survey what it is doing for surgery – allowing us to see deep into the object of study without doing too much damage or removing tissue, which in our case can never grow again.

The principal applications of site survey are in evaluation, where the objective is to know as much about a site as possible before deciding what to do about it (its design), and in research, where its methods are deployed in the implementation stage with a view to chronicling the development of a settlement or cemetery without digging it.

Techniques

Site survey techniques group into five: using maps and documents, topographical mapping, surface collection, geophysical survey and sample excavation. Some of

Site survey

- USING MAPS and DOCUMENTS

- SURFACE MAPPING
- Topography
- Vegetation

- SURFACE COLLECTION

- GEOPHYSICAL SURVEY
- Metal detector
- Resistivity
- Magnetometry

- SAMPLE EXCAVATION
- Shovel testing
- Bore holes
- Quadrats and trenches
- Strip-and-map

FIGURE 5.1 Techniques for site survey.

these we have met already (FIG 5.1). Like all surveys, this one starts indoors in the archive and map room, where we can often discover surprising things about the study area, particularly what happened to it during the more recent centuries (FIG 5.2). It is good to know where recent hedges were grown and ditches dug – if only to discount them as ancient things. It is also good to know where houses once stood and tracks once ran. It is equally important to know where modern pipes carrying water, oil or electricity are buried, as these are going to affect our remote mapping instruments. In the UK it is mandatory to discover where public service cables run before a project

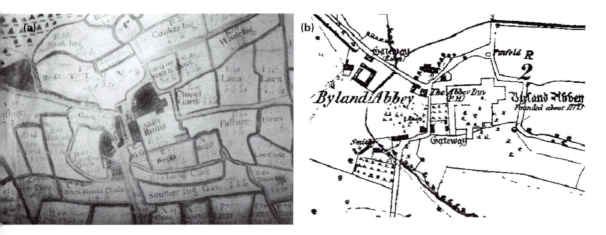

FIGURE 5.2 The medieval abbey at Byland on maps of the 18th century (a) and the 19th century (b). These maps were used to give the basic layout of the monastery in advance of an evaluation project in 2008 (FAS Ltd).

starts, by telephoning the agencies concerned – a procedure known as "dial before you dig".

Our area of study, say a patch of countryside 500×500m in extent, is marked out on the map together with everything we know about it so far. The modern terrain – the way the land is being used now – will determine which methods are going to work best, e.g. topographical mapping where the ground undulates, surface collection on ploughsoil, magnetic survey away from electricity carriers like pylons. The area is therefore divided into zones, with a list of operations (interventions) drawn up for each zone (see Chapter 3). Topography is mapped using a TST (see Chapter 4) and the points turned into a hachure plan, a contour map or a digital terrain model (DTM). Hachures show the breaks of slope (whatever their height) so are often more expressive of ancient earthworks (FIG 5.3). Contours show points at the same height above

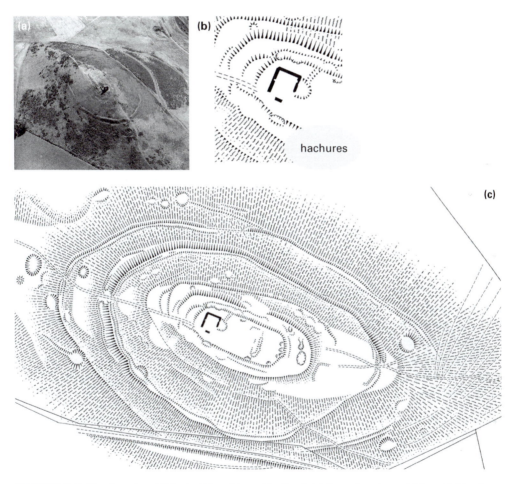

FIGURE 5.3 The Iron Age hill-fort of Dunnideer, Scotland: (a) from the air; and (b) and (c) hachure plan (Crown copyright RCAHMS).

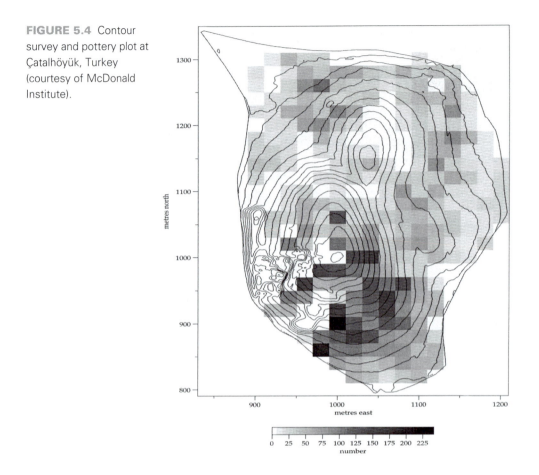

FIGURE 5.4 Contour survey and pottery plot at Çatalhöyük, Turkey (courtesy of McDonald Institute).

sea level joined by a line (FIG 5.4). Surveyors gather points on the break of slope using a TST or GPS. Computerised plotting programs use the resulting database to plot either hachure or contour plans as required and the contour plans can be made so that they too show the breaks of slope. A DTM uses a computer program to model the topography as a continuous surface which can be viewed from different directions to put slight bumps into relief using artificial shadow (see FIG 5.5 and 5.15). Sometimes surface features are pretty subtle – ribbons of low banks or stones which remember ancient trackways for example. They may not show from the air (or we may be in a no-fly zone), so we need to build up the picture piece by piece by survey. FIG 5.5 shows an example from Egypt.

Surface collection for site survey will generally use total rather than sample coverage, since at this scale we want to see variations from metre to metre rather than mile to mile. The pick-up in this case may require each individual sherd to be plotted (by TST) in three dimensions rather than collected by metre square (FIG 5.4). As well as a two-dimensional map, the three-dimensional co-ordinates of the pottery plot can give us a contour map of the surface: a steady rise and fall may indicate that the modern

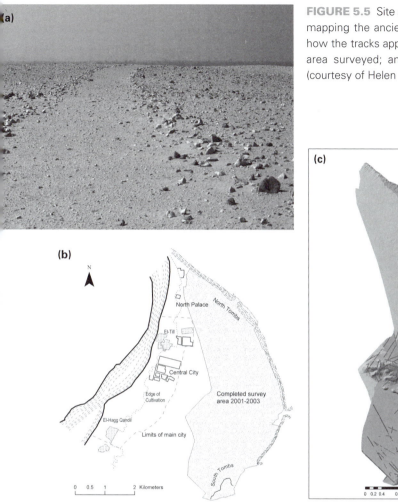

FIGURE 5.5 Site survey at Tel el-Amarna, Egypt, mapping the ancient road lines with a GPS: (a) how the tracks appear on the ground; (b) map of area surveyed; and (c) the road lines located (courtesy of Helen Fenwick).

farmers had nearly ploughed away an earlier medieval system of ridge and furrow. In addition to pottery and flint and topography, surface inspection may address itself to other parameters: the concentration of phosphate has proved revealing, particularly in Scandinavia. Phosphate is a decay product of many human and animal activities; plotting the quantities of phosphate present in the soil gives an indication of where these activities were concentrated (FIG 5.6).

On turf or pasture, floral patterns can signal the history of the land (FIG 5.7). Mow the grass in autumn and wait for the spring flowers and shrubs to appear. Bracken and brambles like a disturbed, well-aerated soil, such as is left by a rabbit warren – or a robbed grave. Moss grows on sandy subsoils where the topsoil has been removed. Thick-leaved grasses like well-watered rich soils – and so on. One way of improving the legibility of turf is to plough it yourself, and then field-walk it to retrieve

FIGURE 5.6 Site surveys carried out at Sutton Hoo. The surface finds are marked by a dot, the double lines are plotted cropmarks, and the greyscale squares are phosphate measurements.

the artefact pattern. This is justifiable if you can show that the land had already been ploughed before, and in this way the new ploughing does not count as fresh damage.

There is now a considerable variety of electromagnetic sensing devices which we know as *geophysical*. The simplest are the metal detectors beloved of treasure seekers, some of them highly sophisticated (both machine and user) (Chapter 4, FIG 4.4 has a picture). As well as metals these instruments can pick up a signal from certain kinds of pottery. But they find only artefacts not features, and their problem is that it is hard to know what kind of an object makes the beep and how deep it is, without digging it up. This means that the metal detector does not conform to the site survey specification of being "non-destructive". They can, however, be very useful in finding metallic traces that have disappeared. At Coleshill, near Birmingham, a detectorist plotted the fallen beams of a Roman temple from rows of utterly rusted

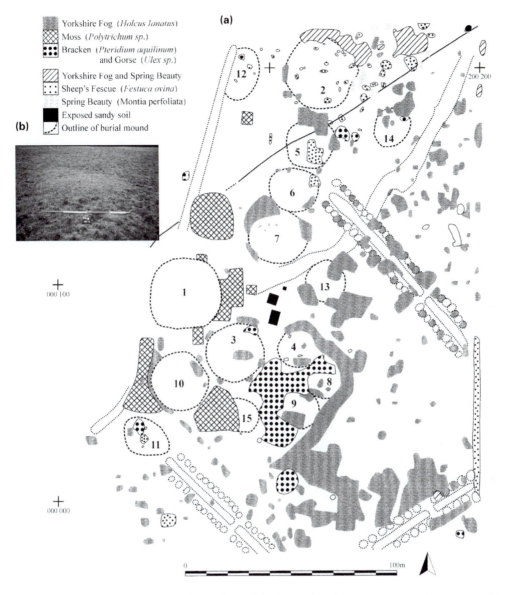

FIGURE 5.7 (a) Floral survey on the surface of the Sutton Hoo barrow cemetery. In the event this pattern mainly indicated the sites of holes dug by recent farmers, tomb raiders and archaeologists; and (b) photograph of an anomaly.

and invisible nails found by a metal detector. At Sutton Hoo, a metal detector was used to discover lines of metallic signals where iron from wire fences had dripped onto the ground. The fences had gone, but knowing where they had been allowed lawyers to demonstrate the former extent of the landowner's property – and in this case resulted in a gift of land to the Sutton Hoo Trust. Metal detectors can also help

FIGURE 5.8 Geophysical surveyors in action:
(a) soil sounding radar; (b) fluxgate gradiometry;
(c) magnetic susceptibility; (d) resistivity meter;
and (e) caesium magnetometer (N. Macbeth).

to locate areas that are rich in metal debris, which are therefore unsuitable for some kinds of geophysical instrument.

The more sophisticated instruments in the geophysical toolbox divide into electrical, magnetic and radar devices (FIG 5.8). Electrical instruments pass an electric current through the ground and measure the resistance or resistivity or conductivity at that point. The resistance to electric current varies with the type of soil and the amount of moisture in it, so this kind of instrument will distinguish between, for example, a ditch and a wall. Magnetic instruments (magnetometers) read the lines of force of the earth's magnetic field and note where they are being reinforced or weakened by buried conductors. Other magnetic instruments read the magnetic properties of the soil (its susceptibility) directly. Baked clays and some decayed wood are strongly magnetic, so this kind of instrument is good at finding hearths or big post-holes.

Whether it measures electric resistance (ohms) or magnetism (teslas), the object of the survey is to map out the relative strength of the signals from the ground at intervals (say 50cm) and observe the pattern, which in turn can be attributed to buried features. Instruments are getting better all the time, but in general they can only "see" features a metre or more across (FIG 5.9). The Caesium vapour magnetometer has succeeded in mapping post-pits only 50cm across, and improvement is promised (FIG 5.10). However, at present the biggest single challenge to geophysics is to find and map human burials, which are usually small (2×1m) and often close together, denying the instrument the contrast it needs. This problem needs solving since, of all site types, the cemetery is the one most in need of prior site survey, for reasons of both research and conservation.

The performance of a geophysical instrument depends on the terrain and the type of buried feature. This is often hard to know in advance, and nor are there yet any specific

(a)

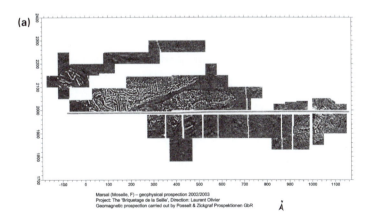

Marsal (Moselle, F) – geophysical prospection 2002/2003
Project: The 'Briquetage de la Seille', Direction: Laurent Olivier
Geomagnetic prospection carried out by Posselt & Zickgraf Prospektionen GbR

(b)

FIGURE 5.9 Fluxgate gradiometry survey of an Iron Age salt works at Marsal, France. (a) Geophysical map, showing furnaces either side of a stream bed. (b) Furnaces under excavation (Laurent Olivier 2007).

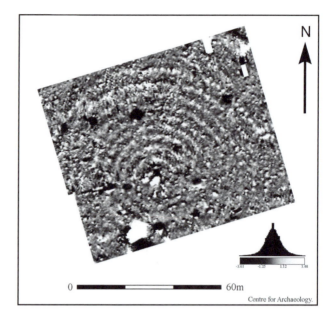

FIGURE 5.10 Caesium magnetometry finds a Neolithic monument made of circles of wooden posts at Stanton Drew, England (courtesy of Andrew David).

rules as to which machine will perform best. We can assume that resistivity will respond well to buried ditches (they are good conductors) and that magnetometry will find hearths and other kinds of burnt earth (it has a high magnetic susceptibility). But often the quickest way in is to do a test: select an area, run several machines over it, and then excavate it to determine which machine could see which kind of feature (FIG 5.11).

Radar works on a different principle: it fires a bunch of radio waves into the ground and measures the time they take to bounce back. The time represents the depth, so this instrument ought to be able to construct "time slices" or radio sections and, given enough readings, produce a three-dimensional underground map. In practice, there are so many variables that the computer modelling is still very challenging and the results are still fuzzy. The radio waves can bounce off any kind of interface from the surface of the subsoil to a random stone; the waves travel at different speeds in different kinds of soil and they are easily attenuated (i.e. lost) by damp. Payson Sheets and Lawrence Conyers had some success at Ceren, El Salvador, mapping 22 houses and a substantial piece of prehistoric landscape at the surface of a Maya site buried beneath 6m of volcanic ash. At Wroxeter in England, Dean Goodman and Yasushi Nishimura have made a series of time-slices through the buried Roman town. Mike Gorman made radio sections through mounds at Sutton Hoo, showing the profiles of burial chambers and early excavation trenches. At York, John Szymanski used a GPR to locate the voids of tombs under a church floor, and, also by detecting voids, was able to show the City Council where its medieval wall needed repairing. These are early examples of what promises to be an underground three-dimensional mapping device of great power.

Excavated area

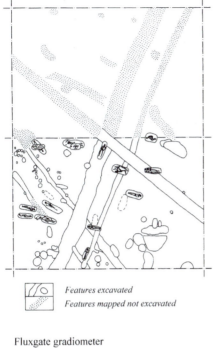

Proton magnetometer

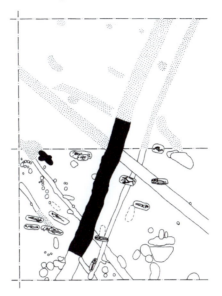

Features excavated
Features mapped not excavated

Fluxgate gradiometer

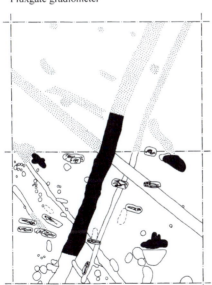

Resistivity

0   20m

FIGURE 5.11 Which could see what at Sutton Hoo: geophysical instruments perform on a test area, subsequently excavated.

FIGURE 5.12 Augering for urban evaluation (Hungate, York): (a) the auger is a hollow cylinder about 10–15cms in diameter which is driven into the ground by a mechanical hammer. When extracted it brings with it a sample of the deposit – a core; and (b) cores indicate the depth of natural and human deposit (FAS Ltd).

Although non-destructive mapping remains the site surveyors' guiding principle, there are occasions where digging is appropriate or inevitable. The aim is still to get a sneak preview while disturbing the archaeological strata as little as possible. Top of the range ethically is to re-use a hole already dug by someone else, by emptying it and looking sideways at the section. This is a neat trick in town sites, which often have old cellars in them. Take out the walls of the cellar, with a mechanical back-actor, and then clean up the earth wall behind. At Worcester, I found a Roman road behind an 18th century cellar wall; it was made of gravel and iron slag and so immovable that the 18th century builders had given up trying to get rid of it, and incorporated it into their foundations. At Sutton Hoo we used a farmer's old silage pit to gain a "free section" through the prehistoric site at a point where it was best preserved.

However, the only recourse often is to go in deep, with a test trench, test-pit or auger (FIG 5.12). At Bagnolo San Vito, near Mantova in Italy, there was a special problem to be solved at the site known locally as Forcello – a whaleback by the river Mincio. Was this a natural hill, or an Etruscan "tell" as implied by sherds of decorated pottery kicking about in the maize field on top? The prescription was to use augers to make *carotaggi,* or bore-holes, about 10cms across to drill down at intervals and inspect the character of the deposit – and see whether it was natural or manmade (FIG 5.13). Here it was indeed man-made, containing sherds, bones, charcoal and crumbling mud brick, and the overall pattern of deposit depth revealed by the bore-holes mapped the site's buried shape and edges.

Digging test-pits and trenches always risks damage – but it is sometimes the only way to peer into a particularly inscrutable site. On the Scottish island of Uist, Steve

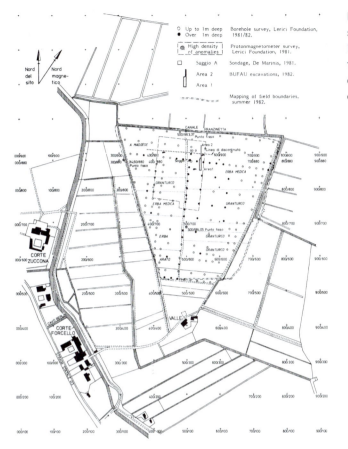

FIGURE 5.13 Bore-hole survey at Bagnolo San Vito, Italy, confirming and mapping the low mound of the Etruscan city (deep deposits in black circles) (M. Hummler).

Mithen used an array of 1×1m test-pits to find where Mesolithic flints were concentrated, guiding him to the most fruitful place to look for settlement evidence (FIG 5.14). Test-pits and trenches are especially effective if time is short and the site is scheduled to be destroyed; they are widely used to evaluate large areas (see applications, below).

A last type of "soft" digging well worthy of mention is at once the most revealing and the least destructive (Colour Plate 1a). This technique, known as "strip and map", involves the removal of the turf or topsoil that covers the site, and then cleaning and recording the surface that shows (see Chapter 6 for more). In effect this surface is the interface between the disturbed topsoil and the intact archaeology. In rescue work, the method is not used as much as it might be because it requires a large work force and the commercial profession either cannot afford them or finds it hard to integrate volunteers into their work programme. For this reason they resort to the use of the more damaging and less informative, but easier to manage, test-pits and trenches dug by machine. Large cleaned areas not only offer a much more reliable and non-destructive forecast of what lies beneath, but can be enhanced by

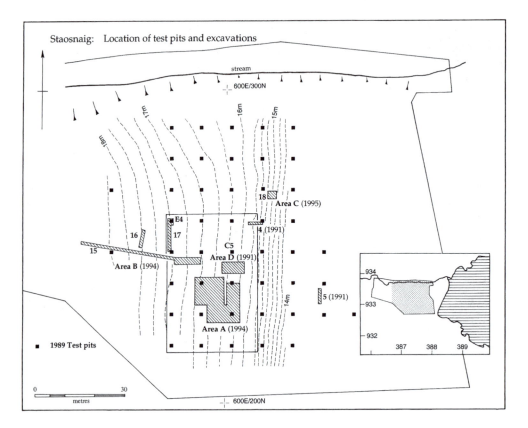

Staosnaig: Location of test pits and excavations

stream

600E/300N

17m

16m

15m

18m

18 Area C (1995)

E4

16

17

4 (1991)

15

C5

Area D (1991)

Area B (1994)

934

5 (1991)

933

14m

Area A (1994)

932

■ 1989 Test pits

387   388   389

0   30

metres

600E/200N

FIGURE 5.14 Test-pits used to focus the activity at a Mesolithic site in Uist, Scotland (courtesy of McDonald Institute).

geophysical survey conducted at the stripped level – that is on the surface of the subsoil. Surfaces that have been recorded, but are not needed immediately can be protected with polythene sheeting and reburied ("strip, map and wrap").

Applications

Site survey for evaluation

The bundle of site survey techniques finds its most frequent application at the evaluation stage, and particularly in that part of evaluation designed to model the deposit. As we shall see in Chapter 14, it is an important principle of deposit-modelling not to be too greedy. We are not trying to write the history of a site, only to discover its potential to write history.

In the countryside, surface site surveys can paint a sophisticated picture, offering a sequence of occupations in the same general area, evocatively and non-destructively.

FIGURE 5.15 Site survey at Hindwell. The topographic survey was generated from numerous points captured digitally by TST and exported as a three-dimensional CAD file. The result is presented as a Digital Terrain Model (DTM). The magnetometer survey, which mapped a Roman fort and a Neolithic palisade and numerous other features, was laid over the DTM to provide a combined model, in this case viewed vertically. Surveys by Helmut Becker and Barry Masterton for Clwyd Powys Archaeological Trust.

At Hindwell in Wales, the Clwyd–Powys Trust conjured a Neolithic, Bronze Age and Roman site from a smooth grassy open field (FIG 5.15). The topographical survey showed the former Bronze Age barrows, and caesium vapour magnetometry mapped a Neolithic palisade and Roman fort. These maps were laid digitally together showing a detailed sequence that can be viewed vertically or from any other angle. This kind of composite digital terrain model is a window into the future, when we should be able to resolve the sequence of shallow sites over several hectares without digging.

Towns and forts of the Roman period produce good results for geophysical mapping – particularly when they have a regular layout. Nicopolis ad Istrum in Bulgaria was an abandoned Roman town that was fairly evident, but it had attached to it a later annexe, and a research project was launched there to find out what this was (FIG 5.16). The Roman town gave a satisfying linear result with resistivity, which meant that this instrument could be trusted to see what lay within the more irregular post-Roman annex (the main research objective). Here resistivity and topographical survey mapped a number of anomalies, which were then investigated by targeted excavation to reveal a street, two basilicas and a number of other buildings.

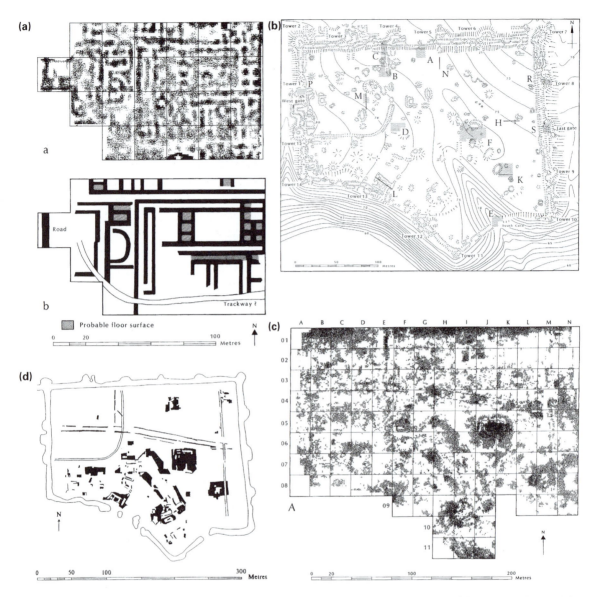

FIGURE 5.16 Site survey at Nicopolis, Bulgaria: (a) resistivity survey of Roman building and its interpretation; (b) topographical survey (hachures and contours) of the post-Roman annex; (c) resistivity plot of the annex and (d) interpretation of the annex (courtesy of Andrew Poulter).

Roman period sites also produce plenty of pottery and tile, so detailed maps of the extent of occupied areas can be made quickly. A small Byzantine fortification, known as a *quadriburgium*, was identified at Louloudies in northern Greece by archaeologist E. Marki during rescue excavations in advance of the high speed rail link between Athens and Thessaloniki. This discovery was soon followed in 1995 by a survey designed to find out whether the site had stood alone or was part of a larger complex. The broad survey zone covered 17ha (42 acres), most of it under intensive cultivation, and the 25 fields in the search area had different crops and different degrees of access: 11 were planted with cotton, 2 with vines, 3 with fruit, 7 had been planted with cereals, and 2 were under grass. The cereals had been harvested and their fields were stubble or plough, but in the cotton fields the plants stood about 1m high and 0.9m apart. The team found that visibility was excellent on the plough and it was possible to search the strip of soft topsoil between the standing plants and pick up pottery without damaging them. Visibility was also good and pick-up practicable between the rows of vines and fruit trees, but on the stubble and grass, surface material was too thin to merit recovery. Surface collection was carried out by click survey (see Chapter 4) followed by pick-up survey in 5×5m areas. By contrast, stubble and grass provided the surface most accessible to geophysical survey, which was carried out with a resistivity meter in 20×20m squares. The pottery and tile scatters showed the site had been occupied in the Hellenistic period (3rd century BC) and in the early Roman empire (1st to 4th century AD) before being developed as a Byzantine fort in the 6th. This survey, completed in a single three-week season, thus discovered a previously unknown late Roman defensive enclosure perhaps 4ha (10 acres) in extent, and mapped an earlier settlement sequence of nearly a millennium without a hole being dug.

Evaluating highland, upland and forested sites, especially for cultures with no flint or pottery, presents bigger problems. High precision topographical survey, using TST on the ground and lidar in the air presents the first recourse. Phosphate mapping is effective where the ambient phosphate (e.g. from fertiliser) is not overwhelming. Geophysical responses can be poor where the ground is boggy, spongy or wet. It is understandable that evaluators in this terrain quickly resort to digging test-pits and trenches. Even then, the rewards may be sparse in terms of artefacts, and the main function of the pits becomes to provide samples. At Achany Glen, Rod McCullagh and Richard Tipping set out to evaluate the corridor of a new road 3.5km long and 300m wide. They first searched the archives in Edinburgh for records of earlier discoveries in reports and on aerial photographs, then they divided the corridor into 50×50m blocks and examined each block by surface inspection in transects at 5m interval spacing. As a result, 752 features were recognised in 237 blocks, although 13% of these were later rejected as being natural humps and hollows. Detailed topography and vegetation boundaries were also recorded, together with samples of soil depth. This stage was completed by 16 fieldworkers in 22 weeks. Some 30% of the sites located were then selected randomly and visited by a field team who cut a 2×1m trench through each one. This led to the excavation of 27 sites and the taking of 4,000 environmental samples. The eventual yield from the project included a detailed environmental history and descriptions of an early Bronze cairn, Bronze Age round houses and clearance cairns, an Iron Age defended site, numerous field boundaries and a late 18th century long house.

Deposits in towns, encumbered by modern buildings, also present a powerful challenge for site surveyors. Town archives can be very rich, so that some of the intimate
history of a town site can be sketched in advance. There are also opportunities for
"free-sections" such as that behind the cellar wall at Worcester (earlier). Resistivity
and radar have been used on town sites, but without very convincing results. The
objective is to model the deposit in three dimensions, to find out as much as possible
about its depth, what it contains and its state of preservation. This in turn suggests
the research targets available, the recovery levels that are appropriate, how long the
excavation will take, and consequently how much it will cost. Sometimes this can be
inferred from bore-holes, but in nine times out of ten only a trench cut through the
site (or along one edge) can offer a reliable forecast. Such a trench, dug stratigraphically rather than cut by machine, allows the excavator to encounter most of the likely
rewards and problems at first hand.

SITE SURVEY FOR RESEARCH

As in other sciences, archaeological techniques and objectives are in dialogue,
each encouraging and enlarging the ambitions of the other. As remote mapping
techniques improve, so research projects that rely solely or mainly on site survey for
their success are becoming more common. The high cost of excavation and its increasingly specialist and time-consuming character are also leading some researchers in
this direction. Certain types of site (e.g. gardens and graveyards), and other types
of research-emphasis (e.g. an interest in space rather than sequence, and in some
cases a focus on later, better preserved, periods) have also created a new following.
In Gloucestershire, Mick Aston and Chris Gerrard, assisted by a mighty cohort of
volunteers, examined the village of Shapwick and its surroundings, inside and out
over many years. They applied topographic survey, shovel testing, geophysical survey
and chemical survey – among other achievements finding a lost medieval church from
the concentration of lead in its churchyard. This early example of "community archaeology" provided a fertile social context, in which many local people could become
active participants as well as stakeholders in the campaign. The result was a
meticulous model of a Medieval settlement, its buildings, woods and fields from its
earliest inhabitants to the great changes of the Reformation in the 16th century.

Ever since James Deetz showed their research potential in New England, USA, the
memorials in the *graveyards* of recent times have become attractive to archaeologists
and social historians. The inscriptions on the tombstones reveal the type of people
who are being commemorated, and when. The iconography, with its cherubs, spades,
coffins, hour-glasses and skulls, chronicles the contemporary attitudes to death, and
shows up links between families. The dates on the stones mean that the development
of the burial ground can be mapped, this being amplified by records of the deceased
and of land grants. Accordingly the data required by the survey is a map of all the
memorials, a topographical map of the cemetery, a record of all the inscriptions and

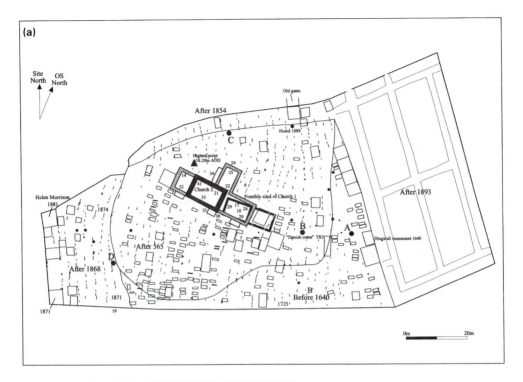

FIGURES 5.17 The churchyard at Portmahomack, Scotland, showing the boundaries as deduced from the dates on the gravestones (above); recording memorials (below) (author).

the folk art and as much information as possible on the history of the land and the community that used it to bury their dead. These surveys have tended to focus on Christian graveyards, which are relatively well documented (like Portmahomack in FIG 5.17), but there is no reason why they should. Every burial ground is a material archive of its people, worthy of study as it is worthy of memory.

Two other kinds of site, battlefields and gardens, conclude this brief review. Before the advent of trench warfare and the building of redoubts, sites used as *battlefields* were potentially covered in debris dropped during the battle. The North American site of the Little Bighorn, Montana, extending to some 500 acres, was the scene of

General Custer's Last Stand against the Sioux and Cheyenne in 1876. Researchers wanted to know how the lines were drawn up, what happened during the battle and how it ended. The sources of information were thousands of bullets and cartridge cases and a number of graves. More than 4,000 items were located using a metal detector, and subsequent ballistic analysis showed that they had been fired by 215 firearms of 30 types. Researcher Richard E. Fox interpreted the patterns of the bullets and graves as indicating that the Plains Indians had had a number of rifles themselves, used to good effect against an enemy who were expecting a mass advance on the Medieval model.

The battle of Towton was Medieval, and is thought to be the bloodiest encounter to have taken place on British soil. On 29 March 1461 many thousands of knights and soldiers lost their lives on a snow-covered field in central England. The site was marked on early maps, and remembered to this day as Bloody Meadow. In 1996 builders constructing a new garage discovered part of a mass grave, and archaeologists subsequently analysed the skeletal material, which showed terrible wounds from swords and armour-piercing arrowheads. Metal detectors were used to attempt a map of the course of the battle, but the quantity of ferrous material in the field from recent agriculture meant that the distribution could not be obtained from the signals alone. Curiously the 15th century material that was actually recovered came mainly from horse harness and personal ornaments rather than weapons. Battlefield surveys

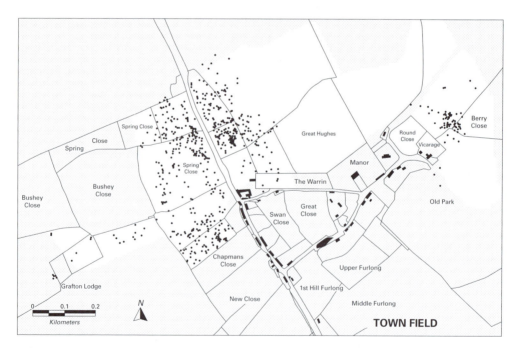

FIGURE 5.18 Civil War battlefield at Grafton Regis, with a plot of shot found by metal detector (Glen Foard).

have had more success at later (17th century) battle sites, such as Grafton Regis, since the metal detector can be used to plot the distinctive lead shot from muskets and pistols (FIG 5.18).

The rediscovery and study of formal *gardens*, usually 17th to 19th centuries in date, throw light on the lives of the occupants of stately homes, and their present managers are attracted by the prospect of restoring them. This type of site mainly contains broad and shallow deposits, often with strong geometric alignments. At Pfauinsel, Germany, Michael Seiler located paths laid out by Peter Joseph Lenne (1789–1866) from early maps and topographic survey and then sampled them with test trenches. The paths were found to have been made up with a layer of yellowish red shingle compacted with clay, which provided a pleasing contrast to the green lawns. Seiler used a metal detector to find the cast-iron pipes which supplied the fountains.

The more sensitive geophysical methods developed in recent decades have proved to be a boon for garden archaeologists. Shallow geometric features such as former paths and beds are often easily detected and mapped without recourse to excavation. The repeated tilling and manuring of a flower bed give rise to long-term moisture retention and enhanced low-resistance anomalies. Magnetometry responds well to magnetically enhanced sediments and burning, so locating typical – but ephemeral – garden features such as bonfires and middens. The standard resistivity procedure for a garden site will take readings at 1m intervals (since the paths will be generally at least this wide), with a twin-probe spacing of 0.5m giving a depth sensitivity of about 1m, but greater depth (wider spacing) is needed to find underground conduits and features beneath terraces. It is harder to discover what was once growing in the flower beds by digging them, since humus provides a highly active micro-environment in which roots and seeds are eventually recycled.

In theory gardens can be of any age, but in practice their formality and recreational features confine them to the great houses of the rich. The earliest found in Britain was the Roman garden with avenues and ornamental tree stances excavated at Fishbourne by Barry Cunliffe. But the majority belong to a later age of grandeur – the 18th and 19th century. For this reason the point of departure for the survey is often an old map, then amplified by geophysical surveys or trenching used to locate paths and the water supply, as in Wessex Archaeology's investigations at Lydiard Park (FIG 5.19). Subsequently, the paths may be restored, and old flower beds and shrubberies replanted as part of a restoration programme. Thus the site survey is also a blueprint for restoring an old garden to new life.

In sum . . .

Site surveys produce detailed maps in two or three dimensions of features that could have archaeological significance above and below ground. The techniques include

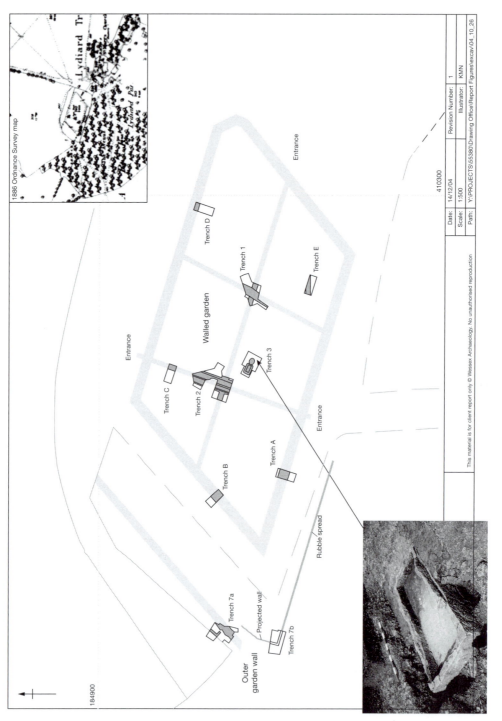

FIGURE 5.19 Garden archaeology: locating a vanished 18th century walled garden at Lydiard Park, England, using a map of 1886 and trenches. In the centre of the area formed by garden paths was the water supply – a well with a stone basin lined with clay (Wessex Archaeology).

documentary records, surface inspection and collection, remote sensing devices and test digging in pits, trenches or strip-and-map. In evaluation, the main target is the extent and the character of the deposit, its potential rewards and problems. In research, site survey can sometimes sail alone, charting the history of a village, a cemetery, a battlefield or a garden without the need for large-scale digging.

Briefing

Site survey for its own sake is still rare, so some very successful site surveys are hidden in large research excavation reports or even more in the thousands of pre-construction evaluations carried out worldwide every year. Since these are conducted for governments or private clients (see Chapter 15), they rarely make their way into the literature. Within the profession therefore, there is a wealth of experience that is hard to tap other than by being in it. For those in a hurry, M. Carver 2005 (Chapter 2) offers an introduction to a range of site survey techniques applied to a rural site in order to make a resource model.

History and Principles

Aitken et al 1958, Aspinall 1992, Donaghue 2001, M. Carver 2003. **What is a site?:** Lucas 2001, 168, Dunnell 1992, Darvill 2005 (framework for a site and its environs, Stonehenge).

Techniques

Archives and maps: There are lots of examples of investigations using early site maps in the journals *Medieval Archaeology* and *Post-Medieval Archaeology* (e.g. Fleming and Barker 2008); Framework 2008 (246, 260) for an Essex deer park endorsed hunting lodge by an old map and by excavation (see Chapter 12); see also landscapes (Chapter 4) and gardens (below). For general discussions on maps, documents and sites see Crawford 1953, Deetz 1967, C. Taylor 1974, Rogers and Rowley 1974, Beaudry 1988, Rippon 2004.

For examples of **topographic surveys** (contour and hachure plans) and DTMs (Digital Terrain Models), see RCAHMS 2007, M. Carver 2005, 16, Hodder 1996, Gibson1999. Systematic **vegetation mapping** was used in M. Carver 2005, 17. **Geochemical mapping:** Craddock et al 1985, Ball and Kelsay 1992, Bjelajac et al 1996 (for phosphate) and Lippi 1988 (in the jungle). For mapping other chemical elements in the soil see Bintliff et al 1992, Aston et al 1998, Heron 2001, Cessford 2005. Bull et al for detecting manuring. **Geophysical mapping** (including resistivity and gradiometry) is discussed in Aitken et al 1958, Clark 1975, Weymouth 1986, Clark 1990, Aspinall 1992, Becker 1995, Arnold et al 1997 (jungle), Lyall and Powlesland 1996 (fluxgate), Masterson 1999 (Tara), Sternberg 2001, Gaffney and Gater 2003, David et al 2004, Gibson 1999 (caesium magnetometry). Pasquinucci and Trément 2000 has sections on geochemical and geophysical methods applied in the Mediterranean. A **metal-detector survey** was applied formally at Sutton Hoo, M. Carver 2005, 18. **Dowsing** has been claimed as useable in Bailey et al 1988, Locock 1995. Ground penetrating or soil sounding **radar** appeared as prototypes in Sharer and Ashmore 1979, 166–7, Aitken and Milligan 1992, Batey 1987, Imai et al 1987, while Goodman and Nishimura 1993, Goodman et al 1995, Conyers and Goodman 1997, Goodman and Nishimura 2000 and Sheets 2002 (Ceren) put the more high performance modern instruments through their paces. For discussion about **test-pits** see Nance and Ball 1986, Hester et al 1997 (58–74), Mithen 2000 (for Uist) and see Chapter 6 (excavation); for **strip and map,** Crawford 1933; Carver 2005, 43–7.

Applications

General: David 2001, Donaghue 2001.

Large-scale site mapping: Gibson 1999 (Hindwell topographic and geophysical model), Gaffney et al 2000 (large-scale mapping with a fluxgate at Wroxeter), Powlesland et al 1997 (Vale of Pickering). **Site evaluation** is discussed in M. Carver 2003 and for some specific examples see Clay 2001, David 2001, English Heritage 1995, Gaffney and Gater 1993, Weymouth 1995 (Ohio), Hodder 1996 (Çatalhöyük), Poulter 1995 (Nicopolis), idem 1998 (Louloudies), M. Carver 2005, Chapter 2 (Sutton Hoo). Examples of fine **research surveys** are Newman 1997 (for Tara), McCullagh and Tipping 1998 (Achany Glen) and Aston and Gerrard 1999 (Shapwick). Mytum 2000, 2004 for how to record and interpret **graveyards**. **Battlefield** archaeology is usefully reviewed in Freeman 1998 and Freeman and Pollard 2001. Fox 1993 for Little Big Horn, Fiorato et al 2007 for Towton, and Foard 2001 for Grafton Regis. **Garden archaeology** is blooming in Europe; see Taylor 1983, Brown 1991, Currie and Locock 1991, Miller and Gleason 1994, Jacques 1997, Cole et al 1997 for examples of geophysical surveys, Doneus et al 2001; Cunliffe 1971 (Plate II and III) for Fishbourne, Wessex Archaeology 2004 for Lydiard Park.

6 EXCAVATION

First day on a dig

Eight people line up in front of a patch of ground, each one armed with a bucket, a builder's trowel and a hand shovel. The earth is freshly exposed with the turf off, an uneven and sandy surface with numerous stones. You all kneel as though taking your marks for a race, but you do not race forwards; rather you go slowly backwards, kneeling or crouching or bending over. To the right and left are other diggers – one apparently a veteran of a hundred campaigns; another new and nervous like you, only you don't know them yet. Behind the line the site assistant hovers and fusses, giving instructions and opinions in an argot that is at first difficult to follow. "Jack, keep on the 45 easting; person next to Jack, pay attention to the black sticky feature, when you get to it. Leave it proud, OK? Elaine, here is a bag, and you can have the spare bags. Everyone, just clean off the loose. No pulling roots; we'll return and snip. Work round pebbles, just get the horizon. We're leaving Level D until the weather settles. We'll try for two modules by lunch."

It seems you are "the person next to Jack". What black sticky feature? The dirt in front of you looks just like that: dirt. Are you to stroke it gently? Or dig out the stones and leave the soil? Or remove it all with this stupidly small implement? Clean the loose what from what? What is a module? Which horizon? You glance to left and right, hoping the others will guide you. And then the line crawls slowly backwards, but in 10 minutes it has hardly moved. There is so much loose soil to remove before you get to a harder horizon you can feel beneath – ah, of course "the loose", "the horizon". The loose earth goes into the bucket with the aid of a hand shovel, and when the bucket is full it is emptied into a wheelbarrow. The next stroke of the trowel, and up comes a piece of pottery, small, crumbly, brown and grooved, but certainly pottery and you don't need a degree to recognise it. This is the moment which makes a thousand archaeologists. Paralysis can set in, as with the first sighting of a lion on safari. But this paralysis is simply the first symptom of a lifelong addiction. It breaks the ice with your neighbour: "Umm, look." "Hey, good." Into a bag it goes, your sherd. Then it's your turn to empty the wheelbarrow and you ask the site assistant where. "Over there,", she says, vague and busy, waving a hand behind her. But the track to the spoil heap (backdirt pile, as they say in the USA) is easy to follow; along the planks to the edge of the site and then to the edge of the heap, where the path is long and winds uphill all the way.

At the top of the heap the track stops, you up-end the barrow, and stop and turn and look back, and there is the site you are working on, an acre of dark brown, with the tiny strip cleaned and some dark patches in it already showing. Beyond are the tents and the hut where you had breakfast. And beyond that the trees and then the river. Yesterday it was like the first day at school, and you felt like the only person who brought a pink lunchbox. Today it is like the first day on a film set, and you are a player. You return to the line; in 30 minutes you are talking, and the ground in front of you is smooth and orange and shows dark patches and clusters of stones. It is covered in bags containing pot-sherds and Elaine has none left. After two hours, surveyors are beginning to plot and gather the bags, and at the far end Jack has been sent back to snip roots. The black sticky feature now shows like a monstrous dark bruise, raised very slightly up ("proud") from the flat surface. On it was a flint flake and a piece of charcoal and something that may have been a bone. In four hours the line has moved about 16m, the first two modules (each 4×8 m) have had their initial definition, and it's lunchtime (FIG 6.1).

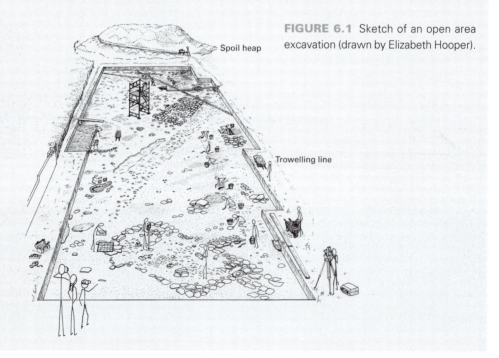

Spoil heap

Trowelling line

FIGURE 6.1 Sketch of an open area excavation (drawn by Elizabeth Hooper).

This is one kind of excavation – there are a great many others, examining places from the top of a mountain to the bottom of the sea, and we shall visit some of them presently. All of them have certain things in common. First a Design Stage in which all the hard decisions are made: How do we intend to recognise and define the strata and how shall we dissect them? What needs to be done, in which order, where to dig, at what size, to what level of precision, making which records? These questions are all answered by means of prior evaluation and the answers are incorporated into the Project Design (see Chapter 14 for more). Hopefully, the Project Design has been published or circulated, and everyone has (theoretically) had a chance to read it and comment on it, whether they be a local resident or a distant academic. So, by the time that the team assembles on the site, they (and everyone else) can answer the visitor's question: "Why did you decide to dig there?" We should know where the edges of the excavation are to be, where the spoil heap will be, where the offices are, where the cars are to park, where visitors may go, what information is there for them, where is the nearest doctor and the nearest pub, and if there is a campsite, where that is. This is necessary for all excavations from the largest to the smallest, from the most leisurely research excavation to the most urgent evaluation.

Excavation takes you to out-of-the-way places – some of them hardly accessible to a small human; others lie in the town centre; others in farmland full of testy neighbours. Excavation is dangerous: it involves heavy machinery, sharp tools and – often – loose deep edges (FIG 6.2). So it's safety first (FIG 6.3). Excavation is also the greatest fun imaginable – exciting, companionable, poetic: like a theatre group, there for each other whether the run is to be long or short (FIG 6.4). Matters of local know-how and expressions of mutual support are covered in the first briefing on the evening of the first day. So although arriving at an excavation as a new member of the team can be lonely and scary, that first day you should close your eyes feeling wanted and useful.

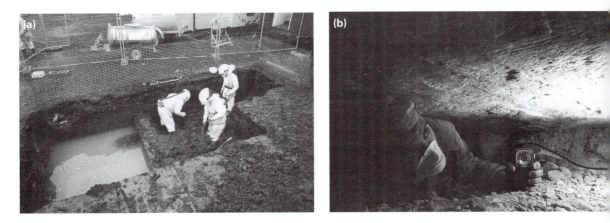

FIGURE 6.2 Tight places: (a) test excavation in chemically contaminated site (FAS Ltd); and (b) excavating a tunnel in a flint mine at Defensola, Italy (Galiberti 2005).

SAFETY FIRST

Prevent
Depth – maximum 4ft, 1.3m

*A man was killed in Scotland in April when the 2.5 metre unsupported trench he was working in collapsed on top of him;
*A man was killed whilst working on a conservation development in East Sussex in May when he jumped into a 3 metre deep trench which then collapsed on him;
*One man was killed and another injured in July when a 3 metre deep trench collapsed on them in an unsupported area of work in Yorkshire.

Injury – risk assessment, accident book, first aid, tetanus AB, doctor's phone

Protect
Hat, boots [No hat, no boots, no job]

Practice
Train team to use tools safely

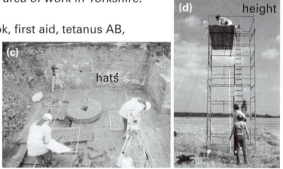

FIGURE 6.3 Safety first: four main causes of accidents on excavations (a–d).

FIGURE 6.4 Excavation team at Achir, Algeria, 1993: students, academics, civil servants from the heritage ministry and national museum, local residents and volunteers (author).

On method: three ways of dissecting strata

The task of the excavator is to dissect a deposit to understand how it was formed and what happened there in the past. The deposit itself is a fossil composed of a thousand different actions, each of which may be significant to the story, and the trick is to isolate each of them, interpret them and put them into a sequence. Partly due to the terrain in which they work, and partly out of tradition, excavators in different countries address this task in different ways. Here I summarise them as three main types (FIG 6.5). All three, like surgery, involve slicing and looking, although, as in surgery, we expect to do less of this and use more non-destructive techniques in the future (see Chapter 5).

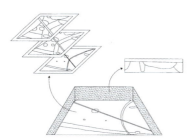

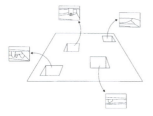

The first method is known by the German term *Schnitt* (slice), which I call here *geometric* (FIG 6.6). A rectangle is laid out, and the earth within it is levelled into a perfectly flat horizon and taken down in slices of equal depth (*spits*), usually about 5–10cm thick. Since life does not happen on a perfectly flat plane, this procedure reveals a surface composed of numerous truncated layers seen from on top – a series of *horizons*. As you go down, the sides of the rectangle gradually rise as vertical cliffs, again consisting of numerous sliced-off layers seen sideways (*sections*). The record of the deposit thus consists of a set of a horizontal and vertical slices which are carefully recorded in drawings and photographs. This is a ruthless – but efficient – method. Its advantage is that it produces a three-dimensional model of the whole deposit which can be cross-checked between every section and every other. Its disadvantage is that the layers are never seen for what they are, so that the humanity of the deposit is lost. This method is widely employed, particularly when the deposit is very difficult to read (i.e. few layers show), or when the work force is

FIGURE 6.5 Three ways of dissecting strata: (top) the *Schnitt* method: the excavated deposit is recorded as a series of horizontal and vertical slices; (centre) sampling in quadrats; the deposit is explored by digging square boxes, separated from each other or side by side; (bottom) stratigraphic excavation. The deposit is taken apart by defining the many episodes that created it (FAS Ltd).

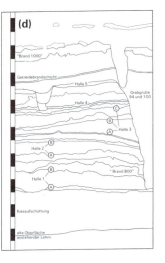

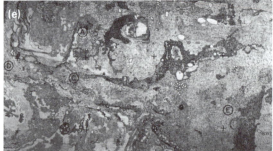

FIGURES 6.6 Geometric or *Schnitt* excavation at Starigrad/Oldenburg, Germany (a, b). The horizontal (e) and vertical (c, d) surfaces are recorded precisely in colour (courtesy of Michael Müller-Wille).

unskilled, since they need follow only one basic instruction ("keep it flat"). The skilled part of the work force then makes the records of each surface.

The second method, *sample excavation*, is a variant of the first and equally widely practised. Here the deposit is studied in a number of *test-pits*, small square boxes, perhaps 2×2 or 5×5m in area. Within each box, the soil may be taken down in slices (spits in the UK) or *arbitrary layers* (in the USA), or dug stratigraphically (coming next). Each box then gives you a mini-sequence of the deposit at that point. Mortimer Wheeler put his boxes side by side, and variants of this "Wheeler system" are still practised in many parts of the world today (FIG 6.7). The boxes form a grid separated by baulks, which are recorded in section when each box has been dug to the bottom. The baulks are then removed leaving columns of strata at each corner as last witnesses of the layers that have been cut. Then the columns are removed in their turn. The object is to keep a tight control, and always to have some record standing vertically to show where the excavators have been. How high the baulks can stand

FIGURE 6.7 Box excavation in China in 2006. The boxes are excavated leaving four walls for each, carrying sections (left); after recording the greater part of the walls are demolished leaving columns at the junctions (centre); these columns are then removed (right) and the lower part may be dug in open area (Cultural Relics Press).

will depend on how solid the soil is. But in general, the walls of an excavation in Europe cannot usually stand more than a metre high, either physically or legally. The tell, with its solid 30m high sections plainly belongs to a different world (Chapter 1, FIG 1.8).

A common approach in the USA is to place the boxes over the study area in isolated positions, chosen randomly or symmetrically as seen in Michael Schiffer's "Joint Site" (FIG 6.8). Theoretically (in all senses, positive and negative) this provides a sample of the activities on site, unbiased by preconceptions. Other boxes can be added later in extra places that need investigation (judgement samples). The walls of the boxes (sections) can also be linked to each other, so that the sample sequences collectively give an account of the sequence overall. The use of sample pits may thus be applied in stages, random boxes, judgment boxes and expanded areas, as in Charles Redman's projects at Qsar es-Seghir and Cayönü. The advantage of the method is that the digging is easy to manage and quick to do. The disadvantage is that it only offers the sequence at a point, with a lot of blank spaces in between. And as in any human settlement, every point is different and the sequences in the boxes may be difficult to link up. The method obviously suits terrain where the strata are fairly thin or demonstrably homogenous. The most important general application of this method

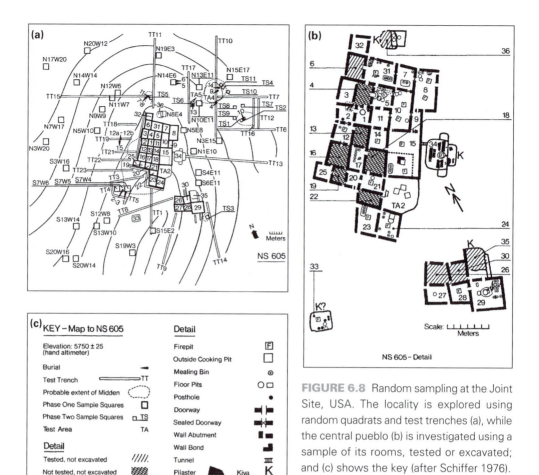

FIGURE 6.8 Random sampling at the Joint Site, USA. The locality is explored using random quadrats and test trenches (a), while the central pueblo (b) is investigated using a sample of its rooms, tested or excavated; and (c) shows the key (after Schiffer 1976).

is during the reconnaissance and evaluation stages, since the boxes can most readily answer the question: "What kind of deposits are there?" In research investigations, the success depends on the terrain, and the busier the stratification, the less useful the boxes.

Stratigraphic excavation addresses a predetermined area, and studies the layers as they lie. The excavation starts at the top and each element of the deposit is defined and removed as it appears. The difficulty of doing this depends on the terrain: in some sites the layers are nice and sharp and colourful, and everyone can see them. On others the decay of the deposit has gone so far that it all seems to look the same. Dissecting a deposit thus requires a large number of individual decisions. The excavators' task is to find the edges of new contexts and decide which is the next one to come off. A *context* (see Chapter 1) is any stratigraphic unit: a layer, a clutch of stones, a vertical cut – the many types of element out of which a deposit is formed.

Stratigraphic excavators carry a "stratigraphic vocabulary" in their heads, and the more experienced they are the better chance they have of matching what they see to this vocabulary (see Chapter 1, FIG 1.14). Unlike the previous two methods, where most of the recording is done at the end, in this procedure each excavator records as they go along – define, record, remove, record. In addition to the description of the context, many excavators also carry out more in-depth, more interpretative inquiries – how did the context get there, what role does it play in a human activity, which other contexts does it belong with? In this more comprehensive approach, groupings of contexts are defined on site using another, higher order, stratigraphic unit – the *feature*, recorded on a feature card (see later).

In Europe, where the stratigraphic method reigns supreme, it tends to be applied in broad continuous open areas, which are turned into a large number of individually recorded contexts. This allows you to reconstruct the whole area of the deposit, each of its elements and the way they arrived in the ground – giving you the whole history, with no blank areas. The main disadvantage of this approach is that, since the only records are of individual contexts, there is no overall check on the stratification – no maps or sections. The method is suited to terrain where the strata are numerous and visible, especially sites with multiple occupation like tells and towns. A skilled workforce is clearly necessary for its success and reliability.

Nevertheless, flexibility must not be abandoned, and every excavator should declare ownership of every method, since our task is not to be "correct" but to be appropriate. Where context definition is difficult (and it often is) all excavators like to examine the deposit in both plan and section if possible, to give themselves two chances of seeing the edges, one horizontal, the other vertical. The interface between two layers that are lying on top of each other is not easy to determine when you are trowelling them away: you are dependent on a sixth sense that the character of the soil is changing, and that sixth sense is often lacking. Viewed sideways, however, the median line of the interface is clearer and can be measured. One useful way of achieving this double-view is to dig geometrically using the *Schnitt* method (above). A related, but less drastic variant is to use *quadrants* (Colour Plate 4a; FIG 6.9). In this case, the site is laid out in rectangles, and the insides excavated, leaving a "pastry strip" between them. However, these are not the same as Wheeler's boxes, since the baulks are offset so that the edges of adjoining rectangles offer a single vertical plane viewed from alternate sides. The baulks can be of any height, as low as a couple of centimetres and as high as a few metres (depending on terrain and safety), and any size – applied to a whole site or to a single pit. The baulks can be drawn and removed at any point. Quadrants do not therefore carve up a site prematurely and damage it. They can be applied just when and where the stratification demands it, in order to see better. A whole site can be divided into quadrants, especially for the depth of the topsoil (where the strata is poorly defined), and these quadrants then form the basis for capturing horizons. By the same token within an amorphous fill – like the backfill of a grave – an excavator may well employ spits to lower the fill in a controlled manner

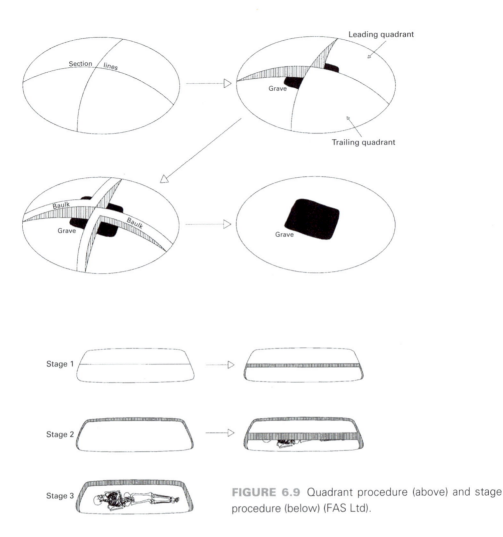

FIGURE 6.9 Quadrant procedure (above) and stage procedure (below) (FAS Ltd).

in *stages*, recording the horizontal surface and the part-section at each stage (FIG 6.9).

Thus in practice, whatever their proponents may claim, the canny excavator makes use of each and any of these methods as and when they are needed. Test-pits dug in spits are widely used in the reconnaissance and evaluation stages, to find sites and to assess their legibility. Research investigations on well-stratified sites tend to make use of stratigraphic excavation in open area. But even these usually begin with the cleaning and mapping of the first horizon (strip-and-map, see Chapter 5). And the best stratigraphic excavators will dig in spits where three-dimensional recording is desirable but the layers have become invisible.

We need similar versatility and open-mindedness in the matter of recording. Stratigraphic excavators will sometimes report their findings just as a sequence of contexts (more in Chapter 11), but no one who cares what a site means can be content merely with a stack of records of individual contexts. There are many occasions where stratigraphic excavation is greatly aided by horizons and by sections – and later researchers are very glad that earlier excavators made these records. The section still has the power to provide a snapshot of how things actually were – often vital in corroborating a controversial point of sequence. As we shall see in some examples below, most excavators try "to have their cake and eat it", by digging stratigraphically, context by context, but continually cleaning and mapping the surface of the site (context map) as they go down, and drawing the vertical sides of the excavation (sections) at the end. They combine stratigraphic inquiry, geometric precision and on-site interpretation to give them the best understanding of the strata on site from all angles. And this is sensible: an archaeological deposit is a three-dimensional artefact, only seen once and never seen whole. It deserves an analytical approach that is special to itself: not just to be dissected and recorded, but to be studied.

The new excavator is going to have to confront many challenges, embarrassments and discomforts: missing the obvious feature, smashing the fragile find, suffering from aching muscles and dirt up the nostrils. But none of this compares with the danger of dogma. Some archaeologists will urge you to believe that all excavation must only be carried out stratigraphically, must use only one type of record (the context), and each of these must always be drawn in outline on a single sheet. Of course there are times when these things are appropriate. But such excavators are like street musicians with only one song or carpenters with only one tool in the box. Excavation is not an unvarying ritual, but a creative study, carefully redesigned every time it's done. The methods used depend on what you want to know, the site and the social context in which you work. These are always different, everywhere.

Here I will focus on the procedures that relate to a stratigraphic area excavation on a flat site in open country, since they can be adapted easily enough for use in boxes or trenches. In the next chapter we shall visit a variety of situations where a variety of investigation methods are applied: in caves, in towns, underwater and on upstanding structures. Each of these situations demands different approaches, using selections from the same basic set of skills: defining the parts which make up the object of study, describing and measuring them, and then (usually) removing them. But there is something that needs saying first.

There is a single controlling factor in excavation, and one that can never be given too much emphasis. We are about to dissect a unique three-dimensional deposit and turn it into a set of records, written, drawn, digital and photographic. An excavation is a laboratory for a surgical activity, not a kind of gardening. Dirt is dirt and it gets everywhere, but an excavation cannot succeed if it is untidy. This means that keeping clean is the main and continuous activity on a site. It means having very straight well-protected edges, planked pathways so that people do not tread on cleaned surfaces.

It means having no sprouting vegetation, no loose earth left in piles – except on the spoil heap. It means having clean tools and continually cleaning them in use. It means not trying to dig if the site is soaked or baked solid. Pretty basic you would think. But the archaeology profession is unfortunately full of people who cut corners and think no one can see them. Visiting some excavations and seeing others on television can give completely the wrong idea. They are often disgracefully messy, with ragged edges, tools lying about and earth everywhere. There's plenty of activity and chat; but tidiness comes before talk. If any proper research is intended, there is no substitute for keeping everything permanently and ridiculously clean.

On procedure: Recovery Levels

Here's a basic axiom for digging: *the strata we see depend on the measures taken to see them*. In other words, archaeological contexts are not lying there for the taking; they must be looked for and defined. If you do this standing up with a shovel, you will see rather less than you will kneeling down with a trowel. And yet a shovel is appropriate in some cases, and a trowel in others – the whole of a site is never dug with the same tool. But if different tools are used, then the number and size of contexts defined and artefacts seen will be different. It follows that we must record the tools we use, otherwise we will not be able to compare the contexts we excavate.

This leads to the idea of *Recovery Levels*: a series of procedures with increasing levels of precision and thus increasing levels of finds recovery (FIG 6.10; Colour Plates 3 and 4b). My system usually has six levels ranging from Level A (use a bulldozer) to Level F (the finest). But you could have more or fewer levels than these, and decide that different types of work could take place within them. Recovery Levels provide a sturdy basis for an excavation design. The recording should match the digging: if you excavate a pit with a shovel, its edges probably do not deserve to be mapped to the nearest millimetre, because they were not defined to the nearest millimetre. But a grave tableau lovingly defined with a spatula deserves close-up photography and high precision survey (Colour Plate 6). Since the tools, techniques and records vary in each case, describing Recovery Levels in action is a neat way to introduce them.

Recovery Level A is used to open up sites in town and country, and these days makes use of a mechanical excavator. Sites are often cleared by contractors using massive earth-moving machinery. But this is usually unsuitable for archaeology and sometimes results in ruin. For this reason we prefer to hire machines of our own (FIG 6.11). In archaeology, those that drag (a back-blade) are more useful than those that push (a front-blade or dozer). For removing concrete and rubble from town sites, we do as the builders do and break up the top with jackhammers or a steel point, and then scoop up the pieces with a toothed bucket. In the countryside, the topsoil is taken off with a broad toothless bucket on a back actor or "back-bladed" with the inside edge of a front bucket. In either case the cutting arm of the machine moves backward

LEVEL	COMPONENT	FIND	CONTEXT	FEATURE	STRUCTURE	LANDSCAPE	EXAMPLE
A	(Not recovered)	Surface finds PLOT 2-D	OUTLINE PLAN	OUTLINE PLAN	OUTLINE PLAN		Machining
B	(Not recovered)	Large finds RECORD EXAMPLES KEEP EXAMPLES	Defined by shovel DESCRIBE	Defined by shovel SHORT DESCRIPTION. OUTLINE PLAN	As features	PLOT STRUCTURES on OS Map	19th century house
C	(Not recovered)	All visible finds RECORD ALL. KEEP EXAMPLES. MAY PLOT BY m^2	Defined by coarse trowel DESCRIPTION (Munsell for mortars and natural)	Defined by coarse trowel FULL DESCRIPTION. DETAILED PLAN HEIGHT	Defined by coarse trowel EXCAVATE AS ONE. PHOTOGRAPH	1:100 PLAN PROFILE	16th century pits
D	SAMPLE SIEVING of spoil on site for presence of specified material (spoil not kept)	All visible finds PLOT 3-D and KEEP ALL	Defined by fine trowel DESCRIPTION (incl. Munsell) PLAN 1:20	Defined by line trowel FULL DESCRIPTION DETAILED PLAN 1:20 (colour coded) CONTOURS PHOTOGRAPH (B/W)	Defined by fine trowel EXCAVATE AS ONE. PHOTOGRAPH by PHASE	1:100 PLAN CONTOUR SURVEY	Timber trace building
E	TOTAL SIEVING of spoil on site for presence of specified material and KEEP SPOIL	All visible finds PLOT 3-D and KEEP ALL	Defined minutely DESCRIPTION (incl. Munsell). PLAN (natural colour) 1:10 or 1:5 contour	Defined minutely FULL DESCRIPTION PLAN (colour) 1:10 or 1:5 CONTOUR PHOTOGRAPH	Defined minutely EXCAVATE AS ONE. PHOTOGRAPH by PHASE	(As LEVEL D) CONTOUR SURVEY	Skeleton
F	MICRO SIEVING soil block in laboratory	(As component)	(As LEVEL E) and LIFT AS BLOCK	(As LEVEL E)	(As LEVEL E)	(As LEVEL D)	Storage pit fill

FIGURE 6.10 Recovery Levels – a general example. These are re-designed to serve each excavation project.

FIGURE 6.11 Digging at Level A:
(a) Hymac with long arm and teeth,
and pneumatic drill break up concrete
in London; (b) monitoring a box-
grader lowering the topsoil in Russia;
(c) JCB using back-hoe and (d) Drott
back-blading .

like the arm of a giant troweller. Machine operators who work regularly with archaeology become extremely good at it and can follow contours and create a surface within
a centimetre of the desired height. They are guided by an archaeologist who stands
by the bucket and signals when to stop. (How do they know when to stop? It's all in
the evaluation, see FIG 14.8.)

The recording at Level A is fairly basic; spotting finds is haphazard and the horizon
exposed is worth a photograph, but the edges are pretty fuzzy. Machines can also be
used to empty known features such as huge deep ditches at speed, using the long
arm of the *back-actor* (US *back-hoe*). Level A digging requires high level supervision.

If the bucket goes too low it destroys the strata you want to study; too high and it leaves a lot to do. If one front-bucket of earth is left behind by a mechanical excavator it will need about 20 wheelbarrow trips to remove it.

Recovery Level B is used to tidy up the surface left by Level A, and involves soil shifting with shovels or hoes (FIG 6.12). Level B can also be applied to badly disturbed or very recent pits, where we might feel justified in emptying them with a shovel. The "English" shovel has a short handle, a flat face and flanges, and is operated by slicing forwards and scraping back. It is good for sand and soil. The "Italian" shovel has a long handle and a face like the ace of spades (obviously), and is operated by pushing the handle with your knee. It is good for rubble. Archaeological shovellers have refined shovelling into a skill verging on an Olympic sport, the object being to hurl a shovel-full of debris several metres into a wheel barrow without spilling a crumb.

The artefacts seen during a shovelling operation will tend to be large and infrequent, but a shovel can often define the edges of pits or walls clearly enough to be recorded. The fact that they aren't is generally due to the fact that the horizon (or feature)

FIGURE 6.12 Level B in action: (a) shovelling out a ditch after machining (Italy); (b) breaking a surface with rakes; and (c) surface collecting (England).

FIGURE 6.13 Level C cleaning: (a) trowelling line; (b) brushing loose gravel; and (c) defining with trowel (FAS Ltd. and N. Macbeth).

concerned is usually to be given another – maybe even two more levels of definition at higher recovery levels.

Recovery Level C represents the normal level of intensity at which everyone works to keep a site tidy (FIG 6.13). On very rocky or dry sites, the main tool used is a brush, but on earthy sites (the vast majority) the favourite tool is the trowel. These are builders' trowels not gardeners', and they have a flat triangular pointed blade welded to a tang set into a wooden handle. A trowel with a robust blade and an edge about 100mm long will do on most kinds of earthy, sandy, stony soils. The blade is used to clean a surface, the point to winkle out dirt from between stones. On clay, a useful variant of the tool has a narrow blade about 150mm long and is thin, bendy and very sharp, so the clay can be sliced like cheese. In the 'first day on a dig' we met some Level C trowellers kneeling in a line, cleaning the surface with a trowel, and brushing large stones with a brush, putting loose earth into a bucket with a hand-shovel and emptying the bucket into a wheelbarrow.

Recovery Level D is the normal level of intensity used to define and excavate contexts. The difference between Level C and D is really one of degree and one of purpose. Level D is slower, more meticulous, and is aimed not just at cleaning, but at defining edges. At this recovery level, finds are normally recorded individually in

three dimensions (although this kind of decision is one for each project design). On rural sites, the first task is to prepare a *horizon*, the level at which intact archaeological strata first appear beneath the topsoil (Colour Plate 1a). We have met this horizon when discussing strip and map (Chapter 5), and the procedure is the same. On plough soils, "Horizon 1" refers to the level to which the most recent ploughing has reached (usually defined at Level A and B). "Horizon 2" refers to the top of the subsoil, the level at which archaeological features can be first defined (usually defined at Level C and D). To achieve a horizon, topsoil is cleared with a machine (Level A), tidied with a shovel (Level B), cleaned with a trowel (Level C) and super-cleaned at Level D.

The detail that is achieved in a horizon will depend on the investment made, and this is a balance between the time taken to trowel a surface and its maximum contrast – the point at which the contexts show best (FIG 6.14). On most kinds of deposit in temperate climes this tends to be a matter of humidity: the drier the surface the less you see, and the longer you take, the drier it gets. Some terrains such as sand can take any amount of water and are workable very soon after rain. Others, as on clay, are ruined by rain and take an age to drain. Thus for successful horizon records, the surface must be workable, which may mean waiting for it to dry or waiting for it to get wet. Theoretically in some climates this means waiting for six months. Water can be sprayed on if you can get it, but in hot climates it is usually in short supply and most needed by thirsty people. Nevertheless, the excavator must face up to the fact that the high level definition of contexts is not possible if you can't see them, and you can't see them if the site is too dry, too wet or too messy. If the humidity cannot be controlled artificially (for example under a shelter with a water supply), then the selection of the season to dig in becomes an important part of the excavation design.

FIGURE 6.14 Recording horizons: (a) spraying, (b) tagging and (c and d) plotting with TST (N. Macbeth and FAS Ltd).

In general each context is defined, planned and described before the next one is removed. The limits of a context are visible in the surface when that surface is clean, and the cleaner it is the more visible the context. Then it can be planned and described (see recording, later). Even so there will be many occasions where a context is only partially visible – that's the nature of the beast. For this reason it is helpful to regard the recognition and recording of contexts, and all other elements of the strata, as an act of definition, not an act of observation.

The art of definition in general consists of not going faster than you can see and not removing anything you don't understand (FIG 6.15). The things we don't understand – a clutch of stones, a row of bones, a linear stain, a stray artefact – these are the things we are after. They say: Caution! Look harder. Such anomalies will be defined as contexts, and where contexts are closely associated with each other in space, the expectation is that it should be possible to define a higher-order entity, the feature. So where a set of contexts is suspected of belonging together to form a pit, a wall, a floor and so on, a feature study will be initiated too.

If the context can be seen to be one of several lying in a feature, some kind of depression or pit, then there is a decision to take. Should we remove the contexts one at a time, seeing them only from above? Or should we cut a section, thus seeing

FIGURE 6.15 Leave it in place! Level D definition; freeing a pattern of bones with trowel and paint brush (FAS Ltd).

them from the side? Experience tells us that both these prescriptions have advantages; the decision depends on how much we can learn from each. We can't do both. If the pit contains a broken pot we would learn more about it by excavating in plan. But if the pit contains a vanished post we would learn more about its history (whether it was leaning, whether it was pulled out) by seeing it in section. So how do we know which to do? We don't; if we are very lucky the evaluation may predict what pits are likely to have in them; otherwise only the experience on the site will point in the right direction, after a few errors.

The excavation of a feature commences by cleaning, studying and recording the surface in which it shows, and then studying it by dissection and then studying what is left (Colour Plate 5; FIG 6.16). The records at Level D are therefore more comprehensive: plans and photographs before, during and after excavation, detailed records of each context, and if appropriate, detailed study of a set of contexts at the higher conceptual level of the "feature" (see Recording, later).

Recovery Level E, in my scheme of things, is held in reserve for graves (Colour Plate 6; FIG 6.17). In principle, a grave is just a pit with a body and (sometimes) objects in

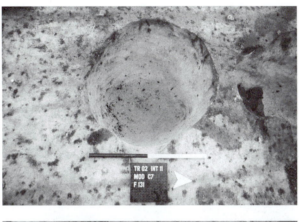

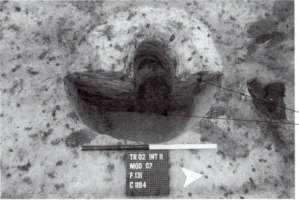

contexts

FIGURE 6.16
Feature portraits, during excavation (below) and after (above) (FAS Ltd).

it, but the difference lies in the idea that the body and the objects are still in situ. Potentially they contain more information than other features, both because they lie as they were placed in the ground and because they refer directly to a human being. Given our current research agendas and our current techniques, graves deserve increased time and thought. More care is needed to dissect the layers – we are looking for the traces of decayed timber for example – and to define individual artefacts – which may be very smashed and fragmented. A range of special instruments, wooden and metal spatulas, dental picks and spoons are at the service of the Level E excavator (FIG 6.17). To try and capture the vertical and horizontal variations in the

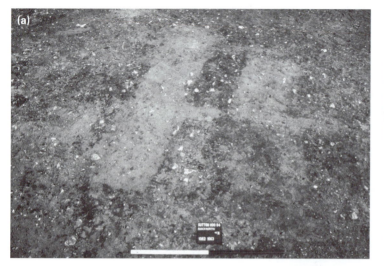

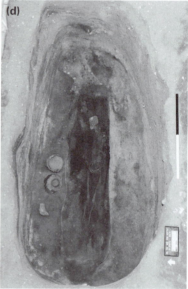

FIGURE 6.17
Excavating graves:
(a) how burial pits
show on a gravelly
surface; (b) finding
the body by
lowering the fill
in stages; (c) the
Level E toolkit;
and (d) a complete
tableau
(N. Macbeth).

(a)

grave fill – even the variations not visible to the naked eye – the inside of the grave is taken down by spits (5–10cm in depth) in *stages* (see FIG 6.9). At each of these stages, the surface is mapped (FIG 6.18). Each stage is taken down one half at a time, so that a section 5–10cm high is exposed, along the long axis of the grave. The face of this section can then be used to take samples (e.g. samples for chemical analysis, to understand decay processes). The other half is then taken away, leaving the flat surface of the next stage. The *running section* is put back in exactly the same place for the next stage. The precision of the records is commensurate with the digging: planning of bones, artefacts and

FIGURE 6.18 Level E burial excavation records: (a) a stage photograph and (b) context maps at particular stages (N. Macbeth/A. Roe).

(b)

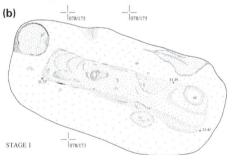

STAGE 1

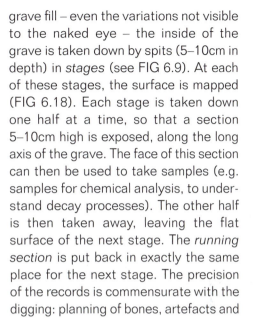

STAGE 2

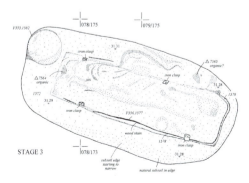

STAGE 3

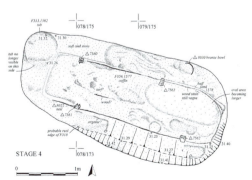

STAGE 4

EXCAVATION **133**

anomalies in the soil to the nearest mm, detailed descriptions of everything observed, and detailed photography, filming and thinking out loud in a journal.

Needless to say there are other kinds of feature for which Level E may be appropriate: a floor scattered with objects or a metal-worker's hearth. Some finds present special challenges: for example a wooden wall of the Viking period still standing in York, or a mail coat found in an Iron Age chariot burial at Kirkburn. The ideal way to study such a complex feature or artefact is to lift it and examine it in the laboratory, away from wind and weather. This is a job for Level F.

Recovery Level F comes in two main forms: micro-mapping on site, and lifting a block of soil and taking it off site to examine in the laboratory. Micro-mapping might employ

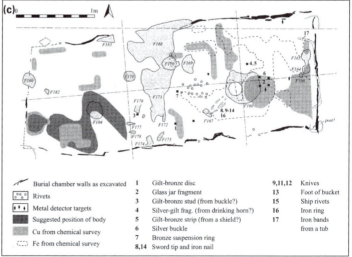

FIGURES 6.19 Level F chemical mapping: (a) sampling the floor of a burial chamber (b) at Sutton Hoo; (c) the result of the analysis (N. Macbeth).

Burial chamber walls as excavated	1	Gilt-bronze disc	9,11,12 Knives
Rivets	2	Glass jar fragment	13 Foot of bucket
Metal detector targets	3	Gilt-bronze stud (from buckle?)	15 Ship rivets
Suggested position of body	4	Silver-gilt frag. (from drinking horn?)	16 Iron ring
Cu from chemical survey	5	Gilt-bronze strip (from a shield?)	17 Iron bands
Fe from chemical survey	6	Silver buckle	from a tub
	7	Bronze suspension ring	
	8,14	Sword tip and iron nail	

a metal detector to plot the decay products where metal once was (see Chapter 5), or chemical mapping, where rows of samples are taken to detect the traces of otherwise invisible activities in the ground. At Sutton Hoo chemical mapping was applied to the floor of the robbed chamber in Mound 2 to see whether the position of the body and any grave-goods could be located in what was in effect an empty room (FIG 6.19). Some 640 30g samples were taken from the sandy floor of the chamber and then examined by ICP (inductively coupled plasma) spectroscopy to list the chemical elements present in each sample. A rich pattern of iron showed where an iron chain had been lying; a circular patch of copper-rich sand probably marked the site of a cauldron, and concentrations of phosphorus, strontium, barium and aluminium showed where the body had lain. In some graves the shape of the body is visible, but formed of sandy earth and still hard to capture on record. As well as survey, photography and sampling, silicon rubber moulding can be used to replicate and capture the earth contours exactly (FIG 6.20).

Lifting a block of earth for dissection in the laboratory can be applied to a piece of earth that contains evidence of special importance – at Chalton (England) it consisted of the shadows of timber posts in a trench (FIG 6.21). Or it can be used to lift a whole burial chamber as Dagmar Selling did at Högom, Sweden, when she realised that the burial chamber under her Mound 2 was intact. The area around the chamber was excavated, and iron plates driven beneath it with jacks. The whole was then boxed up and taken off to town on a lorry, where in the peace and quiet of the laboratory, wind-free and well-lit, a warrior on a bed was slowly dissected (FIG 6.22).

FIGURES 6.21 Level F excavation: taking the post-holes home; lifting a section of earth consolidated with PVA on a chalk site (Chalton, England).

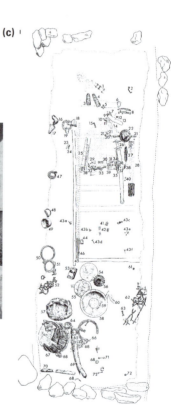

FIGURE 6.22 Level F excavation: taking a burial chamber home at Högom (Sweden); (a) the burial is jacketed in a wooden crate; (b) the crate is lifted and taken to the lab on a lorry and (c) the excavated burial: a 5th century AD warrior in bed (courtesy of Per Ramqvist).

No attempt was made to lift the Sutton Hoo Mound 17 burial in one piece, but a block of earth up one end of the man's grave had showed the glint of metal and the dark lines of rotted leather straps. It was the remains of saddle and bridle, and taking it apart (in order to put it together again) was clearly a job for a museum (FIG 6.23). The block was exposed by digging all round it and jacketed with polystyrene foam to make a strong packing. A steel plate was hammered beneath the block, and then lifted with straps attached to the back-actor of a mechanical excavator, transferred to the boot of an estate car, and driven to the British Museum in London. There the parcel was X-rayed, then unwrapped and excavated in a basement with even lighting

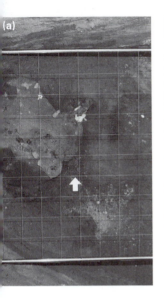

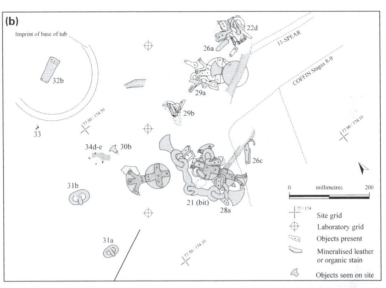

FIGURE 6.23 Level F excavation: Lifting the Sutton Hoo Bridle block: (a) consolidation and location of the block in the field; (b) the plan, with site grid and lab grid; and (c) dissection of the block in the lab (N. Macbeth; A. Roe).

and delicate instruments. Certain pieces of metal and tell-tale markers showing on the sandy surface of the block had been planned on site, while the block was still in its grave; and these were planned again in the museum. In this way the full plan of the bridle with its gold and silver fittings could be repositioned as it had lain in the grave (although we had never seen it there).

Recording

Among the most important records to be made on an excavation are the finds, the artefacts and the biota, which are retrieved by lifting, sieving (screening) and sampling. Both the records made of their location, and the finds themselves, survive at the end of the dig, and are the subjects for a major programme of analysis. Although

FIGURE 6.24

Recording: (anti-clockwise)
(a) photographing a structure;
(b) planning at 1:10;
(c) deciding Munsell colour;
and (d) writing journal (FAS Ltd).

the retrieval, the conservation and some of the analysis starts on site, I hope readers will forgive me if we visit this in an integrated manner in Chapter 9.

By contrast, an excavated deposit survives only in the records that are made of it. It would be hard to exaggerate the responsibility that this imposes. Recording is a matter of pride for some, and a chore for others. Some people can sit all day with a pencil and notebook making notes and sketches like a naturalist, while others have to be nagged, or physically restrained to stop digging and write something down. The trick is to make room for the job, and realise that at Level D or higher more time is going to be spent recording than moving earth (FIG 6.24).

Recorders *study* strata, that is they describe what they see, investigate it and comment on it. The records thus say what it looked like, how it was defined and what it might mean. These records are made in three main media – written, drawn and photographic – all of which may be gathered and stored digitally these days. The main classes of record used on excavations are context, feature and structure records (FIG 6.25). Each of these has its own number and is recorded on a proforma accompanied by one or more drawings and photographs. These multi-conceptual stratigraphic units are subsets of each other (see Chapter 1).

The subject of a *feature record* is an individual feature (FIG 6.26a). The subject of a *context record* is an individual context, its location, how it was defined, what it was made of (its components), its stratigraphic relations to other contexts (FIG 6.26b). Contexts will normally be individually planned at Level D. A set of contexts makes a feature, so the study of a feature results in records of the feature (as an idea) and

Stratigraphic excavation records
multi-concept

- **Component** - (grain of sand), amongst which are
- **Finds** – (anything kept), and these belong to the following:

- **A CONTEXT** – any defined set of components – a layer, a surface.
- Recorded with a Context card, plan, section

- **A FEATURE** is a defined set of contexts
- Recorded with a Feature card, plan, section, photographs

- **A STRUCTURE** is a defined set of features
- Recorded with a Structure card, plan, photographs

- **A HORIZON** is a defined interface between truncated contexts
- Recorded with a survey, a plan and photographs

FIGURE 6.25 Multi-concept records.

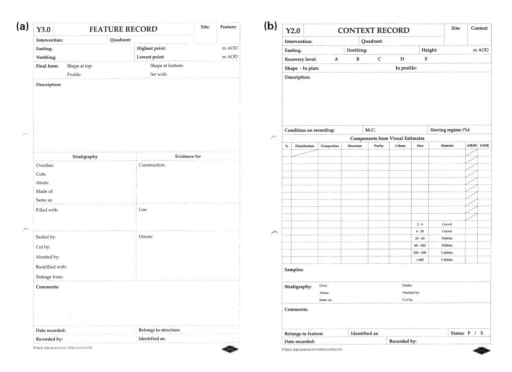

FIGURE 6.26 (a) feature record and (b) context record.

studies of all the physical contexts that make it up. The main burden of a feature record is to say which contexts make it up, which will on occasion be mapped together (FIG 6.27). This is because a feature does not itself exist physically; it is a set of contexts (which do). A feature is thus a higher order of stratigraphic record, relying on a larger amount of interpretation; thus it asks different kinds of questions: How was the feature defined? How did it begin? How did it function? How did it end? And most important, what was it? These questions cannot be answered every time; but it is sensible to ask them about something you can still see.

A structure is defined by a set of features (FIG 6.28), and a *structure record* maps the features that make it up. The structure exists at a still higher level of interpretation and is still less *material*, more of an idea, than its features. Structures are sometimes reasonably obvious – the extant walls of a Roman villa for instance. But more often they have to be hunted: on site by getting up high and off site by discovering which features may have been contemporary, and mapping them (more in Chapter 10). A key piece of information for all three types of record is "Which recovery level was used?" since only contexts, features and structures excavated at the same recovery level are strictly comparable with each other.

Horizons and sections – sets of truncated contexts viewed in a flat horizontal or vertical plane demand recording procedures of their own. To be useful their surfaces

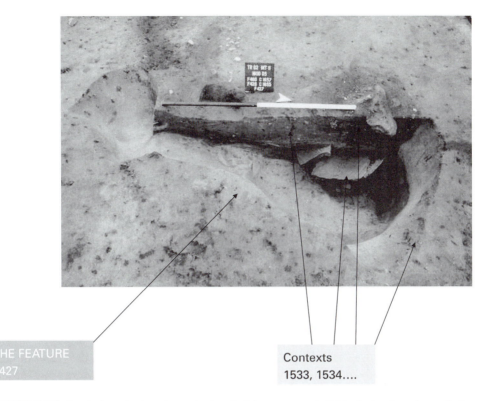

THE FEATURE
F427

Contexts
1533, 1534....

FIGURE 6.27 A set of *contexts* makes a *feature*: in this case a post-pit (the feature) made up of pits, a stone post-pad and backfills (contexts). This feature had a "life": an upright post on a stone pad was replaced by a vertical post and a leaning buttress post in adjacent pits; and both these posts were subsequently removed (FAS Ltd).

must be super-clean, and since nothing stays clean for long, the smart move is to record them photographically immediately, and then make an analytical drawing: either in colour with the edges merging, or more interpretatively as an outline. Contrasts are maximised using fine spray, the horizon is photographed and to capture context edges on a fast fading horizon, white tags can be used, which can then be plotted as soon as the TST is free (see FIG 6.14). The pattern of the contexts leads to the identification and subsequent excavation of features. Tagging is a fairly unobtrusive method of remembering where an edge was in a fading horizon. Other approaches are more emphatic: a practice known in Japan outlines the edges of excavated features with whitener so that they show up well in an overhead photograph (FIG 6.29). Improvement of contrast to make high impact photographs (for example for publicity) assumes that the primary observations have been already made. The first purpose of recording is to tell it how it was, and only then to add tiers of interpretation, recognised and recorded as such through some concept such as the "feature" and "structure".

FIGURE 6.28 A set of *features* makes a *structure*. Rows of post pits (features) excavated into chalk. The presence of a structure is inferred from the pattern that the posts make in the ground.

FIGURE 6.29 Feature map by overhead photography (Japan). The edges of features are enhanced with whitener (courtesy of Kaname Mayakawa).

Sections, like horizons, show the character of relationships between contexts, so that the information recorded amounts to more than the sum of its parts (the contexts). The interfaces exposed in section are recorded with respect to a horizontal line with known three-dimensional co-ordinates, so it is anchored in space (FIG 6.30). A section can also present the character of a structure and the way it was built in a uniquely dramatic form (FIG 6.31). And it must be admitted too, that sections may reveal interfaces that can elude the most diligent troweller on the flat. In short, the reported "death of the section" is premature.

Recording generates written records and spatial records, using the clean faces exposed by digging. A *plan* is a drawing of a single entity, while a *map* shows more than one entity. All the maps and plans made on a site are related to the universal grid and to the height above sea level, so that anyone in the future will know exactly where they were. (Since the sea level is not as permanent as we might have hoped, these heights are related these days to a fixed datum point in each country.) For

FIGURE 6.30 Drawing a section. A tape is stretched along a horizontal datum line with a measured height above sea level. One archaeologist measures the horizontal distance along the datum and the vertical distance up from the datum (with a hand tape) and shouts out the measurements to the other, who is making the section record, annotated and drawn to scale (author).

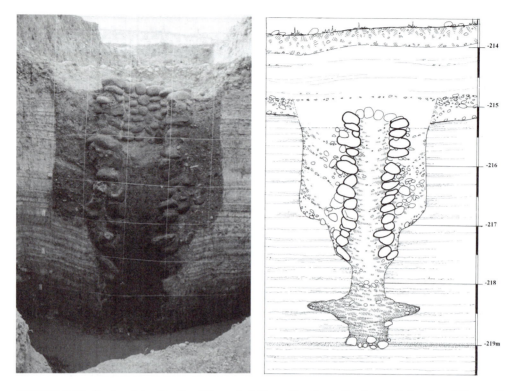

FIGURE 6.31 Section through a Neolithic well at Sha'ar Hagolan in the Jordan Valley, Israel. The well has been cut vertically through to expose its structure and its well pit: (a) photograph with a grid, and (b) section drawing, carried down below the water table, where the camera cannot reach (Yosef Garfinkel).

horizons we make a map of contexts. Contexts, features, structures, horizons and sections thus each have written, drawn and photographic records, systematically made following a cycle that every site has (FIG 6.32). Every piece of earth on site has a context record – nothing that we see escapes being defined as a context. Features and structures on the other hand are not always successfully defined on site. They may need further analysis at the end of the dig: for example, to believe in a structure made of wooden posts, we would need the use of chronology and spatial analysis to determine which post-holes were actually contemporary with each other (more in Chapter 10).

Feature and structure records formalise preliminary interpretations and log them. But interpretations at a still higher level also figure in a *notebook*. The main purpose of the notebook is as a journal, to say what you did. For the supervisor of an area, the site notebook is usually full of things to do, tasks for diggers, timetables, preliminary interpretations, speculations about troublesome anomalies, notes for future analyses, conversations with specialists. For site directors, it is a record of decisions made, of what was done, when and why – what should be done now, soon or sometime.

Excavation Records
Recovery Level

WRITTEN RECORDS

Context card
Feature card
Site diary - Project history

DRAWN RECORDS

Horizon map
Context outline (single context plan)
Context plan
Context map
Feature plan
Feature map

PHOTOGRAPHIC RECORDS

Horizon photo
Context portrait
Feature portrait (before/after excavation)

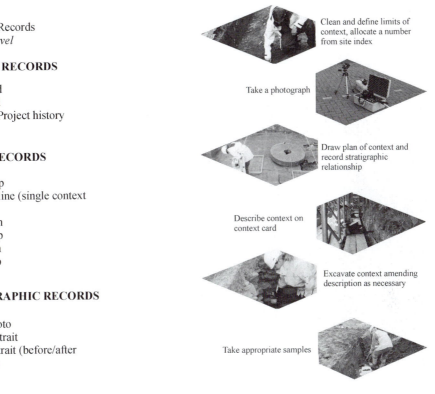

Clean and define limits of context, allocate a number from site index

Take a photograph

Draw plan of context and record stratigraphic relationship

Describe context on context card

Excavate context amending description as necessary

Take appropriate samples

FIGURE 6.32 Excavation records (left) and the recording cycle (right) (FAS Ltd).

It can be seen that there is a spectrum of records from the very factual to the quite fanciful: while some of the records made are data, measurements, drawings, photographs and soil descriptions, for example, others are more speculative, feelings and opinions about what something might have been, what people may have done. Why is this? Excavators work in a world in which the boundary between fact and interpretation is continually being redefined. A damp patch in the sand marks a cylindrical socket, which, once it is emptied, and its width and depth measured, is recognised and named as a "post-hole" (or "post-mold"). The progress of the anomaly from damp patch to post-hole was the result of a series of small acts of definition. The description of the anomaly passes from the more certain to the less certain; it climbs into ever higher levels of inference, and is supported by decreasing degrees of consensus. Whereas each of these concepts, the damp patch and the socket, required definition, only the last, the naming, is labelled as an act of interpretation – but in practice the business of interpretation is seamless. These days there is often a high degree of consensus for the existence of a post-hole (now a common enough feature) but less for its function. That it formed part of a structure may be readily agreed; but once enough is known about the site, it can be designated as part of a roof support for a

Course of an excavation

Setting up and laying out

Opening (Level A)

Cleaning (Level B, C)

Horizon definition
(Level, C, D)

Recording of horizon:
context mapping (Level D)

Feature location and
recording: context planning
(Level D, E, F)

Sheeting, backfilling and
decamping

FIGURE 6.33 The course of an excavation (FAS Ltd).

building; that building may become a feasting hall, and in subsequent interpretations it may be hailed as the post on which the chief hung his hat. The urge to create ever more vivid interpretations is controlled by the need to support them with accurate observations. Thus the ladder of inference remains visible; and if it seems to stretch out of sight in an excess of imagination, we can always return to the last firm rung, the last identification that attracted a reasonable consensus. In the study of humanity we do not trade in unequivocal information, but use observation, experience, argument and persuasion to build a concordat, reinforced by trust. This does not disqualify us from being scientists.

The course of an excavation

Armed with these few basic techniques let's end with a potted history of an excavation from its beginning to its end (FIG 6.33). Before opening any patch of ground, it should be surveyed and photographed. This may show nothing at all, but that doesn't matter. You still need the photograph to record what was or wasn't there in the event of a legal problem. Then lay out the area to be excavated and decide on the location of the spoil heaps, the site huts, the camp site and how to park cars and manage visitors. You may have to rope off deep areas into which visitors, given the chance, will tumble.

The site will generally be opened with a machine, working at Level A, which will remove the modern top soil or rubble and either place it in a heap (if it is to be used for back-filling) or in a lorry if it is to be taken away and sold. After machining, all hands are deployed in tidying up with shovels. The surface is scraped to remove the loose earth, and the edges are marked straight and orthogonal, and cut clean and vertical with a spade and then a trowel. The edges are then marked with a tape or fence to keep everyone from treading on them. An excavation is judged by the precision of its edges, and rightly so. Now it is starting to look like a real piece of research as opposed to cleared ground. Planks supported by sandbags are laid out on the surface to provide walkways; they will have to be moved about regularly to reflect the areas being worked.

The first horizon is then prepared, using Level C and then Level D digging. The success of this operation depends on matching tools and techniques to terrain; having water if it's too dry, and having drainage if too much of it is falling from the sky. A tower, or some way of getting up high, is essential on virtually any terrain. From up there you can see what is happening, what is coming next, and you can take those overhead shots on which all readers of reports depend. It is impossible to conduct any excavation that aspires to obtain a research result without planks, sandbags, water control and a high-lift. Some excavators feel obliged to bypass these necessities, but it will result in sub-standard work and we will all be the losers in the end.

FIGURE 6.34 Daily life on a dig: (clockwise) (a) site cabin for recorders; (b) filling sand bags; (c) tea break; (d) end of the day – cleaning the tools (author).

As in any other industry, once certain provisions have been shown necessary to achieve a standard required by the public, those provisions must find their way into the costing of projects, whether for research or rescue. Excavation is more satisfying, and no less fun, for being disciplined, well-organised and diligent (FIG 6.34).

Finishing an excavation is much harder than starting one. Here the two cultures of rescue and research are at their most distant. Rescue excavations must finish. The developer employs archaeologists as professionals working in a commercial company, and a commercial company must finish its contracts on time or it will never make any money. The health of the archaeology here is almost entirely in the hands of good evaluation and design. Good planning and good advocacy means adequate time and a valuable result. Once the digging is done, the construction contractors may take over immediately and the archaeological opportunity is at an end.

Research excavations are not apparently under the same constraints, and as a result some never finish at all. I say "apparently" because in practice, exactly the same constraints of time and money apply: the excavation is being carried out for the community, and stakeholders are owed a result. The project design should determine the access to the resource, exactly what is to be done there, how much it will cost and the condition of the site when it is handed back. There are important issues of conservation and display here, which should be detailed in the design (more in Chapter 14). After an excavation is complete, a research excavator will need to budget for at least one more season dedicated to tidying up and consolidating the site for its new future (FIG 6.35).

Excavation

Design
- Location
- Size
- Methods

Techniques
- Geometric
- Stratigraphic
- Recovery levels

Applications
- CRM Mitigation
- Research

FIGURE 6.35 Excavation summary.

In sum . . .

The course of an excavation is determined in advance by a design, drawing on an evaluation. This design will specify an approach which is in turn dependent on the terrain (what type of land), the objectives (what we want to know) and the social context (which will determine the stake-holders and the work force). Open-minded attitudes are essential to unlock the knowledge from any piece of land. Excavations may be geometric, or sampling, or stratigraphic; they may be small square boxes or large open areas. The trick is not to stick righteously to a rule book, but to be appropriate to the task. The two main theatres in which we work – the research theatre and the rescue theatre (see Chapter 15) – will also be determinant. There will be differences but also many shared values and practices between them.

While I believe strongly in a flexible approach to excavation, of being appropriate rather than dogmatic, I am aware nonetheless of having exercised certain opinions, strongly held: that excavators must have a clear design, stated Recovery Levels, a disciplined ethos, a multi-conceptual recording system, adequate equipment, control of humidity and a way of getting an overview from high up – and that sites should always be insanely clean. For me this kind of stipulation ought to apply universally, but in all other matters I would give way to the invention and creativity of the response to a particular challenge. Design is all, design as the way that, in every case, the objectives, the character of the land and the interests of stake holders are married in clear programmes of research and conservation.

In the next chapter I propose that we should visit a variety of projects in different countries to see how terrain and objectives and social contexts influence field workers and modify their methods. Although excavation will feature prominently in all these examples, note that most projects today use landscape survey, site survey and excavation in different combinations to address their research questions or to rescue their sites. Whether they are paid for as research or rescue is not so important – the aspiration at least is that both types of circumstance should equally serve the past.

Briefing

Of all parts of archaeological investigation, excavation is the hardest to appreciate from a book. For the history and development of the art (or science) see Chapter 2 and examples given in Fagan 1996. Among the classics, modern Europeans tend to follow a trajectory that runs from Pitt Rivers 1886–90, Petrie 1904, Wheeler 1954, Barker 1977 and Roskams 2001. These are all how-to-do-it books focusing on stratigraphy. For US practice, the modern classics are probably Hester et al 1997 and Thomas 1998. The books on field archaeology (see Chapter 2 *Briefing* for others) only give a rather partial view of what is actually being done. The main source ought to be in the design and method section of excavation reports, but excavators remain strangely reticent about including this information in any detail. A strong theme of the present chapter is that although there is a range of standard techniques, their application is very varied and depends on what you want to do, in other words, the design. So while this chapter reviews the basics, the next offers a series of examples of site investigations, mainly by excavation, in different types of terrain. The two chapters should be read as one.

The rationale of excavation **design** is best appreciated from Chapter 14 where it is put in context. In my acquaintance the most detailed and accessible accounts of which methods were used and why are Hope-Taylor 1977, Chapter 2 and Carver 2005, Chapter 2 and 3, but there ought to be others. Every excavation should have a **safety** manual which will probably draw on Department of the Environment 1973, 1974, 1975, Roskams 2001 (82–9), Allen and Holt 1997 (in the UK), and Niquette 1997, US Army Corps of Engineers 1996, and Poirier and Feder 2001 in the USA. The picture of a digger in a tight spot is from Galiberti 2005.

Geometric methods: my example of the *Schnitt* is from Starigrad/Oldenburg (Müller-Wille 1991). For spits and artificial and natural layers see Hester et al 1997 (p. 88) where it is called the unit-level method or arbitrary level: "The unit-level method is undoubtedly the most common method of excavating sites that show little stratigraphic variation." **Sampling** procedure is well described in Schiffer 1976 (the "Joint Site"), Hester et al. 1997 (37–9), drawing on Brown 1975. Redman 1986 for Qsar es-Seghir. **Stratigraphic excavation** has a long tradition in the UK, e.g. Pitt Rivers 1880, Wheeler 1954, Barker 1993, Roskams 2001; **open area excavation** was arguably practised by Koldewey (1914) at Babylon, but its rise to favour in modern Europe can probably be tracked to Hatt 1938, Steensberg 1940, Biddle and Kjølbye-Biddle 1969, and P.A. Barker 1969, 1993.

Recovery Levels as an idea has been previously presented and discussed in M. Carver 1987, 130 (urban) and M. Carver 2005, 25 (rural). Machining and tool use can't be learnt from a book and it's dangerous to try. For lifting soil blocks see Franken 1965, Cronyn 1990, 43–57; Payton 1992 for the Viking wall and Iron Age mail coat. M. Carver 2005, 124 for the Sutton Hoo bridle; Ramqvist 1992 for Högom. For chemical mapping in graves, see Bethell 1991, M. Carver 2005, 49 and 159–61.

Records and recording: Many firms have generated their own standardised recording systems, among which MoLAS 1994 is one of the more widely adopted. Context-only recording is discussed and promoted by Roskams 2001. The multi-conceptual recording system has been previously presented and discussed in M. Carver 1979a, b, 1987, 1999a and 2005 (41–2); see Framework 2008 (p. 8) for an adaptation and development of the system in a large-scale commercial project. I suspect there are many similar variants being successfully practised in the field.

7 PROJECTS GALORE: INTEGRATED FIELD RESEARCH

Introduction

This chapter will take us on a trip round the world looking at projects on different types of terrain, from a cave in Greece and a shell-mound in Kentucky to a town in England and a submerged village in France (FIG 7.1). It is something of a package

FIGURE 7.1 Map showing locations of projects discussed in this volume (FAS Ltd).

tour, with every visit too short, but even a brief chat on site can often be more illuminating than a formal report. In each case, we will see how the project director has matched the objectives and the social situation to the terrain to achieve the best result, and how a value-led approach was often taken, overtly or not. The result offers a small celebration of the ingenuity of archaeological investigations and some pointers to the consequences of their great variety.

A cave site in Greece (FIG 7.2; no. 2 on FIG 7.1)

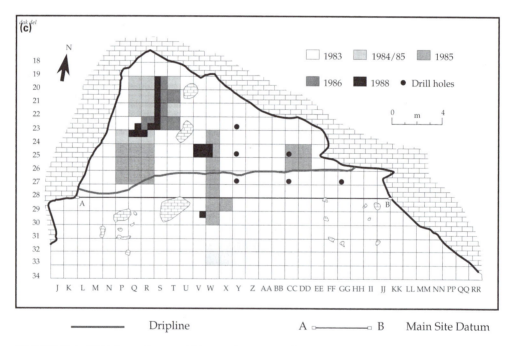

FIGURE 7.2 Klithi Cave, Greece: (a) inspecting a core; (b) excavating in quadrats; and (c) the cave plan with location of cores and areas excavated (courtesy of Geoff Bailey).

My first port of call is a *cave* – and the one I've chosen is Klithi, a limestone rock shelter on the right bank of the Voïdomatis River, in mountainous Epirus, northern Greece. To get there, Geoff Bailey and his team from the University of Cambridge had to man-pack every item of excavation equipment along a goat track, a half-hour journey from the nearest vehicle access. The rock shelter was 25m wide, 10m high and 10m deep, and the finds density proved to average 34,000 items per cubic metre. No finds are permitted to leave Greece, so all finds processing and analysis had to be carried out during the five-week season. The camp site was on a terrace by the river 300m away, and the river itself provided water for wet sieving – which was necessary to pick up diagnostic fragments of bone and artefacts less than 10mm across. Very detailed retrieval was crucial, since the date of the occupation was 21000–17000 cal BP.

The design confronted the dilemma of whether to apply the resources they had to getting a vertical sequence or to exploring the shelter in plan – and so understanding something of the social use of space in the upper Palaeolithic. Director Geoff Bailey commented: "There was a continuing tension throughout the excavation between the requirements of digging deep and digging wide." There was also a tension between attempting to define contexts stratigraphically or retrieving samples in arbitrary layers (spits).

The team divided the area covered by the rock shelter into metre squares and began in 1983 with two exploratory pits at the front edge. The next year they opened two areas with a total of 12m squares which produced a hearth and 45,000 finds (mainly flints), giving an idea of the rich assemblage. In 1985–7 more squares were opened and by 1988 the team had examined an estimated 3% of the deposit. At this point they took cores with a percussion rock drill that extracted samples from a known depth in a hollow steel tube. A core 6.93m long yielded 41 samples suitable for AMS c14 dating, and bedrock was later reached at 7.1m. This showed that intensive human occupation of the rock shelter was limited to the top 2m of deposit.

In his comprehensive two-volume 1997 report Geoff Bailey points out that if they had continued to use their selected methods of recovery it would have taken another 16 years to reach the bottom. With the advantage of hindsight, it can be seen that if coring had been used in a preliminary evaluation phase at the start of the project, it might have then been noted that the upper two metres contained the occupation sequence. A test-pit (at Level B or C) cut through these 2 metres would have provided a preliminary deposit model, including an assessment of the logistics of processing a large assemblage on site. The consequent design could then have given priority to slow excavation in area (at Level D) in order to examine the use of space by upper Palaeolithic people. On the other hand, a test-pit 2m deep, and dug rapidly, followed by a large scale excavation in plan could be viewed as unacceptable in a still unexplored cave, and might still have taken 16 seasons. The cautious approach actually taken tried to match maximum yield with minimum impact.

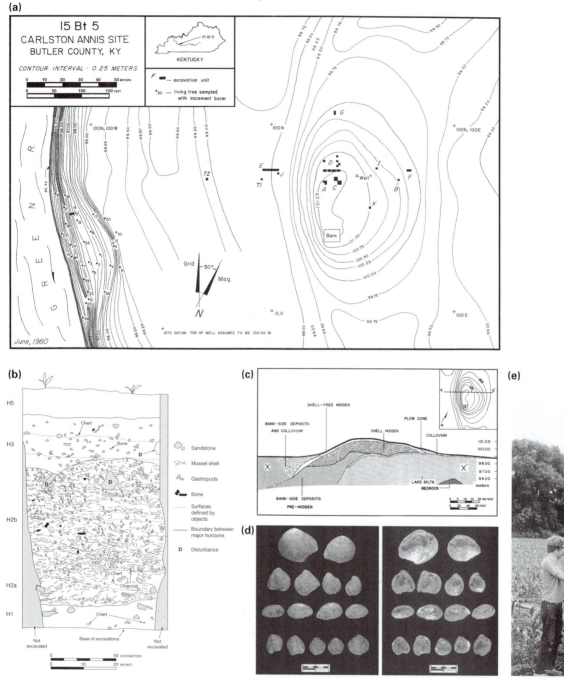

FIGURE 7.3 Carlston Annis shell mound, Kentucky: (a) contour map; (b) a deep section; (c) profile; (d) types of shell; and (e) coring with the Giddings Probe (William Marquhart).

The period that followed the ice age, the post-pleistocene or early Holocene is one of the most challenging for excavators. Among the more obtrusive targets are giant mounds of shells such as figure prominently in the prehistoric landscape of western Kentucky. The Carlston Annis mound (otherwise 15Bt5), measured more than 100m across and rose 9m above the Green River (a tributary of the Ohio River). It was first the subject of investigations under a WPA (job creation) programme of 1939–41, but new investigations were initiated in 1972 when William Marquardt visited it with some fellow graduate students from Washington University. Marquardt and co-director Patty Jo Watson were to study the mound for over 30 years. The original objective of the SMAP (Shell Mound Archaeological Project) was to throw light on the origins of agriculture, but the agenda continually broadened. As the directors remarked in their final publication: "Repeatedly we have defined a research issue and begun to attack it, only to have the problem evolve and redefine itself as if it had life and volition of its own."

The investigation took the form of a research excavation by sampling, supported by regional surveys. To dig the mound away completely would be both unethical and uneconomical; but vertical samples should report the generality of a subsistence sequence, since the make up of shell and midden was expected to be broadly homogenous in cultural terms. The project began with mapping and surface collection. Then a number of 1×1m test-pits was cut to varying depths in order to sample the mound make-up and pre-mound layers. The team devised a water flotation device to float seeds and other organic debris from the deposits found in the test-pits.

In 1975, interest widened to the locality, and test-pits were dug in neighbouring rock shelter sites. In 1977, geoarchaeologist Julie Stein was recruited to study site formation processes and David Baerreis began a study of climate through the gastropod fauna. In 1978, test-pits were dug on top of the mound, cores were taken with a Giddings Probe and a 9×1m trench was excavated at the edge of the mound to investigate the geology. In 1981, Thomas Gatus located sources for the chert used by prehistoric tool-makers, and specialised studies were undertaken on chert, molluscs, plant remains, faunal remains and geology that allowed a summary conclusion to be published in 1983.

Understanding continued to mature with additional studies that put the Carlston Annis mound in context. Between 1983 and 1993 Christine Hensley analysed the local chipped stone industry and explored non-shell mounds many of which proved contemporary with 15Bt5. The analysis programme was concluded and the synthesis of 30 years' work was published in 2005, when the initiators, directors and authors, Marquardt and Watson, summed up the contribution made by their project in terms of early hunting gathering, horticultural and agricultural strategies. These Shell Mound Archaic people flourished between 5700 and 2500BP, and were not farmers.

This project shows how on some sites a complete programme can be hard to predict in advance. Materials for prior evaluation and a strong design may not be in reach initially and the project may evolve through time, especially as here when there is a prominent multi-disciplinary theme. A 30-year timespan for the research study of a single site is not unusual in archaeology. For every new piece of strata you see, you wish you could see more; every piece of analysis done suggests more data are needed. The questions start simple (that's how grant-givers like it) but the answers are always complex. In a way, this should reassure archaeologists that they are succeeding in their investigations: it means ancient life was just as complex as modern life.

On the gravels: a timber palace in northern England (FIGS 7.4, 7.5)

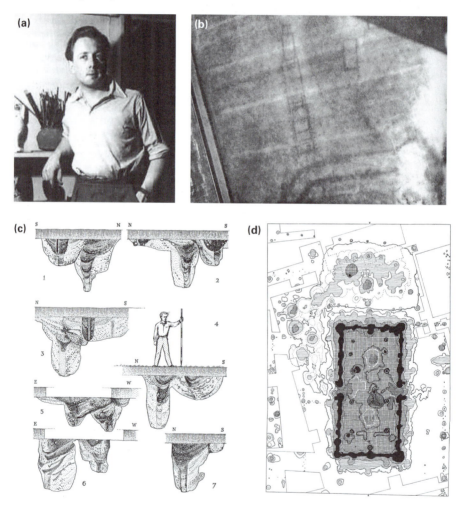

FIGURE 7.4 Anglo-Saxon palace on the gravels at Yeavering: (a) Brian Hope-Taylor, the excavator; (b) aerial photo; (c) sections demonstrating different kinds of upright timber, now vanished and (d) structure plan with depth of features (Brian Hope-Taylor).

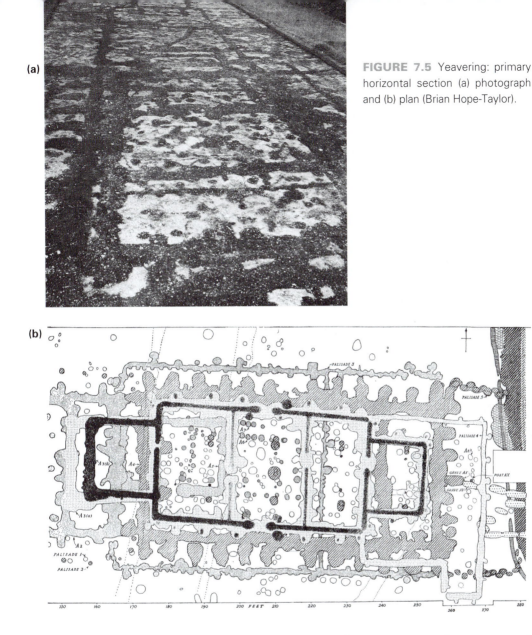

(a)

(b)

FIGURE 7.5 Yeavering: primary horizontal section (a) photograph and (b) plan (Brian Hope-Taylor).

Plough-damaged sites in open country are among the most commonly encountered: popular with researchers because well-drained sand and gravels subsoils were always preferred by early farmers too. They also appear frequently on the menu of commercial archaeologists because these same sands and gravels are extracted in modern times for road building. Additionally, the nature of the subsoil means that excavators can often be guided by cropmarks.

Although undertaken in the 1950s, the excavation of the early historic cropmark at *Yeavering* in Northumberland (UK) by Brian Hope-Taylor remains a classic investigation on gravel and he pioneered a number of enduring techniques. The cropmark seemed to show a group of rectangular buildings originally constructed in timber. The excavator was faced with a site where nothing at all was visible on the surface and, at first, very little under it. The location where the cropmarks had been spotted was a gentle rise (the "whaleback") beside the River Glen. The first stage was to draw up a contour map on which the positions of the cropmark features could be located. Trial excavation on the sites of the buildings at first failed to see anything, but knowing they must be there, Hope-Taylor experimented with larger areas and different methods of cleaning the gravel surface. The excavation seasons took place in autumn and winter, beginning in September after oats had been harvested, and continuing into January or February when snow lay on the fields. This is a dark and damp time of year in Northumberland, with high winds, but Hope-Taylor and his small hardy crew showed in the course of their work that the definition of features would have been nearly impossible in dry weather.

Areas for excavation up to 100m long and 30m wide were stripped by spade and then cleaned by trowel. The gravel surface of the excavation area was first cleaned and re-cleaned by trowel, and then with large hand-brushes with stiff bristles ("churn-brushes"). Applied with a slightly circular motion these functioned, to use Hope-Taylor's phrase, "like a thousand tiny trowels". The exposed surface prepared in this way was called the "primary horizontal section" (equivalent to our *horizon*). Optimum visibility of features in the horizon was achieved by dampening the site, allowing it to dry and viewing it from a tower 12m high. Some experiments were undertaken with artificial dampening (a fire-hose pumping water from the River Glen), but nothing was so effective for dampening a horizon as the light drizzle of Northumberland. When the rain stopped, the imprint of the buildings would gradually grow before the excavators' eyes, like a developing negative. The horizons were photographed at half-hour intervals until the moment of optimum clarity and then planned. Post-sockets, foundation trenches, pits and graves all appeared as slight variations in the orange and brown gravel of the subsoil.

On the ground, Hope-Taylor found that he could detect the edges of features scarcely visible at ground level from a slight change in the noise made by the trowel as it passed from the gravelly subsoil into a more humic fill. The excavation produced practically no artefacts. Bone had on the whole deteriorated in the acid porous gravel to a fragment or a stain; burnt wood was present, but the majority of wood was inferred from dark patches and strips in the gravel. Hope-Taylor used the horizons to examine the relationships of negative features in plan; and vertical sections to capture the form of upright timbers, or in some cases, where timbers had been. This was partly just practical: if he had attempted to remove the latest context (the post stain) from the earlier (the packing) the tableau would simply have fallen to pieces with nothing gained. As it was, digging by *Schnitt* gave an extraordinarily detailed account of the architecture of a dozen monumental structures, including halls, a temple, a church, and a segment of an amphitheatre, which had been built, destroyed, or dis-mantled by Anglo-British kings in the 6th to 8th centuries AD.

One of the most valuable aspects of Hope-Taylor's report was Chapter 3, in which the course of the excavations, the problems encountered and how they were addressed were explained in detail. Such expositions are sadly rare. He showed how he adapted his objectives to the terrain – to make it show what he knew was there. It was a pity that in the 20 years it took for the report to appear, this experience remained largely hidden from other practitioners.

On the sand: a Neolithic village by the Seine (FIG 7.6; no. 6 on FIG 7/1)

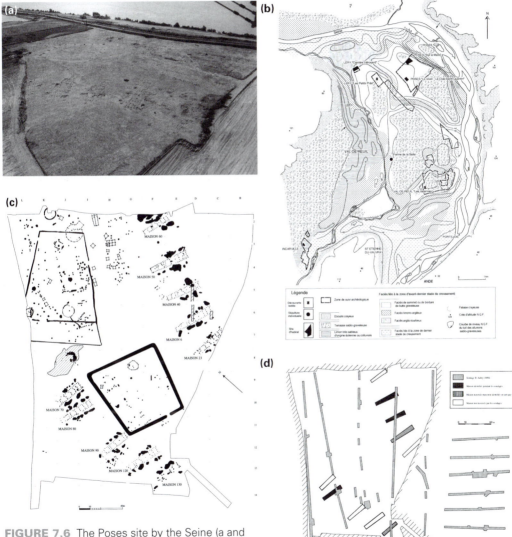

FIGURE 7.6 The Poses site by the Seine (a and b), and the exploratory trenches that found the Neolithic longhouses (c and d) (Françoise Bostyn).

Fifty years later and in France, archaeologists working on similar terrain at *Villeneuve-St-Germain de Poses* (Poses for short) had to excavate without guidance from an air photograph and under severe pressure from quarrying. The area of interest, located on a terrace in a loop of the Seine in Normandy, was already well known to a network of local enthusiasts, who were picking up Neolithic and later pottery and keeping an eye on the encroachment of contractors who were extracting silt, sand and gravel. Between 1973 and 1986 archaeologists had intervened at intervals as best they could, but from 1986 official agreement was obtained to maintain watching briefs at the quarries. The systematic management of the resource began in 1994 with a review by B. Aubry which led to a plan for the investigation of a proposed new area of quarrying at Poses.

Excavator Françoise Bostyn who directed the work, was well aware of the dangers of relying on too superficial a reconnaissance or evaluation. Not only was there no air photograph, but two seasons of fieldwalking drew a blank. However, a study of the geology showed that in this alluvial zone, early land surfaces were being continually buried or eroded, and the subsoil surface carrying prehistoric dwellings lay at variable depth. Total stripping of the whole area would be financially prohibitive and might damage the stratigraphy of hidden occupation levels. Accordingly, the archaeologists opened long trenches 20m apart, using a mechanical excavator with a toothless bucket 2m wide. As they noted, such a method tends to favour the discovery of linear features such as ditches, but it did also succeed in locating post-holes subsequently shown to belong to Neolithic long-houses. The Neolithic features lay hidden in a layer of brown silt up to a metre down. A further protohistoric phase, including a large enclosure, was in general contacted some 15cm higher.

Having unlocked the formation process by means of these trenches, an area of 4.5ha was stripped and excavated over a six-month period. Ten post-hole buildings were defined, each around 40m long and well spread out, belonging to the Neolithic period (4000BC).

In her thoughtful report Bostyn shows that the definition of the prehistoric settlement was greatly dependent on the terrain, the yellow sandy silt, brown silt and gravel all offering different visibility to features and different preservation of artefacts and bone. This exemplifies the challenge of recovering archaeological evidence from huge areas that are about to be completely destroyed by quarrying. The ancient buildings and settlements may be invisible from the surface, well spread and well-buried on an undulating surface now ironed flat by the plough. The time needed for the evaluation phase is often far too short, and yet it is time and thought that are needed to explore such a threatened area thoroughly, to locate and select suitable targets for detailed excavation. The "staged" approach, essential for archaeological research, is some-times not appreciated by those contracted to deliver gravel.

A turf hall in Norway (FIGS 7.7 and 7.8; no. 7 on FIG 7.1)

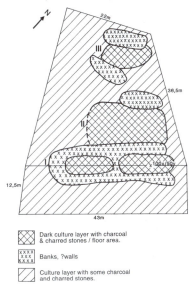

(b) Borg, Vestvågøy, Nordland. May 1983.
Sketch of possible features visible after ploughing.

Dark culture layer with charcoal
& charred stones / floor area.

Banks, ?walls

Culture layer with some charcoal
and charred stones.

FIGURE 7.7 Borg, Lofoten Islands, Norway: (a) excavation; (b) surface survey and (c) appearance of Horizon 2 (Else Roesdahl).

Borg in the Lofoten Islands, northern Norway, lies above the Arctic Circle but warm currents at the end of the Gulf Stream allow cultivation, and cultivation means ploughing. The late Iron Age settlement (here AD200–300) was found accidentally in 1981 when an alert farmer turned up unusual amounts of charcoal and charred stones, and consulted local archaeologist Kåre Ringstad. Surface mapping of the field showed that there had been buildings there with turf walls, or more properly sod (earth with roots). The site had not been ploughed for long: members of a local family remembered playing hide and seek in a turf ruin in the 1920s. A special committee was formed to take the project forward with the support of Tromsø Museum, the Nordic Cultural Fund, the Nordic Committee for Research in the Humanities and the local authority. Excavations were carried out under the direction of Tromsø archaeologists Gerd Stamsø Munch and Olav Sverre Johansen, and the prominent Viking

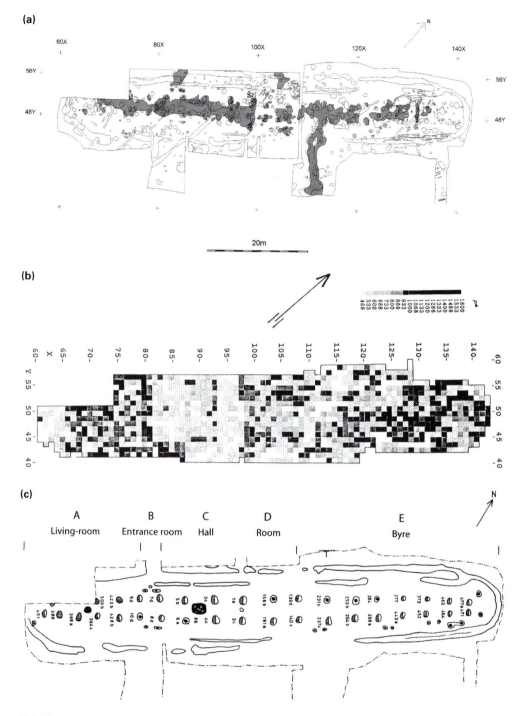

FIGURE 7.8 Borg: (a) feature map; (b) phosphate plot; and (c) interpretation (Else Roesdahl).

specialist at the University of Århus, Else Roesdahl, and the project culminated in a landmark publication in 2003.

On the surface, zones of charcoal and stones already pointed to the likely positions of buildings and these were explored by trial excavations in 1983–4. Test-pits 1×1m were used to investigate the depth and extent of the cultural layer (that is, the layer where turf walls and midden had raised the thickness of soil). Test-pits that proved to be too small for observation were enlarged to 3×2m. A test trench was excavated to confirm the presence of a building at the south part of the field. This building, designated Borg I, became the principal focus of research and was investigated by area excavation. An area of 2000m² was scheduled, protecting the immediate area of the building from further ploughing.

In the area excavation at Borg I, Level 1 (i.e. Horizon 1) was defined in the cultural layer 5–10cm below the surface of the recent ploughsoil. Features were here recorded at 1:20 and then photographed vertically. Level 2 (= Horizon 2) was the surface of the sterile subsoil. The patterns at this level were recorded by planning and a mosaic of overhead photographs. In its fully developed form, the building proved to be 80m long and constructed with timber posts and (originally) with turf/sod walls. Negative features were well defined against the yellow sand subsoil: they contained stone slabs and dark sandy soils derived from the cultural layer. Ploughing had reached the subsoil, but some of the unploughed cultural layer survived intact along the long axis of the building.

To improve knowledge of the way this large building was used, all objects were individually plotted, and phosphate samples were systematically collected from both horizons. Samples for C14 were taken from hearths and other carbon sources and the 34 dates obtained provided the main method of sequencing in the absence of stratification. Some 4,500 Iron Age finds were retrieved and processed, 72% of which were recovered by hand, 16% by sieving (screening) and 1% by metal detector. The remaining 11% were recovered from the immediate region without a firm provenance (stray finds). The detailed mapping of the distribution of the finds: sickles, fish hooks, beads and gold plaques led the archaeologists to propose the uses of the different rooms – as living-rooms, hall and byre for animals. They also reflected on differential use by men and women based on the character of the artefacts.

Buildings constructed with ephemeral materials such as turf and earth are hard to see and demand excavation in plan. The form of the building and the character of the deposit was anticipated here not from preliminary test-pitting, but from local ethnoarchaeological knowledge. Note that it would not do to have machined this site to the subsoil – even though that was the level at which features were easiest to see. It was the combination of detailed finds-plotting from the top, and the discovery of bands of denser soil left by rotted turf that led to the understanding of the structure and the way it had been used.

A stone fort in Sweden (FIG 7.9; no. 9 on FIG 7.1)

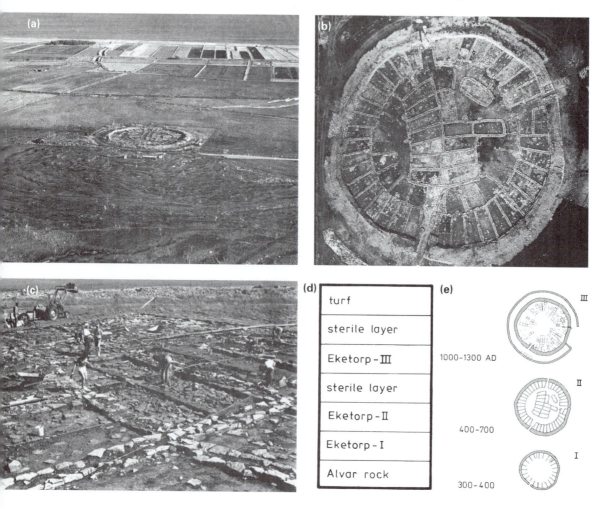

FIGURE 7.9 Excavations at Eketorp, Sweden: (a) location; (b) the excavated ring work; (c) excavators at work; (d) scheme of stratification; and (e) sequence (Borg et al 1976).

Before its excavation in 1964–72, the ring-fort at *Eketorp*, Sweden, appeared as a circular stony bank. Trial excavations by Mårten Stenberger in 1931 had already shown that the interior contained buildings, and from comparable circular enclosures in Scandinavia, such as Trelleborg, it was surmised that Eketorp might belong to the late Iron Age (Vendel or Viking periods). Excavation began with a trial trench in the west interior, where an aerial photograph had revealed traces on the surface attributed to radially placed buildings. These were confirmed as houses built of slabs of limestone with the wall cores filled with broken stone; there was no clay or mortar bonding. In 1964–5 one quadrant of the ring-fort was opened up and excavation continued every year until 1972, by which time virtually the whole site had been exposed down to its first phase.

Since the buildings were constructed from dry-stone walling and had largely collapsed, the excavators had to learn how to read the wall lines and separate them from the rubble, while also reading the rubble for its use as paths, yards and other features. For this, the only prescription was to get up high and view the site from above. Immediately under the turf were the remains of the latest stone-built settlement Eketorp III, dating from the medieval period, detected from stone sills among the rubble, with numerous finds dating from the period. Beneath the stones of the medieval settlement was a fine and fairly even earth surface. Within this layer the prehistoric occupation began to appear with house foundations and "many interesting stone constructions". The stratigraphic separation of Eketorp III, the medieval phase, from Eketorp II, the prehistoric (Viking) phase, was thus relatively legible. Eketorp I (pre-Viking) was implied by the form of an early, faced wall protecting the ring-work, and is thought to have been largely empty of structures.

The buildings revealed after clearance of loose stones were recorded by overhead photography and then surveyed. The settlement was phased using the very thin strata, where it was present, and otherwise using joints between walls, their alignments and the position of finds, all 25,000 of which were individually plotted. By this means and by associated dated finds and 53 radiocarbon dates, the settlement was resolved into its three main phases.

The moral from Eketorp is that in such a collapsed stone structure it is difficult to see what you are doing without a tower, which is in permanent use on site. This not only helps the excavator to appreciate relationships in plan between features that have already emerged, but indicates where the work should go next. Only from a height can the regularities of buried wall lines be "sensed". Without the thin layers of intervening strata, the sequencing would have depended almost wholly on the spatial patterns of stones and objects.

A tell site in Syria (FIG 7.10; no. 10 on FIG 7.1)

Other kinds of collapsed structure require to be seen both from above and sideways, perhaps the best known examples being those made of mud-brick. *Tell Brak* is a famous prehistoric settlement mound extending over 40ha in northern Syria. Like other tells (see Chapter 1, FIGS 1.8 and 1.9) it is composed of a succession of mud-brick buildings, constructed and collapsing over several millennia, in this case being finally abandoned around 2000 BC. Erosion and deflation has reshaped the tell, cutting wadis (watercourses) and depositing fans of alluvium on and around it, and exposing copious sherds of pottery on its sloping surface.

Excavations by David and Joan Oates since 1976 had defined two periods (the late fourth and late third millennia BC) during which *Tell Brak* had been a major regional

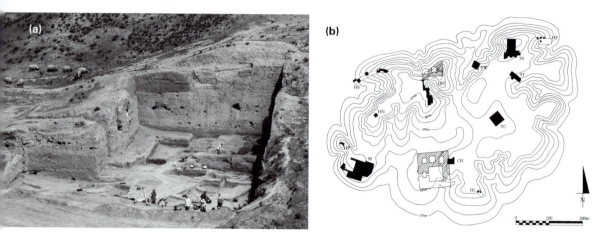

FIGURE 7.10 Tell Brak, Syria: (a) excavations in progress in Area TW looking east; and (b) location map of excavations (Joan Oates).

centre. In a new project in the 1990s, the objective of archaeologist Roger Matthews was to investigate the periods before and after and in between. With Wendy Matthews as principal on site expert, he was also to use the occasion to develop the special analysis of *micro-assemblages* (minute animal, vegetable and mineral remains) to map the detailed use of space.

Erosion and deflation (wind blow) meant that the sides of the tell would be truncated and so strata of different periods would be exposed on the slopes. Accordingly the project began in 1993 with surface collection over an area of 1000m² on the north-west spur; 8,684 sherds were recovered, which showed a clear chronological banding – pottery of late 5th millennium dominated the bottom of the slope, while the late 3rd millennium was represented at the highest point. Site survey continued with a strip-and-map, carried out with broad-bladed hoes in 10×10m squares, in which the thin topmost crust of earth was removed to reveal the tops of walls.

This evaluation phase led to the siting of a series of six area excavations carried out in 1994–6, each terraced into the slope, one above the other. Each area excavation began as 10×10 or 5×10m and was reduced as the depth increased beyond a metre. Stratigraphic units (contexts), that could refer to features (walls), layers (floors) or to arbitrary layers, were defined and recorded with written descriptions and drawn plans and sections. The units were grouped in *levels* that represented those phases of occupation that could be identified on site. For example, in trench HS1, seven levels of occupation were identified within the 2m depth of stratification. Numerous samples were taken from floor levels and used to throw light on the use of the space concerned (see Chapter 9 for more details). The sequence was ordered and dated by stratification, pottery and 39 radiocarbon dates, taken from charred cereal grains recovered in context.

Western Asian tells produce copious quantities of pottery, at once a blessing and a curse. On the basis of his surface collection Roger Matthews estimated that the surface of Tell Brak is at any one time covered with around 6 million sherds. The pottery is ubiquitous and provides an almost continuous sequence of dates, but the quantities are challenging. Each excavation trench had its own sherd-yard where the pottery was processed and recorded. At the end of each season some objects were selected by the Syrian Government for submission to the museum at Der ez-Zor. The remainder stayed on site, stored in the excavation house on the mound.

Tell sites represent a formidable challenge to excavators who want to know about both the sequence and contemporary use in space for a particular period. They are too wide and deep to dig *totally*, either from the point view of engineering or ethics. Where a research question concerns the history of occupation, excavators often dig at the edge in the hope of contacting the earliest strata where they are least encumbered. If the earliest strata lie deep in the centre, then the intervention is necessarily narrow, and it is especially hard to study the activity of the earliest people in plan. Other well-known tell projects like Çatalhöyük and Asikli höyük use a combination of deep area excavations at the edge and open area excavations on the summit where the mudbrick buildings have a chance of being contemporary with each other. In this way tell excavators try to match the twin goals – depth and area, historical sequence and the social use of space.

A terp site in Holland (FIG 7.11; no. 11 on FIG 7.1)

Wijnaldum-Tjitsma in Holland belongs to a type of site well-known along the north-west coast of Europe, where cultural layers build up into a mound known as a *terp*. The build-up of a terp is due to the accumulation of rubbish, or to the deliberate raising the settlement out of the reach of the encroaching sea by dumping. A *terp* thus resembles a wet tell, composed of earth rather than broken mud-brick. In 1991 it was decided to use the terp in question (already a protected monument) to examine the role played by this kind of site in the making of the kingdom of 6th/7th century AD Frisia, and at the same time to see how well preserved its archaeology was and the degree to which it was suffering from erosion. The project design thus included both research and CRM objectives.

Surface collection was carried out as a test over an area of 16×30m, followed by a programme of boreholes to establish the total thickness of the cultural layers to subsoil. Area excavation was then programmed in a cruciform transect laid over the highest part of the site where erosion was expected to be at its worst. The areas were 8m wide and 210m long north to south, and 8m wide and 76m long east to west – an area of more than 8,000sqm. In the centre, the excavation found the subsoil at 3.5m below ground surface, while at the north end it lay at 1.8m deep. Extra trenches

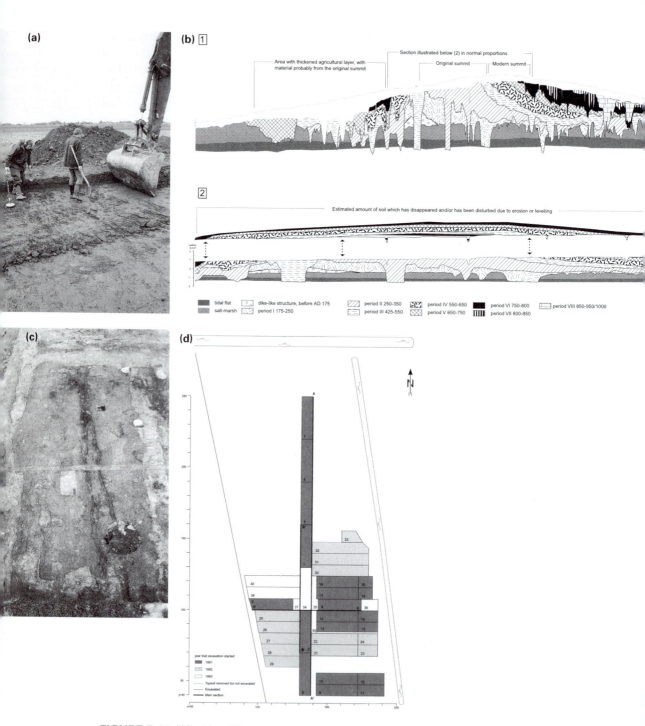

FIGURE 7.11 Wijnaldum-Tjitsma, a terp in Holland: (a) scraping the surface; (b) profile; (c) long-house features showing on the surface, including turf walls and post-holes; and (d) plan of excavation trenches, with section points and year in which excavation started (Besteman et al 1999).

(8–16m wide) were used to extend the area examined at different levels. The operation was completed in 1993.

The usual method of excavation in Holland on sites with soft soils and an almost horizontal but scarcely visible stratification is to strip horizontally. At *Wijnaldum* the variation in the height of the *terp* could be appreciated in advance. The areas were excavated with a mechanical excavator using a toothless back-hoe c1.8m across, and the driver was able to dig almost to the millimetre in spits 50mm deep (the equivalent of Level C, although using a machine). The site was recorded in 4×4m squares. When a spit revealed anomalies it was designated as a *level* (i.e. horizon): "A *level* was documented as soon as the features changed considerably from those of the preceding levels." The first level generally appeared at between 40–60cm below the surface. Subsequent *levels* appeared at vertical intervals of 25cm or more.

The excavators were looking for traces of buildings constructed in timber (post-holes) and clay lumps. These clay structures were very difficult to see when the surface dried out, or if it got soaked by rain (when the sand lenses would run). Many of the clay lumps had originally been cut from the salt marshes, and could be detected from the thin lines left by storms in the thickness of the clay ("storm surges"). The coursing of the clay walls was marked out with the point of the trowel when showing well, and drawn naturalistically in colour. Other contexts were charcoal layers and burnt loam. Middens and actual timber were unusually rare and it was suggested that most of this had been recycled as fuel. In each square, objects were individually plotted and the recovery of metal finds was enhanced with the use of a metal detector. The spoil excavated from features was wet sieved at 4mm: producing sherds of glass vessels, beads, charcoal, fish bones. A total of 12,000 finds was recovered, including soil samples.

As a result of this intensive excavation, the history of a high status farm was chronicled from about AD250–850. The site had experienced much erosion and decay due to flooding and agriculture, drains and ploughing, and its surviving state of preservation was very variable over the terp. The objectives were achieved, but Danny Gerrets, the principal supervisor, had some interesting comments to make about the control and recording of a large excavation conducted at speed. In order to work to programme they needed to work fast, and increased the work force accordingly; in 1992, there were more than 100 excavators on site. This proved counter-productive, since the controlling factor was not the number of excavators, but the number of supervisors who knew what to do. The additional hands did however greatly assist the comprehensive sieving programme. There was also an attempt to automate the recording system: records were put directly onto a database (Dbase IV) and drawings were digitised in Autocad. Features were not numbered in the field because it was thought that every feature could be reconstructed retrospectively in 3-D and the artefacts could be later assigned to them using the digital record.

In practice, this led to loss of information at both ends of the process. On site, records of strata became inadequate because excavators were not seeking to define features (only contexts). Off site, the reconstruction of the features from the digital record actually still required the input of human (i.e. interpretative) decisions. In the event, the whole stratigraphic sequence was reconstructed using relationships shown in the traditionally drawn colour plans, which fortunately had been maintained throughout. Gerrets feels that computerised automation means "that one tends to concentrate on the input of data and . . . postpone the analysis. In this way excavation becomes an industrial procedure." Not for the first time in this book, it can be noted that excavation and recording systems need to allow archaeologists not merely to observe the ground, but to study it.

A Maya ruin in Belize (FIG 7.12; no. 12 on FIG 7.1)

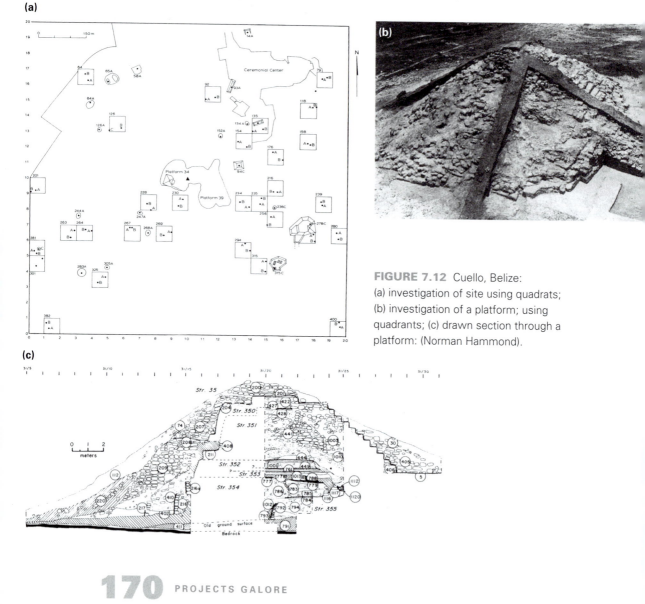

FIGURE 7.12 Cuello, Belize: (a) investigation of site using quadrats; (b) investigation of a platform; using quadrants; (c) drawn section through a platform: (Norman Hammond).

If a site remains as a ruin, the wall lines and spaces offer invitations where to dig, and influence the project design. But given that the total excavation of a site is unethical (because none of it will then remain for future researchers) a choice is necessary. And where the terrain is opaque to remote mapping, both the site and its immediate hinterland may have to be explored by excavation. One strategy is to place sample trenches or quadrats both within the ruins and outside them. These can be placed so as to address specific questions, based on prior knowledge of the site and its culture, or in the event of little being known, the sample areas can be placed randomly. In this latter case, they function as reconnaissance rather than research.

At the Maya settlement of *Cuello*, defined during regional survey in 1973–4 by the British Museum–Cambridge University Corozal Project led by Norman Hammond, work began with a site survey that mapped the extant remains above the surface. The relatively intact Platform 34 and its neighbouring Platform 39 were selected for area excavation, using quadrants, while a 1km (0.6-mile) frame containing the known site was subjected to 80 exploratory quadrats, 60 of which were sited randomly while 20 were aimed at visible mounds. Within each 50×50 m quadrat, two sub-areas were excavated. Where these cut into mounds they measured 1.5×1.5m (4.9×4.9 ft), and between mounds they were 1.25×1.25m (4×4 ft). All were excavated stratigraphically where strata were visible, otherwise they were dug in arbitrary levels 200mm thick.

The test-pits revealed the formation processes of the soils and of the archaeological deposits. As a bonus, seven of the test-pits also struck hitherto unknown platforms. Pottery was densely distributed in the flat tests, a distribution interpreted as resulting from temporary or vanished houses rather than general cultivation scatter or soil movement. On the basis of this it was possible to map changes to the settlement pattern from the pre- to late Classic (500BC to AD800) within the 1km^2 of the known site.

This example shows that quadrats, quadrants and area excavations can all be deployed on the same project – what counts is their purpose. Each is there by design, and not just adopted as a standard way of digging.

A villa by the Adriatic (FIGS 7.13 and 7.14; colour plate 7; no. 13 on FIG 7.1)

In spite of their prominent character, relatively intact stone-built sites may still have been rescued by excavators at short notice, even to this day. When a project for the creation of a dam on the Celone River in Puglia was proposed in 1986, little was known of the archaeology of the area. A few Roman *dolia* had been found and stood in the grounds of a neighbouring farmhouse. Some reconnaissance was carried out in advance of the dam construction, but without raising any alarms. Only in 1995, when the dam was nearly completed, did two local archaeologists notice traces of

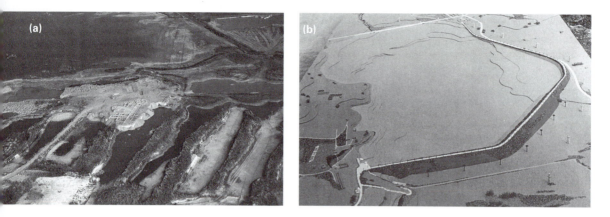

FIGURE 7.13 Villa and churches at San Giusto, Celone, Italy; rescued (a) and drowned (b) (courtesy of Giuliano Volpe).

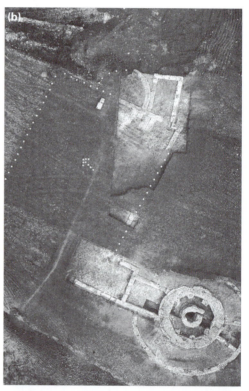

FIGURE 7.14 San Giusto, Celone: (a) general plan; (b) overhead photography by balloon (grid points are marked by paper plates); and (c) excavating fallen masonry (courtesy of Giuliano Volpe). See also colour plate 7.

walls within the area being cleared for the reservoir. Architectural blocks and Roman dolia, crushed by the contractors' machinery, began to appear over a broad area suggesting the site of a Roman villa by the sea.

At this point the Soprintendenza Archaeologica requested help from the Department of Archaeology at the University of Bari to carry out an emergency excavation, to be financed by the Province of Foggia and the Commune of Lucera, together with money hastily raised by the Consorzio di Bonifica. The University contributed its staff and teams of students and in particular Roman specialist Giuliano Volpe as director. On the basis of the distribution of surface remains, a cordon was thrown round an area of 1.2ha, to be excluded from earth removal for the reservoir and left on an island with a causeway leading to it. Three hectic seasons followed in 1995, 1996, 1997 using a team of 10–15 archaeologists and students and five labourers.

From their first day on site, the archaeologists were aware of the grievous shortage of time and expected each season to be their last. They began by opening three areas at the edge of their "island", to discourage further encroachment (Saggi I–III). The strata lay to a depth of c50cm, and each archaeologist excavated and recorded the equivalent of 20m^2 per month. However, the speed of recording naturally slowed down greatly for burials, and for the study of destruction layers of what emerged as a church and the cleaning of mosaics. Use of a helium balloon for overhead photography meant that they could make regular views of the developing plan. In eight months the team had unearthed and defined the walls of a Roman villa, and the two early Christian churches and baptistery that had succeeded it.

Much thought was given to the question of the preservation of this remarkable sequence, rarely seen in Italy or indeed anywhere. What could be done to save the site? In the end, cost and the difficulties of access meant that the excavated monument would have to be surrendered to the waters. The archaeologists completed the excavation as far as possible in the time, lifted the mosaics and laid plans to create an archaeological park elsewhere, with a reconstruction of the main church and an exhibition of finds and architectural elements.

Even in regions with well-regulated heritage management, archaeologists can still be taken by surprise. Relative success in this case was owed to an excavation director and a team of exceptional flair and energy, and also to the visible and solid character of Roman building practice.

Tomb tableaux in China (Colour Plate 8a; no. 17 on FIG 7.1)

Three tombs of the Warring States period (476–221 BC) excavated in December 2006 show the richness of detail that can be recovered by modern archaeologists even when structural wood has all but disappeared. In stiff silt, the wood often leaves a vacuum that can be filled with plaster, recovering the shape. The tombs of Majiayuan in Zhangjiachuan, Gansu province, took the form of passages approached by steps, sometimes with an additional chamber. Tombs M1 and M3 contained chariots of leather with wheels and axles of wood. Showing remarkable ingenuity, the excavators succeeded in making a tableau – that is a three-dimensional soil-shape – recreating that of the original chariot and its fittings. The leather chariot body, the lacquer on the front panels and the bronze, silver and gold ornaments on the wheels were all revealed and presented in situ. These skills have developed to the point at which it is possible to recover the pattern of red varnish on chariot panels, as in Tomb 21 at the Marquis Jin cemetery (Northern Zhao period), also excavated in tableau in 2006.

It would have been simpler, of course, to lift all the tiny pieces as soon as they were encountered, or to explore the whole deposit in vertical and horizontal slices (*Schnitt* method), or to record the soil marks and other anomalies as single contexts one at a time, each with its own plan. In theory, these data could be used with digital manipulation to reconstruct the whole form of the deposit off site. But the skill of the archaeologists (from the Gansu Province Institute of Cultural Relics) in excavating the scene and photographing the tableau in situ has given us not just the archaeological data, but a historical image of extraordinary power. They captured not only the form of the burial but something of its humanity.

Studying standing buildings

The ultimate usable ruin is one that is still occupied, and the study of houses that are still occupied (or were until recently) is an expanding area in field archaeology. There are two reasons for this. First, historic buildings legislation means that any alterations – up to and including demolition – must be preceded by careful record of the fabric. And second, the research value of relatively modern dwellings has increased alongside interest in the archaeology of the 18th to 20th centuries more generally. In the USA, historic properties are listed in the *Historic American Buildings Survey (HABS)*, and before any alteration or repairs, a standard recording response is required from archaeological contractors. TABLE 7.1 shows an inventory form used in Kentucky.

This checklist provides the essentials for a structure to get into the register of historic properties and, suitably adapted to local conditions, could be used anywhere. It constitutes in essence a reconnaissance and evaluation – the business of locating a historic building and giving it contemporary value.

If a property is to be researched or demolished, then the recording and analysis is in consequence very much more detailed. There may also be an opportunity to delve into the joints between walls and windows and roofs and determine their order of construction – this may not be at all obvious on the surface. Historic buildings or parts of them burn down and this means detailed recording is required, either before complete demolition or with an eye to restoration (FIG 7.15).

TABLE 7.1 Instructions for completing an abbreviated Kentucky Historic Resources Individual Inventory Form (extracted from the Kentucky Historic Resources Survey briefings at http://heritage.ky.gov/natreg/histbldgsurv/)

The attached form was developed for use in countywide surveys and for coding data for entry in our computer file. As you use this form to record a single building or complex, it is not necessary to fill in the segmented (__/__/__) spaces, and not all numbered categories must be completed. Instructions on what to complete follow.

1. **Historical name of resource** (name of first owner or most important owner).
2. **Street address;** or if rural, indicate the road located on, how far from the road and how far to the next intersection.
[3. Do Not Complete–Staff Use Only.]
4. **Owner's name and address.**
5. **Your name** – indicate affiliation if you are surveying the site for an organization.
6. **Date the site was inspected** and photographed.
[7.–9. Do Not Complete.]
[10.–11. Fill in appropriate answers.]
12. **Date.** Give general date under "estimated," unless actual date can be given under "documented." If documented, give source under 28 "history."
13. Estimated or known **dates** of major additions and remodellings.
14. **Fill in the construction material** of the original building and earliest additions, e.g., log, frame, etc.
15. **Give actual dimensions if known.** If unknown, give height in number of stories and leave width and depth blank.
[16.–18. Do Not Complete – Staff Use Only.]
19. **Foundation**. Type should be "piers," "continuous," or "other."
20. **Primary wall material** refers to exterior wall covering, e.g., "weatherboard" under original, "asbestos siding" as replacement.
21. Fill in covering **material** if known, e.g., "wood shingle," "standing seam metal," etc.
22. **Give condition:** excellent, good, fair, poor, ruins.
[23. Do Not Complete – Staff Use Only.]
24. Take **photographs**, preferably in black and white, showing all sides of the primary structure and any outbuildings. Important interior and exterior details should be photographed.
25. If important **historic support resources**, such as farm outbuildings, are associated with this structure, complete this section with appropriate answers. Key to site plan drawn under #26. with letters.
26. Draw a simple **site plan**. Complete even if #25. was not answered to show relationship of building to major roads, streams, etc.
27. **Map.** Please mark the location of the site on a county highway, U.S.G.S., or city planning map and attach it to the inventory form.

Optional Additional Information. Attach continuation sheet(s).

28. **Plan.** If the building surveyed was a house, draw a simple floor plan or an outline of its shape. Show porches and additions with dotted lines.
29. **History.** Provide a short history of this building. This should not discuss family genealogy or the previous history of the institution for which the building was constructed, but should focus on who built it, why they did so, the building's original and subsequent uses, and its original and later appearance. Copies of pages from local histories, who's who, newspaper clippings, etc., should be attached if available.
30. Write a short statement about why this building is important (or typical) in the history or architecture of your community or area; for example, "a rare survival of an once common type of log house in this area," or "only remaining 19th century tavern in _____ county."

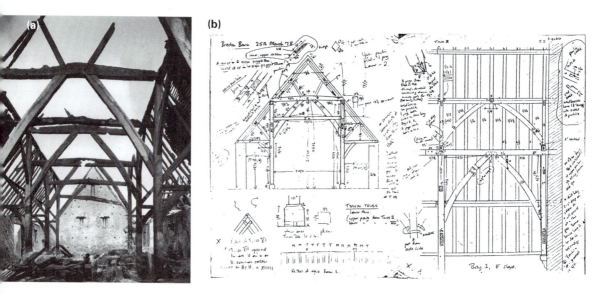

FIGURE 7.15 The burnt-out barn at Bredon (a) and an example of recording sheet for emergency survey (b) (photo by Martin Charles and record by Patricia Borne).

Standing stone walls used to be recorded, rather laboriously, by drawing every stone in the elevation, as one would draw a section. Photogrammetry and rectified photography, which use photographs taken at a set distance in a set plane, are quicker and more accurate methods. Modern reflecting laser survey instruments can record the surface of a wall in space with a carpet of precise three-dimensional points, without having to place a prism on the target. So the fabric of a stone building (like Balquhain Castle in Aberdeenshire, Scotland, FIG 7.16) can be rapidly recorded as a two-dimensional plan in which all the anomalies, and thus the different phases of building, show clearly. Remote mapping methods are also in development which can "see through the wall", for example an infra-red thermographic photograph can show the form of timber beams hidden by a layer of plaster. These methods add to the power of initial non-destructive survey, which is usually as far as building investigation goes.

In some cases, however, the investigation of a building goes hand in hand with excavation and may use very similar methods of dissection and of making records. At Pride Hill Chambers, Shrewsbury, England, a much altered and ruinous town house was scheduled for refurbishment (FIGS 7.17 and 7.18). The roof had disappeared, and fallen brick and tile lay inside the ground floor or had been shovelled out of the frameless windows onto the meadows beneath. The main advantage of this state of dereliction was that the wall plate was clear, thus reducing the danger of falling masonry. The bulk of the house was mainly 14th century with a plan adapted so as to rest its south footings on the stub of a 13th century town wall. The house, surviving to two stories originally, overlooked the meadows bordering the River Severn which encircles the city of Shrewsbury.

(a)

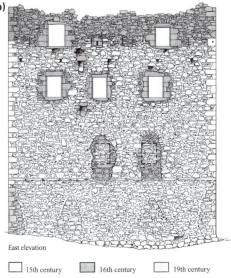

(b)

East elevation

☐ 15th century   ▨ 16th century   ☐ 19th century

(c)

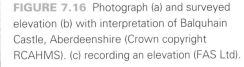

FIGURE 7.16 Photograph (a) and surveyed elevation (b) with interpretation of Balquhain Castle, Aberdeenshire (Crown copyright RCAHMS). (c) recording an elevation (FAS Ltd).

(b) PRIDE HILL 1974   S2   F512   INTERIOR

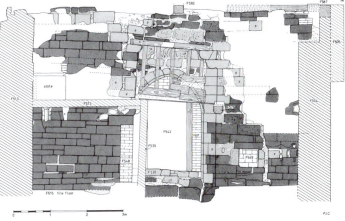

FIGURE 7.17 Derelict medieval and later building at Pride Hill, Shrewsbury (a), now a McDonald's. Analytical (contexted and featurised) drawing of side wall (b).

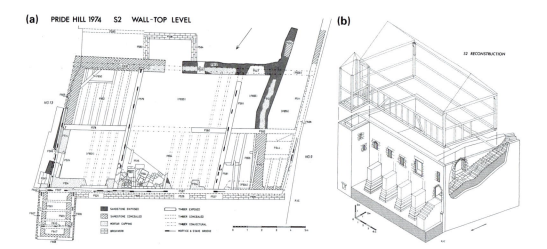

FIGURE 7.18 Pride Hill: (a) plan of wall plate; and (b) reconstruction of vanished timber super-structure.

Excavations took place on the street side, which proved to have been already levelled to the sand subsoil, but contained rubbish pits dating from the 10th to the 14th century. Inside the building, the floor had also been levelled onto the terraced subsoil apart from one patch of re-used decorated floor tiles. Outside the building on the river side, the debris lay 2m deep. These strata included layers of stone and then pottery roof tiles which were dated by associated pottery and represented, in stratigraphic order, the remains of roof coverings as they had been discarded and replaced.

Buildings archaeologist Phil Clarke used the excavators' base lines inside and outside the building to make plans at both ground floor and first floor level. Elevations were drawn using datum lines and wall grids, confirmed by many hundreds of direct measurements. Each wall was broken down into contexts and each of the structural elements (including stone walls, openings, steps, brick buttresses and iron reinforcing clamps) was defined and recorded as a feature. Each of the main walls was sequenced independently and then reconciled to give a stratigraphic model for the development of the building as a whole. This was then compared with the sequence of debris provided by the excavation. As a result, the team could propose the form and style of the building in each of its different phases. Stratigraphic ordering for buildings (FIG 7.19) is more tricky than for excavated strata on site, but has the same aim: to represent the sequence in which the building fabric was assembled and modified (more in Chapter 11)

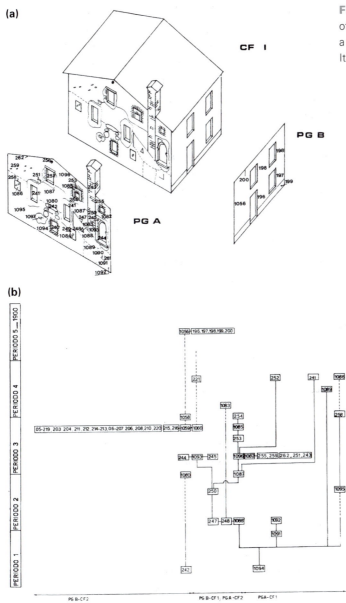

(a)

FIGURE 7.19 Resolution of a standing building into a stratified sequence at Lonato, Italy (Gian-Pietro Brogiolo).

Urban archaeology

Digging in modern towns confronts the archaeologist with four challenges that make it a very special branch of the discipline: complex stratification, depths of 2m and more, the instability of the deposits and neighbouring buildings and (often) a shortage of time, since the site is needed urgently for a new use. The historic parts of a modern town, which usually conceal the nucleus and the place of origin, often coincide now with the busiest and most expensive areas. As excavators, you are exposed in many ways: to the public who love to look and interrupt the work; to investors who have money in the prize real estate of the site and its surroundings; to the impatience of developers, the costs of delay and the dangers of depth and instability. Thus you are more than usually vulnerable socially, economically, personally and legally. In addition, the task is to understand a place that has seen thousands of activities cutting into each other over many centuries, resulting in a stratified sequence so dense as to be often unreadable.

The huge medieval cathedral of *York Minster*, a world-famous monument in its own right, lies above a Roman legionary fortress, one of the most important of the northern empire. In 1967, the fabric of the cathedral began to subside, and soon the glass tell-tales cemented to the walls were cracking, showing that the foundations were on the move. Architects decided that the foundations of the cathedral would have to be doubled in area, but they first had to be dug up. To prevent the foundations spreading when exposed, a horizontal network of steel struts was inserted, and then huge steel bolts were inserted and the piers of the building clad in concrete.

The archaeological deposit representing 1,000 years of European history was between 4–5m deep and the area affected around 4ha. The only access to this great archaeological sequence was through 250 cuttings of around 4×4m each. Director Derek Philips explained: "In order to reveal and strengthen the foundations it was obviously necessary to excavate to a considerable depth, yet it was at the same time essential to minimise the tendency of the subsoil to 'heave' or swell with the removal of overburden, the consequence of which would have been to induce further settlement of the Minster's foundations. Thus, as depth increased, so did the rate of excavation, and when the final depth had been reached it was imperative either to add ballast (e.g. sandbags) or to begin work on new foundations without delay. The only way to buy a little more time, therefore, was to undertake smaller excavations." The base of these cuttings was dark and wet. Water collected on the clay, but the archaeologists were discouraged from pumping it out lest the clay dried and its bearing capacity was affected.

The archaeological investigation (FIG 7.20) achieved under these circumstances was little short of miraculous. Working round the clock, Phillips and his team created a record that was anchored to hundreds of standing sections, meticulously recorded in drawings and photographs and tied to a three-dimensional grid. Phillips found that the best results came from using a large format camera with a flashlight or combinations of flashlights, and from 1968 he insisted on colour photography to bring out the differences between layers.

The walls of the Roman legionary fortress were readily identifiable in that they lay NW–SE, at an angle of 48 degrees to the Medieval cathedral. The Roman plan itself was to some degree predictable, so that short lengths of walls planned in different

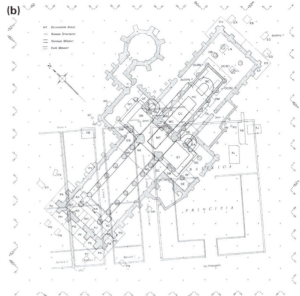

FIGURE 7.20 York Minster emergency investigations: (a) at the centre of the cathedral, with a pier clad in concrete; (b) plan of the Minster with the outlines of the Roman basilica (military headquarters) and barracks beneath; (c) collapsed column of the Roman basilica, with Viking tombstone perched above; and (d) how the Roman fort was mapped: the wall lines found in the 250 excavations (© English Heritage).

cuttings could be linked. But the vital 600 years between the end of the fort and the buildings of the first minster could not be predicted and had to be reassembled from scraps of re-used Roman masonry, layers of cultivation soil and numerous objects encountered in the cuttings. Nevertheless using a number of sequential and spatial analyses a detailed story was put together.

The great majority of excavations in modern towns are carried out in advance of putting up new constructions, rather than holding up old ones. The procedure has become very much more streamlined since the heroic days of the 1960s and 70s and the kind of partnership between archaeologists and engineers eventually forged at York Minster is now routine. The archaeological work is (or should be) programmed from the beginning: ideally the archaeological design is incorporated in the design of new building and the archaeologists are seen as part of the development team. The archaeologists work in professional firms, employed as subcontractors, following site rules and carrying out programmes carefully planned in advance to fit in with the course of construction.

For example in 1998 Pat Miller and Tom Wilson, working for MoLAS (Museum of London Archaeological Services) undertook programmed investigation of an area of 1.25ha in central Northampton (UK) before its redevelopment (FIG 7.21). At the same time, the office buildings that stood on the site had yet to be demolished, so they placed 15 trial trenches between the buildings to determine the depth and character of the strata. This evaluation phase led to the project design. On the west part of the site, there was to be little construction, and deposits were expected to survive the new building. In this area there would be five evaluation pits, and there would be also archaeological observation of the service trenches when they were dug by the contractor (a *watching brief*). On the east side, the offices were demolished in 1999 and were found to have stood on timber piles that were pulled out. It could be assumed that nothing much had survived beneath the office footprint. That left the space between the office foundations as eligible for area excavations. Seven areas, having high archaeological potential, were marked for excavation in 2000, time being allowed by the contractor. Of these, Area 3 was to be unaffected by the development and was subsequently redesignated for preservation in situ. The remainder were opened by machine, and then excavated by hand to subsoil – but only where the destruction was expected to penetrate to that depth. The archaeological sequence lay in silty sand on weathered ironstone. Identified features included sunken-floored buildings of the 10–11th century and medieval timber town houses, kilns and refuse pits (12th to 16th centuries).

It can be seen that the incorporation of archaeological research into construction in towns has a number of pros and cons. Archaeologists and developers both benefit from advance programming. The excavation can be funded more willingly by the developer because it is designed in detail in advance and represents only a fraction of their overall budget. But not unnaturally, the sponsors may only wish to pay for

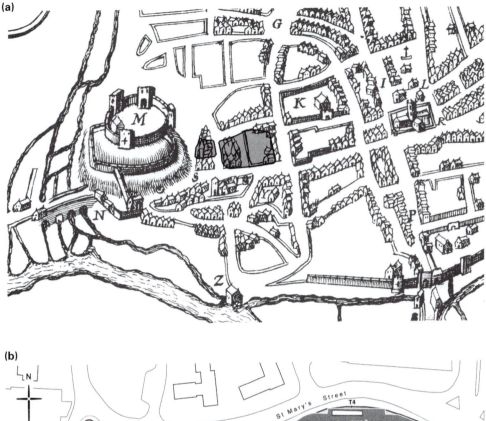

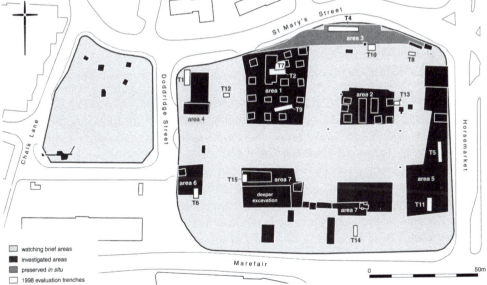

FIGURE 7.21 Commercial mitigation in Northampton: (a) Speed's map of 1610 with the development area superimposed; (b) trenches and exploratory pits used by the archaeologists (Pat Miller and MoLAS).

the excavation of what will be damaged – a position often supported by local officials (curators) responsible for CRM. This is frustrating since the area we are paid to dig may not make sense in terms of research. On the credit side a useful sample of artefacts and biological material is usually retrieved and the sequence underneath European towns is becoming increasingly well known, so that even a small intervention can often contribute by adding another comprehensible piece to the jigsaw.

But this does not really amount to designed and programmed research and in practice most of the many hundreds of archaeological interventions commissioned in towns each year can be regarded as exercises in reconnaissance and evaluation, continually refining the knowledge of the deposit and the increasingly subtle research questions that can be addressed.

Getting wet

Wet sites make very special challenges to the archaeological investigator – so special that wetland and underwater archaeologists have begun to think of themselves as almost belonging to a separate discipline of their own. The most famous asset of these sites is their propensity to preserve wood and other organic materials. Just to give a flavour, from a huge and expanding subject, I offer three examples, each one slightly wetter than the one before.

The Windover site was discovered accidentally by developers while constructing a road in their Windover Farms housing development near Titusville, Cape Canaveral, Florida during the early summer of 1982. Recognising the archaeological potential of the site, the developers not only re-routed their road, but were instrumental in raising more than US$800,000 from federal government to pay for investigation.

The site was a pond 1–3m deep in a swampy area, and the prehistoric material was buried in peat more than 2m (6.6ft) below the bottom of the pond, so access for excavation would require de-watering. An initial experiment succeeded in creating a workable area measuring 12×25m (40×82ft), and in 1985–6 the entire pond was de-watered by being encircled by well-points and pumped out. Anthropologist Glen Doran, who was called in to investigate the site, describes the system: "Each point consists of a long pipe, or riser, connected to a perforated plastic and steel well-point. Points were installed by boring a hole into the peat with a high volume jet pump. A well-point and riser, 4–6m long was then dropped into the hole and approximately 25–50 gallons of coarse sand placed around the point to act as a filter to keep fine particulate matter from clogging the well-point. The points are connected to a header pipe system put under vacuum by a large rotary pump . . . Initial pumping volumes were around 700 gallons per minute in two to three weeks continuous pumping. Gradually volumes tailed off to around 200 gallons per minute for the rest of the season and once into the 'dry' season (less than 5 inches of rain a month) the pump

could be run only at night or on alternate nights, depending on circumstances. It was a very effective method of dealing with the water . . . [but] at a conservative estimate the cost was $120,000".

Within the peat below the pond base were found the remains of human bodies which had been deliberately buried there. The chemistry of the water was neutral with a pH of around 7, and there was good preservation of both organic matter and bone. The human remains thus survived as skeletons (27 male, 27 female and 9 indeterminate), but there was also brain tissue preserved inside the skulls. Many of the bodies had been held in place by wooden stakes; but some had slid down the sides of the pond and become disarticulated. Most lay in a flexed position, on their left side with their heads to the west.

The burials yielded 87 well-preserved examples of handwoven textiles, of five twining or weaving types, "the oldest, largest and most sophisticated group of flexible fabrics found in the Americas". There were macroscopic plant remains, but they proved difficult to identify because processing had removed the outer layers of fibre; Sabal palm and saw palmetto were thought to be the most likely plants of origin.

Other finds included bone awls, pins, shaft straighteners. and a wooden bowl, pestle and trap. Shark teeth and dog teeth set in wood were used as cutting implements. An antler tine was embedded in the hip of a 35-year-old man who had died from the attack. In this rich assemblage however there were only 11 stone artefacts: six bifaces and five flakes over the whole excavation area: a reminder of how partially the stone assemblage, often all that survives, represents a community.

Some details were highly informative: one adult male had consumed 550 elderberries, 40 grapes and a prickly pear cactus fruit just before he died. The brain tissue was analysed with X-ray, CT scanning and magnetic resonance imaging. Its condition, showing little deterioration, suggested that burial had taken place within 48 hours of death. Sedimentary analysis showed that at the time of burial the maximum water depth had been about 30cm (12 in). Radiocarbon determinations around 8000BP show this to be of the earliest known hunter-fisher-gatherer sites in North America.

In a shallow Alpine lake (FIG 7.22; no. 22 on FIG 7.1)

The Charavines project, 1971–93, was a programme of investigations carried out on the bed of a lake – the Lac de Paladru near Grenoble in south-east France. The memory of the Charavines sites was either never lost or was revived by objects retrieved from time to time by fishermen. In any event, the legend of a former town, drowned because of the wickedness of its inhabitants, was still prevalent in the area in the early 20th century. In 1866, the water level fell to reveal an island and timber posts, but the opportunity for research came as a result of proposed developments

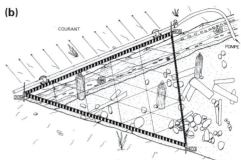

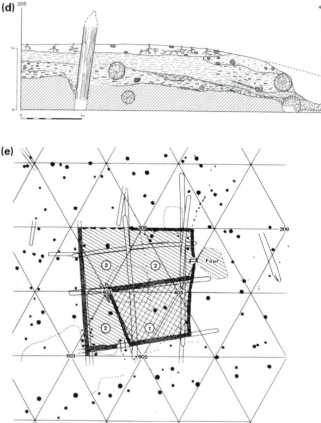

FIGURE 7.22 Excavations in shallow water at Charavines, Lac de Paladru, France: (a) the lake, with diving point; (b) triangular grid used for underwater planning and plotting; (c) coring the lake bed; (d) with the "winnowing" current that keeps it clear of silt; section drawn along one leg of the grid; (e) site grid (Michel Colardelle).

in the early 1970s – the building of a marina at Coletière and a bathing beach at Les Baigneurs. Archaeologists were alerted to the potential threat to the underwater timbers by life guard Eric Lavigne du Cadet, in charge of the existing municipal beach at Charavines.

Rescue operations were mounted in tandem, with the prehistorians at Les Baigneurs and the medievalists at Coletière collaborating on strategy and sharing resources.

Situated in a basin of chalk, the water was fresh, cold (8°C) and alkaline. In form the medieval site was a mostly submerged peninsula, intermittently an island, measuring 50m from north to south and 20–5m east to west. The water level varied from year to year, but rarely exceeded a few metres in depth. Here scuba diving could be undertaken, without the problems of decompression. A base camp was set up on dry land and a wooden walkway constructed leading from this to a floating platform above the site. On the platform was a lifeguard, an intercom for communicating with the base camp and air compressors. Staff on the platform filled the air bottles with compressed air, looked after the divers and received the buckets of deposit which the divers retrieved from the bottom of the lake, checking their labels and taking them to the base camp for processing.

Teams of two divers operated in the water each half-day, the maximum number that the system could handle, given the volume of deposit which was extracted for processing. The site was mapped and all deposits located using the "triangular grid" conceived by R. Laurent in 1962 for operating in murky waters, but hitherto untried in practice. A base line was pegged under water, running north–south to the west of the settlement, and a zero point chosen and marked as the origin about half-way along. The grid was formed by equilateral triangles with sides 5m long, each divided with cord into 25 smaller triangles, 1m each side. The first triangles were laid against the base line, while subsequently triangles could be added to the first, forming a grid capable of extension in any direction without line of sight. Each 1m triangle was numbered as a unique space on the lake floor. The grid was checked during the drought of 1989–90, when 700 planned and labelled timber posts appeared above the surface of the water and were surveyed using a theodolite and photogrammetry.

Only the area of one 5m triangle was dug at any one time. The sediment on the lake floor included fine chalk which clouded the water at the least movement and took several hours to disperse. To create reasonably clear working conditions a Swiss "water curtain" or artificial current powered by pumps was used. Excavation was generally carried out with bare hands, these proving the most sensitive instruments in the poor visibility. An experienced excavator could sense small changes in strata, structures or object, even the most fragile. The deposit in each 1m triangle was excavated, placed in a bucket and sealed with a lid. A diver then delivered this bucket to the diving platform, announcing its number and letter code, whereupon it was labelled. Numerous experiments were made with torches and flashes, but photography rarely succeeded. Plans were made on plastic sheets. Since the stratification was impossible to see or dig underwater, it was recorded in advance: at the north apex of every 5m triangle a core was taken with a rigid pipe 90mm in diameter and 1.5m long, driven into the lake bed with a mallet. The core was extracted by means of an aqualift – an air balloon capable of raising 200kg. These cores formed the record of the strata and were later linked together to provide a summary of the stratification across the site. Samples were taken for dendrochronology from 150 timbers. It was discovered that sapwood and bark were never preserved in posts standing in open water, but only on those which had been buried by sediment. Sampling for dendrochronology was therefore selective and limited to timber likely to carry the full sequence of years.

Organic objects were preserved but had no structural strength, so that a piece of leather or basketry would quickly break up with the least pressure of a current of water. The greater part of all the damage to objects occurred during their excavation, so it was here that the greatest care was needed. Larger finds were lifted en bloc, by easing in weighted plastic boards around the soil block at least 100mm deep and then sliding a thin steel sheet beneath the block, having sawn a passage for it.

On arrival at base camp, the labelled buckets were lined up by their codes and then sieved (screened) with water jets through 8mm and 4mm meshes in turn. The largest mesh caught the stones, fragments of hearths, charcoal, pottery, metal objects, pieces of leather, large animal bones, whole nuts including beech nuts and chestnuts, and animal droppings. The medium-size mesh caught most of the plant remains – cereal grains, grape pips – and fish bones. The sift for screening at the finest level was transported to the Laboratoire de Chrono-écologie at Besançon. It was noticed that screening on site captured only 6% of the total plant taxa that were eventually recovered with the aid of the 2mm screening. But on-site screening did capture species which were not represented among the taxa captured in the laboratory.

The dating programme gave an informative demonstration of the different kinds of date offered by different methods. Had the site been dated by pottery and metalwork alone, the stated range would have been 9th to 12th century. Radiocarbon dating would have placed it in the 10th to 11th century. Dendrochronology showed that the settlement had actually been constructed in 1003–4, and that the last repairs to buildings were being made with timber cut in 1034. This was readily reconciled with the documentary record.

Diving deep off Turkey (FIG 7.23; no. 23 on FIG 7.1)

The classic excavation undertaken by George Bass on Yassıada off the coast of Turkey, was the opportunity for numerous pivotal experiments in deepwater excavation, and the published account offers us an invaluable account of experimentation with techniques that now form the basis of standard practice (FIG 7.23). In the summers of 1958 and 1959, reconnaissance operations by Peter Throckmorton located a number of wrecks while sailing and diving with Bodrum sponge-divers off the Turkish coast. Yassıada I appeared as a mound of amphorae measuring 16–17m (52–6ft) by 9–11m (29.5–36ft) protruding from a thick sediment of calcareous sand (derived from mollusca and the parent limestone of the island). A stack of iron anchors could be seen at one end, presumed to be the prow, and broken tiles and cooking pots implied a galley (kitchen) at the other. Shipworm had eaten the exposed timbers, but timbers were uncovered just beneath the sand, suggesting that part of the ship's

FIGURE 7.23 Diving to the Yassıada wreck off the south coast of Turkey: (a) lifting finds with air balloon; (b) planning with a planning frame; (c) ship's timbers under a square grid; (d) excavators; (e) a photomosaic plan of the cargo of amphorae; (George Bass).

hull had survived where buried (it proved to be 10% of the whole). The depth was measured, using a taut wire stretched from a surface float on a calm day, as 32m (105ft) at the shallower and 39m (128ft) at the deeper end.

The cargo was first recorded in a "trial strip" 2m (6.6ft) wide, which ran across the wreck. The amphorae and other objects were removed until, beneath a third layer of cargo, ship's timbers were encountered; these were then temporarily reburied in sand. This "trench" through the cargo was intended to reveal the condition of the hull, while its sides would show the form in which the amphorae had been stacked. It was exactly analogous to a trial trench dug on land. A second trench was then taken across the "galley" area, which revealed many small pottery and tile sherds, and other objects. Metal objects were found to have become concreted voids; by cutting the concretion in half, a mould could be made of the void and the form of the original object determined.

The primary objective was to study the form of the ship, and then to study its cargo. Another important objective of the project was to explore the practicalities of excavating wreck sites and experiment with different techniques, and the record of these experiments and methods has proved of enduring value. The cargo was sampled, with a selection of the 900 amphorae taken to the surface and analysed, while the remainder were stacked and left on the sea-bed. Additional examples from this stockpile were still being raised for study 30 years later as techniques of analysis improved. Once the cargo had been removed, the surviving timbers of the ship could be defined, planned, dismantled, and taken to the surface.

The team included a physician whose duties included noting the time a dive started and signalling the end of it by hammering on an iron bar that hung into the water from the barge. There was a concrete block hung at exactly 3m (10ft) deep to which divers could hold while decompressing to avoid the "bends" (decompression sickness). The decompression times depended on the depth and duration of the dives, and whether people had already been diving earlier in the same day, and thus had residual nitrogen in their bodies. Working at 33–9m (108–28ft), divers were allowed a total of 43 minutes a day underwater in two dives, with 3–6 hours between (details of safe limits may now be found in the diving tables of organisations such as the US Navy). Thus a team of four divers, working broadly in two shifts, could do no more than 3 person-hours per day. This shows the very different cost, pace and intensity of excavations underwater as against those on land.

The normal method of removing sand and silt from the wreck area was with the "air-lift", a long pipe held upright with a float which was fed with compressed air, creating an updraft, like an aspirator. It was supported by stays attached to old oil drums filled with rocks to stop it escaping to the surface. The water which was sucked in might take up finds with it (although it rarely did), so a catch bag was hung at the top where the silt dispersed. In areas of delicate excavation, the sand could simply be fanned or "winnowed" down the slope, the airlift being used to remove the heaps so created. Experiments in planning included the use of plane tables and planning frames, and finally photogrammetric mapping, using a rod anchored to the sea bed with concrete blocks and held horizontally 6m above the target area with air cans. Two marks 1.2m (4ft) apart showed the positions from which the stereo pairs were to be taken. The camera was suspended from the rod with gymbals made from hinges and levelled with a bull's eye (spirit) level on the camera base; a metal ring around the lens hood had three adjustable weighted screws on stalks which could be moved until the bubble centred. Viewing the stereo pairs allowed a direct measurement of the parallax and the distance to an object seen in the three dimensional image.

The amphorae in the cargo were raised to the surface, at first by turning them upside down and filling them with air from a diver's mouth piece, and then by the safer method of transporting them in a basket raised by a balloon filled with air from an air hose from the barge. Small objects were carried to the surface by hand or in wire baskets raised by balloon. The timbers were transported in a 6m (20ft)-long cradle by four or six divers wearing tennis shoes (rather than fins), who walked them underwater up the slope to the beach, a distance of 150m (490ft).

It can be seen that underwater archaeology has a framework that is not dissimilar to the practice on land, using reconnaissance, evaluation, design, survey and excavation. Underwater techniques and recording have since developed greatly, particularly as a result of initiatives by George Bass and colleagues at Texas A&M at other sites; but Yassıada remains a pivotal project: the moment that conventional field archaeology took itself into the sea.

In 1964, experiments were made with a submarine, *Asherah*, the first to be designed and built for archaeological exploration. Thus, in the last stage of this early campaign of modern underwater archaeology was born the machine of the future, the Remote Operating Vehicle (ROV) a submersible equipped to carry out low-invasive investigation at great depths. A developed model of the ROV eventually reached the Titanic at a depth of several kilometres of water under the Atlantic. The sea is now being explored with a range of submersible vehicles and with towed remote sensing devices such as sonar or side-scan radar. A brilliant indirect survey has been carried out by Kenneth Thomson, Vince Gaffney and Simon Fitch over the Dogger Bank under the North Sea, using the drilling records of oil companies (Colour Plates 9a and b). Aided by GIS, the cores of the drillers (like augers on land) were used to construct an undersea landscape of hills and valleys – "Doggerland".

In sum . . .

Field research projects make use of a hugely varied technical toolbox to meet the questions anticipated by research in a wide variety of terrain. A project is designed on the basis of reconnaissance and evaluation exercises (which may include test excavations), and that project will include landscape survey and site survey as well as set piece excavation, and excavators may well need to record a building or get wet.

Reconnaissance finds sites and defines landscapes for further investigation. Evaluation assesses how feasible an investigation is likely to be – how to match the research questions to what is there, and whatever modern social constraints may be operating. The project design brings these assessments together and comes up with a programme – an integrated programme – of field research. Of course each project has its emphasis, as we can see: some are virtually all excavation; others, just site or landscape survey. But most integrate the different methods to give a fuller picture of ancient society. After all, no human ever lived all their life in a single hole (whatever they might have felt about it). Every excavation needs a context, which site survey and landscape survey provide. And every survey needs an excavation to give it sequence.

The great variety of the situations in which field researchers find themselves means that rigid procedures and recording systems have been quickly adapted or abandoned. Rightly so. Dominating prescriptive methods have always been the curse of our subject, which has a creative and curiosity-driven character, not helped by the straight-jacket of a standardised practice. The analogy is rather with writing novels: there is an accepted framework: a story with a beginning and end, purchasable in a portable form between two covers. Field Research Procedure also provides a framework; but within it we expect every story and its telling to be different.

Each of our protagonists told their story with unusual thoroughness, what they did, what they found and what it meant – which made them good case studies for us. Getting archaeology from the trench to the bookshelf is no easy matter: it requires detailed reporting, careful analysis, imaginative presentation and targeted publication – all subjects of the next part of the book.

Briefing

Grateful thanks and a blanket apology to the authors and directors of these case studies, all of which have probably suffered from compression. For **Klithi** cave, Bailey and Thomas 1987, Bailey 1997; digging deep and digging wide, 46. For cave archaeology in general Bonsall and Tolan-Smith 1997 and good examples in Thomas 1998 (157–62) (Gatecliffe Shelter) and Henshilwood et al 2001 (Blombos); **Carlston Annis** shell mound, Marquardt and Watson 2005 (p. 629 for the quote); **Yeavering** – a protohistoric palace on the gravel, Hope-Taylor 1977; **Poses** – a Neolithic settlement on the gravel, Bostyn c.2004; **Borg**, a turf hall, Munch et al 2003; **Eketorp** Borg et al 1976; **Tell Brak** (and other tells) Oates et al 1998, 2001, 2007; W. Matthews 1995; W. Matthews et al 1994, 1996, 1997; R. Matthews 1999; Rosen 1986; Hodder 2005 for Çatalhöyük; for Asiklihöyük see Chapter 1; The **Wijnaldum-Tjitsma** terp, Besteman et al 1999 (pp. 19 and 21 for the quotes); **Cuello** Hammond 1991; **San Giusto, Celone**, in Puglia, Volpe 1998; **Warring States Tombs' China:** State Administration of Cultural Heritage 2007, 91–8.

Studying standing buildings has become an attractive and expanding sub-discipline, made very precise with laser surveying instruments. **General**: McAlester and McAlester 1984, J. Wood 1994, S. Brown 1997, K. Clark 2001, GBG

(Geotechnics Ltd) 2001; **recording:** English Heritage 2000b, Watt and Swallow 1996, Swallow et al 2004, Hurman and Steiner 1995 (photogrammetry); NSW Heritage, 2002a and b (handy guides for CRM projects in Australia); RCAHMS 2007 for Balquhain Castle; **conservation:** Weaver 1997; **building materials:** Alcock N.W. et al 1996 (timber), Warren 1999 (earth), Howe 2001 (stone), Historic Scotland 2001, 2003 (lime mortar), Historic Scotland 2002 (plaster). **Analysis:** Bänteli 1993, R. Samson (ed.) 1990, and see Chapter 10. Atkinson 1995 is a nice example of the stratigraphic dismantling of a whole building. For **Bredon**, Charles 1997; **Balquhain**, RCAHMS 2007 (176); **Pride Hill Chambers**, Carver 1983c.

For **urban archaeology** Grimes 1968 is still salutary and Manacorda 1982 still exemplary; R.A. Hall 1984 provides an all too rare first-hand narrative of the conception and completion of a large scale urban project, with Rowesome 2000 a graphic account of a more recent one in London; M. Carver 1987 is a survey of English urban digging at the height of the "rescue" movement, and M. Carver 1993 a polemical discussion of urban archaeology in Europe. The examples chosen here were **York Minster**, Phillips and Heywood 1995 (I, 17 for the quote) and **Northampton**, Miller et al 2005. See also Burnouf et al 1991 for a fine interdisciplinary research project in Lyon. Too many other urban projects take place (and they are numerous) without their excavators revealing why they did what they did.

Working in the wet is also a specialist area, and one demanding special training. No one should venture into the water without a professional escort and a course of instruction. Some idea of the problems can be gained from NAS 1992 and HSE (Health and Safety Executive) 1997. My examples were: **wetland**, Purdy 1988, B. Coles 1992, Coles et al 1999, **Windover** Doran 1992 (for quotes), 2002, Coles and Coles 1996; **shallow water: Charavines**, Colardelle and Verdele 1993; **deep water:** Muckleroy 1978, Gregory 2000; Bass 2005; **Yassıada:** Bass and Van Doorninck Jnr 1982, and for later developments Bass 2005. **Coastland:** Flemming 2004. **Doggerland**, Gaffney et al 2007.

PART 3
WRITING UP

8 ANALYSIS

The tasks: manage, assess and analyse

The vehicle full of boxes that brings us back from fieldwork is parked with a sense of both satisfaction and apprehension. "Writing up" is in many ways the most exciting and creative part of field archaeology; but it can also seem frustrating and to take an eternity. As with fieldwork itself, a staged framework can help. But nothing beats appetite – the wish to understand what you have found and tell others about it. The next six chapters deal with this.

Unlike most writers, who just need a desk, books and notes, archaeologists need something approaching a warehouse, with floor space, a big table, plenty of light and storage (FIG 8.1). First, we have to unload and organise the boxes and put them

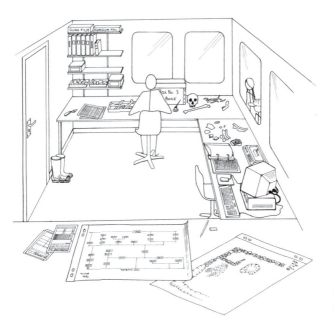

FIGURE 8.1 Writing up (sketch by Liz Hooper).

somewhere accessible. There may be many hundreds of them, containing objects or containing records. In the field, the objects have already been sorted into soil samples (heavy), slags, animal bones, human bones, iron, pottery and stone, and those special finds ("small finds") kept separate because they are delicate and need conservation. Like a consignment of freight, the boxes will have codes written on them – the project code (e.g. "WAS 08", the site of Wasperton, 2008 season), and codes for materials (e.g. Sl for slag, AB for animal bone, Fe for iron), so we know which is which. The contents of these boxes will go for assessment presently to different specialists. Then there are the boxes of records: notebooks, A4 files of context sheets and feature sheets, indexes of objects (the "Finds Index"), drawings at A4 and A1, photographs in colour and black and white; and part or all of these may have a digital equivalent on a laptop, plus back-up on disks, DVDs, data sticks or whatever fancy medium is currently in the shops.

This, our harvest from the field, has first to be *managed*, that is checked, listed and stored (FIG 8.2). This operation has one unvarying rule: it will always take longer than you thought it would. Things go missing, things get wet, disks corrupt and everything must be copied, if it hasn't been already. The task can be daunting: in a hectare of excavation archaeologists will define 10,000 contexts, 500 features and 80,000 finds, generating a consequent volume of records: 30 volumes of sheets, 300 boxes of objects. But all of these are potentially precious, even if nothing further is done. These are the *Field Records*, the input of the writing-up process (FIG 8.3; TABLE 8.1).

Something further will generally be done with these collections, before they go for their long sleep in storage: we need to make history from them. This requires a

Reassessment	Management

Assemblage
– Artefacts: metal, wood, stone
  leather, pottery, glass
– Biota: human bone, animal
  bone
	Records
	– Digital records
	– Context cards/feature cards
	– Maps, plans, sections
	– Photographs
	– Programme of analysis

Chronology – Stratification – Dating sequence	**Objects** – Conservation – Packing and storing – Programme of analysis
Spatial – Contexts to features – Features to structures – Structures to site	**Samples** – Storage – Programme of analysis

FIGURE 8.2 Re-assessment and management.

TABLE 8.1 Field records from different types of project

Project	Written	Drawn	Digital	Photographic	Material
Reconnaissance	Notebook	Map	Digital maps GIS	APs	Surface finds
Evaluation	Notebook Context	Plans and maps	Digital maps		Surface finds Samples
Landscape survey	Notebook	Artefact plots	Digital maps GIS	APs	Surface finds
Site survey	Notebook	Topographic maps	Digital maps GIS	Overviews	Surface finds Samples
Excavation	Notebook Contexts Features	Plans Maps Sections 3-D plots	Context records co-ordinates Digital maps	Overviews Portraits Monitor	Assemblages
Buildings	Notebook Contexts Features	Plans Elevations	Photogrammetry Co-ordinates	Overviews Portraits Monitor	Samples
Wetland	Notebook Contexts Features	Plans Maps 3-D plots	Co-ordinates	Overviews Portraits Monitor	Assemblages Samples

Input: the Field Records

PROJECT FILES (Administration)

SITE FILES (Field Records)

RESEARCH FILES (Research notes and specialist reports)

SITE FILES (one set for each Intervention)

Y00: Indexes to everything
Y01: Journals and notebooks
Y02: Context cards
Y03: Feature packs
Y04: Structures
Y05: Maps, plans sections
Y06: Photographs
Y07: Finds (artefacts, biota)
Y08: Syntheses

FIGURE 8.3 The Input: Field Records.

programme, and the programme requires an *assessment* of what there is (FIG 8.2). Even the most brilliant evaluation will not have predicted precisely what will come out of the ground. And even the best researcher will be surprised by how well or how badly the findings matched the objectives. Findings from fieldwork are a combination of what you hoped for, plus what you didn't expect.

Here are three reasons for doing an assessment: to list what was found, to match it to the objectives of the project design, and to map a new programme of work that takes in both the expected and the unexpected results. In commercial projects (and increasingly in research projects) "post-excavation assessment" is a key design phase, requiring its own programme and budget. This follows the principle of spending money now to avoid wasting it in the future. The re-assessment constitutes in effect an evaluation, assembling the materials and ideas for a new project design which will then guide the work to a successful outcome.

Output: the Lab Reports

FR1: Project History
FR2: Evaluation and Design
FR3: Report on Sector 4
FR4: Report on Sector 2

FR1: Project History
1.1: Project history
1.1.1: Chronological summary 1994–2007 from journals
1.2: List of participants
1.3: List of publications, including films
1.4: Album
1.5: Script for the display in museum
1.6: Script for the database accessible to the public
1.7: Bulletins and interims

FR3: Report on Investigations in Sector 4:
The Church and Churchyard (Int 17, 20, 23)

3.1: Description of the investigations
3.2: Excavation
3.3: Studies of the church architecture
3.4: Studies of burials
3.5: Studies of the memorials
3.6: Studies of the assemblage
3.7: Spatial analysis
3.8: Sequence

FIGURE 8.4 The Output: Lab Reports. Examples of file contents.

The new project design is a *programme of analysis*, a sequence of operations that starts with the records and ends with a synthesis. Everything unloaded from the field had a purpose (or you hope so), and that purpose was to serve the analysis and so play a role in the eventual story (synthesis). In other words every object and field record has an *analytical destiny*, and was compiled or collected with that destiny in mind. That destination, the output from the analytical process, is itemised in the *Lab Reports* (FIG 8.4). These reports include a history of the project, descriptions of the investigations and the sequence and its interpretation in each part of the site. The example in FIG 8.4 gives summaries for the files on the Project History (FR1) and

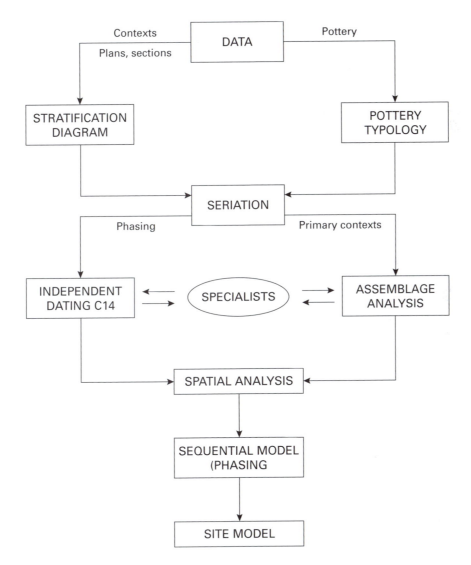

FIGURE 8.5 The Analytical Itinerary (for a site with ceramics).

one of the sectors (the church and churchyard) slimmed down from the large table of contents for the Tarbat project (1996–2010). It is important to recognise that the production of the Lab Reports is part and parcel of the project and should always happen whether or not the project is ever published, in whatever form. Naturally enough, different sponsors and clients have different specifications so there will be variations in the content. But the basic principle is immutable: there must be some record of what the excavators thought they had found, and what it meant, in their own words.

Analysis builds a path from the *Field Records* (the input) to the *Lab Reports* (the output). It takes the material from a lump of stuff in a plastic bag, up to the point where it plays its part in an ancient economic system. This path follows an *analytical itinerary*. So at the start of the writing up stage, we first prepare a programme that maps out the analytical destinies and the analytical itineraries followed in order to get to them (FIG 8.5). The composition of such a programme might seem a formidable task, but the answer (as so often) will be found in design: a statement of the best we can do, with what we have, given what we know, now.

The analytical programme

The elements of most narratives are what happened, where and when, so in general these things are what analysis aims to discover. Out in the field, the daily task was to define contexts and finds, their relative sequence and their location, and these provide the raw materials on which the analysis can work. One convenient way to structure the programme is to view it as three operations in parallel, broadly investigating *what*, *where* and *when*: assemblage, the use of space and chronology. Each of these three sub-programmes has its own agenda, although they talk to each other as they go along (FIG 8.6).

Assemblage considers the objects under two headings: the *artefacts*, and the natural materials (also known as *biota* or ecofacts) (Chapter 9). The assemblage analysis sets out to assign each artefact to its cultural type and decide where it came from. The biota are identified to species. Then the two types of find are quantified and reconsidered as context or feature assemblages. Assemblage analysis leads to the identification of ancient activities – but not only that: for artefacts it shows the range of contacts, and for biota it shows the range of resources and the health of people and their herds.

Understanding the *use of space* is a major goal of excavation and survey (Chapter 10). Space is informative at every scale: the location of objects in a *context* (nails scattered on a floor, chemical plotting in a burial chamber) lead to interpretations of vanished things; the locations of contexts (dark patches, layers, stones) to the identification of *features*; and the relative location of features to the identification of *structures*. So the examination of stone slabs in the ground suggests they were

REDO *Project Design* and write *Analytical programme*

MANAGE ARCHIVE

DESIGN ANALYTICAL PROGRAMME

Assemblage – artefacts – cultures, contacts; biota – resources; assemblages – activities

Chronology – dated materials; stratigraphy; space; sequence

Spatial – objects to activities – contexts to features – features to structures – structures to site

SYNTHESIS: activities – analogies
site model – context
prehistorical/historical/anthropological models

DESIGN PUBLICATION PROGRAMME

FIGURE 8.6 Analysis – the menu.

post-pads, and the distribution of these post-pads shows where a building once stood. Some of these patterns will have been noticed on the ground and will already have the additional advantage of feature or structure studies (see Chapter 6). Others will not: as an example, take the distribution of animal bones over a whole site. Only later analysis will show where animals were slaughtered (heads and feet), eaten (bones marked by teeth and knives) and discarded (carcases and big meat bones). Spatial analysis then moves beyond the site, to the distribution of sites in a territory, and to territories confronting each other over the mountains or across the seas.

Chronology is also studied under two main headings: sequence and date (see Chapter 11). On excavations, sequence is primarily deduced from stratification, while on surveys the main route to sequence is via the distribution of datable materials. Needless to say, each can feed the other – for example, a site like a cemetery, where the graves have objects but all lie side by side without cutting, makes up for its poor stratification by using the distribution of the grave contents in space. A date can be obtained by typology in the case of artefacts, and by radiocarbon or other direct measurements on materials. Armed with these dates the next step is to work out how a dated object actually dates its context. Not so simple, as it turns out. The objects in a grave – a nice sealed context where everything was placed in together – can still be manufactured at different times, leaving the key question (When was this grave dug?) a little uncertain.

Assemblage, Space and Chronology – what happened, where and when – are three parts of the same programme of analysis in dialogue with each other. Surveyors

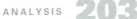

plotting pottery-scatters in the landscape will need to ask *Assemblage* to identify the pottery types, and *Chronology* to work out a dated sequence of landscape use. Excavators studying the structure of a corn dryer from its form in the ground, will need to ask *Assemblage* to identify the grain and the weevils, and *Chronology* to provide radiocarbon dates. It perhaps needs to be emphasised that these are not anarchic discussions or intuitive speculations: it is programmed work. Some of this work can be done in house by the firm or the university that is hosting it. But everyone has to buy in specialists for something – expert botanists, entomologists, radiographers, ceramic historians. These specialists represent a new type of career opportunity for archaeologists: they acquire a broad overview of the part of the subject they like best, and get paid for studying it further (FIG 8.7).

Managing the programme is like assembling a motor car – it is an itinerary in which all the bits eventually come together on the conveyor belt. Assemblage (Chapter 9), Space (Chapter 10) and Chronology (Chapter 11) come together in *Synthesis* (Chapter 12), various versions of which are offered to different sections of the public in *Publication* (Chapter 13). The design and management of the programme is explained, with the other design stages, in Chapter 14.

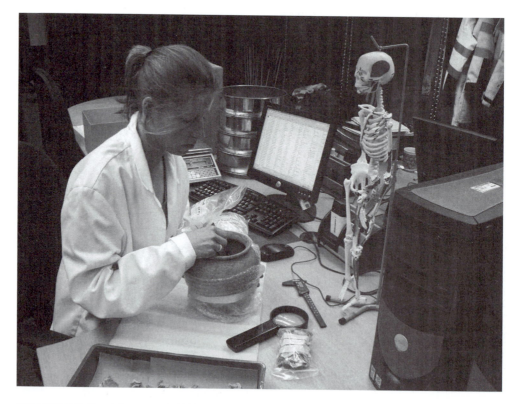

FIGURE 8.7 Specialist at work (FAS Ltd).

There are clear dangers in laying out a template for writing up and publication – as I do here. These can seem very personal matters, and attempts to generalise the process may provoke a certain amount of scoffing. But I take the risk on the premise that one transparent framework is better than none. My experience of writing up has been that many archaeologists, aware of the poverty and complexity of their own records and the rumbling censure of their peers, find it hard to start and still harder to finish. To demystify the process, summarise it, give it a programme and exude encouragement is therefore no bad thing. In Chapter 2, I advanced the opinion that archaeological investigation is to some extent independent of the theories applied to it, because what we do is done in contract with the public, not merely to serve ourselves. I would say this of writing up, too. Whatever the current passions of contemporary scholarship may be, the curation, study and presentation of results won in the field have their own logic. All archaeological investigation has a dedicated outcome, and work can start right away – without waiting for the spark from heaven to fall.

To show how the analytical itinerary works, I am going to take a single case study. It is an urban excavation with organic preservation, because that features a rich range of analysis, and it is one that is already published, so that we can follow the whole journey. I also chose a "rescue" site, not a very big one, so we are not overwhelmed with information; and it is early medieval, not just because that is what I do, but because it is easier for someone without any knowledge of the background archaeology and new to the writing up process, to appreciate the story line.

Case study: Saddler Street, Durham

The site excavated at Saddler Street lay at the foot of the castle mound in Durham City, North England, and it was found to have had a bit of everything. The modern site was densely built up, the buildings climbing from the street a third of the way up the mound (FIG 8.8). University College was planning new accommodation there, for its students, but the existing buildings, although pretty derelict, had yet to be fully demolished. There were

FIGURE 8.8 Durham City: the Saddler Street site.

four points at which archaeologists could achieve contact with mother earth (A, B, C, D; FIG 8.9). Site A was on the overgrown mound itself, B on a sill below the mound, C in the ground floor of a timber hall used for Judo practice and D in the basement of a former theatre. Evaluation showed that A was impracticable, B impossible and

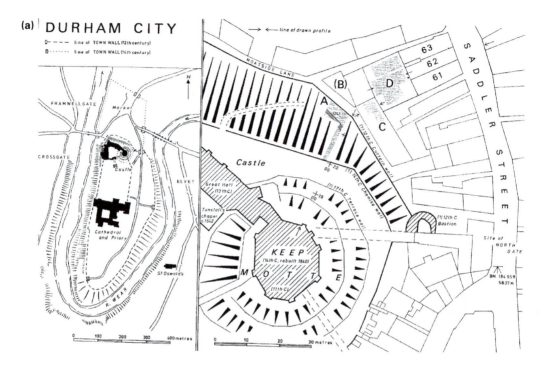

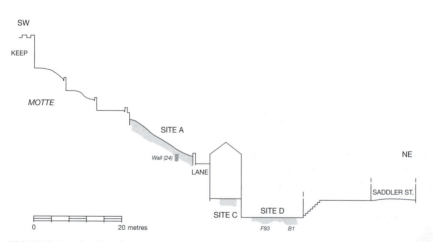

FIGURE 8.9 Saddler Street – location map in plan and profile.

C inauspicious. That left D, which was to produce the premises of a 10th century cobbler in a marvellous state of preservation.

Under the brick floor of the theatre basement was a raft of slightly damp sand, smelling like an airing cupboard, the distinctive aroma of early organic decay in an anaerobic deposit. Small timber posts soon appeared under the sand, forming fences of upright stakes and a large circular clay oven (FIG 8.10). Beneath this were more wattle fences and a hearth (FIG 8.11). There were leather off-cuts everywhere, sandwiched in peaty layers containing a wealth of pottery and organic debris, cloth, moss, twigs, a piece of sheep's fleece and a flower, compressed as between the pages of a book. Each wooden post and layer was recorded individually (context), and as part of a wall or fence or midden heap (feature). The order of the deposition of the contexts was represented in a diagram, and sections were also used to show how contexts related to each other in the ground. At the end of the dig there were context records, plans, sections, photographs and finds galore.

There was a major programme of analysis for the *assemblage*, because the preservation was so unusual (FIG 8.12). The pottery was of an unknown type, so its study had to start from scratch; the copious quantity of leather needed the opinion of a shoe historian; the plants, animal bone, the sheep's fleece and the insects were all

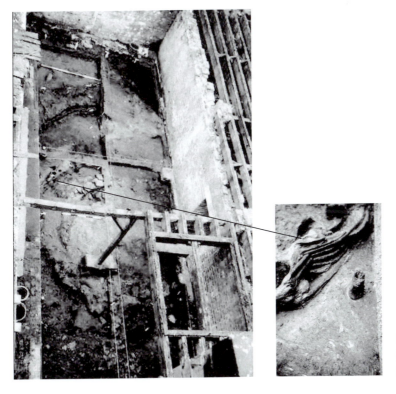

FIGURE 8.10
(a) Under the floor;
and (b) close-up.

FIGURE 8.11 Wattle fences.

sent to specialists for identification and quantification and interpretation (FIG 8.13). In the *spatial analysis*, the map of timber posts showed the shape of buildings and how the land had been marked out by fences. The distribution of artefacts showed that many were clustered in middens, thrown out from the interior of the house into its backyard. Meanwhile the *sequence* was being worked out from the stratification. A context sequence diagram was made by putting the contexts in order and cross-checking with the sections (FIG 8.14), and then features were allocated to replace sets of contexts, so generating a feature sequence diagram (FIG 8.15). A range of radiocarbon determinations gave date ranges for wooden posts and leather scrap which could be positioned in the sequence (FIG 8.16). This provided a framework in which to place material of unknown date – the animal bone and the pottery (FIG 8.17).

Looking at the stratigraphy and the spatial layout, the sequence fell into two main phases. The earliest building, a bow-sided wattle structure, ran alongside the street (FIG 8.18). With its attendant midden heap this dated to the 10th/11th century. It was superseded in the 11th/12th century by a different layout in which there were fences running at right angles to the street, dividing the space into three "tenements" or shops (FIG 8.19).

The information drawn from each of the three analytical programmes and all their contributors could be brought together to make a *synthesis* (FIG 8.20). Radiocarbon dating said that nothing much had happened on this site before around AD900, when a house made of wattle was terraced into the natural hillside. At that time there was probably a track running round the hill and the house had been alongside it. Almost immediately the occupants began producing and mending leather goods – this was clearly their job. They made openwork sandals and sheaths for knives. They used wheel-thrown pink pottery. They had some flesh-eating insects living with them (who doesn't?) and just outside their work area was some wild land with plenty of stinking mayweed. They had oats and turnips and fat hen – all very nourishing, and ate hare, deer, geese, grouse and capercailzie as well as salmon and cod. An iron arrow-head was found. Well-fed people, then, with access to hunting grounds.

Around about 1050, there were some radical changes: the house was demolished and a new one built at right angles to the track. There was a large bread-oven built behind.

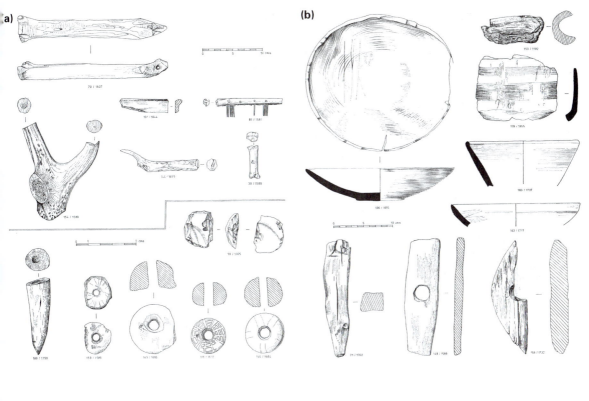

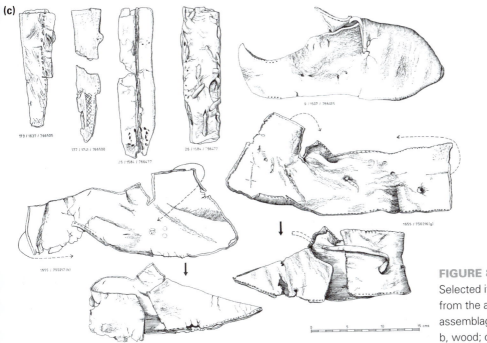

FIGURE 8.12
Selected items from the artefact assemblage (a, bones; b, wood; c, leather).

(a) NUMBERS OF FRAGMENTS OF EACH SPECIES (AND SIZE-GROUP) FOR THE SITE AS A WHOLE

		Primary Deposit	Secondary Deposit	Others	Total
Domestic animals	Horse	18(2)	3	3	26
	Ox	329(39)	47(6)	97(12)	533
	Pig	159(21)	15(5)	31(4)	235
	Sheep/g	162(22)	15(1)	32(11)	243
	Sheep	13	1	3	17
	Goat	5(1)			7
	Dog	43(7)	1	4(1)	56
	Dog or Fox			(1)	1
	Cat	4(1)	1	1	17
	Fowl	77(12)	4(1)	22(10)	126
	Goose, cf. domestic	29	2	6	37
Game	Red deer, *Cervus elaphus*	6(3)		(1)	
	Roe, d. *Capreolus capreolus*	6(4)			10
	Hare, *Lepus cf capensis*	1(1)		(1)	3
Wild Fowl	Cormorant, *Phalacrocorax carbo*		2		2
	Black Grouse, *Lyrurus tetrix*	4	1		5
	Capercaillie, *Tetrao urogallus*	5		1	6
Fish	Cod, *Gadus morhua*	21		8	29
	Haddock, *Melanogrammus aeglefinus*	2			2
	Saithe, *Pollachius virens*(?)	(4)			4
	Ling, *Molva molva*			2	2
	Salmon, *Salmo salar*	1			1
	Eel, *Anguilla anguilla*	1			1
	Gadoid	(1)			1
	Fish, indeterminate	61	33		94
Shellfish	Lobster, *Nephrops norvegicus*	1			1
	Limpet, *Patella vulgata*	1		1(1)	3
	Periwinkle, *Littorina littorea*	1			1
	Common cockle, *Cardium edule*	2			2
	Common mussel, *Mytilus edulis*			1	1
	Pearl mussel, *Margaritifera margaritifera*	3(1)	1	1	6
	Large ungulate	268	52	70	390
	Small ungulate	197	15	40	252
	Large animal	328	36	56	420
	Medium animal	122	4	58	164
	Small animal	18	2	5	25
	Bird and small mammal, indet.	19	3	1	23
	Unidentified	49	3	11	63

TOTAL: 2717

(b) TABLE 13

Species occupying the first ten ranks of abundance in the assemblage from sample 1581

P — Pale individuals recorded

Rank	Species	Number of individuals	Percentage
1	*Oxytelus sculptus*	50 P	11.4
2	*Cercyon pygmaeus*	29 P	6.6
	Leptacinus ?intermedius	29	6.6
4	*Cercyon analis*	28 P	6.4
5	*Carpelimus fuliginosus*	22	5.0
6	*Ptenidium* sp. indet.	18	4.1
	Gyrohypnus fracticornis	18	4.1
8	*Antylus rugosus*	15	3.4
9	*Platystethus arenarius*	14 P	3.2
10	*Xylodromus concinnus*	12	2.7

(c)

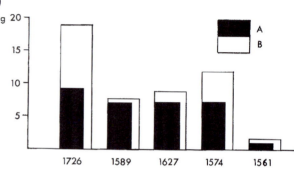

(d)

Context	1726	1589	1740	1562	1576	1575	1574
Description	Ultimate fill of Storm drain, S 15	Midden 1	Midden 1	Midden 3	Primary fill of Cesspit, F 100	Secondary fill of Cesspit, F 100	Midden 5

REMAINS / **SPERMATOPHYTA**

Remains	1726	1589	1740	1562	1576	1575	1574	Plant Species	Group
Achenes	—	—	—	1	—	—	—	*Achillea millefolium* L. (Yarrow)	D I*
Fruits	—	1	—	—	—	—	—	*Aethusa cynapium* L. (Fool's Parsley)	B C
Seeds	1	3	6	40	2	29	5	*Agrostemma githago* L. (Corn Cockle)	B I*
Achenes	1	—	5	12	—	—	4	*Anthemis cotula* L. (Stinking Mayweed)	B C I
Seeds	2	14	12	5	15	9	103	*Atriplex hastata* L./*paula* L. (Orache)	B C H
Carbon. grains	1	—	—	—	1	—	2	*Avena* sp. (Oats)	A
Seeds	1	10	1	3	10	4	3	*Brassica rapa* L. (Turnip)	A B C H I J
Shoots	—	—	—	—	—	—	+	*Calluna vulgaris* (L.) Hull (Heather)	F J
Seeds	—	1	1	—	—	—	—	*Caltha palustris* L. (Marsh Marigold)	E I
Nutlets	—	6	—	—	—	—	4	*Carex paniculata* L. (Panicled Sedge)	E I
Nutlets	3	2	3	—	3	1	—	*Carex* spp. (Sedges)	E
Achenes	—	—	—	1	—	1	—	*Centaurea nigra* L. (Knapweed)	D I
Seeds	15	24	50	16	31	23	48	*Chenopodium album* L. (Fat Hen)	B C H I*J
Achenes	—	—	—	—	—	—	1	*Chrysanthemum segetum* L. (Corn Marigold)	B I
Nuts	—	—	—	1	—	1	—	*Corylus avellana* L. (Hazel)	G I*
Seeds	6	—	—	—	—	—	—	Cruciferae	
Achenes	—	1	—	—	—	—	1	*Daucus carota* L. (Carrot)	A B D I
Nutlets	—	—	1	3	1	1	—	*Eleocharis palustris* (L.) Roem. & Schult. (Spike Rush)	E
Fruits	—	—	—	—	—	—	5	*Filipendula ulmaria* (L.) Maxim (Meadowsweet)	E I* J
Nutlets	1	—	—	2	—	—	3	*Galeopsis tetrahit* L./*speciosa* Hull (Hemp Nettle)	B
Caryopses	6	9	4	7	3	4	2	Graminae (Grasses)	
Seeds	—	—	—	—	—	—	+	*Juncus articulatus* L./*acutifolius* Hoffm. (Rushes)	E J
Seeds	—	—	—	—	—	—	+	*Juncus bufonius* L. (Toad Rush)	C D
Seeds	—	—	—	—	—	—	+	*Juncus effusus* L./*conglomeratus* L. (Rushes)	E F
Achenes	12	2	14	—	2	16	2	*Lapsana communis* L. (Nipplewort)	B C H I
Achenes	—	—	—	—	—	—	—	*Leontodon* sp. (Hawkbit)	D
Seeds	3	7	3	—	—	—	7	*Linum usitassimum* L. (Flax)	A I J
Seeds	—	—	—	1	—	1	2	*Luzula campestris* (L.) DC (Sweep's Brush)	C D
Seeds	—	—	—	—	—	2	1	*Malus sylvestris* Mill. (Apple)	G I*
Seeds	—	—	—	—	—	1	—	*Papaver somniferum* L. (Opium Poppy)	A I*
Seeds	—	7	—	1	—	—	—	*Pedicularis palustris* L. (Red Rattle)	E F
Seeds	—	—	—	—	—	—	—	*Plantago lanceolata* L. (Ribwort Plantain)	D I*
Fruits	30	2	2	2	—	1	7	*Polygonum aviculare* L. s.l. (Knotgrass)	B C I*
Fruits	81	6	1	2	—	1	1	*Polygonum hydropiper* L. (Water Pepper)	E
Fruits	8	1	5	1	2	1	3	*Polygonum lapathifolium* L. (Pale Persicaria)	B C

FIGURE 8.13 From the biota assemblage: tables and graphs showing details on (a) animal bones, (b and c) insects, and (d) plants.

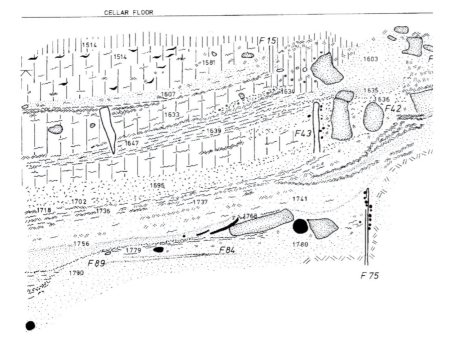

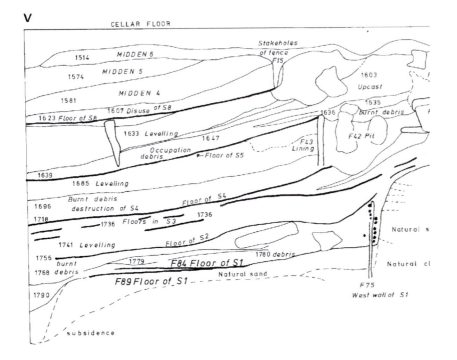

FIGURE 8.14 Relative chronology: extract of section and interpretation.

DURHAM CITY, SADDLER STREET 1974
STRATIGRAPHY, SITE D

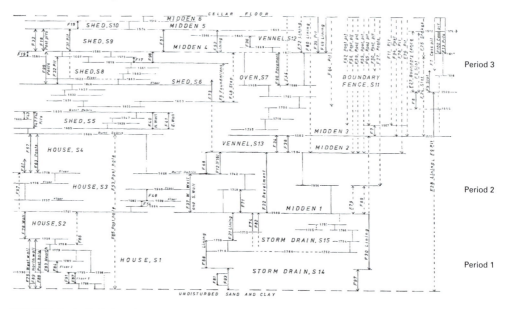

FIGURE 8.15 Relative chronology: stratigraphy, using contexts and features.

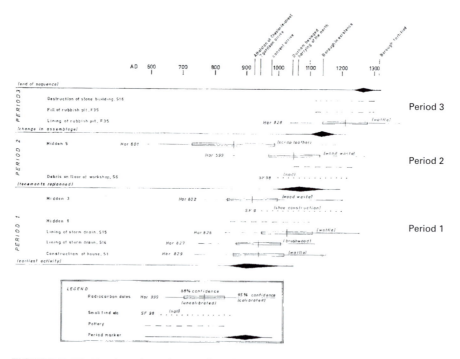

FIGURE 8.16 Absolute chronology: radiocarbon dates.

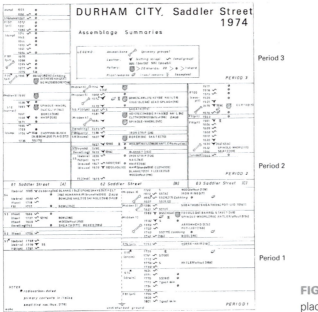

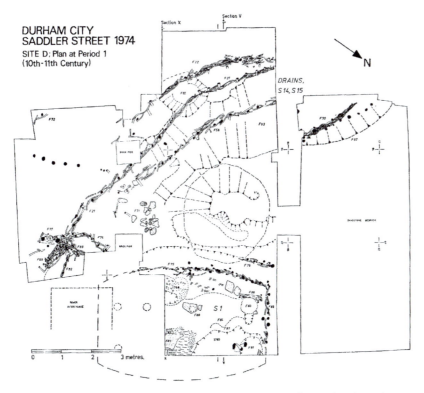

FIGURE 8.17 The assemblages, placed in order by the chronology.

DURHAM CITY
SADDLER STREET 1974

SITE D; Plan at Period 1
(10th-11th Century)

FIGURE 8.18 The spatial layout in the first period according to the chronology .

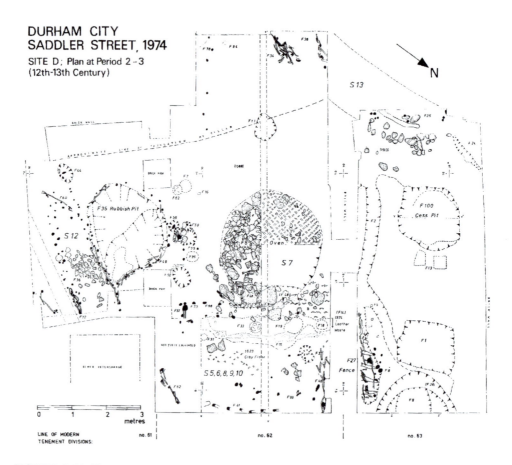

DURHAM CITY
SADDLER STREET, 1974

SITE D; Plan at Period 2 – 3
(12th-13th Century)

N

S 13

F44

F35 Rubbish Pit

S 12

Oven

S 7

F100
Cess Pit

F13

F27
Fence

F1

1623
Clay Floor

S 5,6,8,9,10

0   1   2   3
          metres

LINE OF MODERN
TENEMENT DIVISIONS:

no. 61   no. 62   no. 63

FIGURE 8.19 The spatial layout in the second period according to the chronology.

On either side of it were wattle fences, demarcating, it so happens, property bound-aries that endured to the 20th century. The neighbours were neither bakers nor leather-workers but more residential folk. Coarse earthenware replaced the pink pots, and suddenly there were no more game birds or venison on the table.

This narrative was expressed in outline in a *site model*, the model of what happened here, mostly in words but also as a cartoon (FIG 8.20). That was the first part of the synthesis. The second part attempted to place these events in their context. In this case, the hill within a loop of the River Wear that is now the site of Durham was settled by Anglian people in about 900AD, when other parts of Northumbria were already being settled by Danish Vikings. They no doubt fortified the place, and at the end of the century were to bring there the precious relics of St Cuthbert, Anglian Northumbria's spiritual guardian. On the slopes of the hill was a group of craftsmen, including our own excavated people, the cobblers of Saddler Street, suppliers of boots and saddles to the garrison and to the monastery. William the Conqueror who invaded

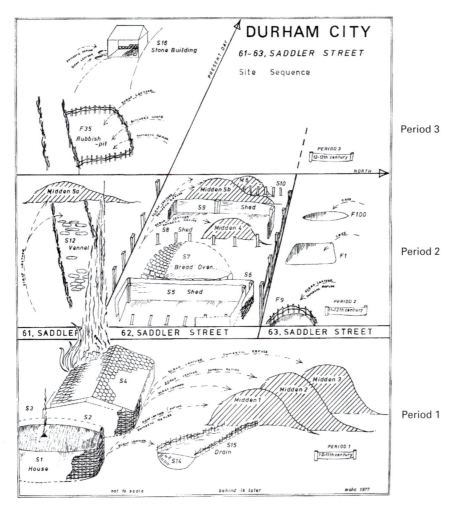

FIGURE 8.20 Synthesis: a sketch of the site model.

England in 1066, subdued the north in a famously brutal campaign in which Durham was besieged. This offers a likely context for the changes between our Periods 1 and 2. The local industries were snuffed out and the tenements re-planned. The people fashioned coarse pottery and had no more access to game. The only wild food is now the blackberry, which probably still grew on the mound, then as now. The workers of Durham seem to have become the victims of Norman urbanism.

Conclusion

Naturally, not every site offers the exquisite detail of an anaerobic deposit, and not every excavator wishes to travel so far along the upward road of conjecture. Nor is

it necessary; an important consideration in compiling a synthesis is the question of who is going to read it. We shall consider this readership in Chapter 13. This case study hopes to offer an example of the way that a synthesis may be woven from the three strands of assemblage, chronology and space. Now let's look at each of the strands in turn.

Briefing

It is hard to find literature on how to study the results of an investigation and write them up – other than in the finished products themselves. But in published reports there is still some reluctance among field archaeologists to say how their results were arrived at or to advertise their failures. Where they exist, post-excavation designs are almost never published, and neither are the unsuccessful analyses. This is often for good reasons of economy of print, and things should improve with the increasing availability of e-repositories in which to hold this potentially very helpful material in the public domain (see Chapter 13).

The state agencies in Britain have issued guides to **managing analytical and publication programmes** in the commercial sector. These have the status of mandatory procedures where archaeologists are applying for money from the agencies themselves (English Heritage MAP; Historic Scotland DSR). There is now some publicly accessible guidance on what should be in a project design for the writing up stage at www.english-heritage.org.uk/upload/pdf/MoRPHE-Project-Managers-Guide.pdf.

Structure of records. The tri-partite system was previously published in Carver 1986. Carver 2008 for Tarbat. Of these the use of site files or their equivalent is routine, but modern structures are more digital-friendly and depend on the concept of record used (see Chapter 6). **Data management packages:** Richards and Ryan 1985 for an introduction to SPSS and other packages. Commercial archaeology firms' researchers have successfully adapted a number of commercially available data base management systems to archaeology. Carver 1979a for the case study.

Analytical methods are discussed holistically in M. Carver 1979a, b and 1999 and in a bit more detail in the following Chapters 9–11. Scientific methods are usefully collected and described in Brothwell and Pollard 2001. Orton 1980, Richards and Ryan 1985, Baxter 1994 and Blankholm 1991 explain statistical procedures for seeking patterns. **Correspondence analysis:** Greenacre 1983, and see Penn and Brugmann 2007 for a recent example of an application to furnished graves.

9 ASSEMBLAGE

Retrieval

Every object starts its new life on site with maximum vulnerability, the moment of its discovery. It is reborn from the earth amid sharp tools and heavy boots, and needs to be well-protected on the first stages of its journey (FIG 9.1). The journey begins with the first task: make a clear record of how the object was found (location), then bag it and take it to a finds hut; there it is lightly cleaned, listed, measured and described, and then treated to prevent decay, labelled and packed in readiness for its analysis and conservation, and, for a few chosen examples, an ultimate appearance in a museum case.

Although archaeology is full of surprises, the chances of finding something at all depend on how big it is and hard you look – i.e. the Recovery Level. Some objects pop out of the ground (a potsherd), and can be lifted and put in a tray or bag, while others must be sought by sieving on site (tiny bones) and yet others (seeds, pollen, insects) need the separation techniques of a laboratory and a microscope to see them – in which case we have to guess that they are there, taking soil samples from targeted contexts. Lifting, sieving and sampling

From the earth to the finds hut

LOCATE (Recovery Level)

BAG and LABEL
(Site/Int/Context/Grid)

CLEAN (wash, brush, dry, seal)

RECORD (Index, inventory)

FIRST AID

PACKAGE

STORE

DESPATCH

FIGURE 9.1 Finds retrieval, from the earth to the finds hut (FAS Ltd).

each have their routines on site, each providing material with its own analytical destiny (FIG 9.2).

Lifting the majority of objects only needs a pair of fingers and a plastic bag. But complex and vulnerable things require precise recording in the ground, because we have high expectations of them (FIG 9.3). For features dug at Level E, there will be a *Finds Location Record* for each object, which says not only where an object was, but which way up it lay and its angle of rest in the ground. This may become relevant, for example, for fragments of fresco fallen from a wall, or a whole pot broken in situ,

Method of retrieval	Record	Targeted material
LIFTING		
Object Levels A–C	Context no. nearest sq. metre	Artefacts
Object Level D	Finds no. Location 3-D to nearest mm	Artefacts Mammal bones
Object Level E	FLR; 3-D to nearest mm; draw and phot. in situ	Artefacts Mammal bones Articulated human bone
Bloc (Level F)	3-D co-ordinates of corners	Artefact or biota complex
Mold	3-D co-ordinates of mold	Artefacts Articulated human body
SCREENING		
Dry (light soil)	Bag to context/nearest sq metre	Artefacts, artefact fragments, small bones of mammals, bones of small vertebrates (e.g. rodents, insectivores, amphibians, bats), birds, fish, molluscs, minerals
Wash (heavy soil)	Bag to context/nearest sq metre	Artefacts, artefact fragments, small bones of mammals, bones of small vertebrates (e.g. rodents, insectivores, amphibians, bats), birds, fish, molluscs, minerals
Flotation	Bag to context/nearest sq metre	Plant remains
SAMPLING		
Grab (bag) 30gm	Context no; 3-D to nearest cm	Plant remains; residues
Grab (bulk) 10 litre	Context no; 3-D to nearest m	Micro-flora and fauna
Column (monolith)	Draw and phot. in situ	Plant remains
Box (Kubiena)	Draw and phot. in situ	Soil history

FIGURE 9.2 Agenda for finds retrieval (author).

FIGURE 9.3 Photographing a find in situ: TR 04 is the site code Tarbat 2004; INT 24 is Intervention no. 24: Module D1 is the 8×4m area: C 2537 means it was found in context 2537; and 6313 is the unique number of the find (FAS Ltd).

or objects in a grave (FIG 9.4). Fragile objects are obviously not just thrust in a plastic bag. They may need (reversible) chemical consolidation on site, and jacketing in fibreglass (like the sword being lifted in FIG 9.4c). Or the whole block of soil containing related objects may be consolidated and lifted together – a Level F operation (see Chapter 6).

When they come out of the ground, objects of pottery and stone are usually recognisable at once. Silver looks black with a purple stain around it, bronze looks brown with a greenish stain and iron may be completely shapeless, with craggy growths of corrosion. The condition of bone, human and animal, varies enormously, and not very predictably, from a strong white structure to a faint stain. Where organic preservation is good, as at Durham, Saddler Street (see Chapter 8), you know at once – that strong sweet wet blanket smell, and the delicate lines of plant stems showing. In badly preserved sites, organic materials can still leave a message; where textiles have been in contact with an iron object, the iron may migrate into the textile and replace it, making a ferrous fossil from what had once been cloth (FIG 9.5). When first detected, objects show us the state they are in, imply the care in lifting and conservation they need and hint at what we can't see, as well as what we can.

FIGURE 9.4 Lifting:
(a) Releasing sherds on
site; (b) sherds marked
with spot to show which
way up they were; and
(c) making fibreglass
support to lift a sword
(N. Macbeth).

Retrieval at the end of a trowel is backed by sieving the earth we trowel up. Sieving
(screening in the USA) is passing the earth through a mesh to catch objects that are
otherwise hard to see (FIG 9.6). The size of mesh determines the size of things that
can be caught – from a button (5mm) to a bead (2mm) to a bird bone (1mm) to a
seed (0.5mm). Plant remains often float, so can be separated out by flotation. This
still leaves some very tiny objects such as pollen grains, insect bodies, grains of
charcoal or chemical elements that we might want to collect and analyse (Colour

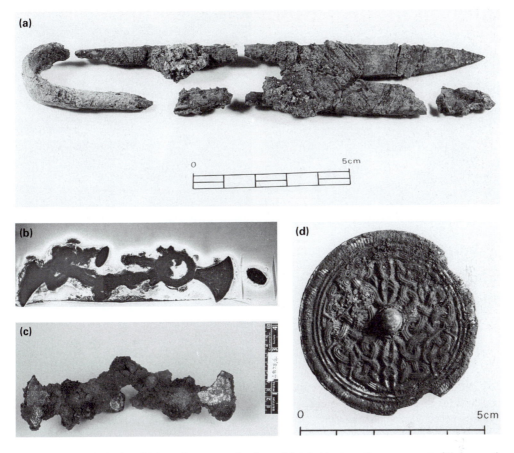

FIGURE 9.5 All that's gold doesn't necessarily glister. Metal objects as they come out of the ground: (a) iron shears with patches of textile; (b) x-ray of iron and gilded snaffle bit, and (c) as found; and (d) a gilt bronze disk.

Plates 10a–c). "*Grab samples*" are little 30gm packets of earth wrapped in cling film, aimed at discovering the proportion of seeds and charcoal or chemical elements in a particular layer. A *Kubiena box*, which takes a 5×5cm block and bakes it, looks to characterise the structure of a layer, to understand how it formed. A soil *column*, which measures about 5cms across and can be 1,000cm high, takes a sample of all the layers one above the other in a vertical column, to identify and count the pollen present in each one. Seeds, charcoal, plant pollen and the tiny granules of earth that make up soils are the components for understanding how the deposits got there, as well as chronicling the environment.

Sieving and sampling on site relate to what we want to know, are decided in the project design and monitored by recovery level. In general, Level E excavation involves sieving of all the dirt before it is thrown on the heap. The size of mesh will depend on

FIGURE 9.6 Sieving (screening): (a) spoil is brought up the ramp (built with earth and planks), and tipped on the meshes for shaking and sorting (N. Macbeth); and (b) flotation – the floating vegetable matter is collected in a fine brass sieve (P. Rahtz).

the target feature, but for a grave, the mesh must be at most 2mm so we do not miss any beads. Finer meshes are used to catch seeds and plant fragments by flotation. With waterlogged deposits, you can be pretty sure they are there, so flotation becomes routine. Otherwise the evaluation may suggest taking "grab samples" – such as one in every ten buckets at Level D. Sampling is similarly targeted – densely at Level E, in intervals at Level D (FIG 9.7).

From the moment of its recovery, every object and sample carries its site code and find number around with it on the bag and on a small impermeable label inside it. Everything then appears in the *Finds Index* – a list of every object and sample, giving its find number, context number, Recovery Level, location (grid reference), brief description and which box it was put in. Delicate objects, which might fall to pieces, are studied on site as far as possible without too much poking, and described in words and pictures on an *Inventory Sheet*. This kind of "special find" (sometimes "small find"), which might be a coin, a brooch or a piece of textile, will be travelling to a conservation laboratory, and possibly to a (different) research laboratory. Everywhere it goes a special find will take its inventory sheet, which acts both as a receipt and

Purpose	Target	Contexts	Amount and container	Destination	Analysis
Identification	Rock	Where it occurs	30g bag	Geologist	
	Charcoal/ wood	Where it occurs	30g bag	Botanist	
Dating	Charcoal/ wood/bone	Where it occurs	0.1 to 400g in sealed bag	Dating lab	C14
	Wood	Sliced from building timber	Largest possible x-section supported in box	Dendro lab	Dendro-chronology
	Burnt clay	Hearths	Lump 25×25 ×6mm plus a background sample from the buried environment	Recovered by specialist	TL
Plant use	Pollen, plant microfossils	All Level D	30g sealed bag	Lab	Pollen analysis
	Pollen, plant microfossils	Selected sequences, e.g. a buried soil	Column 50× 50mm in section up to 1m long, wrapped in cling film and black polythene	Lab	Pollen analysis
	Plant microfossils small vertebrates	All Level D	10ltr in plastic tub	Lab	Screening with 300 micron screen and hand sorting
	Plant microfossils: phytoliths, diatoms, spores	All Level D	1ltr in plastic tub	Lab	Screening and extraction
Ambient conditions	Insect remains	All Level D	10ltr in plastic tub	Lab	Extract with paraffin flotation
Chemical mapping	Concentration of phosphate and other elements	Selected features (house floor, burial chamber)	30g in sealed plastic bag	Lab	ICP analysis

FIGURE 9.7 Types of sample taken on site.

Material	Fabric	Form	Style	History
STONE	Identify type of rock [TS, NAA] – provenance	Function of implement	Date cultural group	Use (blood, polish) symbolism, discard
POTTERY and glass	Identify inclusions [TS, NAA; HM] – provenance plant impressions	Classify form-function culture	Classify ornament and decoration-date and culture	Use, symbolism, discard
METAL	Determine alloy provenance, culture [NMR]	Function of object	Classify form and style – sequence and group	Use, symbolism, discard
Moulds and crucibles	Which metals were worked? [XRF]	Classify		Use, discard
Slags	Metals [XRD] casting, forging or smithing? [MS]			
WOOD	Species of wood [MS]	Classify function	Date, cultural group	Use, symbolism, discard
LEATHER	Species of animal [MS]	Classify function	Date, cultural group	Use, symbolism, discard
TEXTILE	Species of animal	Classify function		
Dyes	Identify [CT]			
BONE, Antler, horn	Species [MS]	Function	Date, cultural group	Use, symbolism, discard

FIGURE 9.8 Artefact study – the menu.

Key: MS – microscope; TS – thin section; CT – Chromatography and see TABLE 9.1, p. 229.

as a record of what was done to it, and what was found out about it. Giving First Aid to finds and packing them is expert work and there are expert books about it, but FIG 9.9 shows something of the range of measures required.

Analysis

"Assemblage" means a collection of objects – either objects of the same kind spread across the site ("the pottery assemblage") or objects of different kinds in the same place ("a grave assemblage"). A context assemblage is simply that part of the context that was kept, i.e. not thrown away, whether it consists of artefacts, bones, plants, insects or soils. Assemblage analysis has three parallel programmes, with cross-overs. The first programme deals with artefacts – things made by people. Here we (mainly

specialists actually) seek to define types, work out where things were made, what they were used for, and which peoples preferred them. The second programme studies the natural materials, or biota, the bones, plants, insects and soils. Here the researchers (mainly specialists normally) identify types of natural matter (taxa) and decide what it means to find them on a site. Mostly these materials refer to the ancient people who lived and worked there: they belong to an anthropogenic assemblage; but some taxa will also refer to the broader landscape and its resources (an environmental assemblage). These two programmes of investigation give a name and a quantity to everything that was retrieved by the fieldwork.

The collaboration between the field archaeologists and the specialists then goes in two directions, both helpful. The field archaeologist brings together the newly identified artefacts and biota that were found in the same context on site. In a pit of burnt debris is a scatter of what turns out to be barley, with what turns out to be grain weevils, with what turns out to be oak charcoal: therefore, a grain dryer fired with oak. The weevil expert meanwhile is pleased to see them so far north and feeding on barley rather than wheat. So while the specialists provide interpretation to the field archaeologists' context, the field archaeologist offers context to the specialists' speciality. It is obvious that the most fruitful working relationships between field archaeologists and specialists are those that begin in the design stage and develop through dialogue on the site itself and then on into the lab.

The third programme investigates the combined assemblages at the level of the context, feature, structure and site, and asks what the combinations mean. Some associations are quickly identified, such as the grave goods in a grave – although not so quickly understood. Others are more scattered – the rubbish in a pit, the charcoal and burnt grain from a dryer – and it is not easy to know what things originally belonged together. Primary assemblages (like the grave goods in a grave) are few and far between; secondary, redeposited, assemblages are the norm, and we need much dialogue with other analyses – spatial and sequential – to re-assemble them. It is worth the trouble: assemblages are our principal evidence for the activities that happened on a site.

Artefacts

Artefact studies are traditionally distinguished by the material they are made of: flint, pottery, textile. It is not such a bad tradition, since objects of the same material are often associated in other ways, such as their function. We live in a world of mass production in which it is reasonably clear where a Peugeot or a bottle of Jim Beam is made and where it is distributed. It might be thought that, by contrast, in the pre-industrial era every artefact was an "original", but that does not seem to have been the case. Communities in their times shared a common vision of what an artefact should look like. Working backwards, then, a type of stone axe, or a type of pot ought

Material	What might be sticking to it	Cleaning	Dangers	First aid	Packaging	To museum
Stone	Paint, gilding	Wash/dry brush	Salts	Dampen	Wrap in black polythene	
Flint	Blood, vegetable matter	Wash/dry brush			Bag	
Shale, jet and amber		Lens brush/none	Change in temperature or humidity		In soil matrix in humidity as found	Immediately
Pottery	Paint, glaze, food residues	Earthenware: brush: otherwise wash-dry	Fragmentation of fabric or glaze	Consolidant	Polythene bag	
Iron	Mineralised organics	Light brush	Corrosion	Keep dry	Perforated polyether packaging: humidity less than 15%	
Copper alloy	Mineralised organics	Light brush	Corrosion		Polyether packaging: humidity less than 35%	
Silver, gold, lead, tin, zinc	Mineralised organics	Light brush	Corrosion		Polyether packaging: humidity less than 35%	
Glass	Metal	Light brush	Damp		Polyether packaging: humidity less than 15%	Immediate
Bone	Paint, pathology	Wash, brush, dry	Mould		Polythene bags	Immediate
Waterlogged organic materials	Vegetable, animal		Drying out	Keep wet and cold, in tank, fridge or damp foam.	Damp foam	

FIGURE 9.9 Finds care and packing.

1A Excavators preparing an archaeological surface showing prehistoric and medieval features at Portmahomack, north-east Scotland (FAS Ltd).

1B Archaeological strata seen from the side. Labelled layers of charcoal, soil and stones lie above the sandy subsoil (FAS Ltd).

2 Aerial photographs of cropmarks: (clockwise) ring ditches showing in wheat fields, ploughed out banks, and a settlement enhanced by infra-red film © English Heritage NMR.

3 Taking off the topsoil. The area to the lower left has been shaved by a back-blading Drott (at Level A). The area to the right has been shovel-scraped, removing the ridges (Level B) and is being cleaned at Level C; the rectangle at the top is being cleaned at Level D, and the graves exposed are being excavated at Level E. The photograph was taken from a kite, operated remotely (see kite string top right).

4A *Quadrants* used to study a mound at Sutton Hoo in 1989 (left). Some 20 years earlier, excavators had used *boxes* to study the adjacent mound at the same site (right).

Level B

Level D

Level E

4B *Recovery Levels* in action: from top to bottom: shovel scraping at Level B, fine trowelling at Level D and excavating a grave at Level E.

5A Feature excavation at Level D. The feature is a square stone hearth of the 9th century, cut away on two sides by later activity. As can be seen this a busy area in which nothing survived in one piece – a common situation in towns (FAS Ltd).

5B Record as you dig. Learning how to describe contexts and draw a plan of a small post-hole on a sandy flat site (Nigel Macbeth).

6 Unto dust we shall return: (clockwise) sand body under excavation at Sutton Hoo; foot of skeleton with preserved shoe (and big toe); skeleton with unidentified white deposit (FAS Ltd).

7 Mosaic pavement being revealed during rescue excavations at San Giusto in Puglia (courtesy of Giuliano Volpe).

8 High precision excavation in recently discovered Chinese tombs. Left: Tomb M3, Majiayuan, China: tableau of the vanished chariot with supporting soil baulks. Bottom right: lacquer surviving on the chariot box; top right: Defining varnish at Tomb 21 in the Jin Marquis cemetery (courtesy of Cultural Relics Press, China).

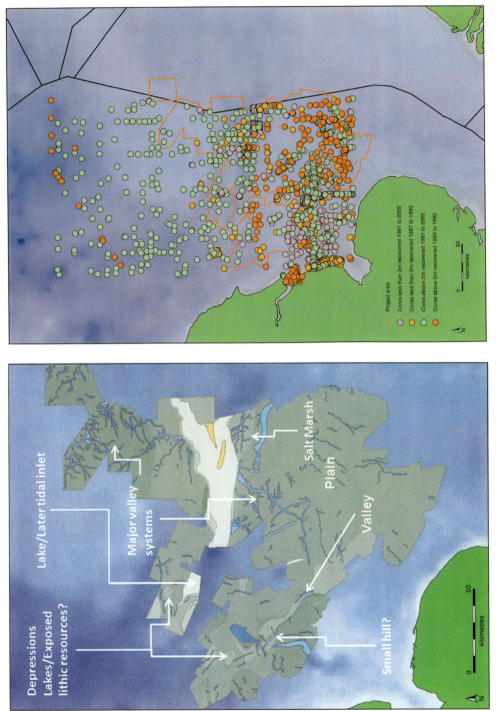

9 Remote underwater landscape mapping of the prehistoric topography of land drowned by the North Sea ("Doggerland") (left) using records from oil drilling (right) (courtesy of Vince Gaffney).

Left map labels:

Depressions
Lakes/Exposed lithic resources?

Lake/Later tidal inlet

Major valley systems

Small hill?

Valley

Salt Marsh

Plain

0   50
kilometres

N

Right map legend:

Project area

Cores less than 2m recovered 1991 to 2005
Cores less than 2m recovered 1987 to 1990
Cores above 2m recovered 1981 to 2005
Cores above 2m recovered 1980 to 1980

0   50
kilometres

N

10 Taking samples on site for dating and palaeoecological studies: (anti-clockwise) sample being taken for radiocarbon dating from a burnt layer in section; a column ("monolith") being taken with a three-sided plastic drain pipe for soil analysis; 30gm samples for soil pollen, their exact location being noted on the drawn section.

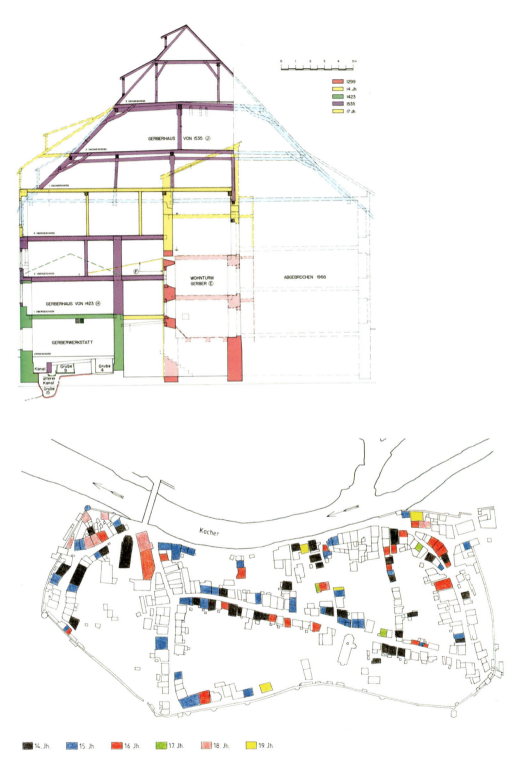

11 Dating structural timbers by dendrochronology: (top) different dates for timbers in the same house in Schaffhaussen; (bottom) a sequence of occupation at Katherinenvorstadt using the latest primary timbers (courtesy of Kurt Bänteli and Burghard Lohrum (1993), and Landesdenkmalamt Baden-Württemberg and the City of Zürich).

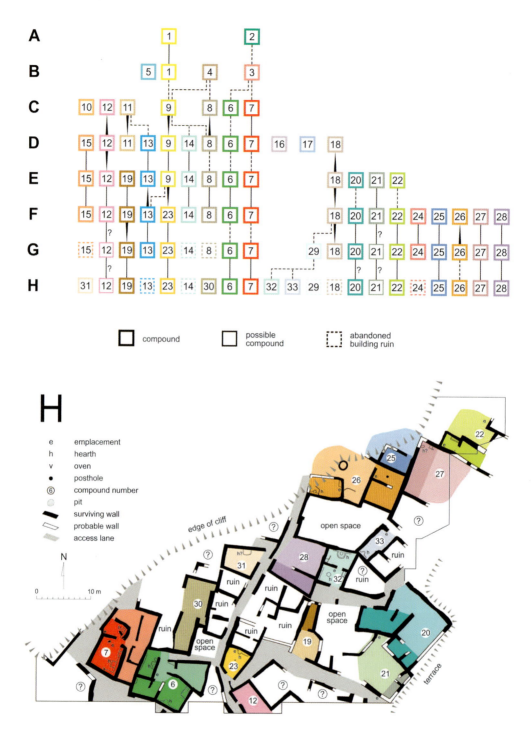

12 Sequencing a building complex at Marki, Cyprus: (top) the lifetimes of the neighbouring rooms, spread over seven phases (A–H), and (bottom) the final phase H (courtesy of David Frankel and Jennifer Webb).

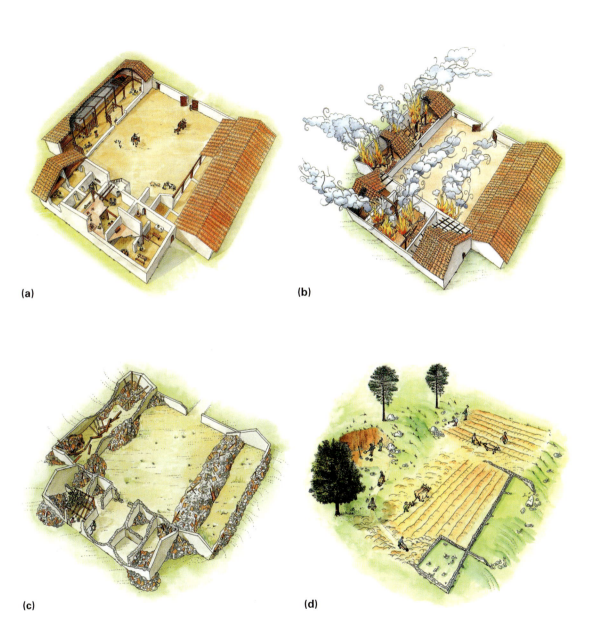

(a)

(b)

(c)

(d)

13 Site model in the form of an image sequence (a–d) of the 7th century palace at Monte Barro, Italy (courtesy of Gian-Pietro Brogiolo and Lanfredo Castelletti).

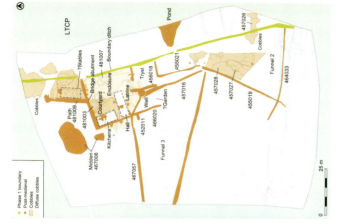

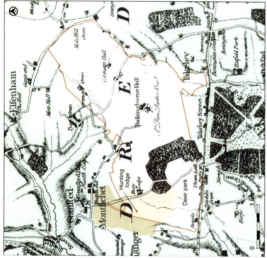

Fallow deer bone

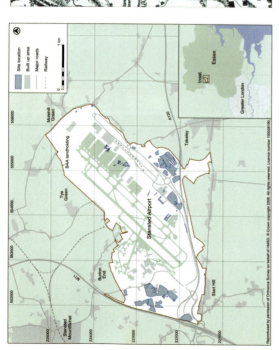

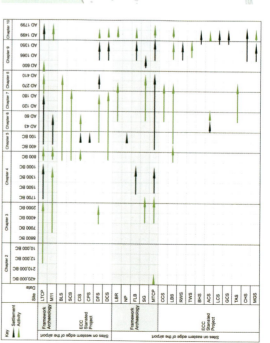

14 Framework's investigations at Stansted Airport: (clockwise) map showing locations of excavations; map of 1777 – the airport was once a deer park; excavated deer hunting lodge, with distribution of deer bones timeline for all discoveries (courtesy of Framework Ltd.).

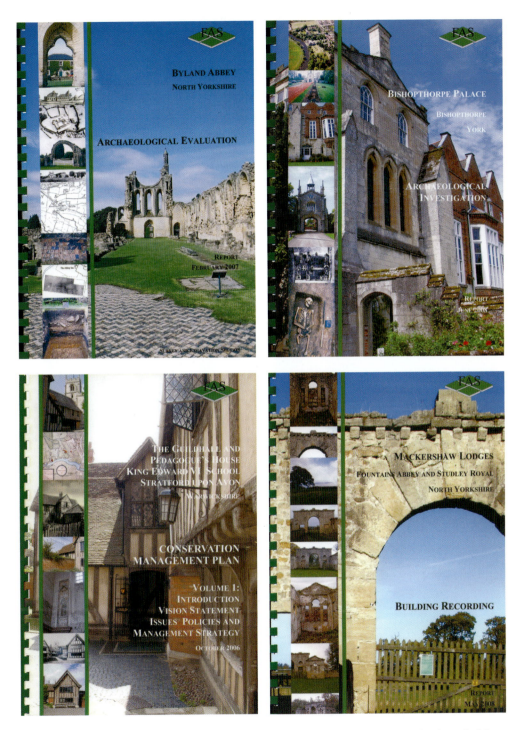

15 Examples of client reports issued by FAS Ltd: (clockwise) an evaluation; an investigation; a buildings recording project; and a conservation plan (courtesy of FAS Ltd).

16 Some professional fieldworkers: (from top): excavator (wearing a name badge, on a building site); excavation supervisor teaching; a buildings archaeologist; an excavation recorder; a finds supervisor; a project manager.

to give us a group of people and a date. A whole branch of the archaeological profession depends on this premise – that an artefact gives a voice to its people and time. There are specialists for flint tools, pottery, metalwork, for carved stone and woodwork, for coins, for upper Palaeolithic figurines, for Roman lamps, for 18th century crockery. And each of these artefact-sets has the capacity to tell us about the economy, social life and the spiritual outlook of their makers and users.

For our purposes, I do not propose to intrude greatly into the specialist workplace, where in any case I am hardly qualified to be more than an admiring guest. But it will be worth outlining the general procedure and some of the methodologies employed, so we know what is going on in there (FIG 9.8). Every artefact is made of something – stone, metal, wood – to which we can give the general term *fabric*. It has a shape, or *form*. And it has a particular ornamental idiosyncrasy, or *style*. Fabric, form and style together combine to make a *type* (FIG 9.10). In addition every artefact has a *history*, or to use the fashionable term, a biography, the story of what happened to it since it was made. Thus a flint tool is made of flint (or chert) quarried from a seam of raw material and has been shaped for a purpose – scraper, arrow-head, axe – and the act of shaping introduces certain peculiarities of flaking or pointing. These stylistic

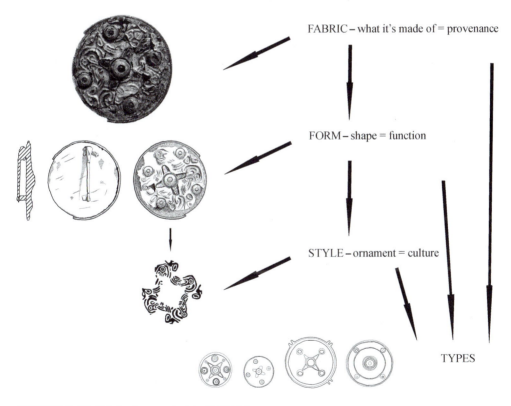

FIGURE 9.10 Fabric, form and style (FAS Ltd).

variants may belong to a general pattern (an arrow-head which is barbed and tanged), or they may be a one-off – your true original. Specialists are in permanent discourse on this topic: is a feature an original or does it link with others? A flint implement also has a history of use. It may have been retouched, to sharpen it up and prolong its life; it may have been given a polish from cutting wheat; it may have the traces of blood on it from a victim's chest. And it may have been broken in use, or broken deliberately and deposited in the ground in propitiation of some god.

In general, fabric leads us to provenance – where something was made, or at least where its raw materials came from. Form implies function – what an object was used for. Style suggests cultural association and date. And history tells us what happened to it, and thereby, its role in its contemporary and later societies. Some of this will only emerge later in the discourse between field archaeologist and specialist. But most of it is firmly on the specialist's agenda.

How do they go about it? Much of the skill lies in familiarity, and we non-experts may be easily impressed. Having seen hundreds of thousands of examples and having a mysterious affection for the objects – flint implements or pots or whatever – the specialist has mastered a kind of language; pots and flints seem to talk to them (not literally one hopes). It seems they only have to look at a bag of sherds or flints to pronounce a diagnosis to its owner, in the manner of a wine connoisseur or Sherlock Holmes: "Ah, I see you have been digging a later Neolithic site in Dorset – a pit group from an interrupted-ditched enclosure? Am I right? I'll take a guess: Windmill Hill, south side."

The modern specialist has lost none of this capacity to amaze, but they draw heavily now on scientific analysis. A whole range of techniques is applied to characterising *fabric*, by breaking it down into its constituents – compounds, molecules, elements and isotopes of elements (TABLE 9.1).

The stone of a stone axe is a particular geological compound (e.g. greensand) and can be traced to the outcrop which must have given it birth (e.g. Langdale Pike). Some rocks have their own giveaway signatures: oolitic limestones have different kinds of fossils. Obsidian, a volcanic glass contains different quantities of zirconium and barium, depending on which volcano it threw itself out of. Metals are usually alloys, and the mix may be significant: a little more tin than zinc in 6th century brooches, a little more silver in 7th century gold coins.

The methods used to determine the constituents of *fabrics* are intended to be non-destructive as far as possible. Some methods identify the component elements or their isotopes, by heating up a sample and looking for the tell-tale light emitted (spectroscopy), agitating the nucleus by bombarding it (activation) or measuring its nuclear spin (resonance). The output is the same: the relative quantities of different chemicals present. The hope is that each mixture is made to a slightly different recipe, so that they can be divided into types, and the types will lead to different dates or

TABLE 9.1 Scientific methods of classifying fabrics

X-RAY Diffraction [XRD] determines the crystal structure of solids (e.g. salt, slag)

X-RAY Fluorescence [XRF] assesses concentrations of trace elements on surfaces (e.g. glass, obsidian, clay crucibles and moulds)

NEUTRON ACTIVATION Analysis [NAA] assesses concentrations of trace elements using gamma rays released by bombardments of nuclei (e.g. flint, glass, coins, pottery)

ATOMIC ABSORBTION Spectroscopy [AAS] assesses concentrations of elements from spectra produced by absorbed light (e.g. metal alloys)

NUCLEAR MAGNETIC RESONANCE [NMR] assesses concentrations of elements from spectra produced by nuclei (e.g. metal alloys)

INDUCTIVELY COUPLED PLASMA [ICP] Emission spectroscopy assesses concentrations of elements in any sample.

ELECTRON MICROSCOPE produces scanning micrographs (like photographs) of very small objects (around 10^{-6} metres) (e.g. pollen, phytoliths, parasites)

HEAVY MINERAL ANALYSIS identifies minerals present in pottery and in the geological deposits used to make them (e.g. ceramics)

THIN SECTIONING identifies minerals present in pottery by inspection of the polished edge of a sherd (pottery)

places of manufacture. However the variations between one mixture and another may be very slight, and the differences between them lie not so much in the presence/absence of one or two elements as in their relative quantities, which vary slightly from specimen to specimen. Every cake contains flour, raisins and sultanas, but their relative quantities vary between the outputs of Mr Kipling and Mrs Beeton. Because the variations are so slight, specialists make use of statistical pattern-seeking packages to define the types. Correspondence analysis, for example, sets up a long line of examples (e.g. of metal alloys) in which each one stands next to the one it most resembles. The result may be to put the objects in groups with similar alloys – which hopefully indicates groups with different places of manufacture (provenance); or a series in which the mix gradually varies from one extreme to the other – which ought to indicate that time is passing (see Chapter 11 for an example of correspondence analysis).

A similar trick can be pulled using *form*. Bronze brooches may not show too much systematic variation in alloy (suppose they are all made from recycled coins?). But the variation in their shape might be more promising. In this case it is the *form* that is broken down into its components, or attributes – the foot, the bow, the catchplate. Pattern-seeking programmes may be used to find similar groups (provenance) or to suggest an evolutionary chain, in which one type of brooch gives way to another, and another and another, through time. Whatever the statistical package applied, the

general practice of putting things in order by virtue of their content is known as seriation. As we shall see, seriation can be applied not just to artefacts, but to whole assemblages.

Style is the part most resistant to scientific analysis, since the system that science is trying to deconstruct is not just elusive – it may never have existed at all. In communities that practised mass production we can perhaps talk of system: the ornament stamped on Roman and Saxon pottery like a trade mark, and 18th and 19th century Wedgwood or Coleport may follow a pattern book that varies by year and factory. But hand-made objects may draw on a wide range of ornament – a combination that is of its time, but highly individual. A Pictish cross-slab from the far north of Scotland, made of local stone, may take its form from Roman models, and in its ornament may refer to Ireland, England and Scandinavia as well as its own local Iron Age. And as for the iconography, it shows some stories that must refer to local events; but others refer to events that are described in the Bible and took place in the Bible lands in the eastern Mediterranean many thousands of miles away.

The way that artefacts change their fabric, form and style is complex and intriguing and there may be no one theory that will work everywhere. Some have seen changing form or style as a kind of evolution, where the artefacts appear to be trying to perfect their form to their purpose. This is a functional view of life. For others the artefact is a little archive of social messages, indicating allegiance to family and folk rather than utility. For others artisans simply copy and refer unconsciously to earlier forms. Our own experience as consumers tells us that within communities sets of particular artefacts are often found in use together – groupings that early 20th century archaeologists termed *cultures or culture groups* and associated with a particular people. Grave goods and objects recovered from single-period sites define these cultures which can be used to build up and map detailed *culture histories* based on their occurrence in certain places at certain periods. This methodology still forms the backbone of the archaeological sequence in most continents. However, we have other ways of dating the appearance of objects on site these days (see Chapter 11), and there have long been reservations that the "culture" can really be equated with a people or ethnic group, rather than being adapted or adopted in whole or in part by particular communities for their own ideological or political purposes. But artefact analysers are tireless in their search for hidden systems, and are becoming ever more skilful at defining and distinguishing the functional and the symbolic, two of the key motivations in manufacture.

As the output of the artefact analysis phase we should look for a typology for the fabric, form and styles of artefacts of each material, with opinions on the date, culture and provenance these indicate. This information will be collected in Specialist Reports, which will find their eventual home in the research files of the Lab Reports, and play a key role in all synthesis and publication.

Biota

Like the artefacts, the harvest of biological material is apportioned between experts (some of whom may of course be already "in-house") for their analysis and reports (FIG 9.11). We are looking for specialists to identify the soils, the bones (human and animal), the plants and the insects. Each of these parts of the natural system has a long tradition of study and there is a massive accumulation of knowledge worldwide. We are now in a field where we can reasonably expect the natural data to be predictable and consistent: here we are not trying to define new types, but to identify taxa (types of animal and plant which already exist and have names). Specialists here work with large "reference collections", which they use to identify the species of animal, plant or insect, of which we have retrieved only a dead bit.

One part of biota analysis contributes to the understanding of what people did on site, their *activity*: for example the remains of cows and pigs and cereals were probably

Source	Material	Identify/analyse	Quantify	Purpose of analysis
Primary contexts	Animal bone	Animal, part of body, trauma, age at death, sex	MNI	Diet, economy
Sieving	Small vertebrates (e.g. rodents, insectivores, amphibians)	Animal	MNI	Micro-environment
Sieving	Birds and fish	Species		Diet, economy environment
Primary contexts	Molluscs	Species		Environment
Sieving	Snails	Species		Environment
Flotation from samples	Insects	Species		Micro-environment
Graves	Human bone	Species: age, sex, trauma	MNI	Health, demography
	Human teeth	C/N isotope		Diet
	Human teeth	O/Sr isotope		Childhood home
Flotation	Plant matter, seeds, charcoal	Taxa		Plant use micro-environment
Column/ grabsample	Pollen phytoliths	Taxa		Micro-environment environment
Kubiena	Soil	Micromorphology		Soil history

FIGURE 9.11 Biota analysis – the menu. MNI is minimum number of individuals.

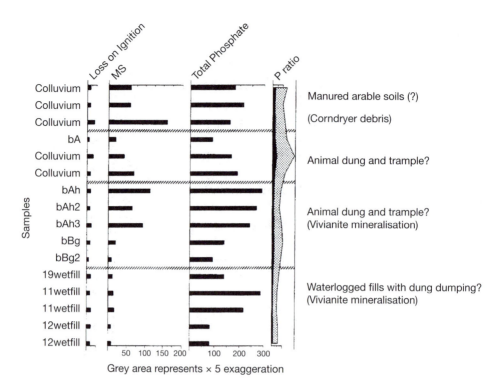

Colluvium — Manured arable soils (?)

Colluvium

Colluvium — (Corndryer debris)

bA

Colluvium — Animal dung and trample?

Colluvium

bAh

bAh2 — Animal dung and trample?

bAh3 — (Vivianite mineralisation)

bBg

bBg2

19wetfill — Waterlogged fills with dung dumping?

11wetfill — (Vivianite mineralisation)

11wetfill

12wetfill

12wetfill

Samples

Loss on Ignition / MS / Total Phosphate / P ratio

50 100 150 200 100 200 300

Grey area represents × 5 exaggeration

FIGURE 9.12 Some chemical signatures of soils (Gill Cruise and Richard Macphail).

farmed and collected by humans for their own purposes (an *anthropogenic assemblage*). The other part informs us about the natural habitat in and around the site, i.e. the rats and frogs and nettles that make their own way in (an *environmental assemblage*). Many types of animals and plants (taxa of fauna and flora) contribute to both: fish, birds and mammals living wild reveal the local habitat. But when captured or killed they become part of the economy.

Each type of specialist has their own rule book, manual and procedures. Soil scientists have defined families of naturally generated soils and can sometimes recognise them (or their disturbed remains) on site. Chemical tests, such as the amount of carbon or phosphorous, distinguish arable soil from midden (FIG 9.12). Micromorphology shows the components of a soil close up, from which experts identify relic lumps of previous natural regimes in the mixture. The soil block taken in the field (in a Kubiena box) is baked and then a thin slice sawn off. Under the microscope this slice carries a memory of the events that formed it: its time supporting a forest, a time of clearance, a time of cultivation, and a lean white soil where it lost its fertility (and became a podsol).

Human bone specialists (physical anthropologists) identify bones by member (e.g. tibia) and for very ancient specimens, by species (e.g. *homo ergaster*). *Homo sapiens*

FIGURE 9.13 The human skeleton. (a) A medieval family in Stafford and (b) skeleton recording form.

(one of us) is usually found in a grave, reasonably complete (FIG 9.13). The specialist assesses the sex, stature and age at death of each individual and any trauma they have suffered that left its marks on the bones. But excavated humans now offer the archaeologist more than their anatomy: memories of diet and birthplace are carried in chemicals in the bones. The things you eat accumulate in bone collagen in the form of stable isotopes of carbon and nitrogen, and the quantities of the particular isotopes differ in fish and in ruminant animals and in the people that eat them. So the bones can distinguish between a maritime and a terrestrial diet. Teeth absorb oxygen and strontium isotopes from water and the water gets a certain isotopic "signature" from the local rocks. The signature of the local isotopes gets into a child's teeth, and stays there. So by looking at the stable isotopes of a dead person's teeth you can (sometimes) locate their childhood home. Recent analysis of carbon and nitrogen results is raising exciting questions on whether Neolithic people ate fish (Mesolithic people did), while the patterns of oxygen and strontium isotopes report on the mobility of people: in Britain they have been pretty mobile since the Neolithic, and in the early

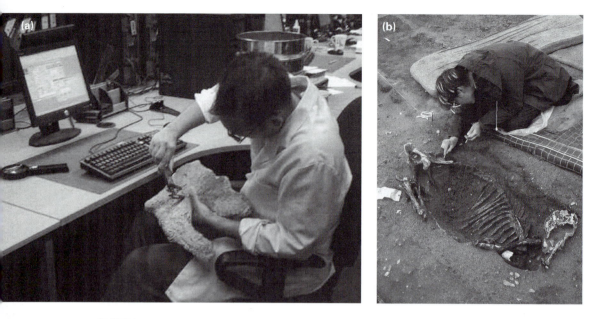

FIGURE 9.14 Analysing animal bone in the office (a) and on site (b).

middle ages moved into England from north, east, south and west. Living individuals and their descendants can be distinguished by DNA, but extracting and reconstructing the ancient DNA (aDNA) from bone or other archaeological remains is proving difficult to do. Progress with biomolecular analysis (see later) should soon close this gap.

Animal specialists (palaeozoologists) identify all the bones by member (tibia) to species (*bos primogenus*) and work out the minimum number of individuals (MNI) present (one leg implies at least one animal) (FIG 9.14). From anthropogenic assemblages you can then appreciate the ancient preference of sheep, cow, pig in the diet, phase by phase – also whether they are being bred for meat, or milk or traction, and together this adds up to a statement of the economy. Animal specialists are also interested in the species of the animals themselves, domestic and wild, and the ecosystem they belonged to. They have their own questions, so collaboration is important to all parties.

Snails and insects (not usually farmed) show something of the surroundings, on site and off it since they flourish in certain specific environments. Snails (FIG 9.15) distinguish open country and woodland. Insect specialists (palaeoentomologists) probably have more taxa to cope with than anyone else (FIG 9.16). Insects are anarchic creatures: they get everywhere. But because the different types are specific feeders they choose their pitch carefully: a pile of dung, a patch of grass, someone's head. Some insects prefer to be outdoors, others live inside. Insect assemblages are thus indicators of vanished local conditions.

Zone	Species	Environment	Radiocarbon dates BP
y	*Pupilla, Vallonia* and *Vitrina*	Periglacial	13 160 p/m 400 to 11530 p/m 160
z	*Pupilla, Abida, Vallonia, Trichia, Columella, columella, Nesovitrea hammonis*	Open ground	11 530 p/m 160 to 9820 p/m 90
a	Decline of *Pupilla;* appearance of *Carychium tridentatum, Vitrea, Aegopinella*	Open ground	9760 p/m 100 to 9530 p/m 75
b	*Carychium tridentatum, Aegopinella, Discus ruderatus*	Woodland	9460 p/m 140 to 8630 p/m 120
c	*Discus ruderatus* replaced by *Discus rotundatus*	Woodland	8630 p/m 120 to 7650 p/m 80
d	*Oxychilus cellarius, Spermodea, Leiostyla, Acicula*	Woodland	7650 p/m 80 to 5620 p/m 90
e	*Re-expansion of Vallonia.* Decline of shade-loving species	Open ground	5620 p/m 90 to 3980 p/m 70
f	Appearance of *Helix aspersa*	Open ground	From 2870 p/m 70

FIGURE 9.15 Snail story. Environmental sequence obtained during the Eurotunnel Project, at Holywell Coombe (Folkestone, Kent), as derived from land snails found in successive radiocarbon-dated zones. (p/m means plus or minus).

Order *Ordonata* (dragonflies) – aquatic deposits

Order *Dermaptera* (earwigs) – dead and decaying plants and animals

Order *Phthiraptera* (biting and sucking lice) – biting lice associated with birds and blood-sucking lice with blood of mammals

Order *Hemiptera* (true bugs) – sap of plants or blood-sucking; some are host-specific

Order *Coleoptera* (beetles) – occur in every terrestrial and aquatic habitat; some species host-specific; aquatic and some aquatic coleoptera are specific to stagnant or free free-flowing water.

(This is the order with the greatest palaeoecological value)

Order *Siphonaptera* (fleas) – feed on blood of birds and mammals

Order *Diptera* (flies) – identifiable larval heads of *Chironomidae* (midges) can be very common in lake sediments; sensitive to water quality and temperature; *Spaeroceridae* (sewage and seaweed flies) have proved useful in identifying middens and cesspits

Order *Trichoptera* (caddis flies) – some species fastidious in their water requirements

Order *Hymenoptera* (bugs, wasps and ants) – apart from the honey bee *(Apis mellifera)* and ants, have proved very difficult to identify; galls formed in plants to protect larvae survive in deposits

FIGURE 9.16 Examples of orders of insects found on archaeological sites and what they indicate.

Plants are the stuff of life, and make both anthropogenic and environmental contributions to the story. Plant matter is brought into a settlement for an infinity of reasons: to eat, for medicine, to sleep on, to thatch the roofs, to build, to make things, to burn as fuel. Sadly, conditions on the majority of sites destroy the botanical fraction almost entirely. Where plants survive, on anaerobic and wetland sites, we are always astonished at how important they were. By contrast the generality of deposits, rich in bacteria, may leave us little more than burnt seeds and spikelets carefully extracted by flotation and treasured. Pollen on the other hand is well nigh indestructible, but is highly mobile, blowing off trees and other plants and collecting in soils at a distance. Most useful is the pollen in lakes and bogs accumulated over time, which chronicles a sequence of the environment, relating to a region rather than a specific site (FIG 9.17).

(a) STAFFORD KING'S POOL

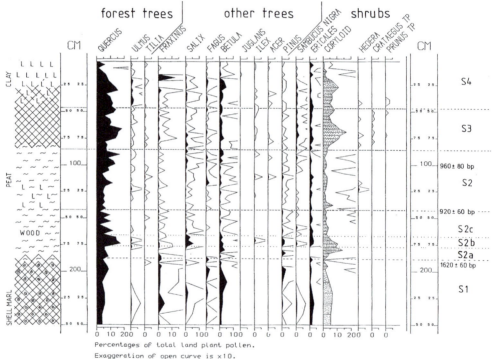

Percentages of total land plant pollen.
Exaggeration of open curve is x10.

(b)

FIGURE 9.17 (a) Pollen diagram, showing the variation in plants with depth from a marsh outside Stafford town; (b) how the samples were taken, with a Russian borer.

Investigations at micro-chemical level are proceeding at a great pace, and will surely revolutionise not just the interpretation of an assemblage, but the whole way we do archaeology. Early progress was made in finding what was in a pot by extracting the residues (lipids) of plants and animals that had been absorbed in the fabric. In this way pork, beef and dairy products have been detected and distinguished in pots that are apparently now empty (FIG 9.18). New methods have managed to extract and identify proteins – for example proteins derived from whale blubber were detected in potsherds from Alaska. Proteins are identified from their sequence of peptides, and the number of combinations is mind-blowing (estimated as 4.9×10^{211}). "Archaeoproteomics" is thus a method of huge potential, anticipating the identification from minute quantities of plants and animals and even of animals that are now extinct.

As mentioned above, the potential of aDNA should soon be realised. Work reported from Greenland as I write describes a sequence of "dirt aDNA" from a soil column that offers a dated narrative of grazing animals, human occupation and human disappearance, matched in this case by the excavation sequence of a neighbouring Norse farmhouse. It seems likely that "The Farm beneath the Sand", as the site was called, will be seen as the point of departure for a new kind of archaeological investigation, in which the story of human and other biological activity in any place on the planet can theoretically be deduced.

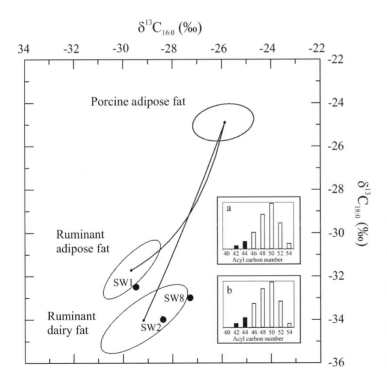

FIGURE 9.18 Lipids extracted from three prehistoric potsherds (SW1, 2 and 8) compared with results from modern pork, beef and dairy products . . . (Berstan et. al. 2008).

Interpreting site assemblages

The potential output for the assemblage analyses is informative at several different scales. Some analyses define types of artefact and natural materials and where they come from. These may refer to a general predominance on the site, or a particular phase or even a particular feature (like a grave). These materials are imported by people (anthropogenic) and are put to use by the inhabitants, so can be read as part of their economy or their symbolic lives. Other analyses show microenvironments, for example where insects have gathered at a particular place on the site, indicating what was there. Other taxa, such as snails and pollen, are informative about the broader environment of the surroundings: its woods and rivers and wildlife. The assemblages thus feed directly into these questions: what were the activities that took place on site? What resources, for food, for building, for ritual, were drawn on by the inhabitants phase by phase through time? And what was the local environment like, and how did it change?

Of these, reading activity from site assemblages is currently the most difficult – and the most rewarding. Some have a long tradition of study: the contents of a grave for example (FIG 9.19). There is not much doubt what a grave was for, but considerably more about what it means. The body was placed in a hole and laid out there, together with chosen objects placed in certain positions. This forms a tableau which must have

FIGURE 9.19 Assemblage: a richly furnished grave: Tomb M895 at Liuwan, Ledu, Qinghai, China (Sarah Allan 2005).

had an intended expression – it had *agency*. Experts have seriated grave assemblages, using correspondence analysis, hoping that they show changes which reflect the passage of time. And so they may. But the idea of agency is that a person (an actor) can put in what they like – they may choose heirlooms to signal a deep ancestry. So it can be safer to put graves in order using scientific dating (radiocarbon) and then decide how the assemblages change (more on this in Chapter 11).

Other kinds of activities are traditionally interpreted from a scatter of objects: broken pots and animal bones suggest cooking or a feast; flakes of plaster, nails, fragments of daub show where a building had been. A pit full of dark brown gunge is said to be a cess pit and a pit full of bits and pieces a rubbish pit. These identifications are weakened where there is no good organic preservation. Pits also often live a double life – in use and afterwards. The famous Pit 13 from Cuckoo Lane, Southampton, had a wooden floor and was originally a cess pit with a rich assemblage of plum stones and apple pips in its dark lower levels. But when its residents departed they threw an incredible quantity of jugs, glass, metalwork, leather and even architectural blocks into their privy. These things had obviously not passed through the human system, but had sunk to the bottom by their own weight, a sample of life in the 13th century house of which this was the smallest room.

However we are much less satisfied by these top-of-the-head identifications these days: artefacts, biota and chemical analyses increasingly work together to give a more detailed and individual aspect to on-site assemblages. Just three examples will have to suffice. At a protohistoric monastery in Scotland, Cecily Spall recorded and retrieved a curved knife, a bone needle, three pumice stones, 16 flints, 25 small round pebbles, three rows of cattle metapodials and a pile of alkaline ash from the yard a house (FIG 9.20). Analogies drawn from modern practitioners showed that these are the waste products of parchment-makers: a tank for tawing the hide with an astringent ash derived from shells, pegs and pebbles for stretching the skin on a frame, stone rubbers for smoothing the surface. So even though there were no hides or parchment or stretching frames in evidence– making parchment is almost certainly what they were doing.

At York, Allan Hall and Harry Kenward have combined plants and insects to propose "indicator groups" for certain crafts and even for stages of manufacture (FIG 9.21). Making textiles potentially leaves behind indestructible pollen of hemp or flax, fragments of sheep keds and lice, and the occasional rather particular tool – spindle whorls, loom weights and tweezers. Fragments of teasels show that cloth was being finished; and of madder, woad, and clubmoss, that it was being dyed.

My last example looks to the future power of the microassemblage. Studying strata on tell sites in Mesopotamia, Roger and Wendy Matthews could see that floor areas consisted of many thin layers; these were sampled, examined under the microscope and broken down into their components. Looking at the thin lenses in micromorphology samples, they could see where the ground had been trodden, and where it

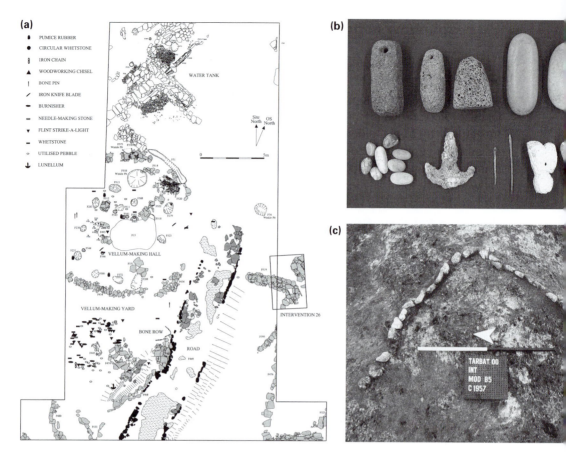

(a)

- PUMICE RUBBER
- CIRCULAR WHETSTONE
- IRON CHAIN
- WOODWORKING CHISEL
- BONE PIN
- IRON KNIFE BLADE
- BURNISHER
- NEEDLE-MAKING STONE
- FLINT STRIKE-A-LIGHT
- WHETSTONE
- UTILISED PEBBLE
- LUNELLUM

WATER TANK

VELLUM-MAKING HALL

VELLUM-MAKING YARD

BONE ROW

ROAD

INTERVENTION 26

(b)

(c)

TARBAT 00
INT
MOD B5
C 1957

FIGURE 9.20 The detection of parchment-making at Portmahomack. The plan (a) shows the distribution of knives, pebbles, pumice rubbers and needles (b) and bones, (c) that are diagnostic of the craft (FAS Ltd).

had been exposed to wind and rain, so distinguishing indoors from out and mapping pathways. Phytoliths from plants showed where mats had been laid. Small pellets of calcium carbonate were the mineral traces of vanished cattle dung, either from standing cattle, or from dung brought into houses as fuel. At Çatalhöyük colleagues plotted chemical components in the floors using ICP spectrometry and noting variations in the quantities of titanium, aluminium, calcium and potassium. Ethnological studies (i.e. variations found on the floors of modern Turkish farm buildings) helped to explain the patterns: for example calcium showed where floors had been finished with plaster, and potassium mapped the ash in the cooking areas (FIG 9.22). Recent analysis of middens at the same site distinguished charred grasses, wood, seeds, phytoliths, ash, dung, plaster, mud-brick, bone and faecal samples including deoxycholic acid indicating human bile: the microstratigraphy of the middens showed a cyclical rhythm of deposition.

	Plant remains	Animal remains	Artefacts
Fibre production, extraction and initial processing	Remains of hemp (*Cannabis sativa* L.) and flax (*Linum usitatissimum* L.)	Wool (and bones of sheep!): sheep keds (*Melophagas ovinus* (Linnaeus)); sheep lice (*Damalinia ovis* (Schrank))	Bale pins, wool-combs, the ripples, flax pounders, flux scutching tool
Spinning			Spindles, distaff, spindle whorls, yarn fragments
Weaving			Loom weights, sword-beater, pin-beaters, weft-bobbins, wet beaters, heddle cradle and rod
Dyeing	Remains of following: roots of madder (*Rubia tinctorum* L.), stems of dyers' greenweed (*Genista tinctoria* L.), pods of woad (*Isatis tinctoria* L.) and stems of a clubmoss (*Diphasiastrum complanatum* L.) Perhaps also seeds of 'weld' (*Reseda luteola* L.)		
Fulling and lentering			Tenterhooks, shearboard hook, tweezers
Finishing (including teasing)	Receptacular bracts of teasel (*Dipsacus sativus* L.)		Slick-stones linen-smoothers, shears, needles
Finished textiles			Fragments of cloth, remains of recognisable articles of clothing.

FIGURE 9.21 Hall and Kenward's Craft Indicator Package (Allan Hall).

This kind of microanalytical procedure resembles the methods of police work as employed in Crime Scene Investigation. Indeed it has acquired the erroneous tag of "forensic" (= lawcourt) archaeology, but it might be better named *trace archaeology* since we use it to track the passage of ancient activities from minute traces. These are early days for the detective science of the microassemblage, but it has a great future.

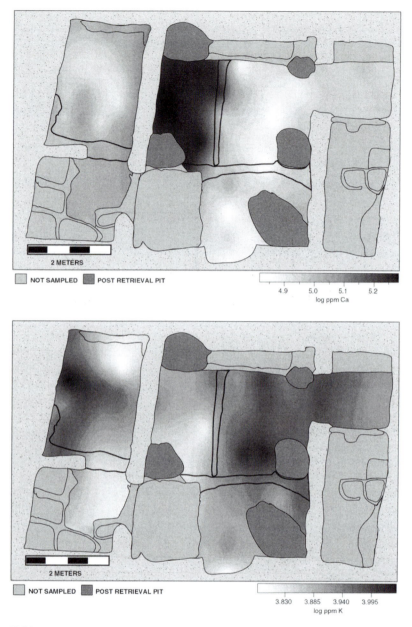

2 METERS

☐ NOT SAMPLED ☐ POST RETRIEVAL PIT

4.9   5.0   5.1   5.2
log ppm Ca

2 METERS

☐ NOT SAMPLED ☐ POST RETRIEVAL PIT

3.830 3.885 3.940 3.995
log ppm K

FIGURE 9.22 Chemical mapping at Çatalhöyük. Calcium (above) and potassium (below). (McDonald Institute).

Briefing

Mannoni and Molinari 1990, Brothwell and Pollard 2001 and Bahn and Renfrew 2008 give succinct **overviews** of techniques of analysis for artefacts and biological material.

For **retrieval on site:** James 1997; Payne 1972 (sieving); Payton 1992 (lifting objects), Shopland 2006 (onsite handling), A. Millard 2001 (state of bone), Davidson and Simpson 2001 (soil samples). **Conservation:** Watkinson and Neal 1998 *First Aid for finds* is the handy handbook for protecting artefacts on site; for what happens in the lab: Plenderleith and Werner 1971 (the classic), Cronyn 1990 (the modern).

Hodges 1989 and Henderson 2000 are comprehensive general reviews of **artefacts** and what they are made of. Richards and Ryan 1985 (15–18), for how to break down artefacts into data; Read 2007 is an advanced treatise on classification by a mathematician with a wealth of analytical experience (especially ceramics). For identifying and classifying **lithics**, Edmonds 1995, 2001; **ceramics:** Rice 1987, Middleton and Freestone 1991, Gibson and Wood 1997, Freestone and Gaimster 1997, Henderson 2000, Chapter 4, Whitbread 2001, Peacock 1969 and Williams 1990 (use of minerals in rocks to track the provenance of ceramics); **glass:** Henderson 2000, 2001; **metals:** Tylecote 1986, Henderson 2000, Chapter 5 (with large bibliography); **slags**, Backmann 1982; **bone, antler, ivory, horn:** MacGregor 1985; **residues in pots:** Berstan et al 2008, Evershed et al 2001, Heron and Evershed 1993. Examples of the use of gas chromatography and mass spectroscopy to determine **provenance** from the proportions of trace elements and compounds will be found in Mukherjee et al 2008 (amber), Henderson 2000 (309–14), Carter et al 2008 (obsidian).

On **cultures and ethnicity** see Trigger 1978, 83–4.

Start to explore the giant field of **biota** with Evans and O'Connor 1999. Points of departure for different aspects of the natural world will be found in Brothwell and Pollard 2001, and for **soil and sediments**, Kubiena 1953 (inventor of the eponymous box), Calaway 2005, Barham and Macphail 1995, with micromorphology in action further explained by Davidson et al 1992, Davidson and Simpson 2001 and French 2003 (and see Chapter 1); Cruise and Macphail 2000 for microstratigraphy, and see micro-assemblages, below. **Human remains:** Brothwell 1982, Cox and Mays 2000; **cremated remains:** McMinn et al 1987, McKinley et al 1993, McKinley and Bond 2001; **teeth:** Hillson 1986; **faeces** Canti 1998; **blood residues:** Cattaneo et al 1991, Hyland et al 1990, Loy and Dixon 1998; **plague victims:** Gowland and Chamberlain 2005; **analysing skeletal remains in USA:** Grauer 1995; **animal remains:** best is probably O'Connor 2000 with the same author's edited collection (2005) on bone survival, diagenesis. Also Schmid 1972, Hesse and Wapnish 1985, Rackham 1994, Reitz and Wing 1999, Jones and O'Connor 2001; **birds:** Gilbert et al 1985; **fish:** Wheeler and Jones 1989; **shells** Claassen 1998; **land snails** Evans 1972; **diatoms** Matiskainen and Alhonen,1984; **insects:** Kenward 1978, Robinson M. 2001; **plants:** Renfrew 1973; Hillman 1981 (charred grain). **Ancient environment:** Fieller et al 1985, Evans and O'Connor 1999, Dincauze 2000, French 2003 (sediments), Moore et al 1991 (pollen).

M.K. Jones 2002 for an overview of **biomolecular** methods (especially DNA); **ancient DNA:** T.A. Brown 2001, with Mulligan 2006 on why it's hard to do; using

stable isotopes in bones to indicate diet and teeth to identify childhood homes, Bentley et al 2007 (Pacific), Budd et al 2004 (Britain). Lipid residues in pots: **milk products:** Copley et al 2005, Craig et al 2005; the annual conference on Biomolecular archaeology is a good way to keep track on progress in studies of aDNA and **proteomics** and see *Antiquity* for accessible summaries of the new methods.

Inferred activity: Platt and Coleman-Smith 1975 for the Cuckoo Lane pit, Carver and Spall 2004 (parchment-making at Portmahomack); **micro-assemblages:** Wendy Matthews 2005, Middleton et al 2005 (floors at Çatalhöyük), Shillito et al 2008 (at Çatalhöyük); **indicator groups:** Hall et al 1983, Kenward and Hall 1995, Hall 2002, Hall and Kenward 2003.

10 SPACE

Scales of space

Space informs us at every scale. On my desk is a laptop, various piles of half-done work, some borrowed books and a cold cup of coffee – the typical organised chaos of student, teacher or writer. Within my room, the disposition of the furniture indicates function (card-playing, eating, TV watching, sprawling) and proclaims taste and economic circumstances (late 1970s random acquisition style). Inside the house, the plan of the passages and doors reports on the number of resident people and pets, their relative energy, their work, play, sleep, coupling. In the garden are bushy bits and open bits – more function and taste. The village has a plan too – 4 farms, 43 houses, a pond and a pub which map out into an arena of working agriculture with twee residential patches. The village is one of five along the River Derwent's flood plain, all medieval in origin, with fields, water meadows and dykes. After that we could have a look at the larger picture – Yorkshire, the North Sea community, the new Europe, the Atlantic alliance and so on. So the use of space is social use and spatial analysis is about people, and it happens at very different scales.

In the field, the capture of space begins at the design stage, with work programmes for mapping the site, its immediate surroundings and its region, each of them a target for investigation (see Chapter 3). On a site, *location* is the parameter that every record has in common, and in archaeology location is measured very precisely – normally to the nearest 5mm. The distribution of objects tells us what is going on in a context. The relation of contemporary contexts may suggest a feature; contemporary features may make a structure. The map of structures and the paths between them weave the lattice of a settlement. Settlement patterns show the economy and ideology of a people. Peoples confront each other across land and sea, exchanging or resisting ideas. Space is studied, as life is lived, in a series of areas of different scales, one nested within another like Chinese boxes.

The menu for spatial analysis can be conveniently divided into three, corresponding to the three main sources of spatial data: excavation, site survey and landscape survey. The chapters on these methods (Chapters 4, 5 and 6) have already offered a few examples of spatial patterning and we will refer to them here from time to time. These three sources of evidence also broadly address increasing scales: excavation looking at the most intimate patterns on the ground, site survey looking at the environs of a site and landscape survey at larger spaces still. The smaller distributions, of finds and features, feed the larger, of structures, sites and territories, so there is some logic in proceeding in this order, from the smaller to the larger scale.

Spatial patterns from excavation (FIG 10.1)

Every find, context and feature recorded on site has a location, so can be put on the same map. Spatial data provide three dimensions for each point: two of them give the location, and the third may be the height (for a topographical survey) or the type and/or quantity of artefact (e.g. of pottery) for an artefact survey, or the concentration of one or more elements (e.g. phosphorous) for a chemical survey, or the strength of a reading, e.g. in nanoteslas for a magnetometry survey. There might be a tendency to overload the map with the different kinds of information carried by the

Field Records	Task	Outcome	Significance
Artefact index Context Index Plans Photographs Sequence diagram	Plot artefacts that belong to the same stratigraphic horizon	Map(s) of artefact types	(1) Activity areas (2) Sequences
Artefact index	Plot conjoining sherds	Map showing related fragments	Formation processes
Context records, Feature records, plans, context sequence diagram artefact and context maps	Plot contemporary contexts	(1) Identify features (2) Identify structures	Activity area
Feature index Plans Photographs of features	Plot all features	Map showing all features	Identify structures
Structure records Structures Photographs Site notebook	Plot structures	Map of structures	(1) Settlement form (2) Phases
All maps Site notebook	Map showing ranking of contemporary structures	Use of space	Social organization

FIGURE 10.1 Menu for seeking spatial patterns from excavation.

"third dimension", but this is not necessary with digital plotting. Using the site records, the distributions of objects, conjoining sherds, contexts, features and structures can each be mapped separately and then overlaid. There may be considerable redundancy in this work, but it is usually economical to indulge in a certain amount of trial and error. For many years this comparative process involved copious amounts of copying, scaling up or down and tracing; but now, with digitisation, archaeologists reduce maps and plans to the same scale, overlay them, merge and combine them, after serving only a short apprenticeship with a digital drawing program (such as Corel Draw, Adobe Illustrator or Autocad). The ultimate instrument for comparing the spatial relations of everything is the GIS (Geographic Information System), which can be applied equally well on site and off it. A GIS allows the information to be stacked in separate layers, any two or more of which can be combined. In this way we can inspect the coincidence (or not) of types of pottery with types of building, types of building with types of animal bone, types of ploughmarks with phosphate – and so on. The results are often startling and unexpected.

Understanding the use of space on site should only involve things that were contemporary, so common sense might tell us to first isolate those artefacts, contexts, features and structures which were in use at the same time, using the chronology. In practice, we do not necessarily know which objects were in use at the same time – only those that were found together in the same stratigraphic context. The analyses are in dialogue with each other: contemporary objects and features may report on the contemporary use of space, our primary goal. But the map of all objects and all features also has a use in revealing areas that might be contemporary because they share artefact types or an alignment and so make reference to each other. Finds may have been in contemporary use originally, but are all mixed up in later layers (residual) as found. Therefore finds-plotting is nearly always informative, even for finds now out of their contexts. Graves may be interpreted as contemporary because they line up, a track might connect two houses or a field boundary may avoid a mound. These are spatial relations but they can feed the chronology. It must be stressed that space (this chapter) and sequence (the next) are in a dialogue of equals. The two types of analysis work in harmony to try to recreate the changing culture of a community out of the scrambled or gappy narrative that excavation provides.

Plotting objects

Mapping objects in a context may indicate how an activity operates. The pattern of flint flakes around a hearth allows us to surmise where cores were prepared, blades were broken off and even where the knappers were sitting. Not only can the flints be related if they lie near each other, but also if they came from the same core, determined by physically *refitting* one fragment to another (FIG 10.2). *Conjoining sherds* by contrast report on former associations that have been dispersed, since nothing is being made, only broken. It is not easy to interpret these breakage patterns;

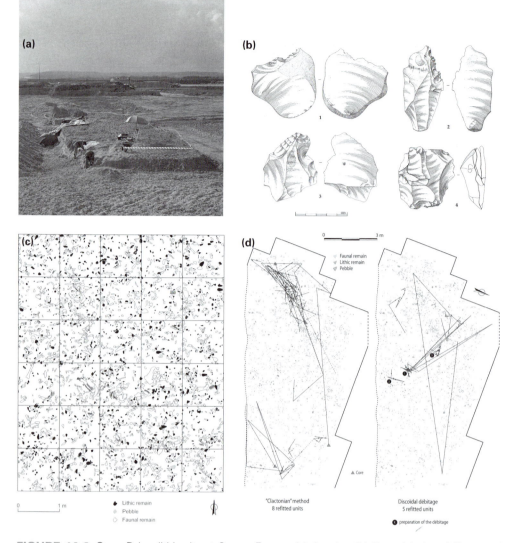

FIGURE 10.2 Open Palaeolithic site at Soucy, France: (a) the site; (b) flints; (c) plot of flints; and (d) conjoining fragments (Vincent Lhomme 2007).

at the least they give a clue to the degree of disturbance and how the deposit has formed, and can suggest where contexts that are otherwise unrelated might have been in use at the same time.

Within a feature, expectations of close association increase, and are occasionally dramatic (FIG 10.3). Artefacts in a grave have a layout we can call ritual, divided into personal stuff (clothes) and objects for feasting (cauldrons) or hunting (spear) or fighting (shield). A vivid picture can come from mapping things other than artefacts. In a classic example of Level E digging, archaeologists at Rickeby, Sweden mapped all the burnt fragments in a large bonfire under a cairn, and found them to be the relics of a funeral pyre, where a person, a horse, four dogs and several birds of prey had

FIGURE 10.3 The importance of accurate plotting: shell patterns depicting a tiger and dragon from the base of tomb M45 at Xishuipo, Puyang, Henan pr. (Sarah Allan 2005).

(a)

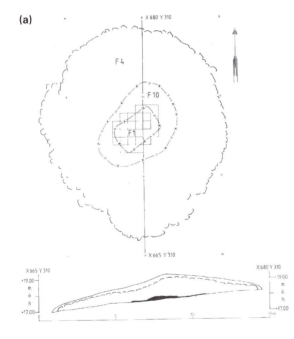

(b)

FIGURE 10.4 Finds within a feature: plot of cremated bone recorded over a grid under a cairn (a) at Rickeby, Sweden, revealed the tableau of sacrificed animals burnt *in situ* (b) (National Museum Stockholm).

been cremated in situ (FIG 10.4). Plotting finds within structures has the potential to show how the structure was used. The distribution of beads and other artefacts within the hall at Borg prompted the interpretation of the status of the rooms and their distinction from the byre (where the cattle lived) (see Chapter 7, p. 162).

Mapping features and structures

Stratigraphic units are often only planned individually, and may have been excavated some days apart and out of sight of each other, so it can be illuminating to see them on the same map: this is the way to throw up spatial associations which were not observed directly on site. The distribution of objects may define a context, and the distribution of objects and contexts may define a feature, and a combination of features may be defined as a structure. Thus the spatial pattern of finds, contexts, features and structures each helps to define the next level up (FIG 10.5, and see Chapter 6).

The earth-fast timber building (which has dominated residential life on this planet up to now) leaves little after its collapse apart from the sockets where the posts were dug in – post-holes. Mapping the post-holes that are contemporary should give us the shape of the building (FIG 10.6). In practice, the period to which a post-hole

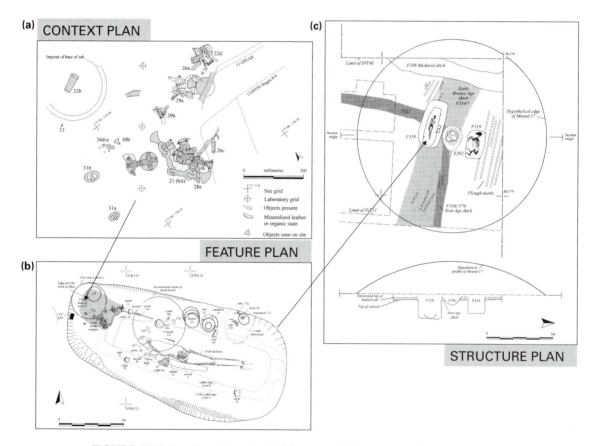

FIGURE 10.5 Location: (a) context, (b) feature and (c) structure plans.

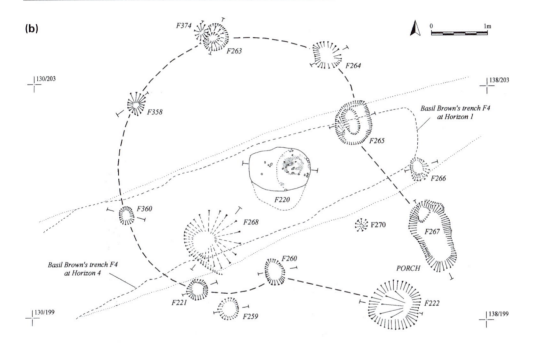

FIGURE 10.6 A ring of post-holes makes a structure: a Beaker-period building at Sutton Hoo. (a) photo, (b) plan (N. Macbeth/M. Hummler).

belongs is notoriously hard to measure precisely, even in a strong sequence. Thus, where the stratification is poor, as is usual on most prehistoric settlement sites, all the post-holes may appear as though cut from the same level, even though they were not contemporary. Here a type of pattern-seeking is applied, cheerfully known as "joining the dots", where the posts are linked to make structures of the expected shape – usually round or rectangular. This is rewarding, but there are uncertainties in the art; many prehistoric peoples now dwell in rather too symmetrical houses created on a modern drawing board.

Spatial patterns from site survey (FIG 10.7)

Field Records	Task	Outcome	Significance
Topographical survey	Map	Contours, hill-shade	Location of features
Artefact survey	Map by type	Dated occupation areas	Sequence of occupation
Chemical activity	Map by parameter Seek patterns	Location of chemical anomalies	Location of possible features
Geophysical survey	Map parameters Seek patterns	Location of anomalies	Location of possible features
Monuments	Map by type	Plot of dated monuments	Location of monuments through time

FIGURE 10.7 Menu for spatial analysis of site survey data (see also Chapter 5).

Plotting finds on *excavated sites* contributes to activities and to dating. Coins discarded at the Roman temple at Uley, England, showed where coin users (and droppers) were focusing their attentions at the beginning and end of the 4th century (FIG 10.8). Mapping pottery will show where sherds were concentrated – but this information needs to be carefully examined. It could be that concentrations of pottery are caused not by use, but by the subsequent formation processes. For example at Sutton Hoo the bulk of prehistoric pottery was concentrated in the early medieval mounds – since they had been constructed from the deposits of the prehistoric settlement. The distribution of pottery showed the location not of Neolithic farmers but of later vanished aceramic mounds. Similarly, exploring the ceramic pattern over the surface of the abandoned 7th century town of Teotihuacan, the distribution of the fine ware known as Regular Thin Orange appeared to be plentiful in certain areas, which therefore should have been the quarters of the richer class of citizen. However, when the quantities of this fine ware were plotted as a percentage of all the other types of pottery, its distribution was much less pronounced (FIG 10.9). In other words, the concentrations indicated areas rich in all types of pottery, so fine wares would there be plentiful, as would all other contemporary types. The distribution indicated areas of dumping, rather than areas of high status. The distribution of objects in space can thus be tested for site formation processes, to find concentrations of activity, for discovering the nature of the activity or for the chronological use of the site (see Chapter 11 for more).

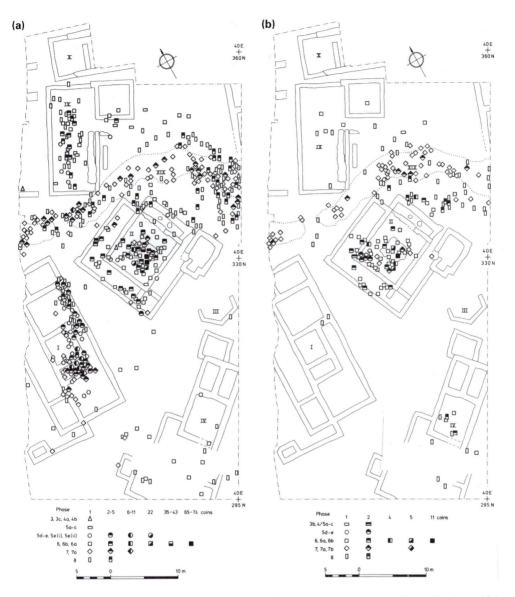

FIGURE 10.8 Finds within a site: coin plots at the Roman temple complex at Uley, showing which buildings were active, using coins of the early (a) and later (b) 4th century AD (© English Heritage).

The survey of *unexcavated sites* is designed to capture anomalies on the site and in its immediate environs. The menu for spatial analysis (FIG 10.7) draws on topography, artefact maps, chemical maps (especially phosphate), geophysical surveys and surveys of monuments (examples of these can be found in Chapter 5). Plotting the material around a site gives it a local context and is often how an excavated site was defined in the first place. After excavation, these local surveys provide an insight

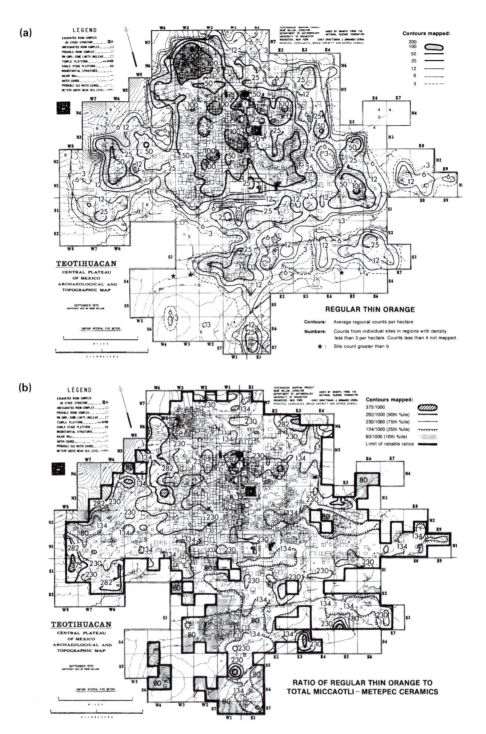

FIGURE 10.9 Pottery distribution at Teotihuacan: (a) total quantities of Regular Thin Orange fine ware; (b) showing proportions of pottery as a whole (George Cowgill).

Field Records	Task	Outcome	Significance
Geology	Summarise and map main geological features	Resources Agricultural potential	Living space
Placenames	Map by period/ language	Linguistic map	Location of language use
Known sites and previous finds	Map	Cultural map	Location of cultural groups
Surface collection	Map parameters Seek patterns Date clusters	Location of sites	Location and sequence of occupation
Location and rank of sites	Thessien polygons	Location of centres	Hierarchy of occupation Territories

FIGURE 10.10 Menu for spatial analysis of landscape survey data (see also Chapter 4).

into the parts of the site that could not be dug. Other site survey projects that look at graveyards, battlefields, gardens and the evolution of a long-lived settlement also rely on mapping and spatial analysis (see Chapter 5 for examples).

The distribution of buildings in a settlement, its pathways and the enclosure that surrounds it, all add up to its spatial character. We are looking for social relations in the space: a hierarchy of structures, a network of preferred routes. We are looking for function: where is the rubbish dump, the meeting place, the cattle pen, the water supply? We are looking for chronological development too: implied in the alignment of buildings, as well as from datable architecture or artefacts. This shows how excellent it is to have the whole of a settlement plan. Excellent, but infrequent. Whole settlements are not often on offer in commercial archaeology, since the area to be developed does not coincide with it; or in research excavation, since ethics normally discourage us from digging all of anything. However, site survey and excavation working together can often give us a strong tilt at a whole plan. The surface survey of a site, using methods outlined in Chapter 5, and its subsequent excavation in area (see Chapter 6) provide a powerful combination to tackle the use of space.

A "site survey" lies somewhere between an excavation survey and a landscape survey, but the differences are marginal and the analyses are interchangeable. As well as the analytical results that come from plotting things on a map, we can improve our recognition of patterns by using pattern-finding programs on a computer. So we will move on now to the landscape scale, and then at the end of the chapter consider four analytical routines that can be applied at any scale.

Spatial patterns in the landscape (FIG 10.10)

The local context for a site may be widened to the study of its hinterland, defined (for example) as "all the land within a day's journey of a site" or by an arbitrary space, such as an area 50km radius with the site at its centre (see Anuradhapura in Chapter 4 for an example). Such a region is studied for its provision of resources to that site (*catchment*) or the degrees of social control exercised by the site's governors. Alternatively a region may define itself from the distribution of certain types of site or artefacts that display similarity to each other (FIG 10.11). These create 'culture

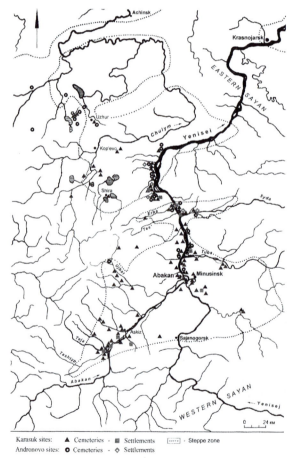

Karasuk sites: ▲ Cemeteries - ▦ Settlements   [·····] · Steppe zone
Andronovo sites: ○ Cemeteries - ◇ Settlements

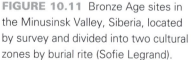

FIGURE 10.11 Bronze Age sites in the Minusinsk Valley, Siberia, located by survey and divided into two cultural zones by burial rite (Sofie Legrand).

zones' that may be held to represent a community of people that think in the same way, or areas which share a trade agreement (FIG 10.12) or the location of recipients who have similar status (FIG 10.13). As indicated in Chapter 4, one of the goals of landscape survey is to use pottery scatters to find settlements, and infer their status from their size. Since the pottery also offers a date, the outcome should be a settlement pattern that changes over time, and among those changes are changes to

(a)

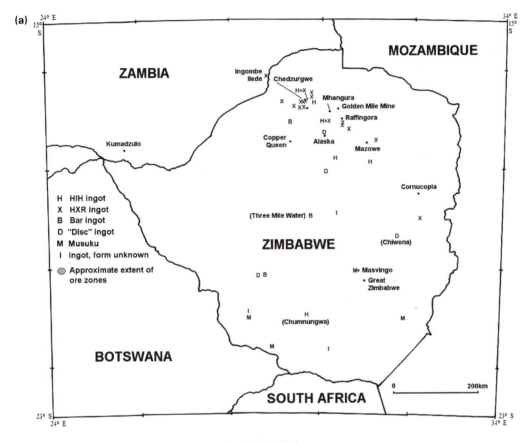

(b)

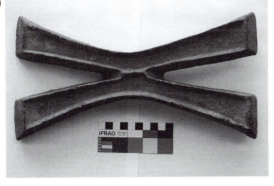

FIGURE 10.12 Distribution map of x-shaped iron ingots in East Africa, marking out an area of high status (a) and photograph of ingot (b) (Lorraine Swan).

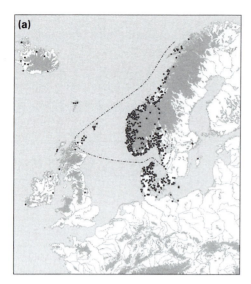

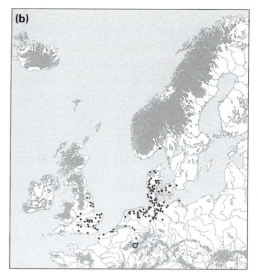

FIGURE 10.13 Distribution map of steatite bowls (a), and Mayen quernstones (b). The dashed line marks the natural occurrence of steatite, and the black circle the site of Mayen; (c) is a photograph of the objects (Arthur and Sindbaek 2007).

settlement size, function and status (FIG 10.14). Contemporary landscape surveys may thus have ambitious goals of social and economic interpretation, all essentially dependent on mapping and pattern-seeking.

Pattern-seeking by computation

Analytical routines developed by geographers have helped archaeologists to squeeze more meaning out of their patterns. Key data, like the number of people living in a village, the ratio of men to women, the acreage under the plough, the amount of grazing and the routes routinely travelled are often available, if at all, rather indirectly. One well-tried geographical analysis infers the location of territories from the size of the towns that served them: the bigger the town, the bigger its territory. Assuming the edge of the territorial boundary between two towns lies proportionally nearest to the smaller of the two, territories emerge as geometric shapes around each town

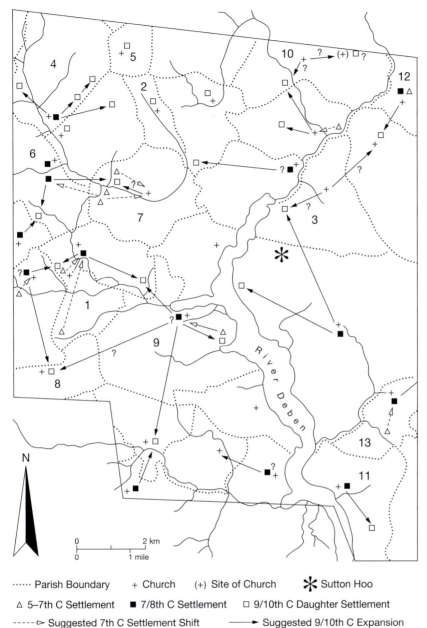

Parishes mentioned in the text:-

1. Little Beslings
2. Boulge
3. Bromeswell
4. Clopton
5. Debach
6. Grundisburgh
7. Hasketon
8. Kesgrave
9. Martlesham
10. Pettistree
11. Ramsholt
12. Rendlesham
13. Shottisham

FIGURE 10.14 Settlements located and dated by surface scatters of pottery and metal-work in the Deben Valley, Suffolk. The arrows suggest how later settlement budded off from earlier (John Newman).

(Thiessen polygons). Not having any towns or population figures for 6th century Norway, Bjorn Myrhe adapted the idea to what he did have: furnished graves, hill-forts and ship-sheds (rectangular hollows where ships were laid in winter). He plotted these sites on a map noting that they clustered in certain places, and then ranked each site type: the graves by their imported gold, the hill forts by their size and viewshed and the ship-sheds by their length. Using these measures of status he was able to construct Thiessen polygons for SW Norway and was gratified to find that they gave a pre-echo of the later county boundaries (FIG 10.15).

The patterns offered by a distribution map of pot-sherds, flints or settlements are usually a lot more fuzzy than this, but can be given more meaning in a number of ways. A *trend map* counts the objects by metre square to provide an average at the points where the squares meet. The resulting contour shows concentrations that for the eye were hard to find. Patterns can be sharpened further by using a computer to find the most probable clusters, using programs that make and compare thousands

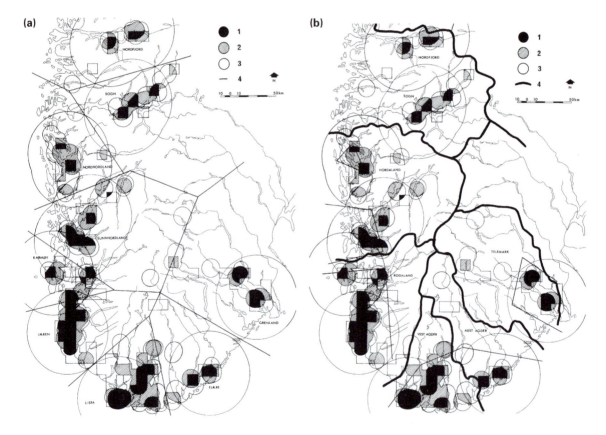

FIGURE 10.15 Territories in 6th century Norway, based on ranked central places: (a) Thiessen polygons; (b) Modern administrative boundaries (Bjorn Myhre).

of individual calculations. *k-means* analysis searches an untidy pattern of points and tidies them up into clusters. The computer calculates the distance between every point on the distribution map and locates a central point for them (the centroid). The other points are then divided into groups by their distance from the centroid. Those groups farthest away are given new centroids of their own and assigned to new *clusters*. The degree of association of any cluster is measured as the sum of the squares of the distances of all the points in the cluster from its centroid (*SSE*). The program keeps trying to reduce this figure by forming new clusters; it will not end up as one cluster for each sherd, unless they were evenly spaced (in which case, the pattern was obviously not significant in the first place).

In many cases, especially in survey, our distribution contains more than one type of object – pot, flint, animal bones, slag, pot-boilers, tesserae or tile. The variations lie not only in where the material is concentrated on the ground, but in which things occur together. So here there are a number of variables, and possible combinations of variables, but we do not know which are the most significant for showing where centres of activity might lie. *Local Density Analysis* calculates the local densities of each variable within a pre-selected neighbourhood distance (r), and then searches for neighbourhoods with similar compositions of finds. The "neighbourhood" can be predefined on archaeological grounds, for example by saying that a vanished midden heap should not be more than 5m across. The local density analysis then finds neighbourhoods of this size with similar compositions – and the result is a hypothetical map of middens. *PRESAB* (Presence-Absence) analysis defines neighbourhoods as in Local Density Analysis, or uses grid squares, but compares their populations by the presence or absence of each variable (type of pot, bone, etc.). This allows large complex assemblages to be compared which have a large number of different types of material. Hans Peter Blankholm, Professor of Archaeology at the University of Tromsø, Norway, has reviewed a number of these methods, by applying them each in turn to a complex distribution of different objects around a modern hunting camp (the "Mask Site" recorded by Lewis Binford). He found *k-means*, *correspondence analysis* and *PRESAB* to be the most helpful in finding patterns in space (FIG 10.16).

In a rock shelter on the River Rhône in France, Pascale Yvorra plotted the lithics and clustered them by trend-mapping and by k-means. He then looked at the types of lithic in each cluster and used the result interpret the activity that had dominated each area. In this way he was able to propose the way in which Palaeolithic people had managed their living space (FIG 10.17).

Where walls and rooms survive, spatial analysis can get more sophisticated. *Access analysis* studies the importance of rooms in a building by calculating how difficult they were to get to – i.e. whether you need to open one, two, three or more doors. The resulting patterns help to distinguish between different kinds of social use. Paolo Brusasco did an access analysis on buildings in Babylonian period Ur, and compared the resulting diagram to those obtained from modern Arab houses in Iraq and modern

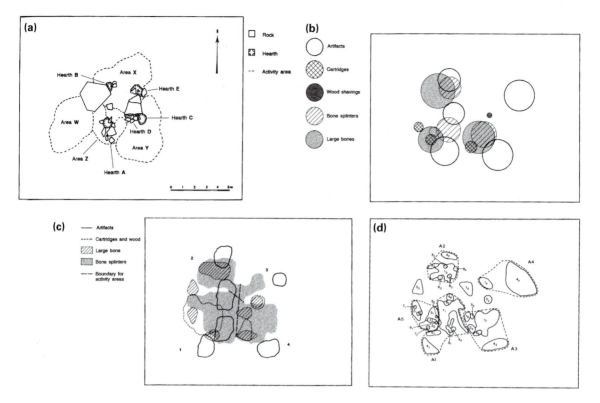

FIGURE 10.16 Pattern-seeking using different programmes: (a) The Mask Site, after Binford 1978; (b) clustering object types by k-means; (c) Local Density Analysis and; (d) PRESAB (after Blankholm 1991).

African Ashanti residences (FIG 10.18). He found that the ancient Ur houses most strongly resembled the modern Arab ones. They had a hierarchical reception process, with one way in and a gradual admission to areas of increasing privilege. The African examples, by contrast, had a pattern that reflected their matrilocal society, in which the chief male residences were integrated with the female and the system had many more ways in and out.

Exploring the way that centres of population interacted with each other assumes that there will be preferred pathways rather than random connections, and that these pathways will themselves promote the establishment of new settlements on the route. The actual pathways can sometimes show up, as in the case of the prehistoric roads found in Corona satellite photographs (see Chapter 4). Otherwise they can be inferred from topography and settlement locations. The assumption here is usually that human beings like to travel with as little effort as possible, and so nearest is best (*proximal point analysis*). However, although nearby places are popular with travellers, so are places that have a special importance even though they are far away. People owe allegiance to the village they live in, their place of work, but also may have a son

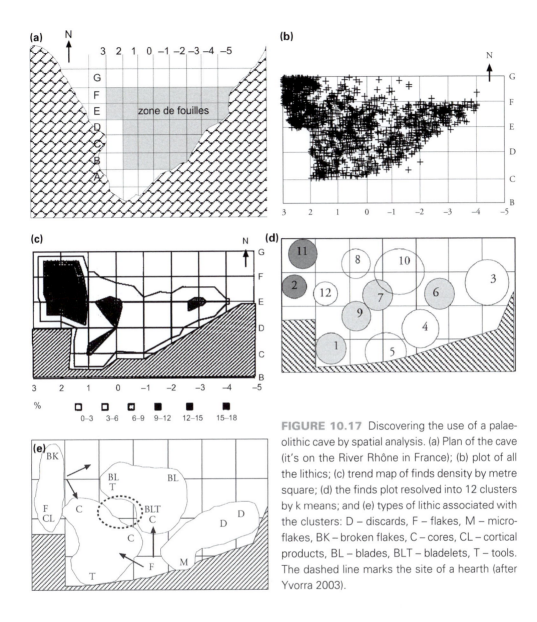

FIGURE 10.17 Discovering the use of a palaeolithic cave by spatial analysis. (a) Plan of the cave (it's on the River Rhône in France); (b) plot of all the lithics; (c) trend map of finds density by metre square; (d) the finds plot resolved into 12 clusters by k means; and (e) types of lithic associated with the clusters: D – discards, F – flakes, M – microflakes, BK – broken flakes, C – cores, CL – cortical products, BL – blades, BLT – bladelets, T – tools. The dashed line marks the site of a hearth (after Yvorra 2003).

in New York and a daughter in Rome, not to mention a favourite holiday destination in Ireland. In other words, we all have spatial networks which are greatly enlarged and skewed, especially through faster modes of travel. Prehistoric people did not have airlines, but they certainly used the sea. Maritime networks operate over much longer distances than territorial networks, since travel is up to five times faster. Furthermore, within the constraints of tide and wind, travel is equally easy in all directions. To discover preferred routes one approach compares the attraction of settlements for each other across the sea with the physical laws of gravitation. Carl

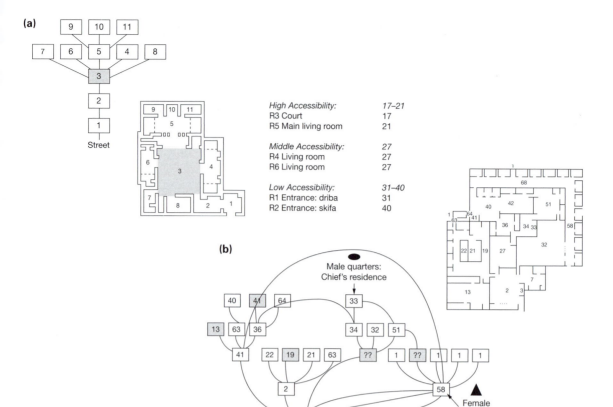

(a)

	9	10	11	
7	6	5	4	8

3

2

1

Street

9 10 11
5
6 3 4
7 8 2 1

High Accessibility:	*17–21*	
R3 Court	17	
R5 Main living room	21	
Middle Accessibility:	*27*	
R4 Living room	27	
R6 Living room	27	
Low Accessibility:	*31–40*	
R1 Entrance: driba	31	
R2 Entrance: skifa	40	

(b)

Male quarters:
Chief's residence

40	41	64		33

| 13 | 63 | 36 | | 34 | 32 | 51 |

| 41 | | 22 | 19 | 21 | 63 | | ?? | | 1 | ?? | 1 | 1 | 1 |

2

58

Female quarters

Street

(c)

E.M. SITE

FIGURE 10.18 Access analysis. (a) Plan and access diagram for an Islamic town house in modern Iraq. (b) Plan and access diagram for an African Ashanti residence. Access analyses for Babylonian Ur (c), show most affinity to modern Iraq (Brusasco 2004).

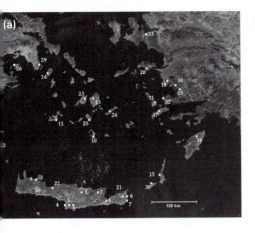

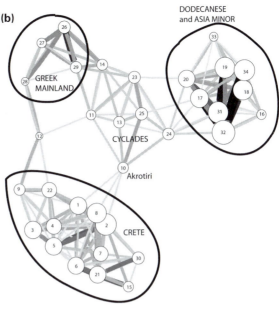

FIGURE 10.19 Maritime networks in the Bronze Age Aegean, based on optimised resources for 34 settlements, and the ease of passage between them (a) map of sites; (b) inferred routes (Carl Knappett).

Knappett and his mathematical colleagues used a gravitational equation to study the network between 34 coastal sites in the Bronze Age Aegean Sea. Assigning a probable wealth of resources to each site, and fixing the time of travel between them, they showed which routes were preferred by the network in its optimum, most stable condition (FIG 10.19). Having built the model, they could also show how it most probably adjusted itself following the removal of a key node in the network – in this case the port of Akrotiri on Santorini, destroyed in a volcanic explosion.

Conclusion

This chapter addressed the question: why do archaeologists spend so much energy recording the precise location of everything? It is because those locations, mapped on the same maps, give us a wealth of information coming under the general heading of "the use of space". Spatial analysis reflects the different scales at which people live their lives. For our convenience when writing up, we make distribution maps of artefacts, contexts, features and structures on site. All of this is possible to do rapidly these days, thanks to digitisation and high-precision surveying instruments. Trial and error as well as deliberately designed analyses throw up relationships which can reflect ancient activities and social practice and also indicate sequences of activities. These analyses come out of excavation, site survey and landscape survey and the results are being used to address ever more extensive and fundamental social questions: trade, religion, marriage, slavery and exploration.

Thus in precise spatial mapping lies some of the greatest potential for the understanding of societies. As fieldworkers we can also note that location is the one parameter that is always available. We may have no assemblage and know no dates, but whenever we have something to observe, however obscure, we will still be able to map it.

Briefing

For **general reviews and ideas** Hodder and Orton 1976, Allen et al 1990 (and GIS); Kroll and Price 1991, Blankholm 1991, Gillings 2001, Robertson et al 2006. For **spatial patterns in excavated sites (intrasite analyses)**, Blankholm 1991 shows how different analytical procedures aid pattern-recognition for artefact distributions on site; for good examples, Hietala 1984, Bartram et al 1991 (huntergather camp), Stevenson 1991, Yvorra 2003 (rock shelter), Cowgill et al 1984 (Teotihuacan), Cunliffe 1987 (Hengistbury), Frankel and Webb 2006 (Cyprus), Sjösvärd et al 1983 (Rickeby), Larsson 2007 (Uppåkra), Woodward and Leach 1993 (Uley), Marcus and Flannery 1996 (San Jose Mogote); **chemical mapping:** Conway 1983 (phosphate), M. Carver 2005, Chapter 3 (a grave).

For **spatial (use) patterns in buildings:** the access analysis classic is Hillier and Hanson 1984. Foster 1989 applied the analytical principles to prehistoric structures. An attractive introduction to social and symbolic analysis of living space is Samson 1990, in which the editor sets out a nice clear theoretical basis and then offers us examples from Neolithic tells and villages, Roman villas and houses of the Medieval period and later. This shows as well as anything why we make accurate plans and elevations and how this information leads to new understanding about people. Brusasco 2004 is an example of a recent attempt to read social uses of space in ancient Mesopotamia using analogies from Islamic houses and from modern Africa.

For **spatial patterns in landscape:** Legrand 2006 (Minusinsk), Swan 2007 (Zimbabwe), Arthur and Sindbaek 2007 (steatite and Mayen), Myhre 1987 (Norway); see Chapter 4, Middleton and Winstanley 1993, Brandt et al 1992 (GIS). For processing and manipulating spatial data using **GIS**, Chapman 2006. This shows how data acquisition from ground survey (TST) and air survey (lidar) can be used to make three-or four dimensional maps overlaid with finds distributions. The emphasis here is to visualise ancient land use as thoroughly as possible rather than to fill in the gaps with mathematical models. For **gravitational networks**: Sindbaek 2007 for Vikings, Knappett et al 2008 for the Aegean in the Bronze Age.

11 CHRONOLOGY

The business of chronology

In this chapter our aim is to establish a chronology – to put events in order and give them a date. We have two targets in our sights: objects on the one hand and contexts on the other; and we have two tasks for each: first, put them in a relative sequence; and second, provide them with a calendar date. "Chronology" is the combined operation (FIG 11.1).

Our programme can be baldly summarised at the outset. Artefacts, which have form and style, can be ordered by typology, the morphological "language" spoken by

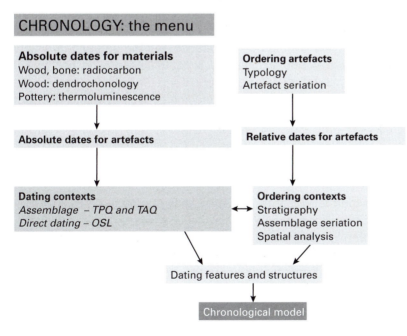

FIGURE 11.1 The business of chronology.

different communities that allows us to recognise them in the ground (Chapter 9). Materials, principally those of organic origin, i.e. wood and bone – can be dated by scientific methods. These measure the length of time an object has been buried, or the time that has elapsed since it was living. Dated objects can then be used to date the contexts they are found in, layers, pits and graves. But the relationship is not a simple one. Objects can live a disorderly life between their date of manufacture and their eventual rediscovery in the ground, perhaps many centuries later.

Contexts can themselves also be scientifically dated: a date for a layer of sand can be computed by measuring the time it has been out of the sight of sunlight. But the most fruitful route to the dating of contexts lies in their relation to each other in the ground – the stratification. The art of stratigraphy is to work out the order in which contexts were deposited – and thus their relative date. Where stratification is poor (and it often is), the ordering of contexts has to rely more on their contents (artefacts and datable materials). As we will see, context seriation is a way of doing both: improving the stratigraphic model by using datable objects.

Many different methods are therefore put to work in the business of chronology. Every site will demand its own emphasis, but excavators can rarely afford to depend on just one method. Rural "flat sites" are famously short on stratification, and must bring in spatial and artefact dating. Urban "deep sites" often enjoy good stratification, but may have mixed up assemblages. These are crude distinctions of course. Even in the countryside there will be large mounds, pits and ponds, where the strata are dazzling and sharp. And even in the best urban excavation there will be areas where the stratification seems to give up. Most sites are neither very well nor very poorly strat- ified but somewhere between the two. For every excavator there are two horses pulling, between the ordering of events by stratification and the ordering of events by objects. The key here, as in all field archaeology, is not to be dogmatic: don't insist that *only* stratigraphy or *only* artefact dating matters. Keep the toolbox open and the mind free. The chronology, which aims to be the outcome of this analysis, is the best dated sequence that can be produced, using every tool in the box.

Typological dating of artefacts

Since artefacts vary in their fabric, form and style, they can be put into a relative order of manufacture, on the basis of how similar they are to each other. Traditional typologies have been carefully built up over the centuries as a result of types of object discovered at many sites, some now with historical dates or scientific dates (FIG 11.2 and see Chapter 9). Large numbers of undated, but stylised, artefacts can be dated by putting them in order of similarity or *seriating*. This uses the principle that for any one form of artefact – a lamp or a cooking pot – one type succeeds another through time, its influence waxing and waning like a president. In a long-lived site, one dominant type gives way to the next as time goes by.

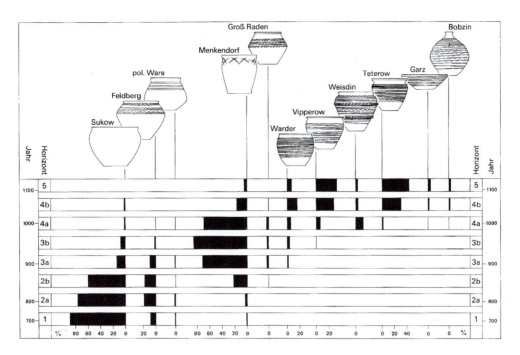

FIGURE 11.2 Ordering pottery types by stratification (Müller-Wille 1991).

Scientific dating of materials

Materials such as wood, bone and charcoal can be given an absolute, measured, scientific date using a whole range of methods summarised in TABLE 11.1. The best-known methods are those applied to wood and bone. *Dendrochronology* counts the tree rings in a piece of timber and matches them to others to get a calendar date; the pattern of tree-rings is particular to the years in which the tree grew. Unfortunately the date cannot necessarily be applied directly to a building: the timber may be incomplete (i.e. not have all the rings needed to place it in time) or the timber might have been reused in a later building (Colour Plate 11). *Radiocarbon dating* measures the quantity of radioactive carbon (C14) in a sample either by counting its emission of electrons or by weighing the proportion of the carbon isotopes present in minute amounts (AMS – accelerator mass spectrometry). Since the amount of radiocarbon in the atmosphere has varied, the dates have to be calibrated to show where they really belong in time (calibrated dates are marked *cal.*). A radiocarbon date does not offer us just one year (like dendrochronology), but a probable range of years in which the date probably lies. This gets broader the further back in time you go; but the ranges from a set of dates can be narrowed if we know something about the order they should be in: from a succession of stratified layers for example. In this case the laboratory builds a *Bayesian model*, which narrows the date ranges by reconciling

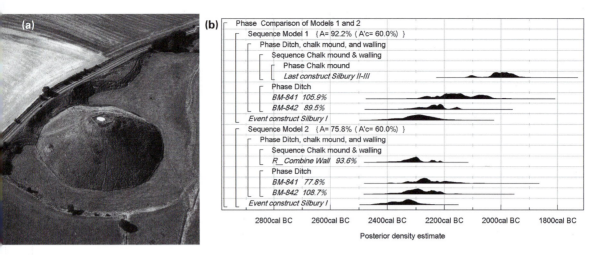

FIGURE 11.3 Radiocarbon dating: refining the precision of the dates by knowing the chronological order (Bayesian analysis). The dates are those relating to the construction of Silbury Hill (a) (compared with other sites). The black wiggles (b) show the date range with (as peaks) the most probable dates (Bayliss et al 2007)

them to their chronological order; this offers the most likely dates with much higher precision (FIG 11.3).

As mentioned above, it is possible to date some contexts directly by scientific measurement, for example a hearth by archaeomagnetism or thermoluminescence, or silts by OSL (optically stimulated luminescence). These methods measure the length of time that the material has been buried, the moment of burial being the point at which it cools down or is deprived of sunlight or the magnetic field inside it is fixed; the clock starts then. Calcium carbonate deposits can be dated using the radioactive decay of uranium isotopes. Thus a cave painting might be dated by radiocarbon from a sample of the pigment, radiocarbon from the soot left by a torch or uranium from a layer of calcium carbonate that subsequently formed on top of it. Monuments of the Nasca lines were dated by OSL measurements of the sand sealed by the stone rows that formed the patterns. Researchers W. Rink and J. Bartoll discovered that much of the system around Nasca had been laid out to guide desert travellers between AD400 and 650. We need more techniques like this. The precise direct dating of contexts is in its infancy, but its further development would be of great value: a date of deposition, completely independent of objects or stratification. As can be seen in Table 11.1, these methods operate with different error ranges and over different time scales; but this fundamental area of research is improving in range and precision with every year that passes.

TABLE 11.1 Methods of scientific dating (with thanks to Janet Ambers, British Museum)

Targets	Method	Minimum Sample size required	Precision	Range of time
OBJECTS				
Wood with visible tree-rings (structural timbers)	Dendrochronology		1 year	From 7200BP (Ireland) 10,300BP (Germany) 8500BP (US)
Objects containing organic carbon (wood, bone artefacts; human and animal bone)	Radiocarbon	1g charcoal 300g bone (emission) 50–100 micrograms (AMS)	within c.50–100 years	From 65000BP (AMS)
Ceramics	TL	200mg/30mm diameter/5mm thick	+/–5–10% on site 25% otherwise	From 100000BP
Obsidian	Obsidian hydration	4–5mm section		From 500000BP
Mammal teeth	ESR			100000–1000BP
Bone	Amino-acid racemization	1g		100000–1000BP
Bone	Fluorine/uranium		relative only	
SEDIMENTS				
Hearths	TL			From 100000BP
Hearths (recent)	Archaeomagnetic			(Depends on available calibration curve)
Hearths (old)	Palaeomagnetic			(Depends on available calibration curve)
Silts	OSL			
Sediments deposited by volcanic eruptions	Tephrachronology		Relative	
Sediments deposited in lakes	Varves		1 year	From 20000BP
ROCKS				
Rock surfaces (rock art)	Cation ratio			10000–100BP

TABLE 11.1 continued

Targets	Method	Minimum Sample size required	Precision	Range of time
Rock surfaces (caves)	Chlorine 36			
Volcanic deposits	Potassium/argon			1 million–100000BP
Calcium carbonate deposits (caves)	Uranium series			250000–10000BP depending on uranium concentration in area

Key: AMS – accelerator mass spectrometry; TL – thermoluminescence; ESR – electron spin resonance; OSL – optically stimulated luminescence

Using objects to date contexts

We therefore have two independent analytical programmes working in parallel: one working on objects, the other on contexts. Needless to say, dialogue between these programmes is vital. Objects occur in contexts, so the date of the manufacture of the objects relates, indirectly, to its date of discard, and the date of discard relates, indirectly, to the date of deposition of the context. Similarly, the date of the deposition of a context relates to the date of manufacture of an artefact found in it. So if we know the date of objects, we have a line on the date of a context; if we know the date of a context, we have a line on the date of an object.

But these relationships are not as straightforward as one might hope (FIG 11.4). The objects in a grave, for example, were deposited at the same time, but not necessarily made at the same time. But we can at least say that they were in use together. The rough date of one item of the grave goods, thus gives a rough date to the others. This method of *cross-dating* has a long tradition in archaeology, and was used in the 19th and early 20th centuries to set up chronological schemes across Mesopotamia, Egypt and other civilisations of the Old World.

But do grave goods actually date the digging of the grave? Not directly. Only one thing can be said with certainty: the grave must have been dug after the objects in it were manufactured. So the date of the grave is later than the latest object in it (if you know which that was), but how much later is not known. This "must be later than" date is known as a *terminus post quem* (TPQ for short) (FIG 11.5). The objects in a layer only give a TPQ to the layer: they do not date it; and the layer only gives a TPQ

Object	Made (A)	Primary context (B)	Secondary context (C)	Tertiary context (D)	Date measured
Human bone	In lifetime	Grave	Disturbed		C14 gives date of death
Human teeth	In life	Grave	Disturbed		ESR gives date of burial
Sapwood	Cut	Used as timber	Burnt	Dumped	Dendro gives date of outermost ring/C14 gives date of cutting
Heartwood	Died up to 100 years before cutting				C14 gives date of death of heartwood
Peat	Grew	Died	Cut	Burnt	C14 gives the date of exclusion from air
Animal bone	Birth	Killed	Eaten	Thrown away	C14 gives date of death
Twigs	Cut	Used	Burnt	Thrown away	C14 gives date of cutting
Pottery	Made	Used	Thrown away	Disturbed	TL gives date of manufacture
Daub	Placed on building	Preserved by burning	Discarded in situ	Displaced	TL gives the date of burning
Hearth	Clay placed on ground	Preserved by burning			TL/Archaeo gives date of last exposure
Silts	Formed on site	Exposed to sunlight			OSL gives date of last exposure

FIGURE 11.4 Date of object and date of context.

to the pit or grave in which it lies. This is a hard lesson and excavators are often tempted to ignore it. So "the floor was dated to the 4th century by a coin of AD345 found in its make-up", is not strictly true. The floor cannot have been laid before AD345 (its TPQ) but might have been laid two or three centuries later. It is different if the coin was found on top of the floor. In this case the relationship is *ambiguous*: the coin might have been dropped on a floor that was already there (a TAQ); or the floor might have been laid after AD345, and an earlier coin subsequently dropped (a TPQ). The relationship between coin and floor cannot simply be read off. The coin may have been around for a long time before being incorporated in the floor – it is then described as *residual*. Or it may have been trodden into a pre-existing floor much later – and it can then be described as *intrusive*. The ideal situation is that it was dropped on the floor in the year both were made, in which case it is *primary*. But we rarely know that. More secure dates can only come from considering the sequence as a whole (see below): for example, there may be a great deal of 4th century material, and nothing else, above and below the floor, making the fourth century date very likely.

The ambiguity is further illustrated by the "cross in the wall" problem in FIG 11.5c. If the cross was part of the original build, the wall is later than the cross, since the cross already existed. But if the cross has been added to repair a pre-existing wall (as in this case) then the cross could have been made later than the wall. But not necessarily; it might have been a very old cross recycled to make the repair. In the first case the wall is stratigraphically later than the cross – but maybe a lot later. In the second case the wall is stratigraphically earlier than the cross, but their dates of manufacture can be the other way round. Luckily we know in this case that the cross is 6th to 8th century and the wall is 19th, and also that it was used to plug a hole. So an earlier cross was added to a later wall. This example is just intended to show that

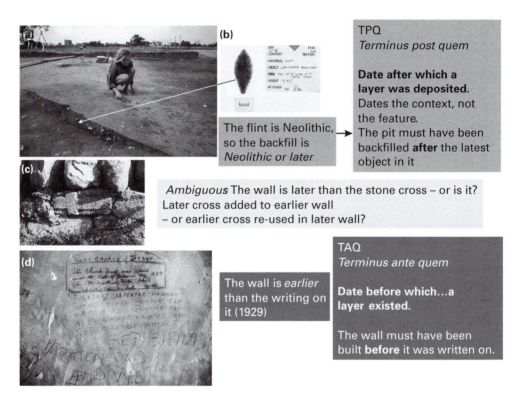

TPQ
Terminus post quem

Date after which a layer was deposited.
Dates the context, not the feature.
The pit must have been backfilled **after** the latest object in it

The flint is Neolithic, so the backfill is *Neolithic or later*

Ambiguous The wall is later than the stone cross – or is it?
Later cross added to earlier wall
– or earlier cross re-used in later wall?

TAQ
Terminus ante quem

Date before which...a layer existed.

The wall must have been built **before** it was written on.

The wall is *earlier* than the writing on it (1929)

FIGURE 11.5a–d Dating contexts with dated finds (TAQ, TPQ).

the story is usually more subtle than just the date of an artefact or the stratification can supply.

Archaeologists appreciate that the circumstances in which objects find their way into contexts is crucial here. Grave goods will be earlier than the grave they are found in, but only years earlier, not centuries. But the artefacts found in ramparts and floor levelling may be very much earlier: tossed around in earth quarried for building, these artefacts can belong to a completely different era. Prehistoric pottery can be found in a Medieval burial mound (or rampart), because the earth used to build the burial mound (or rampart) came from a prehistoric settlement. It happens all the time. Those awkward terms TPQ and TAQ are only useful up to a point: the chronological relationship between a context and an object found in it must be studied and argued for every time.

When sending material for radiocarbon dating, the most important information is the character of the sample, its location and its likely status in the stratification. The laboratory will give a fine date to the sample itself, which may be, say, a small piece of charcoal; but this means little if we do not know whether it was residual, intrusive or primary in the feature where it was found. I had an object lesson trying to date the destruction of a monastery in Scotland. It should have been easy enough: the monastic workshops were covered by a thick layer of charcoal. I selected a nice big chunk and the answer came back in the 5th century, a hundred years before the monastery was built. The wood was heartwood, which had died a century before it was cut down to build the timber houses of the monks at the beginning of their occupation in the 6th century. It had nothing to say about the date of the fire. For this, the burnt layer had to be carefully sifted to extract organic matter that was nearer the fire in date: straw, leaves, insects, a dead bird. In other words material that could be said to be primary to the fire, not just burnt by it. As a general rule: the radiocarbon date of a skeleton dates its grave, a carbonised twig in a hearth dates the hearth, but a piece of charcoal from an unidentified layer does not date anything.

Relative ordering of contexts

Stratification refers to the way that deposits succeed each other in the ground, and *stratigraphy* refers to the act of reading it (Chapter 1, page 20). It is as well to preserve this distinction, since, contrary to popular belief, stratification is not always obvious and our readings of it are often uncertain. Contexts succeed each other by superposition (lie on top) or cutting and these relationships are studied and recorded carefully at the time of excavation (see Chapter 6, page 139). Sections provide an important record of how contexts were related on the ground, but they report the sequence only in one thin slice in one place. The modern art of stratigraphy relates all the contexts that have been defined on site and integrates them into the best continuous sequence.

The stratigraphic information is captured on site by noting that a context cuts or overlies others (on the context card), and/or drawing the edge of every context individually (to make "single context plans"). Either prescription may be sufficient – especially when the relationships are nice and clear. The order of the contexts is then drawn up on a *context sequence diagram* – a modelling procedure with a number of variants, the best known pioneered and promoted by the Bermudan archaeologist Ed Harris as the *Harris Matrix* (FIG 11.6). This diagram shows the contexts as little rectangular boxes joined by vertical lines where they succeed each other, and by double horizontal lines where they are equivalent in the sequence. The art of making these diagrams is to reduce the pathways to the minimum, like a flowchart. The context sequence diagram (ideally) includes all the contexts, so constitutes a total account of every stratigraphic event that occurred, or rather, those that could be observed and recorded (FIG 11.7). In addition to the context records and plans, it will be worth checking the context maps (horizon plans) and sections to ensure the order of contexts is consistent. There will be inevitably some contexts where the strati-graphic position is uncertain – these can be represented by dotted lines. And there will always be others that cannot be included at all, because their stratigraphic position was never determined. There will always be some stratified relationships that

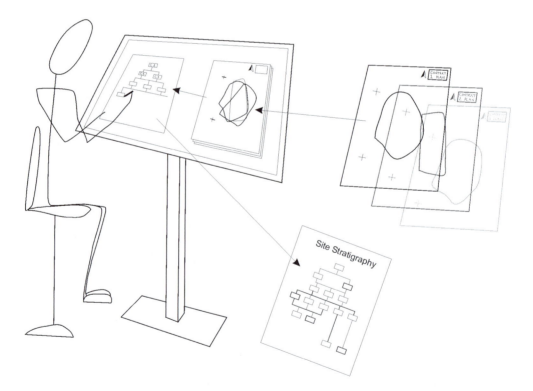

FIGURE 11.6 Representing context sequences in a diagram (the Harris matrix) (FAS Ltd).

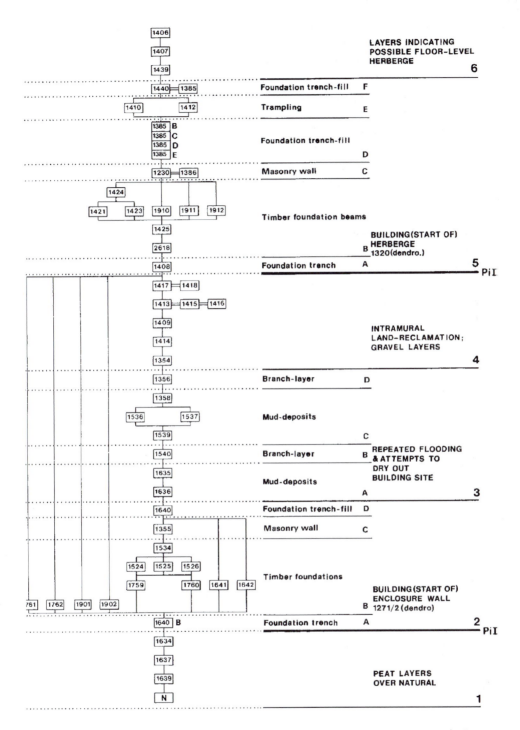

FIGURE 11.7 Context-only stratification diagram (Harris Matrix) for a sequence at Konstanz, Germany (Bibby 1993).

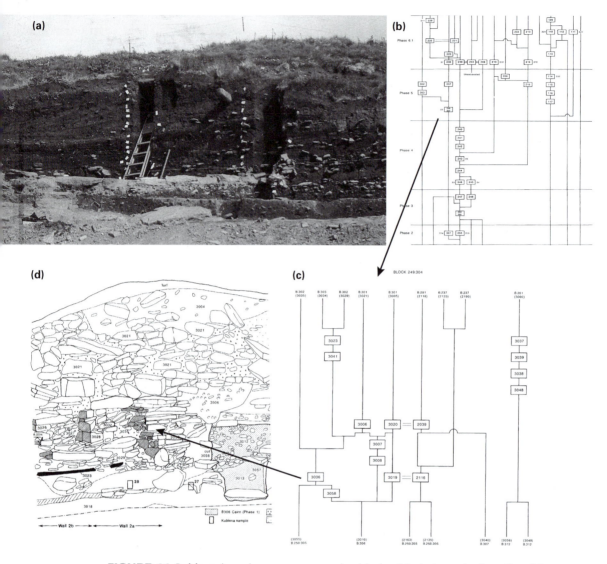

(a)

(b)

(d)

(c)

FIGURE 11.8 Managing a large sequence using blocks: (a) photograph of section; (b) summary diagram of blocks; (c) context sequence in Block 249; and (d) drawn section, with context 3036 marked (Lowe 1998).

are ambiguous. This is not an invitation "to make a decision one way or the other"; on the contrary, it is important to record the ambiguity, with dotted lines. A context that can swing both ways plays an important role in the composition of the chronological model (see the next section). Since context sequence diagrams involve all the contexts they can be very large, but the analysis may be usefully managed in sectors or blocks (FIG 11.8).

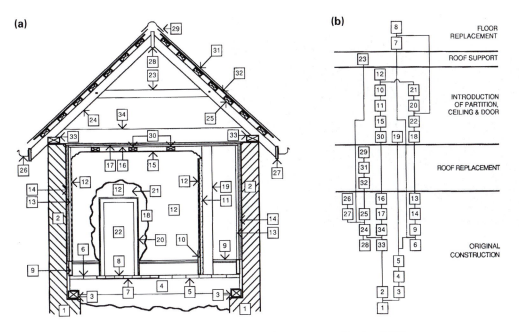

FIGURE 11.9 Representing the context sequence in a structure (Davies 1993).

Buildings, as well as strata, may be broken down into their component stratified parts, i.e. contexts and features, and so the sequence of structure and repair can often be usefully represented on sequence diagrams (FIG 11.9, see also Chapter 7, page 179). The rules are slightly different here, since although a building begins with its foundations and walls, subsequent additions can be made by punching holes in the fabric (insertion) or rebuilding from below (underpinning). This reinforces the idea that stratigraphic relationships, whether in a building or in earthy strata, have to be deduced, rather than simply observed.

Stratification, where it is clear, offers the best evidence for sequence. But there are always grey areas. Some sites are well stratified, with the contexts and their relationships clearly visible – while others are poorly stratified, and seem to have only a few layers that merge into each other. The distinction is marked as between urban sites, where stratification is often good, and rural flat sites, where the stratification can be negligible. Not surprisingly, urban archaeologists swear by stratigraphy and pronounce it the basis of everything, while rural excavators know that they are going to need a lot of other methods for both relative and absolute dating.

Ordering contexts by their assemblages

Where stratification is poor, a way of ordering contexts and features is by ordering the assemblages within them. Most attention has been focused on graves, since these

(a)

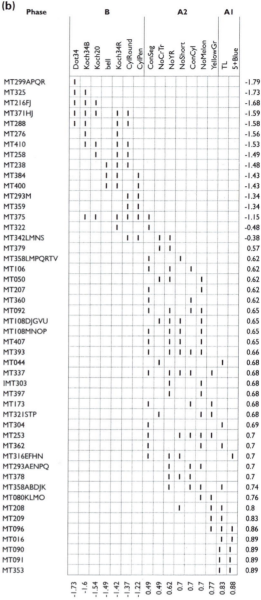

(b)

	Phase				B							A2					A1			
		Dot34	Koch34B	Koch20	bell	Koch34R	CylRound	CylPen	ConSeg	NoCrTr	NoYR	NoShort	ConCyl	NoMelon	YellowGr	TL	5+Blue		
MT299APQR		I																	-1.79
MT325		I	I																-1.73
MT216FJ		I	I	I															-1.68
MT371HJ		I	I	I		I	I												-1.59
MT288		I	I			I	I												-1.58
MT276			I																-1.56
MT410			I	I		I	I												-1.53
MT258				I		I	I												-1.49
MT238					I	I	I												-1.48
MT384					I	I		I											-1.43
MT400					I	I		I											-1.43
MT293M									I	I									-1.34
MT359									I	I									-1.34
MT375			I	I		I	I	I	I										-1.15
MT322						I			I										-0.48
MT342LMNS						I	I			I	I								-0.38
MT379										I	I								0.57
MT358LMPQRTV									I			I							0.62
MT106									I		I		I						0.62
MT050									I	I			I						0.62
MT207									I				I						0.62
MT360									I				I						0.62
MT092									I		I		I	I					0.65
MT108DJGVU										I	I	I		I					0.65
MT108MNOP									I		I	I		I					0.65
MT407									I		I	I		I					0.65
MT393									I		I	I	I	I					0.66
MT044									I						I				0.68
MT337									I		I	I	I		I				0.68
IMT303										I			I						0.68
MT397										I			I						0.68
MT173									I			I		I					0.68
MT321STP										I				I	I				0.68
MT304									I						I				0.69
MT253									I			I	I	I	I				0.7
MT362									I					I	I				0.7
MT316EFHN									I		I	I				I			0.7
MT293AENPQ											I		I	I					0.7
MT378										I	I	I							0.7
MT358ABDJK										I		I	I		I				0.74
MT080KLMO													I	I					0.76
MT208												I		I	I				0.8
MT209														I	I				0.83
MT096														I	I	I			0.86
MT016														I	I				0.89
MT090														I	I				0.89
MT091														I	I				0.89
MT353														I	I				0.89

Bottom axis: -1.73 -1.6 -1.54 -1.49 -1.42 -1.37 -1.22 0.49 0.49 0.62 0.7 0.7 0.7 0.77 0.83 0.88

FIGURE 11.10 Ordering assemblages with finds. Types of glass beads (a) used to put graves into sequence (b) (Penn and Brugmann 2007).

are among the most common features where the assemblage is likely to be primary. Flinders Petrie used seriation to propose an order for his pre-dynastic graves. He reasoned that graves with the most similar pots were nearest to each other in date. This has been extended to other burials, and relies on the idea that the same basic social forces create the assemblage and that time is important to them (neither of which need be true). For example, in a set of late Iron Age Scandinavian graves, the assemblages were seriated, each one placed in order by virtue of the type of glass

Type of site	Stratification	Artefact dating	Context ordering	Context dating
Deep urban	Good	Good	Stratigraphy	Artefacts
Shallow/ disturbed urban	Poor	Good	Assemblage seriation	Artefacts
Furnished cemetery	Poor	Good	Spatial Assemblage seriation	C14
Rural settlement	Poor	None	Spatial	C14, OSL

FIGURE 11.11 Chronological analyses serving different types of site.

beads they contained (FIG 11.10). The archaeologists also produced a "best order" for all the full assemblages (beads, brooches and so on) using correspondence analysis to give the sequence with the smoothest transition (with least differences) from one assemblage to another. Calendar dates are added to this relative sequence, by choosing the likely dates when certain objects first appear. These "likely dates" come from their earliest appearance elsewhere, usually indicated by coins found with them. In this way it is possible to build up a chronological structure, an ordered sequence of assemblages, using the objects alone.

In practice, we shall need to design our programme for chronological analysis with the character of the site firmly in mind: in deep clear stratified sequences, stratigraphy takes the lead; in flat sites with little stratification, we depend on artefacts and radiocarbon dates to give us a sequence and a date (FIG 11.11). But all methods should be held at the ready. Some examples follow.

Chronology for poorly stratified sites

Let's begin with a settlement on flat land – of the type that has left us only pits and sockets in the subsoil, with assemblages of pot-sherds in the pits or spread in the well-mixed ploughsoil above them. Assuming this pottery has been carefully collected and recorded, and assuming that we know its approximate date of manufacture from other investigations, then we have the materials to propose a sequence of occupation by plotting them on a map. The example shown in FIG 11.12 was a settlement site consisting of post-hole buildings and buildings with sunken floors (in which rubbish had accumulated). The datable pottery could be divided into four periods, and these, when plotted on the overall map, indicated where each period was at its busiest. At the same time the buildings could be associated by their alignments, on the principle that buildings aligned in the same direction were probably visible at the same time.

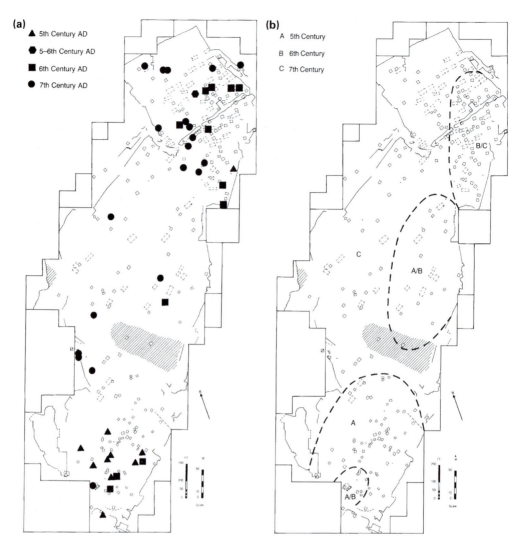

FIGURE 11.12 Dated pottery (a), and alignment of structures give a sequence at the Mucking settlement site, (b) (© English Heritage).

So although stratification was virtually lacking, a model for the occupation of the site through several centuries could be composed.

Now let's take a site type of equally common occurrence – a cemetery on flat open ground. Many communities bury their dead side by side, each new grave respecting the others, with very little intercutting. And then, not realising the graves are there, later people plough away the tops, removing any strata that might have helped to put them in order. Now there seems to be no clue about which graves came first; and yet there are methods available here too.

If the graves are furnished, then the chronological burden falls firstly on the objects. The date of each kind of object is surmised from its inclusion in graves elsewhere and ultimately depends on a date provided by a grave with a coin in it. Particular time-sensitive objects may be put in order by artefact seriation (see earlier). The chronological order of the assemblages is given by the most recent object in each grave, if this is known; or if not, by the best order of the assemblages according to their seriation (i.e. the best order of the assemblages, taking all the grave goods into account). The order of the graves is then equated with the order of the assemblages.

But suppose there are no objects? There are three helpful methods to cope with this situation. Method no. 1 is to radiocarbon-date the skeletons. These dates, like the typological dates given to artefacts, have an error range of about 120 years. In most cases, the death of the person ought to be pretty close to the day the grave was dug; so most of the graves can at least be put into the right century. If there is some other way of putting the graves in order we can get closer than 120 years, as close as 60, by constructing a Bayesian model (see earlier).

Method no. 2 is to use the backfill. For this to succeed there has to be a well-dated deposit on the site which is incorporated into the backfill (or not) when the graves are dug. The famous example is the excavation of the Yeavering palace site by Brian Hope-Taylor (Chapter 7). The excavator had graves with nothing much in them, not even bone, but he noticed that some of the backfills contained pellets of charcoal which must have come from an extensive fire that had burnt down the neighbouring timber buildings. He deduced that graves with no charcoal in them must have been dug before the fire; those with fresh pellets of charcoal just after it; and graves with weathered pellets of charcoal must have followed at some interval after that. This allowed the graves to be ordered into three sets – before, after and long after the fire.

Method no. 3 uses alignments. This only works for inhumation graves which are rectangular so that the axis of the skeleton points in a certain direction. Graves aligned in the same direction may be viewed as contemporary, or follow each other closely in time, since it can be assumed they could see and respect each other. When the alignment begins to deviate, another phase of burial has begun. These three methods can be used to reinforce each other, and of course to reinforce the ordering implied by the assemblages if there are any, and the stratification where there is some. The methods therefore work as a team, to give a sequence that best fits them all.

The early medieval cemetery at Wasperton provides a neat application of this kind of integrated chronological enterprise (FIG 11.13). There was some intercutting and grave goods, so with the three methods just mentioned there were potentially five ways to date the graves (FIG 11.14). There were 26 cremations and 176 inhumations for which some usable data had been recorded. Of these, 118 contained grave goods, and of these, 18 were identified as culturally Roman and 93 culturally Anglo-Saxon. A further seven graves were furnished but not culturally determined. The task was to put all the

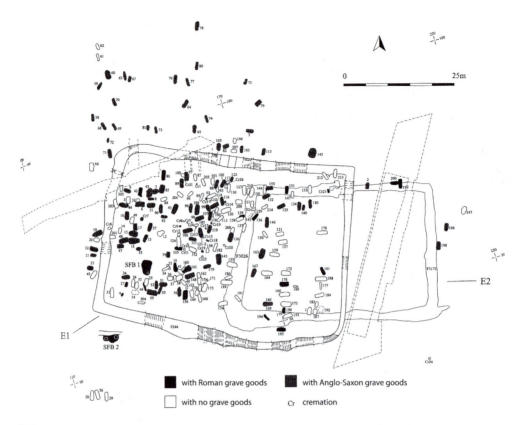

FIGURE 11.13 How do you make a chronology for a very flat site? (Carver et al 2009).

burials in order, whether they had grave goods or not. The difference between Roman and Anglo-Saxon grave goods was not controversial here, so this could be used as factor no. 1 to put the graves into three groups – "Roman", "Saxon" and "don't know". Radiocarbon dating was applied to every burial that had bone: but in practice only three of the inhumations and 20 of the cremations had enough bone left for dating (the soil was very acid, and the bones had mostly rotted away). However, what we knew about the ordering from factor no. 1 meant that Bayesian modelling could be applied. This was factor no. 2. The stratification was minimal but there was some: eight graves had cut other graves or disturbed cremations. This was factor no. 3. Then there was the alignment of the inhumations and the orientation of the body in the grave (factor no. 4). These showed that there were three large groups that chose orientations N–S, S–N and W–E. The instances of intercutting showed that these orientations were chosen in that chronological order, and correlation with Roman and Anglo-Saxon grave goods showed that Romans preferred N–S and Anglo-Saxons preferred S–N. W–E was selected by Romans and Saxons but mainly by people with no grave goods. Although the majority of inhumations fell into these orientations in a general way, the detailed alignments of the graves also offered patterns (factor no. 5). These were

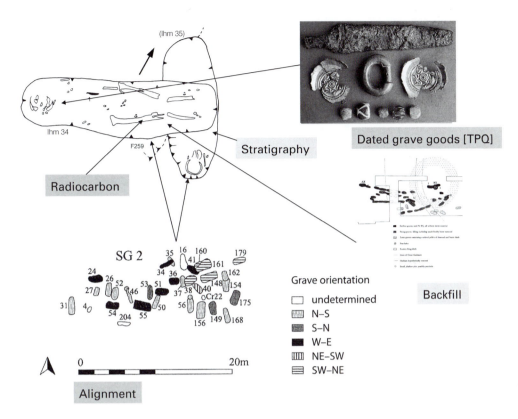

Stratigraphy

Dated grave goods [TPQ]

Radiocarbon

Grave orientation

- □ undetermined
- ▦ N–S
- ▨ S–N
- ■ W–E
- ▥ NE–SW
- ▤ SW–NE

Backfill

Alignment

0   20m

FIGURE 11.14 Five ways to date a grave (Carver et al 2009; Hope-Taylor 1977).

studied for each sector of the cemetery, since similarities of alignment were only thought significant for graves that were near each other.

All five factors used together gave the archaeologists a best fit for the dated sequence. Only then was the order compared with the dates of the assemblages in the Anglo-Saxon graves, as determined by expert knowledge of the objects. The intention here was to compare the likely dates of the assemblages with the dates that they had been put into graves – and so examine the attitudes and allegiances of the burial parties. It probably needs stressing that the business of chronology is to *model* a dated sequence. The model is not a fact: it is the best we can do. At Wasperton, the idea was to argue for the date and order of the graves from the most measurable parameters (radiocarbon, alignment) to the most variable attributes (the grave goods chosen). And it was also important to find a methodology that would include all the graves without grave goods. The result was a sequence credibly divided into half centuries (FIG 11.15).

There are plenty of cemeteries that are not as blessed with chronological data as Wasperton, and many more settlements; in fact virtually every prehistoric settlement

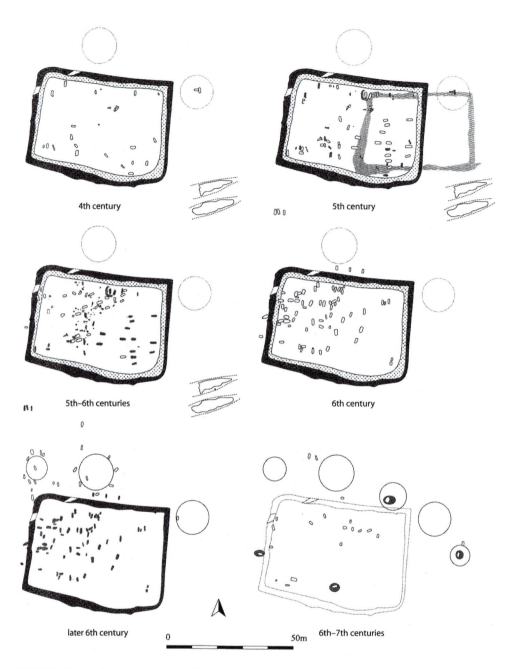

4th century

5th century

5th–6th centuries

6th century

later 6th century

0   50m

6th–7th centuries

FIGURE 11.15 Dated sequence at Wasperton early Medieval cemetery, 4th to 7th century (Carver et al 2009).

site falls into this category. The objects that are directly datable, by typology or radiocarbon – artefacts, bone and charcoal – are mainly in secondary contexts, redeposited in pits and earthworks, or spread over the surface from ploughed-out midden heaps. Here we rely on the distribution of flint and pottery already dated from better stratified sites (graves or caves). The mapping of types of pottery belonging to different periods is the staple analysis for landscape survey, where all the material is secondary, i.e. in the ploughsoil, (see Chapter 4) but it is applied to site survey too (Chapter 5) and in excavated settlement sites it can also be remarkably useful. The premise is that although the pottery has been moved, it hasn't moved far, so that its distribution can show the areas occupied in different periods and thus the way the site developed. I have even used this (in desperation) in a deeply stratified town site, with credible results.

Many of the settlement sites we find are deprived even of the material in the topsoil (for whatever reason: it got machined off, or the pottery was always fragile and got minced by the plough). In these cases, the dating methods are limited to the finds in the post-holes and pits, radiocarbon dating of charcoal and the alignment of the features. It is not only poorly stratified sites that have to battle their way to the best fit using as many methods as possible. As we shall see, well-stratified sites, although they have a huge chronological advantage, need modelling too.

The chronology of well-stratified sites

By definition, well-stratified sites are characterised by well-defined contexts with a clear relation between them. While not every edge is crystal clear, the excavators in this kind of site can take it apart layer by layer and stone by stone, building up a sequence of contexts in their order of deposition as they dig. This kind of site is actually pretty rare in the realm of the human past, but it is mighty prevalent in modern archaeology, because so much development takes place within historic towns where strata lie deep. The methodology of stratigraphic excavation has thus acquired great prominence in literature and practice. Chronology here naturally gives primacy to the stratigraphy, but there is still a role for other data, notably assemblages. Stratification and assemblages come together in context seriation, to be introduced presently.

As can be seen from the examples in the diagrams (FIG 11.7 and 11.8), the relative stratigraphic positions of contexts is reasonably clear vertically, but less clear horizontally. This is because on every site (except perhaps within a narrow ditch or trench) most contexts are out of touch with each other. One only has to think of two pits cut into the same floor or two windows cut into the same wall. Stratigraphically they are equivalent, but they may be of very different dates. The diagram looks rigid, but on close inspection it is possible to move the contexts up and down with respect to others that are not stratigraphically connected, and others that are marked as ambiguous. All context sequence diagrams contain uncertainties, therefore, and the next stage of the analysis attempts to remove a few of them.

Context seriation: Assemblages and stratification working together

The stratification on many sites may be poor or uneven, the dates of objects and samples may be imprecise and their relationship with the contexts they are found in can be uncertain. And yet these are our principal instruments for chronology, for which we seek the maximum precision. One approach to the problem is to let the assemblages and the stratigraphy work together to produce a *rectified* sequence diagram – i.e. to match the best order from the stratification of contexts to the best order of the dated objects that they contain. Ideally this analysis will also show us which assemblages are largely residual, and which have been least disrupted by later material. These latter, primary assemblages, we can more safely use for direct dating, such as radiocarbon.

FIGS 11.16 – 11.18 illustrate the composition of *context seriation diagrams*. The data, drawn from urban sequences, compare the best chronological order of stratification, with the best chronological order of a single type of artefact, pottery, which is durable, datable and ubiquitous. The sequence of contexts, taken from the stratigraphy, is set up on the Y-axis (earliest at the bottom), and the sequence of pottery types is set up on the X-axis (earliest on the left) (FIG 11.16). The amount of each type of pottery in each context is shown as a black disc of proportionate size. If both these sequences

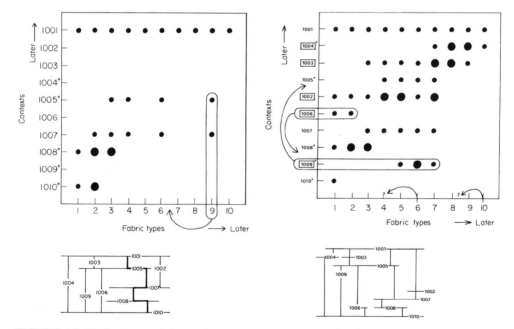

FIGURE 11.16 Context seriation: using a sure sequence to order the pottery (left); ordering the contexts to improve the overall sequence (right).

were perfect, the result would be a diagonal, with all the black blobs along it. Every context would be succeeded by another context, and each type of pot would be buried as the next type of pot came along.

Life is not like that. Many contexts have uncertain stratigraphy, and many others are contemporary, or at least we don't know which came first. The pottery meanwhile follows no gentle itinerary of changing fashion. One type may endure for decades, following which a whole cartload of new types arrives. These are things that are unknown. The object of context seriation is therefore, to reduce as many uncertainties as possible, by shifting the pottery type on the X-axis and the stratified sequence on the Y-axis to get as near to a diagonal as possible. Certain things of course we may not do: we cannot contradict the stratification; and we cannot move a pottery type earlier than we know it to be (Medieval pottery is always later than Roman pottery).

The resulting diagram – never a perfect diagonal – has a number of interesting properties, not all of which have yet been understood (FIG 11.17). A *slope* (Slope A)

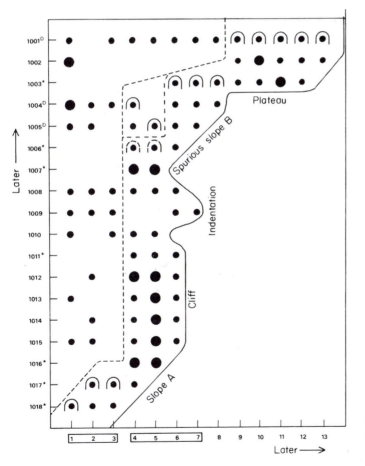

FIGURE 11.17 Context seriation: characteristics (M. Carver 1985).

should mean that as time passes, new types of pottery arrive. A *cliff* should mean that a number of contexts have the same kind of assemblage – they are contemporary. An *indentation* means that the stratified order and the pottery order are not in agreement, and thus that the contexts are secondary and the strata inverted – a load of soil with early pottery has been dumped on a layer with later pottery. A *spurious slope* indicates that although the contexts are put in this order, they contain contemporary pots and therefore could be contemporary rather than sequential. A *plateau* shows a number of new types of pottery without a sequence of contexts. This should mean that a number of contexts is missing from the sequence, i.e. the site has been levelled.

The real example in FIG 11.18 shows some of these properties and others too that invite interpretation. Worcester, Sidbury, was a site occupied in Roman and Medieval times. The sequence was well stratified in the Roman period (1st to 4th centuries AD) and in the later Middle Ages (14th to 16th centuries), but there had been a lot of disruption in between, new building and levelling that had left dozens of pits of different dates in an equivalent stratigraphic position, cut into a Roman road. This is a common situation in ancient European towns, where they liked redevelopment just as much as we do today.

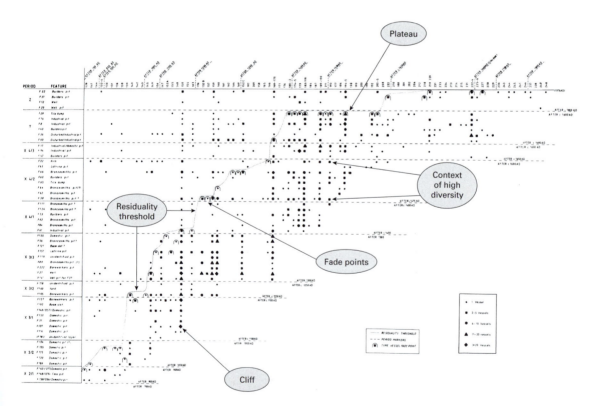

FIGURE 11.18 Context seriation for a poorly stratified site (Worcester) (M. Carver 1985).

In order to improve on this weak stratification, the pottery in the numerous pits was put into its best order, and compared with the best stratigraphic order recorded for the pits – as far as it went. The two orders, on the X and Y axes, were then adjusted within permissible limits to get as near as possible to a diagonal. First let's notice that the majority of the black spots cluster towards the right hand edge. This is excellent news: it means that the chronological order of the stratigraphy and the pottery typology now more or less agree. But on the left hand side there is still quite a lot of pottery – and much of this is clearly residual.

Exactly which types of pottery are residual and which are in contemporary use can be deduced from the way the types vary. One can see that, for each pottery type, there is a moment going up, that is from the earliest to the latest feature, where that type begins to decrease. This is termed the *fade point*: it indicates when the supply probably dried up. The fade points are marked with a little hat, and when the hats are joined with a line they mark the *residuality threshold*. All the pottery on the left hand side of this hypothetical frontier is residual, while the pottery on the right hand side of it was in use together. Two important results spring from this: we can see which groups of pottery were plausibly manufactured and supplied to the site at the same time; and we can see which contexts have no or very little residual material; they are our candidates for primary status.

The face of the supposed diagonal is also full of interest, and it is legitimate to suppose what it might mean. The *cliffs*, where the diagonal suddenly rises vertically, ought to mean that the contexts that contribute to it are broadly contemporary. The *plateau*, where the diagonal goes horizontal, may mean a lot of new types of pottery has suddenly arrived; but more likely marks a levelling operation where a number of pottery-bearing contexts were removed. Basically we are missing a whole part of the sequence, taken away during a redevelopment operation. As can be seen the various cliffs and plateaux of this diagram allowed markers between periods to be put in place, with some indication of where there were time gaps in the sequence. In this way the ordering offered by the stratification alone was greatly enriched.

The virtues of this diagram are by no means exhausted – and we need more of them. But hopefully I have said enough to persuade you that even in the most complex of urban stratified sites, balancing different elements of the chronology against each other has its rewards.

Feature sequence diagrams

Up to this point, the main task has been to produce the best model of the sequence using the stratigraphic order of contexts, refined with as much additional dating and sequencing information as we can muster. This model gives the best order of contexts, a sequence of numerous small events. The next stage is to add to this model the

interpretations of activity that were made on site and recorded as features and structures.

We have already seen that contexts can often be defined as belonging to sets, termed features, which are then interpreted as graves, pits, walls and other human actions. The feature is a higher order stratigraphic unit, incorporating a higher order of interpretation; features are records *additional* to contexts and have their own numbering system (see Chapter 6, page 140). Similarly structures have been formed from sets of features. The features and structures are not only those identified on the site; spatial analysis will have added more (see Chapter 10). A *feature sequence diagram* is simply a higher-order representation of the sequence, in which sets of contexts are replaced by their features.

Some archaeologists like to define features *only* after the excavation has finished, but defining them on site means they have the advantage that they can be studied while still visible. Whether defined on site or off it, the feature asks new questions and provides a richer interpretation of events. Just as the feature is an addition, not an alternative to the context, so the Feature Sequence Diagram, is an *additional*, not an alternative analysis. There is no difference of principle between this diagram and the Harris Matrix; it is merely a more interpretative way of representing the same sequence (FIG 11.19).

However, the resulting diagram does have some interesting additional properties (FIG 11.19; see also Chapter 8, FIG 8.15). Each feature is shown as an arrow, stretching from its earliest to its latest existence, according to the position in the diagram of its component contexts. It therefore has a "life", and the lives of the different features can be compared with each other. A structure can only be composed from features that were contemporary. This is a pretty obvious statement, but in practice it is not always apparent at the time of digging; to know, for example, which, out of dozens of post pits, were in use at the same time. The feature sequence diagram shows which post pits can be contemporary, and therefore which could belong to a structure. This interpretation would be made in collaboration with the mapping of the features in spatial analysis (see Chapter 10).

The feature sequence diagram is also well equipped to show uncertainties, this being one of its assets. This might seem perverse, but the uncertainties show where current knowledge is weak. The diagram needs to be transparent, because it is a major stepping stone on the road to the synthesis. At each step we produce a more vivid narrative, but at the price of increasing approximation. The feature sequence diagram, based on the context sequence diagram enhanced by assemblage seriation, provides

FIGURE 11.19 (opposite) Different ways of portraying the same thing, without and with features. (a and b): context-sequences (Harris matrix); (c and d): the same sequences, featurised (i.e. with an additional level of interpretation) (Malcolm Cooper).

(a)

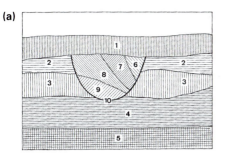

a) A negative impact

(b)

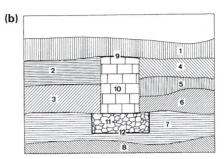

a) A positive impact

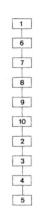

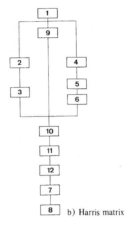

b) Harris matrix

(c)

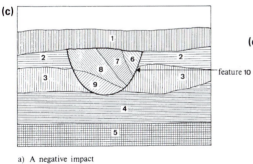

feature 10

a) A negative impact

(d)

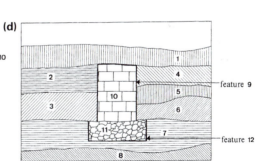

feature 9

feature 12

a) A positive impact

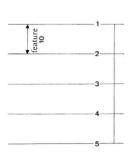

feature 10

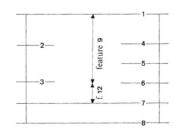

feature 9

f. 12

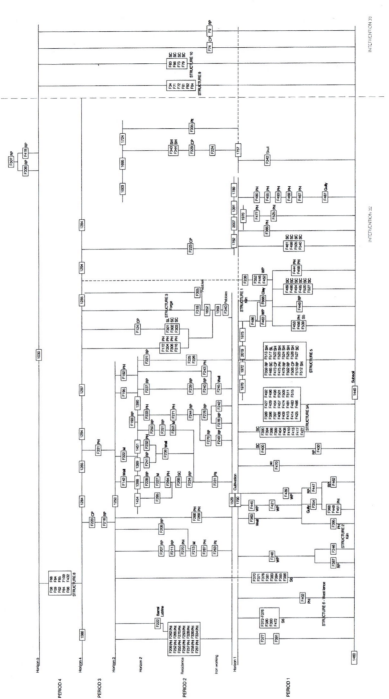

FIGURE 11.20 A feature sequence diagram, with the contexts grouped into features and the features grouped into structures; Tipping Street, Stafford 2009 (FAS Ltd).

a useful platform for site chronology; it combines the best of on-site interpretation with the best of off-site analysis FIG 11.20.

The Harris Matrix, a context-only sequence diagram, was published in 1975, and since then many variations have been proposed, most intended to enrich the sequence it shows. Since the feature sequence diagram presented here was first advanced in 1974, many of these variants have shared its aims. Some, appreciating that contexts were closely associated on site, gather them into groups or blocks at the writing-up stage. Others add distinguishing marks to the stratigraphic units to show that they had structural roles. Others needed to show what was going on over time in a suite of neighbouring rooms all joined together, and so invented a special diagram to do it (Colour Plate 12). This all seems very healthy to me – given the importance of sequence and chronology we should welcome every new experiment in understanding and representing them.

Conclusion

People will have their own ways of making all the diagrams discussed in this chapter. To illustrate the principles, I have quoted several that seem to work, but they are not meant to be prescriptive. The chronological problems encountered are as varied as the sites themselves, and it is right that every excavator works out their own ways of solving them.

The two main assets we have are the stratified order of contexts and the dates of objects or samples. Neither can produce a strong chronology on its own. The art is to put them into dialogue, in which the balance of the argument will lie with the best evidence. In flat sites we depend most heavily on assemblages; in deep sites, most heavily on stratigraphy.

The result of the argument is a model, a story that best fits the data we have recorded in the field. It won't be perfect, but it will be satisfying and tell us a lot we did not know. Of course, you may not think we are here to tell stories. But I do; and if you want a story, this is one way to write the plot. In the next chapter we will consider a few others.

Briefing

For a broad clear overview of chronology, taking in dates from documents and inscriptions and relative chronologies from typology and scientific dating, see Harding 1999. **On dating materials**: Aitken 1990, Goeksu et al 1991, Taylor and Aitken 1997, Hedges 2001; **dendro:** Baillie 1991, 1995; Kuniholm 2001; **radiocarbon:** H. Barker 1958, Bowman 1990, Bronk Ramsey 1995, Bronk Ramsey et al 2006 (calibration),

Bronk Ramsey 1998 (probability), Buck et al 1991, Buck 2001 (Bayesian refinement), R.E. Taylor 2001, Cole and Watchman 2005 (for rock art), Berstan et al 2008 (pottery residues), Rink and Bartoll 2005 (Nasca lines); **TL (thermoluminiscence):** Aitken 1991 (121–40); Grün 2001; **obsidian hydration:** Ambrose 2001, Freter A. 1993 (in Mesoamerica), **ESR:** Grün 2001, **archaeomagnetic and palaeomagnetic:** Sternberg 2001; **OSL:** Aitken 1991: (141–54), Grün 2001; **uranium series:** A.G. Latham 2001; **tephrachronology:** Hogg et al 2003; **racemization:** Griffin et al 2008; **varves:** Thunell et al 1995.

On **dating contexts by ordering assemblages:** Penn and Brugmann 2007 (correspondence analysis); **ordering strata (sequence diagrams):** Harris 1975, 1977, 1979 (1989) for the single unit method; Harris et al 1993, Roskams 2001 (239–66) for examples of its application. Orton 1980 (65–73) for a nice clear account from a mathematician (who also explains what the term "matrix" actually means); Dalland 1984, Hammond 1991, Paice 1991 for later developments of the context-only diagram; Durham 1977, M. Carver 1979a, b; 1980, for examples of the feature sequence diagram. (Note that Harris 1993, 16, and Roskams 2001, 156, mistakenly represent the feature sequence diagram as an alternative to the context sequence diagram, as opposed to an enhancement of it.) The expanding area of study is typified by a series of informal discussions about reading, recording and representing sequence on site called the "Interpreting Stratigraphy" conferences held in UK: Roskams 2000 is a bumper collection. **Context seriation:** Orton 1980 (74–88) (another nice clear account); M. Carver 1985 (context seriation using pottery), Orton 1993 (quantification of ceramics). **Case studies:** Carver et al 2009 (Wasperton), Hamerow 1993 (Mucking), West 1985 (West Stow), M. Carver 1980 (Worcester), M. Carver 1979a (Durham), Hammond 1991b (Nomul), Hammond 1991a (Cuello), Brogiolo 1988 (Lonato) (see Chapter 7).

12 SYNTHESIS

Why write?

Many people become archaeologists to live their lives at one end of shovel – to enjoy the open air, find things and chat about them. Writing does not come easy, and they remember at school (and university) sitting in front of a set essay topic wishing it would go away, much as an earlier generation sat in front of a cold school dinner. Writing a synthesis need not be like that (at least not the way I do it). It is exciting and pleasurable, although it does need work.

Synthesis implies a single version of events, which on first thought seems to go against the post-modern way of letting every voice be heard. However, as with design (see Chapters 2 and 14), my principle is to let every voice speak, but not at the same time. People like to have information organised for them, otherwise the net result is no better than a conversation in the pub, in which nothing is eventually said about everything. Because fieldwork is always a unique expedition, we have a duty to all the people who were not there to report the finds as precisely as possible. We recognise that other people would have seen other things; all the more important to report what we saw. Similarly, this unique experience uniquely qualifies those that had it: they are eyewitnesses. Their story is not the only story, but it is one with a special value. For this reason, synthesis – the outcome of an investigation, arguing for its significance, its value in the present day to scholars and the public – is not an optional stage of archaeological investigation; it is an essential underpinning of the whole investment and must be paid for. This is not always the case (see Chapters 13, 14).

The *Field Records*, containing the many observations that were made on site, were gathered in at the end of Part 2. They are sacrosanct, and will be stored in perpetuity. After the analysis stage, we have gained a new set of results; these too are sacrosanct, even if they are primarily dedicated to interpretation. They are stored in the *Lab Reports*, so that future workers can see what was done and which analysis was fruitful.

Synthesis builds on top of these. It is an attempt to bring together the multiple results and opinions from analysis and present them as a single coherent narrative. There are three diverse characters who might not think this worth doing: the post-modern theorist, who thinks it elitist or simplistic, the lazy fieldworker, who finds it too difficult and the developer, who might have to pay for it. Three other characters, however, consider it vital: the current researcher, the future excavator and the public. These clients want to hear not only what you, the excavator did, and what you found, and what everyone else said – but what you, personally, think it means. This goes to the heart of what archaeology does and what knowledge is. The archaeological investigator employed certain methods, made certain records and did certain analyses. These will all be in the Lab Reports. But only the synthesis expresses the outcome of the shared thinking that powered the design. It is the synthesis that encapsulates the significance of the project and allows it to be assessed by those that use it and those that paid for it. In synthesis, archaeology addresses the rest of the world, and for the statement to be useful, the team must choose someone to speak for them, speak clearly and not be afraid to be wrong in the long term. A project for which there are divers conclusions, and "more questions than answers" will not have a long term and does not deserve one. We owe it to all other researchers, to sponsors and to the public to say without obfuscation, dissembling or self-obsession what we really think happened on site, and what is its significance (if only to give our later readers something to disagree with).

Commercial archaeology does not routinely pay for synthesis, and the world is poorer for it. Presumably some planners or developers or state agencies do not think it to

First stage

Assemblage – artefacts – biota – assemblage meaning: identify ACTIVITIES

Chronology – stratification – dating: lay out SEQUENCES

Spatial – contexts to features – features to structures – structures to site: map USE OF
    SPACE

ACTIVIES + SEQUENCES + USE OF SPACE = SITE MODEL

Second stage

WIDER CONTEXT – the site model in its geographical, intellectual, historical context

INTERPRETATION means recreating human actions, intentions and feelings: living,
    dying, farming, hunting, building, manufacturing, socialising, worshipping,
    fearing … INTERPRETATION begins on site (notebook), and continues using
    parallels, analogies, experiments

SITE MODEL + INTERPRETATION + WIDER CONTEXT = SYNTHESIS

FIGURE 12.1 Materials for synthesis.

be part of the value that mitigation has won back. They are wrong. For the public, it is the primary value: it is the synthesis, not a bulging archive or a sheaf of expert opinions, that made the archaeology worth paying for.

Synthesis can be viewed as a game of two halves: first, make a sequence of events – or "site model"; and second, express its significance within the current state of knowledge. The first of these two stages uses assemblage, space and sequence - the fruits of analysis. The second studies the wider context of this local story. Both parts depend on the measured use of interpretation (FIG 12.1).

Site models

The analytical programme (Chapters 8 to 11) delivered three basic elements for the story we are about to try and write. Assemblage offered activities, human and natural; space gave them a home, local, regional and international; chronology put them in order and gave them a date. Out of these things, the *site model* makes a single narrative: what happened, when and where. How may this be argued for?

The proper starting point is the sequence with which we ended the last chapter. A *context sequence diagram* was constructed from the site records. Then a *feature sequence diagram* was constructed from the context sequence diagram, with an input from the assemblage. With an input from space, this becomes a site model. One way of presenting the site model is simply as a variant of the feature sequence diagram, or its more summary form, the structure sequence diagram.

Where a single building is subject to modification over the years, it is customary to divide its development into phases of construction, and the idea has been extended to express change on a site as a whole. Each phase groups together structures and activities that are deemed contemporary and the site model is presented as a composite plan at each phase (FIG 12.2). The activities are derived from studies of the assemblage, their layout from spatial analysis and their order from chronology, which also supplies the phase with a date (see Chapter 8, FIG 8.20). Phases may be separated with the help of strong horizons, such as a ubiquitous layer of burning. They may be suggested by gaps in the sequence (like the Worcester seriation, Chapter 11, page 290). The services of an artist can illuminate the phases, showing a building at construction, destruction, ruin and eventual disappearance (Colour Plate 13).

It is accepted that phases did not actually exist. But don't worry, historians and prehistorians like to define them for the sake of convenience in argument and understanding. And it is not altogether invalid: even looking back at one's own life, it is tempting to see it as a sequences of phases, marked by successive jobs, houses or partners, in which calendar years are not the first consideration.

If *phases* denote moments of change and turning points, *periods* represent convenient chunks of time. Anything can happen in a period, including nothing. The length of a

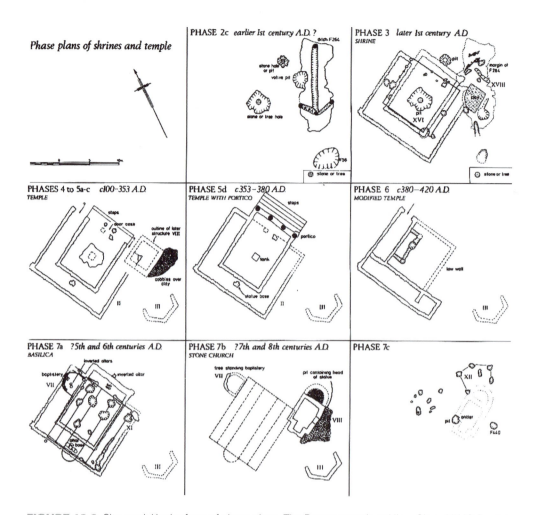

Phase plans of shrines and temple

PHASE 2c *earlier 1st century A.D. ?*

PHASE 3 *later 1st century A.D.*
SHRINE

PHASES 4 to 5a-c *c100–353 A.D.*
TEMPLE

PHASE 5d *c.353–380 A.D.*
TEMPLE WITH PORTICO

PHASE 6 *c380–420 A.D.*
MODIFIED TEMPLE

PHASE 7a *?5th and 6th centuries A.D.*
BASILICA

PHASE 7b *?7th and 8th centuries A.D.*
STONE CHURCH

PHASE 7c

FIGURE 12.2 Site model in the form of phase plans. The Roman temple at Uley, Glos., UK (© English Heritage).

period depends on how precisely it can be measured by the investigation concerned. In surveys, the ceramic dates might only allow a broad sweep: Archaic, Classic, Medieval. In excavations, the periodisation may be more ambitious and have actual numbers of years: Period 1 – c.125–220; Period 2 – c.225–75. A period may embrace several phases, or a phase may endure for several periods. Periods represent all the time that elapses in the sequence, and include those that saw a great deal of change and those that saw little, and those when very little happened. The essential difference between the two is that phases relate to change, periods to time. One method of presenting the site model in periods uses the form of a timeline, where events are tabulated against regular passages of time marked by calendar years. This has the advantage that you can show several different activities that were happening in

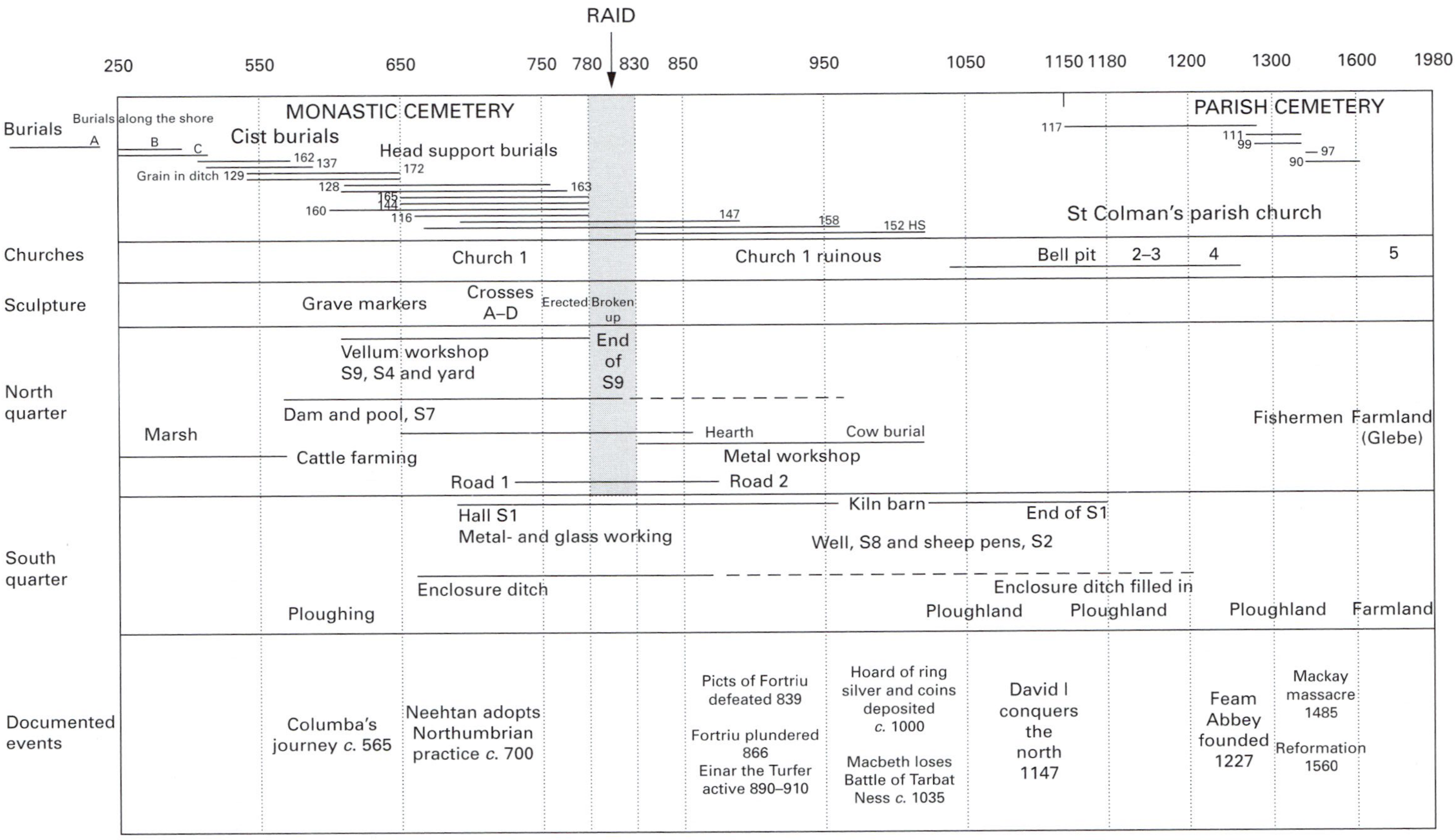

FIGURE 12.3 Site model in the form of a timeline. The story of the monastery at Portmahomack, Scotland. (M. Carver 2008).

different places at the same time, and you can add dates and historical events that took place beyond the site but might have affected it (FIG 12.3).

Interpretation

It is possible to argue for a site model as a sequence of abstract stratigraphic events – "Features 45–50 were succeeded by Structure 3 in which were distributed large numbers of animal bones and broken sherds of Type 32C pottery" – and people do. Synthesis would like to move this forward to something a little more human: "The fence (F45–50) was demolished and replaced by a hall dedicated to feasting off beef and drinking from pottery goblets (of Type 32C)." Running like a thread through this process is the idea of interpretation, which to some archaeologists is simply guess-work or at best an intellectual territory which is either deserted or anarchic. But the territory has been usefully deconstructed and organised for us by scholars like Ian Hodder. In essence, the field archaeologist supports interpretations by using analogies, and these analogies (or "parallels" as we used to call them) come from three main sources: previous archaeological discoveries, current human practices (ethnoarchaeology) and experimental trials.

An archaeologist digs with a head full of knowledge from reading and everyday life. Naturally, interpretation makes use of this. Some activities can simply be "pictured" since they are not in doubt. Oak trees and wheat and grapes are going to look more or less the same in the past as they do today (FIG 12.4). Imagination can be used to fill in some of the gaps – such as threshing and ploughing – without the need for excessive invention. Where parallels are rare, structures are built up from the logic of the ground: there are post-holes and beam-slots, so there must have been a building (FIG 12.5). The result can look a bit rickety, but these buildings stay in the literature until parallels can be found for them or confidence wanes.

An example of the bringing to life of difficult evidence can be seen in a recent report on excavations in advance of the widening of a road in Lothian, south-east Scotland, carried out by the archaeological contractor GUARD. In the evaluation phase, 5% of road corridor was stripped of topsoil with a machine in trenches. A number of sites were located from the spatial pattern of artefacts and stones of different geological origins. The site at Phantassie produced 700 artefacts of the Iron Age in a thin soil above bed-rock or boulder clay, with a carpet of stones that must have derived from the dwellings (FIG 12.6). Using a hydraulic lift to view the stones from above, the excavator recognised paths and lines of walls from straight edges, which could be seen to add to or replace each other. Overall, 15 buildings, with cobbled surfaces and pathways and midden heaps, were identified containing carbonised grain and bone that gave 60 radiocarbon dates mainly between 210BC to AD420. As the excavator tells us, the different types of evidence were then "woven together to create a picture of Phantassie as it evolved". (FIG 12.7).

FIGURE 12.4 (a) Reconstruction of the local environment at the early medieval villa on Monte Barro, with (b) an extract from the plant list (Brogiolo and Casteletti 2001).

(b)

taxon	tipo di resti	anno scavo 1993 / edificio IV / vano f / US 2246 / altre indicazioni A7	1993 / IV / f / 2258 / B5?[4]	1993 / V / e / 2419	1993 / V / 2423	1993 / V / 2442	1993 / V / 2448 / A1
CEREALI							
Cerealia	cariosside						
Hordeum/Triticum	cariosside						
Hordeum/Avena	cariosside						
Hordeum/Lolium	cariosside						
Panicum miliaceum	cariosside						
Secale cereale	cariosside						
Triticum aestivum s.l.	cariosside						
Triticum dicoccum	cariosside						
Triticum cfr. dicoccum	cariosside						
Triticum cfr. monococcum	cariosside						
LEGUMINOSE E ALTRE PIANTE COLTIVATE							
Lathyrus cicera vel sativus	seme						
Leguminosae	seme						
Lens culinaris	seme						
Pisum sativum	seme						
Pisum/Vicia	seme						
Vicia ervilia	seme						
Vicia faba var. minor	seme						
Vicia sativa	seme						
Vicia tipo sativa	seme						
Vicia sp.	seme						1m cfr.
Vicia/Lathyrus/lens	seme						
FRUTTI							
Castanea sativa	"buccia"						
Castanea sativa	cotiledone						4fr
Castanea sativa	"membrane interne"						
Cornus mas	nòcciolo						
Corylus avellana	guscio		1fr				3fr+1fr cfr.
Juglans regia	guscio	3fr	30fr			2fr	52fr+1fr cfr.
Juglans regia	"membrane interne"						
Olea europaea	nòcciolo						
Prunus cerasus/avium	nòcciolo						
Prunus domestica subsp. domestica	nòcciolo						
Prunus persica	nòcciolo			1fr	1m+1fr		4fr
Prunus persica	seme						
Rosaceae	frutto						
Vitis vinifera	vinacciolo						
ALTRE PIANTE							
Lolium temulentum	cariosside						
non determinato		1fr**					
non determinato	guscio						
totale resti		4	31	1	2	2	66

* aspetto "fresco": probabile inquinamento.
** mineralizzato

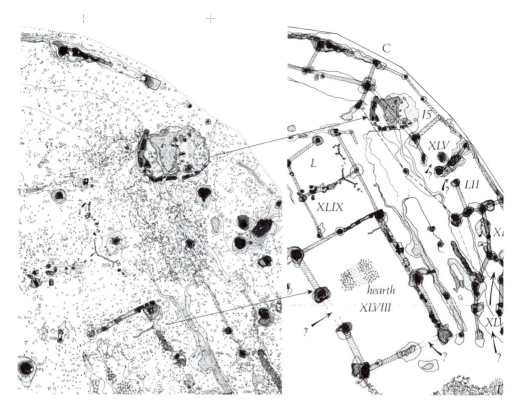

FIGURE 12.5 Interpretation: composite site plan (left) and inferred structures (numbered in Roman numerals, right) at Hen Domen (Barker and Higham 1982).

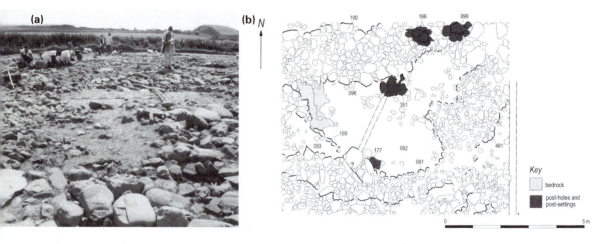

FIGURE 12.6 Interpretation of Iron Age settlement at Phantassie, SE Scotland: (a) part of the rubble complex of Structure 11 under excavation; and (b) the edges of buildings read from prominent stones (Lelong and Macgregor 2007).

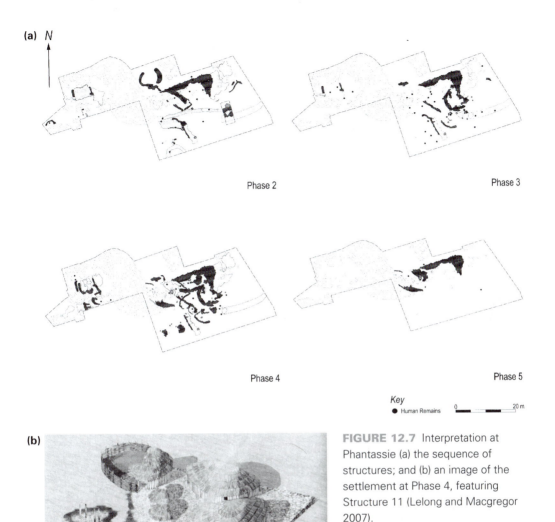

(a) N

Phase 2

Phase 3

Phase 4

Phase 5

Key
● Human Remains   0   20 m

(b)

FIGURE 12.7 Interpretation at Phantassie (a) the sequence of structures; and (b) an image of the settlement at Phase 4, featuring Structure 11 (Lelong and Macgregor 2007).

In their Stansted project, Framework Ltd offer another nice example of different kinds of evidence coming together. In one sector they made use of excavated wall-lines to imply a hall building, and the distribution of animal bones showed that this building had attracted an unusual proportion of roe deer bones. The interpretation could step up a gear when they found that the part of the airport where they worked was still marked as a deer park on a map of 1777; and their hall building could become a hunting lodge (Colour Plate 14).

In most cases, the ideas that are drawn upon to interpret the form and use of artefacts, buildings and settlements can be sourced specifically using a *literature search* – searching the archaeological literature. It might be thought that this task is becoming ever more lengthy and tedious since there is so much literature to search; but the opposite is true. Thanks to digital information highways, like the Archaeological Data Service, and thanks to the fact that the majority of archaeological journals, and many museum collections, are available on line, searching for parallels is an agreeable and often expeditious pastime. But since this is a theoretically limitless process, it is best to give it a limit. It is a reasonable assumption that, even working in a new field, researchers can locate 80 per cent of the useful parallels within a week. After that the references risk becoming increasingly contrived. The literature search will produce direct parallels, as in objects of the same type found elsewhere, or indirect parallels, where similar objects or structures are not culturally related, but provide helpful analogies.

However, there will always be some matters that seem to have escaped the literature altogether, or turn up in it but without really being understood. Some light may be thrown on these puzzling structures and activities by *experiment*. In other words: do it yourself and see what happens. Typical examples known to me are casting a bronze axe (it cracked), building the gate of a Roman fort (the British army enjoyed this),

FIGURE 12.8 Analogy by experiment: (a) experimental grain drier and (b) excavated grain drier (Jon Cane, Cecily Spall).

FIGURE 12.9 Analogy by experiment: tacking a Viking ship (a) and (b) capsizing it (M. Carver 1995).

building an Iron Age temple (it was very dark inside), making a burial mound (it didn't erode; see Chapter 3), testing a corn-dryer with a horse-hair platform (it didn't burn; FIG 12.8) and constructing and attempting to tack a square-sail keel-less Viking ship (it capsized and we all nearly drowned; FIG 12.9). It can be seen that the benefits are various: first you learn about whether the interpretation of the activity is plausible; then how difficult it would be to do it. After it has been built, an experimental structure (correct or not) becomes a monument in its own right. A further benefit, often unintended, is to burn down the building or sink the boat, and so contribute to the study of formation processes.

The problem with experimental archaeology is that it does not reflect ancient practice very directly; it shows what *we* can (or can't) do, but not what *they* did (or didn't) do. The fact that Thor Heyerdahl sailed a balsa wood raft from Peru to Easter island does not mean anyone had done it in antiquity (actually they hadn't). The fact that we are still incapable of making pattern-welded swords, does not mean the Anglo-Saxons did not make them (actually they did).

We can approach a little closer to the way things might have been through *ethno-archaeology* where findings on site are directly compared with activities that are actually being carried out now. Important hunting grounds for ethnoarchaeologists lie in areas where lifestyle, settlement plans and agricultural and manufacturing practice seem to reflect a long tradition. Ethnoarchaeological sources are varied, vivid and everywhere: an old shed falling down, 19th century photographs of ephemeral dwellings (see Chapter 1, FIGS 1.3 and 1.4) or unusual forms of worship and burial, like the clothed corpses suspended in the corridors of the cemetery in Syracusa, Sicily. These are "unusual" in the sense that the observer (not the practitioner) is surprised by them, and so broadens the range of their interpretation.

To bring their site model to life, the excavators of a Neolithic long barrow at Haddenham, Cambridgeshire, drew on first-hand observation of burial practice in

Madagascar. Timber mortuary houses in Madagascar are about 3–5m wide and 5–10m long, and constructed of thick planks so that the corpses never come into contact with the ground. The roof is composed of large timbers which can be removed to make new additions to the ancestors, moving earlier bones as necessary. At Haddenham, the Neolithic wooden chamber (1.5m×6.5m) also resembled a house with a roof and floor, containing disturbed human bones. Since the two burial sites were similar, the features at Haddenham could be tested against the more detailed picture observable in the procedures and rites practised in Madagascar.

We do not always need to go to exotic places in search of usable analogies. The best evidence may lie in the traditional practices of the country where you are working; the chances are that these practices may still be active somewhere, or that someone will remember them, or that there is an archive of photographs or recordings that will make a hazy and tremulous contact with earlier days. An object, of which we excavated only an unidentified piece, may turn up in old photographs or folk museums (FIG 12.10). Sometimes such photographs give us more than objects – they show us structures and interiors – the use of space (FIG 12.11).

For the deeper past, it is often necessary to search the deeper literature: the studies of 19th and 20th century anthropologists, and before that, with circumspection, travellers' tales. But there is always a gap between the interpretation and the reality. Bonnichsen showed this in a famous case study at "Millie's Camp", an indigenous American settlement on a hill-top that had been briefly occupied and then abandoned.

FIGURE 12.10 Analogies from ethno-archaeology: what that iron thing was for – making a straw rope using a *thrawcrook* in the Scottish borders (Fenton 1999).

FIGURE 12.11 Analogies from ethno-archaeology: a crofter's cottage in early 20th century Orkney (Cameron 1986).

The archaeological team surveyed the camp, noting the activity centres with their various artefacts and the paths between them, interpreting how each centre was used. They decided there had been two families living there and assigned their tent stances. At the north end they noted some ovaries hanging in a tree and testicles on the ground, and thought about a ritual area. They then went to consult the former occupants, represented by Millie, about the reality. She explained that there was only one family, but her husband and two adult sons worked away from home during the week at the Grand Cache coal mine. Younger children occupied the grown-up sons' tent during the week which is why there were toys in it. At the north end they had shot and butchered a deer. . .

Does this mean that archaeology is a hopelessly flaky subject, which makes up anything it does not recognise? That would be harsh. Of course initial interpretations are often wide of the mark, and we count ourselves fortunate when we find out that they were. A few wrong ideas do not invalidate centuries of convincing science. Since interpretation is founded on analogy, we can expect a better result when the analogies are familiar. On the other hand, the familiar has been less attractive to the archae-ologist as explorer. Which is only to say that our models get better as we get to know the world better. Millie's Camp was an experiment from 30 years ago; we should know more now, thanks to studies like this, and thanks to improved research relations with the modern indigenous communities.

The wider context

We are probably now ready to draw up a programme for the synthesis stage (FIG 12.12), since most of the tasks and tools have been broadly identified. Let's notice first that it consists, like any other job, of a series of tasks that need to be assessed, planned and completed. This is not achieved by an open-ended stay in a country cottage waiting for inspiration. It is a programme that can be timetabled and costed – so there is no excuse at all for archaeologists *or their clients* excluding it from their funded post-excavation programmes. By the same token, if the writing of reports is to be paid for, then it is right that a sponsor should expect an output that is easy to understand, devoid of conceits and punctually delivered.

The result of the synthesis programme is a dressed-up site model, a site model with blood pressure. However this is not quite the end of the job. The sequence must be placed in its wider context and its significance asserted: the site model gave us a story; now we need to know its place in history or prehistory. Much of the work has already been done in the "literature search" since, in looking for parallels for structures and activities, we will have had a good trawl through the published examples of the relevant cultures. All the same, this is a good moment to bring in colleagues to share in the production of the research results. First, they can critique the site model and second, they can help assess the significance of the findings in terms of the overall state of knowledge. This will be important in the next stage, which is to design the type and content of the desirable publication (Chapter 13).

The task consists of assessing of the success of the field project, the significance of the results, their utility for research and the best course for publication. A useful device is to hold a brainstorming seminar at which the participant researchers and stakeholders are all present. In an unusual case, the proceedings of the one held for Gårdlösa (Sweden) were published, to show what ideas had been considered and accepted or rejected. Following completion of the fieldwork at this Iron Age site, the participants and interested parties compared the preliminary site model with the original research objectives in an all-day recorded discussion. The principal actors were: the director, excavator, artefact specialist, botanist, animal bone specialist, human bone analyst, radiocarbon dating specialist, soil scientist, historical geographer, geologist and historian. And this was their agenda: what was left? The quality of the evidence; where? The site and survey plans; when? The dating evidence; what was it like round there? The resources and environment; what did they eat? The economy; was there manufacture, contact and exchange? What was the evidence for cult? Who lived there, and how many of them were there? What was the social organisation? How did things change? Each topic was presented by one of the participants and then discussion ranged free and was recorded word for word. Alignments of evidence were noted and contradictions were talked through to a compromise. The conversation was published as an end-piece to volume 1 of the research report.

Outcome of analysis	Literature search	Ethno-parallels	Experiment	Models to be created
Identity, sequence and provenance of artefacts	Local material culture studies; comparable artefacts	Similar artefacts in use in comparable cultures	Construction and testing of replica artefacts; manufacture, function, breakage	Uses of artefacts, where they made and how distributed; meaning of symbols
Palaeoecological sequence	Local pollen sequences and excavated assemblages. The current natural landscape and its ecology. Historical accounts of same	Uses of plants and animals How bone, plant and insect assemblages form	How plant and insect assemblages form	Vegetation sequence Micro-environment, animal vegetable and mineral resources and their exploitation; diet, commodities, economy, ecology
Composition of assemblages	Comparable assemblages	How assemblages form and what they mean in comparable examples	How assemblages form	Activities (agriculture, manufacture, ritual)
Identity of features	Features identified on other sites	Features used by comparable cultures	Construction, use and disuse of replica features	Activities
Identity of structures	Similar structures identified on other sites	Comparable structures built by earlier, later or exotic communities	Construction, use and disuse or replica buildings	Appearance, use and symbolic meaning of buildings
Identity of activities	Similar activities identified at other sites	Comparable activities among other cultures	Comparable activities among other cultures	Activities and their meaning
Uses of space	Geography of similar sites, landscapes and settlement patterns identified in the literature	Use of space inside settlements or cemeteries and over landscapes of documented communities	Archaeological distributions resulting from comparable use of space	Meaning of spatial layout within a site Ecological and political meaning of landscapes
Sequence diagrams	Comparable sequences of sites and landscapes and their interpretation	Analogous events in traditional communities		SITE MODEL
SITE MODEL IN CONTEXT	Existing histories/ prehistories	Analogous histories, processes, explanations		Social, economic and ideological systems and explanations for change

FIGURE 12.12 Synthesis: programme of tasks.

Naturally there were annoying gaps in the evidence, and equally naturally the proposed solution was often to do more field-work. But the field archaeologist's response to the final question raised – Should we dig more? – was enlightening. He reckoned that while there was (of course) a great deal we still didn't know, much had been learnt. Digging of itself can only take you so far, and might take you nowhere at all unless it is planned with a proper research question and integrated with regional surveys and environmental investigations. Archaeological excavation was very time-consuming and a limit must be set to every operation. We did in fact have a context for our site, he pointed out, because preliminary work suggested that there were similar settlements and cemeteries on adjacent ridges. There may have been a whole network of such ridge-top sites, with the valley floor little occupied, as the environmental evidence suggests. But tempting as it might be to dig a few more trenches, with the aim of filling chronological gaps and finding companion sites, these are matters that no amount of trenching would resolve. "Let's leave those problems for other projects," he concluded, "and not hold up the publication of ours." Amen to that. Field archaeology is not a magisterial campaign in pursuit of a definitive result. It is a question asked with the maximum respect for the resource, which obtains an answer which must be convincingly expressed. It is not the sole answer, it is today's answer.

As for the presentation of a synthesis, the reader is destined to encounter a broad spectrum between turgid lists and flights of fancy, non-committal plodding and literary affectation, dense thickets which the reader has to hack their way through, and perfumed gardens of delight where the author acts as a hypnotic guide. The case of Gårdlösa might be termed an example of a "consensus" synthesis, which although it is the product of one pen, subsumes and reconciles the many opinions of the participants into one agreed narrative. Other approaches like to leave the different opinions showing, so the synthesis becomes more of an anthology of multiple narratives, into which the reader can dip at will. Others want to supply supplementary comment, since there is always more to a tale than its telling. A popular method is to include asides or boxes of additional texts, which amplify or qualify the main message. Digital reading, where you can drill down deeper into a topic with the click of a mouse, encourages this kind of writing of hyper-narratives; it greatly increases the amount of information that the reader can explore, but reduces its impact. In a world already overloaded with information, the human mind finds one version more memorable than 20. Synthesis will always be a balance between the need to inform and the need to persuade. Some modern authors also like to tell you a lot about themselves and their world-view, in the belief that what they say is ineluctably predetermined by who they are. Leaving behind Pitt Rivers' exhortation to "reduce the personal equation to a minimum", we meet the more highly reflexive archaeologists who like to increase it to a maximum. This assumes a certain complicity in the reader who may actually be rather more interested in the report than its author.

On the other hand, an account of what was done, and what happened, in the field is most certainly significant for the synthesis, and the details are too frequently omitted.

One way of covering both what archaeologists did, and what they think it meant, is to separate the two, as twin-narratives. The first part of the report is then a personal, but factual account of what was done during the project; and the second an impersonal, but imaginative account of what happened in the past. The exact structure of the report will depend on the readership it is intended to serve; and that is matter for the publication chapter, which comes next.

Conclusion

Synthesis is not open-ended dreaming aloud and does not require a blank cheque. It has a programme of tasks which can be timed, costed and completed. The principal outcome is the site model, constructed from the results of the analysis, of assemblage, space and time. Flesh is put on the bones of the site model by interpretation, itself drawn from analogies in the archaeological and ethnographic literature and from experiment. The site model is then placed in its research context to make a synthesis for the research community. It is this synthesis which will be assessed for the next stage – publication.

A synthesis is the more enjoyable and valuable to make, the broader and deeper it spreads its net. The archaeologist is an insatiable reader of curious literature, an incorrigible traveller, a snapper-up of unconsidered trifles. All these can be stored away for a rainy day, and that day will often come while drafting a synthesis. The archaeologist is no jobbing recorder, no digger-up of loot. From the beginning to the end of the process, the archaeologist is a creative artist, bringing the dead to life in words and pictures, as surely as a novelist (FIG 12.13). And as with a novel, the story gets better the more credible it is, the more thoroughly its elements are researched. The better the truth, the better the fiction.

FIGURE 12.13 Artist's impression of a snowy evening at Alfred's 10th century hunting lodge at Cheddar Gorge. Imagined by Alan Sorrell from a site model by the excavator, Philip Rahtz (P.A. Rahtz).

Briefing

Site models: The easiest access to the art is to look at models in reports and see if they work; numerous examples of projects with outcomes have been alluded to in this book, especially in Chapter 7. See Brogiolo and Castelletti 1991 for Monte Barro, Lelong and MacGregor 2007 for Phantassie; Framework 2008 for Stansted. **Interpretation and use of analogy:** excellent textbooks are Hodder 1986, 1991; **ethnoarchaeology:** Fenton 1999, Cameron 1986, Kidd 1996, Hodder 1986, David and Kramer 2001; see Evans and Hodder 2006 (188–9) for the Madagascar analogy to the Haddenham long barrow; **experiment:** Thomas 1998, Chapter 10; Carver 1995 for the ship; Millie's Camp, Bonnichsen 1973; recent examples of **narratives**, Oates et al 1998, 2001; Framework 2008; Hodder 2005 (multiple narratives); Stjernquist 1993 (consensus narrative; Gårdlösa); Evans and Hodder 2006; Framework Archaeology 2006 (hyper-narratives); M. Carver 1998, 2008 (twin narratives).

13 PUBLICATION

Types of output

The aim of publication, the final stage of Field Research Procedure, is to lay the results of the fieldwork before the public. Up to now archaeologists have decided what to do, how to do it, what to record, which to analyse and what it all means. But as any publisher will tell you, when it comes to publication, the verdict lies in the hands of readers, not authors. Since there is more than one kind of reader (see Chapter 3, FIG 3.9), there are many kinds of publication. Here I count eight different kinds of published output designed to serve eight different kinds of client (FIG 13.1). These include the preparation of archives (in their digital form increasingly the principal mode of access), issuing multi-copy reports, and making presentations by lecture, film and exhibitions and the presentation of the site itself to visitors. The perfect field archaeologist will be adept at each of these, just as good at archiving, argument and appearing on TV – but thankfully most people are not that perfect. The task of communication will be a collaborative one, each of us trying to develop the type of communication we do best, and working with others to serve the wider public.

As will soon appear, not every form of publication is necessary or appropriate for every project. Publication begins, therefore, with a design. Traditionally, archaeological gurus have pronounced publication "an obligation". What they really meant by that was an obligation to make findings available to other archaeologists, especially themselves. But the role of publication is a lot broader than that. We are obliged not to keep the results to ourselves, but we are also obliged not to hit the public over the head with voluminous and self-indulgent slabs of data.

At the design stage we identify the potential users, dividing the results of a field project into three: matters that must be made available in perpetuity for others to search; matters that could be of contemporary significance to researchers; and material that might be attractive to the general public. Broadly, these three categories equate to archive, literature and display. These are presented in different media: for example the internet is useful for the archive, multi-copy articles for researchers, and books, magazines, TV programmes, exhibitions and site presentations for the

Mode	Contents	Medium	Clients
1 Field Records	Site records, primary data	Hard copies	Sponsor, other researchers
2 Lab Report	Commissioned studies and analyses	e-repository	Sponsor, other researchers
3 Client Report	Description of the investigation and results	Hard copy with limited distribution ("grey literature")	Sponsors
4 Research Report	Description of the investigation, findings, their interpretation and context	Article (hard copy or online), monograph with multiple distribution	Researchers
5 Popular book	Abbreviated research report	Book	The public
6 Media	Selected significant aspects	Magazine articles, site guide, TV programmes	The public
7 Display	Selected significant aspects	Exhibitions in museums	The public
8 Presentation	The site and its surviving parts; local trails	Conserved monuments; display panels	The public

FIGURE 13.1 Modes of publication. Multiple copies are produced for nos. 4, 5 and 6.

general public. Needless to say each of us has a foot in all these camps. Whoever we are, we might wish to consult an archive on a Monday, read a scholarly article on a Wednesday, read a magazine on a Friday and visit a monument on a Sunday.

Archive

The basic idea of an archive is to keep material for the future. We do not have to justify this ambition: a field archaeology project is a unique operation, and we owe it to other people to keep what was found, and to make a record of it. Centuries of archaeology have taught us how easily this intention is thwarted, by fire, flood, pests, greed and carelessness. Curating an archive is an active, not a passive job. The matter to be curated falls into three parts: the records (called for convenience "the paper archive" even if it is 100% digital), the finds (artefacts and biota taken from the field) and the remains of the site itself.

We have already met the basic format of the paper archive: the *Field Records* which contain the records made on site, and the *Lab Reports* which contain the analyses

and interpretations of the field workers and specialists (see Chapters 8–11). These latter will include the synthesis (Chapter 12). Traditionally the Field Records and Lab Reports took the form of a mass of A4 folders, rolls of drawings, index cards and photographs, transported in numerous cardboard boxes and suitcases. The material was cumbersome, bulky and vulnerable; it still takes up a lot of space in museum basements and claims the time of museum curators. Much of the world still has to cope with this, but hopefully the boon of digitisation will soon become in reach of all.

It is a boon not only because it takes up less space, and because it is so much easier to search, but because its active long-term curation has become that much more feasible. At the forefront of the development of digital archives is the Archaeological Data Service which advises archaeologists how to format and care for digital media, and also itself hosts an immense archive of archaeological projects from all countries online (FIG 13.2).

The finds archive will ideally be found, curated and sometimes displayed, in a museum. In some countries, all finds belong to the state, and the state looks after them in

FIGURE 13.2 Archaeological Data Service, online project archive, front end. Project archives ("grey literature") can be located by place or contractor (ADS).

government offices. In others they belong to the landowner, who can legitimately claim them. As part of the project design (see Chapter 14), archaeologists endeavour to negotiate a deal that allows the finds to stay together in the care of an institution that is publicly accessible. This then counts as publication: the finds are protected and the public can see them (if they ask nicely).

As for the site itself, this is a problem that seldom arises in commercial archaeology, since there is now a brand-new building where the site was. But in research projects on monuments, it is axiomatic that a sizable chunk of the untouched deposits and upstanding ruins should survive for the future. There is therefore a long-term curation programme needed out of doors. In general this task is incorporated into the Conservation Programme that forms part of the Project Design. We will visit this in the next Chapter. For the present it can simply be noted, that where all or part of a site survives our studies, it also becomes our responsibility. Where the part that remains is also presented to visitors, it becomes, in a real sense, part of our publication programme (see page 327).

Client reports

Commercial contractors always provide a report of their fieldwork to the organisation that paid for it. In the business world, this organisation is the archaeologists' client and these reports are *client reports*. Each report addresses the specific work that was commissioned: for example, an evaluation, the record of a building, a conservation plan, or archaeological investigation in advance of development (Colour Plate 15), these being common tasks in the management of archaeological resources (see Chapters 14 and 15). The report begins with a summary and concludes with a brief discussion about the wider significance of the findings and some recommendations for further work. In between, the report is mainly descriptive: a description of the situation that led to the work being undertaken, then a description of the methods used (often standard and pasted in from other reports) and a description of what was done in this case. This is followed by a description of what was found, in words, photographs and plans, and a site model by period. At the end is a series of appendices, listing the contexts, the features, the finds and the samples. The report constitutes evidence that the intended work was undertaken to the intended standard. Without it, you don't get paid.

Commercial archaeology worldwide produces a large number of these reports every month. Academics call them "grey literature" and love to grumble about them: "doesn't count as publication", "stuff we will never know about" and so on. But this is a little old-fashioned. The main reason that the client reports do not get published is that the projects did not set out to solve a research question, but to retrieve material that was about to be destroyed. In this they succeeded. A client report is therefore an archive report, and the only essential is that it should be available in the public domain so that it can freely searched. The real moan is that this does not happen, when it very easily could.

The second matter is also serious: where there *is* a clear research dividend, suitable for multi-copy publication, the client may not provide the money for a proper synthesis (see Chapter 12) or to prepare a publication. Clients are not indifferent to the attractions of a synthesis, but are wary of paying for open-ended periods of study. They may feel that if a mitigation project, designed to rescue data, turns out to have added value in the form of research, then the research community should pay for its further study and dissemination. In order to justify the additional expenditure, the project must first pass the test of research significance. Not every one will – but it is safe to say that they will be many more than at present. This is part of a wider question of what rescue archaeology is for – one that is central to the profession (Chapters 14 and 15 for more).

The commercial sector therefore needs at least to be furnished with an efficient digital archiving service to ensure every project is accessible and easily searchable online; and a system of funded publication for those projects for which a current research significance can be demonstrated. Neither should it be assumed that everything unearthed by a research project is of absorbing interest. All the findings will require to be accessible on archive. But the basis of research publication, in multiple copy, is selectivity.

Research reports

Research is the gold standard of the subject, and there are many ways in which archaeologists wish to communicate new research to each other and to their public, and a variety of published media in which to do it (FIG 13.3). All new information should be archived, hopefully in a form that is accessible to those that wish to search it; but only some of the new information will get published, in the sense of being printed and distributed in multiple copies. Why is this?

To qualify for publication as research, a piece of work must pass the significance test: is this result of immediate interest to the current research community? The future can look after itself: it has the archive to play with. The judges of significance are the publishers' editors and their reviewers, who represent a wide range of potential interests, from the very specialist to the very general. Notice also that a project produces a wide range of potentially hot research: not just the synthesis, but the reports of specialists on artefacts and biota. And not just these, but new methods or a new management experience. In brief, the participants may identify a selection of potential publications – and they will nearly always find an editor that likes it – but you have to shop around. The basic principle is that whereas the archive created a resource in which future researchers can look for what they want, the research report contains matters that you want to place in front of the research community: matters

Type of input	Archive	National publication	International publication
Inventory survey	e-repository	Monograph	
Evaluation survey	e-repository		
Research survey	e-repository Local journal	**Refereed journal**	Monograph **Refereed journal**
Evaluation excavation	e-repository		
Preservation by record	e-repository	Monograph	
Research excavation	e-repository	Monograph **Refereed journal**	Monograph **Refereed journal**
New theory	Local journal	**Refereed journal**	Monograph **Refereed journal**
New models	Local journal	**Refereed journal**	Monograph **Refereed journal**
New methods	Local journal	**Refereed journal**	**Refereed journal**
Politics and debate	Local journal	**Refereed journal**	**Refereed journal**
News	Editorials	Editorials Magazines	Magazines

FIGURE 13.3 Archaeological publication – range of outputs.

which deserve their interest now, matters which have the potential to push the subject along.

The outlets available are journals and books (FIG 13.4). Which is best? For reports of archaeological investigations, the archaeological community remains strongly addicted to books or monographs. Maybe we like their monumental quality, or their comprehensive, inclusive character or the spurious sense of importance they give the author. But for the speedy communication of new research, the journal greatly excels over the book. Journals have a much longer life and a much wider distribution: an article in *American Antiquity* or *Medieval Archaeology* immediately reaches more than a thousand subscribers who have bought it in advance and its results will be archived in public libraries for ever. Furthermore such journals are increasingly accessible and searchable on line. A book (or a monograph – i.e. a book which is just about a single field project) might have a distribution of 500 (if it's lucky), so will only find a home in a few hundred libraries. It is quickly remaindered and disappears into the second-hand bookshops. When archaeologists undertaking synthesis want to search the literature, they naturally turn mainly to the journals, easily accessible and rapidly searchable online, rather than monographs, hard to find and slow to search. The hundreds of lists and appendices that pad out monographs would not only be safer in archive, they would be easier to search and use. So the need for field research reports to appear in multiple published copies of great length in a monograph is one

FIGURE 13.4 Publishing fieldwork – various outlets: top row, left to right: international, national, specialist, national specialist. Bottom row: local, fascicule, monograph, offprint.

that at least deserves careful scrutiny. As a glance at the pages of *Antiquity* or *Nature* will show, there is no piece of significant new research that cannot be presented in under 5,000 words. Ironically, where a report of great length is, for other reasons, essential, it is the online journal, such as *Internet Archaeology*, not the book, that can most economically supply it.

There are plenty who will challenge this championing of the journals. My argument omits the pleasure that books bring, the pleasure of production and the pleasure of ownership. Large projects are often under a political obligation to produce large books, to mark the completion of a task and serve as evidence of money well spent. It must also be acknowledged that in spite of great strides in the provision of accessible archives, on and offline, we don't yet really trust them to be always accessible or even there in a hundred years' time. Again and again we reach instinctively for the comprehensive accounts of great field investigations that ornament our shelves.

Whether to publish in a monograph or a journal will depend on financial circumstances and the intellectual negotiations of the day; and the most desirable outcome may well be to publish in both. Digital dissemination means that the world is changing fast and the current division of material between media might not remain where it is. My own prediction is that the future principal vehicle of professional field research will be the online journal, while the book will remain, or become, the principal means of communicating its research significance to a wider public. Publication reflects the dual aims of synthesis touched on in Chapter 12. We want to make our findings available as quickly and easily as possible to our fellow researchers, knowing that they will know what they are looking for. At the same time we want to invigorate a wider public, who are inveterate browsers and like to have a handsome volume on the shelf. On the one hand, inform and argue, on the other entertain and persuade. It may be that the form of publication, online journal or distributed book will come to divide along similar lines.

Preparing a research report

A research report contains certain essentials, briefly summarised in TABLE 13.1. This is a list with no emphasis, but in reality there will be considerable selectivity, talking up some points and omitting others. The main headings concern what was done, what was found and what it means. The structure will be dependent on the chosen form of publication, so like all other writers archaeologists need to study their intended readers. The easiest way is to look at the products of the journal or publishing house concerned, see what they have published in the past and how they like their reports presented. These publishers serve a broad constituency – the one you are trying to reach – and they know what it wants.

TABLE 13.1 The contents of a research report

Abstract: a summary description of project, pointing up the significant/innovatory matters.

Acknowledgments: adding thanks to those who read the research report in draft and suggested amendments to it.

Introduction: the background, the circumstances which led to intervention, aims, design and subsequent history of the project.

The aim of this report. What were the selected research interests, and why were they selected? These may include innovations in methodology, particular buildings and/or finds, or the sequence as a whole.

TABLE 13.1 continued

Methodology: brief accounts of reconnaissance, evaluation, project design, recovery levels, recording system and deposit quality. This is as important as the "source criticism" which is a mandatory part of any paper on a historical document.

The site model, period by period: this may be presented with a centre piece, such as a sequence diagram, but the reader will always prefer to be talked through it in prose.

Studies of special research interest: for example "The lute from rubbish pit, F45", "The Hall building and its exemplars", "The pottery typology for the middle period".

Digests of specialist reports: cross-referring to the full reports, particularly those which can be related directly to the economy and resources and referring to those that are or will be published elsewhere.

Interpretation of the sequence, and its prehistoric/historic context: this should be argued as a progressive piece of prose.

Index to the Lab Reports and where they may be found.

Examples of Illustrations

FIG 1: A location plan, showing the region and site which was the object of the research.

FIG 2: Master plan with every discovery on it, if possible.

FIG 3: Site model.

FIG 4: Plan of Period 1.

FIGS 5–7: Plan of Period 2 . . . 3 . . . 4 . . .

FIGS 8–10: Selected finds, in support of specialist reports.

FIGS 11–12: Selected analyses: stratification diagram, seriation table, spatial analyses. These are presented in support of interpretations.

FIGS 13–14: Reconstruction drawings of buildings, and the sequence. These are presented in illustration of interpretations.

PLATE 1: Aerial photograph which sets the scene.

PLATE 2: Survey terrain or excavation in action.

PLATE 3: "Period" views, showing key buildings or other structures (e.g. burials) discussed in the text).

PLATE 4: Interesting methodology in action.

PLATE 5: Key artefacts discussed in the text.

The research from a field project can in fact serve several different constituencies – some work mainly from syntheses, others work with flint and pottery, others with plants or animals and others are mad about method. There are readers for all these things – and journals that know how to find them. Some outlets serve quite local matters, the archaeology of Derbyshire for example (FIG 13.4). Others concern

themselves with a region or continent. These are all important publications that do different things. Archaeology, especially field archaeology, is an intensely local subject, and its findings will remain of value in that place for centuries. Some journals cover a period, rather than a place, and seek to link interested researchers internationally: e.g. the *Journal of World Prehistory*, *Post Medieval Archaeology*. Other discoveries or ideas which spring from them will find a more global audience, and will seek the broader outlet: a methods journal like the *Journal of Field Archaeology*, a theoretical journal like *Archaeological Dialogues*, a debate journal like *Public Archaeology*, or *Antiquity*, which does all of these. In other words, publication is for readers, not for authors, and a site may have to be published in several different outlets if readers are to be properly served. This "portfolio" of publication is worked out during the process of publication design.

The design process is eased through consultation. The chances are that friends and sponsors have already expressed an opinion on what they think is valuable, which will help in drafting the publication design. The next stage is to send the design, with its proposed set of outlets, round to other interested parties ("This is what I am planning; what do you think?"). Those entrusted with the dissemination will then be approached. First the archive, whether digital or not, to ensure there is accessibility for researchers. Then the journal editors and/or book publishers. With a measure of support, one or more research reports, with one or more authors, can then be drafted.

Archaeologists communicate in prose, photographs, line drawings, tables and lists and the preparation of an archaeological research report is among the most complex tasks asked of any professional working in the humanities. This is why reports can grow organically in the making until the author becomes entangled in the undergrowth. The key adage is that reports are made for readers, readers need selectivity and selectivity needs design. Design is all. Skilful design can make accessible arguments from large data bases. Framework's Stansted report (already mentioned in Chapter 12) uses "nested" layouts to document arguments that take the reader from a context to a feature to a structure on a single page (Colour Plate 14). This publication is also praiseworthy in that it is an example of a large commercial project that produced a research report (as well as client reports) as part of its output. In this case the client (the Airport Authority) was evidently convinced (for whatever reason) that the production of such a report was an important part of the mitigation required by the public of a developer (they published it themselves).

Drafted reports should always go to friends and advisors for comment, and they always improve as a result. Then the corrected draft is sent to the editor of choice in the form required by that publisher (unless you want it rejected unread). But don't imagine the process ends there. The editors will consult peer-reviewers, and all will have opinions – mainly opinions on how to make your research more telling: "Look at more literature; cut the waffle at the end; include a map." They may ask for the drawings to be redone, for better photographs. This is not a personal assault on the author.

All archaeology is teamwork, and this is only the latest example of it, in the final stages of its production.

The article will come back as a proof, ready for printing, and you have the chance to give it one last check before it is consigned to posterity. Then you can stop worrying. You may never hear another word. Or 20 years on, someone you don't know says: "That site was brilliant; I've used the pollen report such a lot." No, you don't become famous overnight; be resigned rather to a remote whispering of emulation and borrowings, only a tithe of which are ever recorded in citations.

Talking to the public

My other four kinds of publication (popular book, media, display and site presentation) are all designed to serve the public, or since we are all the public, perhaps I can call them popular outputs. They are prepared on different principles and operate on a different economic basis. A popular book has to be taken to a commercial publisher; and commercial publishers are, well, commercial. They are interested in sales. A popular book must be interesting and should be fun. Some publishers like pictures and think that colour photographs of artefacts are what sell archaeology, as they sell art. Others want the book to have a strong historical message; something revolutionary they can put on the cover. But many understand that archaeological investigation is best at recovering stories of ordinary people, and in this lies its charm. The readership for this kind of local parable is growing.

Not every project has a popular output or needs one; commercial projects rarely have them; research projects may not want them. But commercial sponsors sometimes need to woo a wider public, and researchers sometimes like to. If a project has a popular following, the chances are that popular outlets will form part of the publication programme. Such a programme begins in the field, where access for visitors is factored into the project design. Nothing beats the first hand sight of archaeology in action and on most large scale investigations, whether academically or commercially driven, people will come in all weathers to hear tours or see temporary displays, locals to enhance their "ownership" and those from further away to serve a passion for the past (FIG 13.5). Other methods of communication will be more remote, and increasingly the remote facility takes the form of a website or blog. Project staff also expect to give talks, not just to academic groups but to schools and local and national societies, where archaeology's popular support, local and national, is mainly to be found. The interest of the media, from the local newspapers, magazines, TV and radio, is attracted for its own reasons, but it has always a piece of the public in mind (FIG 13.6). Due to the exigencies of the industry, the media presentation of archaeological work can be irritatingly approximate, but its users are no fools and they can read behind the headlines. "Is this news?" is a criterion used by journalists. That is why they lead with questions such as "Is this the first . . . the oldest . . . the most

FIGURE 13.5 Visitors welcome on site, whatever the weather (FAS Ltd).

FIGURE 13.6 On site filming. The film may be broadcast as clips in TV news programmes, in history documentaries or rarely as their own series. TV producers generally use wildlife or history documentaries as models, with presenters and actuality (N. Macbeth).

complete" or, in desperation, "the most exciting thing you have ever found?" The intention is not necessarily to be annoying: all copy has to fight for space and get past the sub-editors. Exposure in the media is good for the profile of the project (there is no such thing as bad publicity) and the projects' sponsors will be gratified.

The primary interface between archaeology and its public is the museum. Since there will be (should be) a museum partner for every field project (see Chapter 14), there should also be a little scheme afoot to put on occasional exhibitions, during and after the fieldwork. Similarly, a museum has to make space for your exhibition, and contain the costs within a shrinking budget. Museum curators will be pleased with a glamorous find, a crowd-puller, and will like the free artwork you can provide. But a full-blown exhibition with finds in context – that needs outside sponsorship.

Presentation of sites

Needing still more serious financial underpinning are the conservation and display of the site to the public – and this time the sponsors have to be in it for the long term. Visitors rarely bring enough revenue to maintain an exciting site presentation, although prominent experiments like the Jorvik Viking Centre in York have succeeded where hundreds have failed. For this reason, a site is safest, and most appreciated and most authentic when it stays in the hands of a public body. If the site is to survive, it should have a programme for conservation and its long-term protection, but also for presentation: access to the ruins and their interpretation with signs and panels and audio-visual aids. The site that has been researched lives on, in archive, in reports

FIGURE 13.7 Consolidation of ruins. The Roman town of Tipasa in Algeria (author).

FIGURE 13.8 Reconstruction and shelter: Knossos, Crete in 2008 (author).

FIGURE 13.9 Reconstruction of a replica Iron Age house at Castell Henllys, Wales (courtesy of Harold Mytum).

FIGURE 13.10 In a Roman garden. Herbarium serving a working Roman restaurant within the Roman fortress at Xanten, Germany (author).

FIGURE 13.11 Re-enactment at West Stow Anglo-Saxon village, Suffolk UK. Volunteers dress up, spin and weave in the reconstructed timber houses, which are based on extensive excavations.

and not least in what remains of it in the ground. In a few special cases, the site itself can form part of the publication programme; to this end it is consolidated, conserved, protected and prepared to receive visitors, or *presented*.

This presentation takes many forms, the simplest being the consolidation of ruins (FIG 13.7). The ruins may be protected with a shelter, and partially reconstructed, as at Newgrange or Knossos (FIG 13.8), or wholly reconstructed, as at Castell Henllys (FIG 13.9). To assist the visitor further in understanding the character of a living site, it may be replanted, like the Roman garden at Xanten (FIG 13.10), or provided with actors who play parts in the story (FIG 13.11). This may include the full-bloodied re-enactment of events supposed to have taken place at the site. Given the best opportunities and resources, presentation begins during the course of the project. The visiting public begin to absorb the site into their world view, and to establish a dialogue with those doing the research. The strategy here looks forward to eventual long-term display by creating a constituency of visitors, both on the site and on the web (FIG 13.12).

FIGURE 13.12 Display and conservation: the magnificent shelter over the 4040 site at Çatalhöyük (author).

The reception of visitors and the provision of materials to aid understanding, including books, panels and tour guides, is a key part of the archaeology profession. It is usually termed *interpretation* (rather than presentation) by those in the business, showing that bringing a monument and its past to life for visitors is an active and creative, not merely a descriptive, task. The word also endorses the idea that the opening of archaeological sites to the public is a genuine part of the publication process. As with communication in print, it has the same duty to serve many different interests and levels of appreciation, without compromising the authenticity and beauty of the place.

Should the archaeologist, as excavator and researcher, be involved in this particular form of publication? I think so – the excavator's verdict should be clearly heard, since it has been forged with much toil and represents the voice of first-hand experience, the voice of the explorer. But of course it need not be exclusive. The interpretation and the visitors' appreciation will be enhanced by the addition of other views on what was found and what it means.

Conclusion

The publication programme for archaeological investigations is potentially broad and varied. Output will be tiered: the bulk of the material in archive, a reasoned selection in a report, and a summary of the selection in TV and magazines. Every field project has an archive containing the finds and primary records. Every field project should generate a set of Lab Reports from the analyses undertaken. All, whether funded by commerce or research, will be required to produce a client report with the basic results. Many will go on to produce research reports to serve the archaeological community. Some will produce popular publications, films and displays of finds and the consolidation and display of the site itself to serve the public. All this lies in the province of field archaeologists, though they will work in teams with publishers, TV producers, museum designers and experts in site presentation.

Publication is the latest of the stages of field research procedure, but we still have two items of unfinished business. At every stage we have referred to the importance of design, and the ascendancy of design over standard procedures when it comes to deciding what to do. Chapter 14 considers the role of design, drawing together some the threads that ran through all the previous chapters.

Our last task will be to place the whole staged process of Field Research Procedure in its economic and social framework (Chapter 15). This is the framework that enables archaeological investigation to serve society, and explains how and why it is possible to earn a living in this most exhilarating of pastimes.

Briefing

Forms of publication in the digital age: Gray and Walford 1999, M. Carver 2007a, b; Richards 2006. **Archive:** Field Records, Walker 1990. **Digital records: ADS (Archaeology Data Service)**, Richards 1997, ADS 1999; Condron et al 1999 is an example of the now numerous ADS guides to best practice in the preparation of digital matter. **Client reports** can be found in the offices of archaeological firms; but increasingly appear also online at ADS (www.http://ads.ahds.ac.uk/catalogue/library/greylit/index.cfn). For **research reports** of many different kinds, see examples cited in Chapter 7; among more recent examples of monographs cited here are Hodder et al 2005 and M. Carver 2005. Edmonds and McElearney 1999 for a publication in the online journal *Internet Archaeology*. For research from commercial archaeology, Framework's *Stansted* (2008) is exemplary with clear structure and strong narrative. Another notable success in reaping the research dividend from massive commercial excavations is Lelong and Macgregor's *Lothian* (2007) and in Ireland Carlin et al 2008. All these projects had a negotiated design although the design was not published, and so remained a private treaty between the archaeologists and the developer. For an overview of how far the recent crop of road excavations serve the research community see J. Carver 2009. **Communicating with the public:** Hall 1984, M. Carver 1998, 2008 are accounts of excavations written for the general public. Rowsome 2000 is nice example of a popular outreach publication; visiting working sites, Binks et al 1988; site restoration, presentation Amendolea (acd) 1995; N. James 1998; for interesting examples see Cooney 2006 (restoration at New Grange) and Papadopoulos et al 2008 (restoration of a burial mound).

PART 4
DESIGN

14 PROJECT DESIGN

Introduction

The idea that archaeological investigation is powered by *design* has run through every chapter up to this one, linking what is done with its purpose, reconciling the diverse agendas that fieldwork must satisfy, balancing its objectives, its ability to read the ground, its social context. Design is the strong flexible axis of Field Research Procedure, kick-starting and concluding every stage. Design makes archaeological investigation productive and dynamic, prevents projects losing their way and becoming stagnant. Design gives archaeology its persuasive edge in the wider world.

Let's also agree the following premise: without a pre-released project design, a field archaeology project must be judged at best inept, at worst unethical. Consider the case of an archaeological site or historic landscape that is about to be destroyed or altered in modern times. The archaeologists need to negotiate the retrieval of the matter of historic value before it disappears – and they need to negotiate this retrieval in advance. To succeed in this negotiation, they must be able to answer the question: Exactly what is it that you would like to do? This is a project design.

Now consider the case of a site or landscape that is to be the target of a research investigation. It is about to be altered too, this time by the investigation itself. This land, like all land, is the subject of many interests, local and global, academic and notional, interests which need to be acknowledged in advance, because once the investigation has happened it will be too late to take account of them. The best way to serve all these communities, academic or social, is to draft a programme of fieldwork in advance: these proposals equally constitute a project design.

A project design is therefore a consultation document that is prepared and circulated widely before serious fieldwork begins. It contains proposed programmes designed to serve research, conservation and other interests. Its importance lies in its acknowledgement that our historic resources are about to be expended and that we seek broad consent. Its utility lies in the exercise of deciding exactly what to do and costing it. Its social purpose is to take field research out of its academic enclave and to place

it at the heart of the modern community. This is achieved by measuring up the archaeological value of a piece of land with all the other values that are placed upon it, and fighting our corner. This kind of archaeology may thus be termed value-led or *evaluative*. Once evaluation has provided the input, the project design can be composed. Its *content* will consist of firm programmes for field research and landscape conservation, and provisional programmes for analysis and publication.

In this chapter we will first revisit *Field Research Procedure*, and note the design elements needed in advance of each stage. We will privilege *Project Design* (stage 3) because this is the stage that results in the irrevocable alteration of the resource. We will see how evaluation assembles and assesses the evidence for the hidden archaeology, the prospects for research and the social interests in play. And finally we will look at the way the project design is implemented: the consultation process and the subsequent checking and monitoring, culminating in the revised programmes of analysis and publication which deliver back to the public the value they entrusted to us.

Field Research Procedure and its design stages

Field Research Procedure (FRP), introduced in Chapter 2 and illustrated in Chapter 3, offers a framework for archaeological investigation in six linked stages. In *reconnaissance*, we explore the landscape identifying sites; in *evaluation* we give the sites current values; in *project design* we decide the best way of realising them; in *implementation* we execute it; in *analysis* we make sense of the results; and in *publication* we publish them. This itinerary was followed, more or less, in Parts 2 and 3. Landscape survey (Chapter 4) was mainly concerned with reconnaissance projects, and site survey (in Chapter 5) focused on the fieldwork associated with evaluation. Implementation uses all kinds of survey, as well as excavation (Chapters 6 and 7). Analysis (Chapters 8–12) and Publication (Chapter 13) followed in their expected order. The reason that evaluation and project design have been left until now is that it is really hard to discuss them without some feel for what happens in the other stages. The composition of a project design requires you to know about how landscape and site surveys are done, the form and consequences of excavation and its enormous output, the challenges of analysis and the options of publication.

Being a staged procedure, FRP expects you to stop and think before each stage, so to some extent design pops up all the way through (FIG 14.1). Some sort of programme is required for reconnaissance projects. Even if these projects are often conducted in a free spirit of exploration, they still cost money and have limits (a search area) set in advance. Evaluations too are designed, in the sense that they require costed work and are not open-ended. But both these stages are, as far as possible, non-destructive and can theoretically be run many times over the same piece of ground without great damage to the archaeological deposits. Project Design, our stage 3, is design of a different order of responsibility, since it concerns the irreversible

Design stage	Input	Output
Before reconnaissance	Scope of survey	Programme for survey
Before evaluation	Location, problem and project scoping	Desk top assessment – site survey – social/ethical context – deposit modelling, research agenda – ethical matters – definition of current value
Project design	Evaluation	Research programme Conservation programme
During fieldwork	Monitor of design	Minor changes in programme
Before analysis	Field Records Assessment of strata and assemblage	Programme of analysis
Before publication	Results of analysis	Publication programme

FIGURE 14.1 Design stages in archaeological investigation.

fate of a part of the heritage. The studies that come together at the Project Design stage decide, for a site or landscape, what will be researched, what will be destroyed and what will be conserved for the future. Project Design also looks forward to the results of its proposed actions: which records will be made and what will become of what is left of the site. It will therefore contain preliminary designs for the programmes of analysis, synthesis, archive, display and multi-copy publication. These analysis and publication designs will need to be revisited after fieldwork, since even the most perfect evaluation never predicts exactly what will come out of the ground.

Readers who already have experience in field archaeology (and especially in its commercial sector) will be aware that different countries have adopted various versions of such design-itineraries over the past 30 years, and may be wondering how they compare. In FIG 14.2 I line up FRP with two of the best known: the Section 106 procedure used in the USA for the management of cultural resources (CRM); and the MAP scheme (Management of Archaeological Projects) brought in by English Heritage with various revisions since 1990 (the latest issue is called MORPHE – Management of Research Projects in the Historic Environment). All three schemes (which have been around longer than their publication dates) use the basic premise that it is desirable to decide what to do before you do it, and to divide fieldwork into decision-making stages. MAP does not include publication, and CRM does not include publication or analysis. Both MAP and CRM are intended primarily for the commercial sector and are focused more on management – obtaining commercial value for money, than on research – obtaining intellectual value for money. The main differences claimed by FRP are, therefore: first, that it sets out to include the whole archaeological process; and second, that it intends to be equally applicable to the academic as to the commercial sector of the profession.

FRP (Carver 1987 and here)	CRM (Neumann and Sanford 2001) USA	MAP (English Heritage 1991) UK
Reconnaissance Inventory survey	Background Surface survey (Phase 1)	
Evaluation Desktop assessment Resource modelling Research agenda	Evaluation (Phase 2)	*Appraisal* Field evaluation
Project Design Research programme Management programme	Memorandum of Agreement Scope of Work/Data Recovery Plan	Project specification
Implementation	Data Acquisition (Phase 3)	Fieldwork
Analysis Programmed design Analysis		*Post-excavation assessment*
Publication Programmed design: Reports Exhibition Site presentation		
'Field Research Procedure'	'Cultural Resource Management'	'Man. of Arch. Projects'

FIGURE 14.2 Fieldwork Design Stages, some different schemes, left to right: (1) Field Research Procedure (FRP); (2) as practised in the USA: Cultural Resource Management (CRM); (3) as recommended by the state agency English Heritage for the Management of Archaeological Projects in the UK (MAP/ MORPHE).

Evaluation in town and country

Evaluation is the assignment of value – in this case archaeological value, the essential prerequisite in the business of deciding what to do. This is the stage at which we generate the information required to feed the proposed research and conservation programmes that will form the content of the project design. What is archaeological value, and how is it measured? In most countries there are authorities which, with greater or lesser transparency, are entrusted to decide what happens to a piece of land (more in Chapter 15). This entails the weighing of particular options against each other – for example, the need for a new school versus the provision of a new shopping centre. Behind these decisions are estimates of value: the value to the community of more school places, versus the wealth created by taxing a retail outlet. One can crudely divide these values into two, according to how they are measured. *Market values*, which create wealth from shopping, or from manufacture, from building homes or just by selling on the property, can be measured in money; and *community values*, which create amenities for health or education or leisure, by building a hospital, school or sports centre, can be measured in votes. There is some cross-over of course; a swimming pool might be semi-privatised and subsist on entry fees, and new housing can also be a vote winner. But on the whole the authority whose planners are responsible for deciding on the benefits of developing a piece of land can assess the value of the outcome in either votes or income.

But there is a third set of values that cannot be so easily assessed – those human values which, while appreciated, do not have a secure footing either in the market-place or the government chamber. The best known and most successful in fighting its corner is the value of natural fauna and flora, *environmental value*. Leaving aside animals that have been found to be useful (since they have either been domesticated or hunted to extinction), there are still wild creatures which occupy the earth. We cannot produce a good financial or political reason for keeping them, but we know we want our children to see them. We might not have a use for the dandelion or the nightingale, but feel the world would be a sadder place without them. Archaeology too falls into this category: for purposes of health and wealth it does not matter greatly whether history happened or not. New cars and safe streets do not depend on the date of Magna Carta. But history is a human need, even if we cannot put a price on it (FIG 14.3).

Many archaeologists are themselves environmentalists who value not only the past human experience itself, but the kind of deep landscape it has left us. Their emotional

---

MARKET VALUES. The value is measured in terms of financial gain
Capital value [profit obtainable on resale]
Production value [profit obtainable from agricultural or industrial development]
Commercial value [profit obtainable from creating a retail outlet]
Residential value [profit obtainable from building houses]

COMMUNITY VALUES. The value is measurable in terms of votes
Amenity value [provides a facility to be shared by the community]
Political value [wins a majority of votes]
Minority value [wins the support of an important interest group,
for example a descendent community]
Local value [conforms to local taste]

HUMAN VALUES. These values arise from membership of the human family
Environmental value [protects the biosphere of wild animals and plants]
Archaeological value [protects the sources of knowledge
about the past]

*Archaeological value is defined by matching the research agenda,
the resource model and the social context*

FIGURE 14.3 Competing values for the use of land. Land has many different values for society, of which archaeological value is but one. All these values compete for primacy when the use of the land changes. A planning system is the legal framework designed to regulate this competition and to ensure that competing interests are heard and debated. Evaluation is archaeology's weapon in this debate.

response to wilderness as a stage setting for prehistory means that the archaeological community is also ready to count natural features as part of the valued heritage, even where no cultural material survives. Archaeologists often take the part of local communities who value the less tangible, less measurable assets of a place: the woods, the skyline, the silence, the emptiness – assets which are, of course, frequently at risk.

Some countries (e.g. the USA) prefer the term "*significance*" to "value", using it for a similar purpose to denote archaeological sites or materials that have the capacity to tell us more about the past, or which matter for other reasons to particular groups. If there is a difference between value and significance it probably lies in the way it is used. Sites that are significant in the USA are included on a *register*, the implication being that they have been shown, more surely than other sites, to merit archaeological attention, investigation or curation. In other words significance is used to rank sites against other sites. Archaeological value ranks the archaeology of sites against other values, the archaeological prospects of a piece of land against what else you might be intending to do with it.

The purpose of archaeological evaluation is thus the assignment of an archaeological value. This value must nevertheless compete with the others: it cannot remain in the province of the wishful; it must become articulate. Planners willing to take the environment and archaeology into account will find it easier if the values and the implications of change are succinctly stated in each case. In Europe and America, this takes the form of an *Environmental Impact Statement*. As we shall see in the next chapter, this statement, its rationale, and the legislation which enables it, has become the biggest single platform for the creation of jobs in field archaeology over the past 30 years. Any potential archaeological opportunity therefore now finds itself in competition with other demands. But on the credit side, every development of land now offers an archaeological opportunity. For their part, the planners, those entrusted with making the decisions about new construction, expect a professional estimate of archaeological value (the evaluation) and a detailed argument for the preferred archaeological option (the project design).

One concise way of composing *archaeological value* is to combine and reconcile its component parts: the research agenda (the archaeological aspects valued by the research community); the social context (the archaeological aspects valued by other stake-holders); and the resource (what's left of the archaeology). In brief, archaeological value is obtained by matching what researchers want to know, with what they can know, given the state of knowledge, the survival of the archaeology and the historical interests of other stakeholders at that particular place, now. This archaeological value can then take its seat at the table in which the future of any site is decided (FIG 14.4).

The *research agenda* will vary greatly over time and place, and it may or may not already exist in a usable form. For example, in a bid to ease the evaluation process,

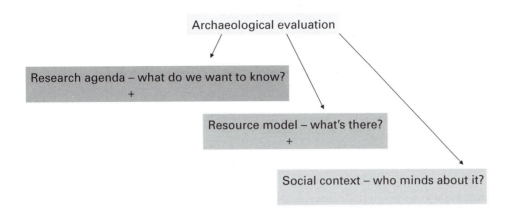

FIGURE 14.4 Evaluation: what we can study, to what end, out of what we want to know, out of what we are permitted to study, now, at that place.

English Heritage has commissioned a number of "research frameworks" which at least provide a point of departure for those out of touch with particular research areas. Their problem is that they go quickly out of date, themes and questions changing rapidly as answers are found or new paradigms adopted. If the project is primarily dedicated to research it will normally have its base in a university and emerge from a research agenda that is highly current. It is no bad principle to strive for university involvement in the commercial sector too, so that even if the project is largely driven by conservation, the *research dividend* can be maximised.

It is perhaps not always realised that the research agenda does not spring from the heads of academics – it has its origin in the contemporary concerns of the public down on the street. It is often the young who, expressing contemporary anxieties – for example, about war or gender – find them articulated by the immediately previous generation in research targets. It is not enough to want to know about such things in the past; the desire has to be turned into well-defined questions, and particularly the kind of questions which archaeology knows how to answer (FIG 14.5).

Archaeologists have had much less practice at assessing the *social context* of a project; and assessment has often arrived too late – in the form of a disaster. Inadequate opportunity to excavate Wood Quay before its redevelopment brought 10,000 people on to the streets of Dublin, led by a Jesuit priest who took the matter to the Court of Human Rights (FIG 14.6). At 390 Broadway in New York City the people of Harlem and Greenwich village put a stop to a development which had not allowed adequate time for the research of an African-American burial ground, which was in the path of a new skyscraper intended (ironically) for the headquarters of the environmental protection agency. These cases are of great interest because they had social implications which were not obvious from the archaeologist's research frame-work – basically, the need to know about aspects of history of special value to the

Contemporary concerns	Archaeological agenda	Field archaeology tasks
Identity: what was the origin and development of "our" people?	*How were communities and territories defined? How were societies organised?*	Studying landscapes, sites and buildings
Nationalism and racial differences. What causes people to regard each other as different?	*What were the people themselves like? How were they organised?*	Studying cemeteries
Gender	*What were the gender roles?*	Studying assemblages and sites
Defining ideologies and Political systems	*What did they think?* *What was their world view?*	Studying cemeteries and assemblages; detection of symbolic and behavioural traits
Economic systems Distinguishing subsistence, trade, tribute, taxation, objects of investment	*What did people eat?* *How did they make and use tools?* *What contacts did they have?*	Studying assemblages; provenance and re-distribution of artefacts; environment
The threatened biosphere	*What was the environment?*	Palaeoecological assemblages
Where are we going?	*Why did things change?*	Sequences; environmental, economic and ideological explanations

FIGURE 14.5 Where do research ideas come from? (left:) Examples of contemporary concerns; (centre:) Archaeological questions (Bahn and Renfrew 2005); (right:) how such questions might be addressed by archaeological investigation.

people currently living nearby. The people of Dublin felt that the past of Dublin's non-Celtic (Viking) predecessors was being ignored. The people of Manhattan, and particularly the residents of Harlem and the then mayor of New York, felt that the heritage of the early slaves of New York was being demeaned. In neither of these examples was a minority group being narrow or obstructive. On the contrary, the arguments in both cases rested on the archaeological provision being too peremptory, too short-sighted, too insensitive and insufficiently developed. In neither case was there a published research design, and it was this that caused the residents to feel slighted – and they were not impressed by an archaeological profession that could apparently function without one. Doing archaeology without a project design was like "driving a car in a foreign country without a road map or a destination", said Laurie Beckelmann in Congress. The construction project was accordingly terminated by President Bush (senior) at considerable expense and the site found a future as a monument in memory of the enslaved people of early America. These examples teach us that, in principle at least, the interests of researchers and other stakeholders may be reconciled in advance, and can be integrated into the project design.

FIGURE 14.6 Social context: demonstrators urge further excavation at Wood Quay, on Westmoreland Street, Dublin, 31 March 1979 (Peter Thursfield courtesy of *Irish Times*).

Making the resource model – rural sites

The most site-specific operation in evaluation is the third component, compiling the *resource model*, in other words assessing the state of the surviving archaeology. We have already touched on some techniques and applications of this activity in Chapter 5, since exploring the deposit predictively is the chief item on the menu of site survey. The idea is to create a three-dimensional image of what survives underground, using instruments and devices that do not damage the strata. In assessing value, we focus on those things that we know will enrich research: a well-preserved artefactual and biota assemblage; legible strata; and the size of the opportunity to do spatial analysis. These can often be anticipated quite well without digging a site, or by digging it but causing as little disturbance as possible.

Resource modelling demands different approaches in town and country. In open country, the assemblage (artefacts, bones, phosphate residues) tends to be visible on the surface where it is used to map the extent of the site and assess its periods of occupation (see Chapter 3 for an example). The presence of underground features and structures can be determined from geophysical survey. Where the results from geophysical surveys are opaque it may be necessary to use limited direct inspection using quadrats and trenches. In general, the need for good visibility means that trenches are more useful than quadrats and best of all is open area strip-and-map, which not only provides the best visibility with the least destruction, but offers another opportunity to use geophysical survey without the topsoil (see Chapter 5 for more on this).

The topsoil or other surface cover is highly influential on the kind of survey that can be applied. Rural evaluations begin by dividing the area to be investigated into "zones" depending on what the surface cover is. A survey programme can then be designed for each zone: surface collection, geophysical, phosphate and then strip-and-map on ploughsoil, trenches in woods and so on. Since the survey techniques will almost certainly be redeployed in the implementation stage, it will be good to test their sensitivity on the terrain concerned, by surveying with different instruments and then digging a test area to see what they saw (Chapter 5, FIG 5.11).

In commercial archaeology, the imminent destruction of the resource, the current limits of remote mapping, the speed and cost of development and the archaeologists' anxieties about missing important deposits all mean that the use of trenches and test-pits remains prevalent. They are quicker and more certain: they are more destructive too, but in this case everything is going to be destroyed anyway, so better safe than sorry. Long trenches spaced at intervals, each cut by machine and then cleaned up and inspected for archaeological strata provide one way of evaluating large threatened areas – like the corridor of a new road (FIG 14.7). Test-pits cut by hand, placed

FIGURE 14.7
Evaluation trenches spaced along a new road line in Lothian, Scotland (Lelong and MacGregor 2007).

FIGURE 14.8 Test-pit (foreground) used to determine the nature and depth of strata. The results will guide the removal of disturbed deposits at Level A (FAS Ltd).

randomly or systematically, do a similar job, with an additional focus provided by stratigraphic excavation – valuable for assessing areas of complex strata, including urban sites (FIG 14.8; and page 100).

A convenient summary of the archaeological character of an extensive piece of land is the *Sensitivity Template*. This is essentially a table showing for each zone which method can detect which size of archaeological find or feature (FIG 14.9a). This can be used as a platform for summarising which methods are likely to be most appropriate for the full investigation of the different zones, the *Deployment Template* (FIG 14.9b). These are useful management tools in both academic and commercial projects, as they allow the detailed planning and costing of a multi-method inquiry applied over several hectares.

Two outputs are desirable from the resource modelling exercise: first, a period map showing which areas were occupied and when, according to the distribution of surface material and buried features. And second, a deposit model showing where deposits lie, at which depth, and how far they have already been disturbed (see Chapter 3, FIGS 3.5 and 3.6). Evaluation does not give you a narrative account of the sequence and does not try to: it offers a physical framework within which the research objectives and the conservation needs of a project can be designed.

(a)

Technique	Features >1.5m across	Features >1.0m across	Features >0.5m aross	Graves >0.4m across	Finds >20mm across	Finds >10mm across	Finds >1mm across
Survey							
Aerial photos	X						
Contour	X						
Surface mapping	X						
Magnetometer	X						
Radar	X						
Fluxgate	X	X					
Resistivity	X	X	X				
Field walking					X	X	
Metal detector					X	X	
Phosphate							
Excavation							
Level A	X				X		
Level B	X	X			X		
Level C	X	X	X		X	X	
Level D	X	X	X	X	X	X	X
Level E	X	X	X	X	X	X	X

(b)

Technique	Zone A	Zone B/C	Zone D/F	Zone E	Top soil	Subsoil surface	Features	Graves	Mounds
Survey									
Aerial photos			X						
Surface mapping	X								
Radar	X								X
Resistivity	X	X	X	X					
Field walking			X						
Metal detector	X				X			X	X
Excavation									
Level A					X				
Level B					X				
Level C									
Level D					X	X			
Level E								X	X

FIGURE 14.9 Evaluation templates: (a) *Sensitivity Template*, showing the ability of different instruments to detect features of different sizes; (b) *Deployment Template,* showing the instruments and Recovery Levels applied in different zones (examples from Sutton Hoo).

Resource modelling for urban sites

Urban deposits – that is, deep deposits beneath occupied modern towns – are unfortunately not usually susceptible to geophysical or electronic surveys. There are, however, two powerful methods not often available in the countryside. Living historic towns tend to have been occupied for two centuries or more, during which time their citizens often included persons with passing archaeological interests. The notes and sketches made by these folk find their way into the municipal archives and create a treasure house of observations. They often do not bear the interpretations put on them by antiquaries, but the locations, depths and dates are usually reliable enough to contribute something to the map of underground deposits.

A second source is found in the observations, equally random, of modern contractors; towns should hold records of drains, services and sewers, and contractors will sometimes wish to investigate the deposits themselves using augers or boreholes. Better still, if the site contains a disused cellar its walls can be removed with a machine, and the cliff of strata cleaned up. This gives a sneak preview of the stratification through which the cellar cut. But, all too often, no previews or non-destructive methods are available and the archaeological evaluator is obliged to sacrifice some of the deposit by digging a trench or pit through it, to establish the character of the strata and its overall depth (FIG 14.8).

None of these methods, of themselves, provide historical information, but they do provide essential pointers to the physical character of the deposit. We need to know how deep it is, how legible is the stratification, and how well-preserved are the structures and assemblages – in other words, the "quality" of the deposit. This can be assessed in a notional way by lining up the assets that can potentially contribute to a historical understanding (FIG 14.10). The more artefacts and biological clues that remain, and the better preserved they are, the more historical information is theoretically in reach. If the stratification is sparse, then clearly not much happened; but if it is exceedingly cluttered, then too much has happened and pit has cut pit with such frequency that their edges cannot be resolved and the assemblages are well mixed up. The ideal, in theory, is a sequence that is both well stratified and legible: rich in incident but not too "noisy". But sequence and depth do not of themselves confer quality. The circumstances of deposition also determine whether there is a strong narrative. A sequence of houses with their hearths offers first-hand primary information on the inhabitants. The deposits in a rampart or burial mound contain displaced, secondary material with less relevance for their constructors. Other assets may be contacted too: areas of peat or disused ponds mean the chance to accumulate environmental evidence, such as pollen (see Chapter 9, page 236). In FIG 14.10, therefore, the "best" site follows the arrows, and although no such site may ever exist, it gives us some kind of standard against which to set the targets of urban evaluation.

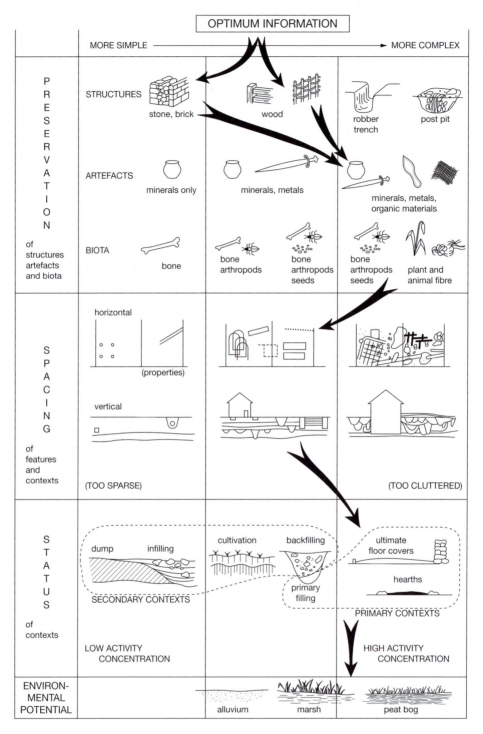

FIGURE 14.10 The quality of a deposit. The "best" site follows the arrows (Carver 1983b).

Being conscious of earlier records and observations somewhat randomly assembled by past citizens, urban archaeologists in the 1970s began to compose more systematic "urban archaeological data bases" to provide a platform from which to plan future research and manage future intervention. FIG 14.11 shows a set of surveys

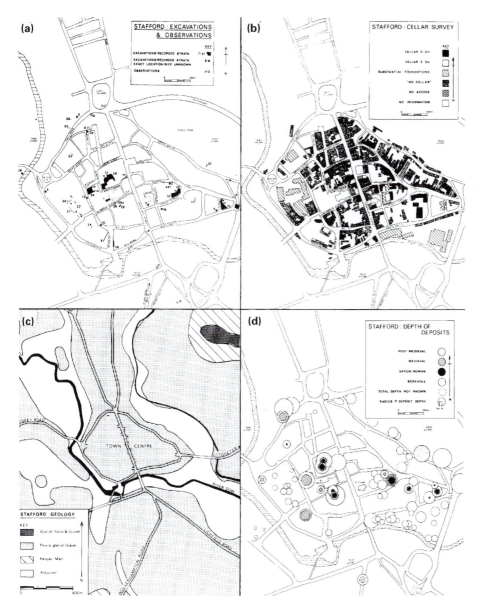

FIGURE 14.11 Four studies of Stafford underground by Jenny Glazebrook: (a) location of all interventions and observations; (b) depth of cellars; (c) the form of the undeveloped site; (d) depth of deposits.

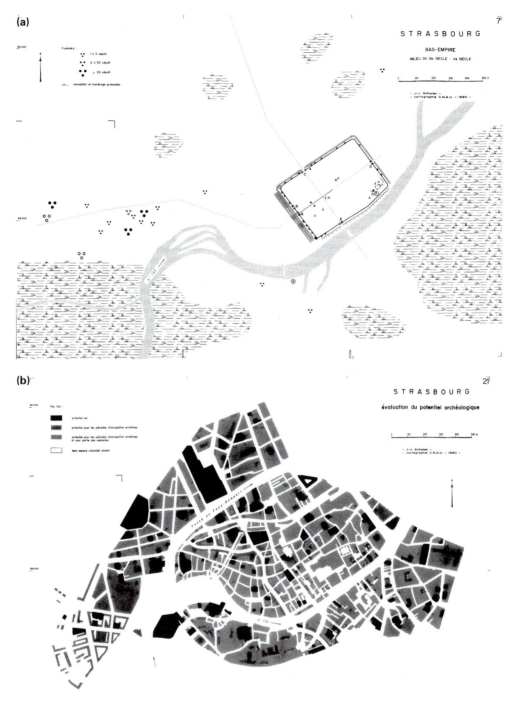

FIGURE 14.12 (a) the site of Strasbourg (France) at the time of the late Roman Empire (mid-3rd to 5th century AD, and (b) a map showing the evaluation of archaeological potential of the urbanised land, divided into no potential, potential for the early periods, and potential for early and later periods (Schwein 1992).

at Stafford, UK (1979), and FIG 14.12 shows a model of Roman Strasbourg, and its current archaeological potential, an example taken from the Centre National d'Archéologie Urbaine's surveys of French urban deposits, termed by them "Les archives du sol". It can be seen that each town has a special underground character which results in the retention of deposits having different depths and distributions. We saw some diagrammatic examples in Chapter 1, FIG 1.7. Some elementary rules emerge: high rocky sites (like Cordes), tend to shed their deposits into the valley – unless there is an artificial barrier, like a town wall. Carcassonne had a rampart and a thick defensive wall from the Iron Age, and this, together with its Roman and Medieval successors, now embraces deposits some 8m deep. Other sites such as Bordeaux have a river running through them, and the valley is gradually encroached by infilling, creating a deep and often anaerobic "archive du sol". North-west Europe boasts a set of towns renowned for their intact timber buildings and organic debris, all preserved in much the same way by encroachment over the river running through

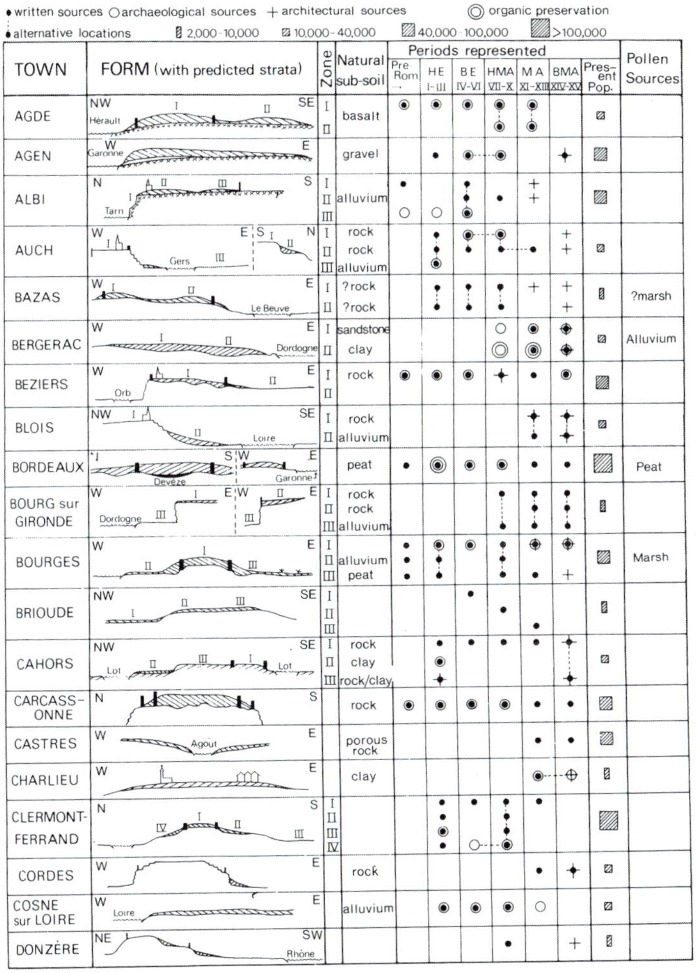

• written sources ○ archaeological sources + architectural sources ◎ organic preservation
⁞ alternative locations   2,000-10,000   10,000-40,000   40,000-100,000   >100,000

TOWN	FORM (with predicted strata)	Zone	Natural sub-soil	Pre Rom →	HE I-III	BE IV-VI	HMA VII-X	MA XI-XIII	BMA XIV-XV	Present Pop.	Pollen Sources
AGDE	NW ... SE, Hérault	I, II	basalt								
AGEN	W ... E, Garonne		gravel								
ALBI	N ... S, Tarn	I, II, III	alluvium								
AUCH	W ... N, Gers	I, II, III	rock / rock / alluvium								
BAZAS	W ... E, Le Beuve	I, II	?rock / ?rock								?marsh
BERGERAC	W ... E, Dordogne	I, II	sandstone / clay								Alluvium
BEZIERS	W ... E, Orb	I, II	rock								
BLOIS	NW ... SE, Loire	I, II	rock / alluvium								
BORDEAUX	S / W ... E, Devèze, Garonne		peat								Peat
BOURG sur GIRONDE	W ... E, Dordogne	I, II, III	rock / rock / alluvium								
BOURGES	W ... E	I, II, III	alluvium / peat								Marsh
BRIOUDE	NW ... SE	I, II, III									
CAHORS	NW ... SE, Lot	I, II, III	rock / clay / rock/clay								
CARCASSONNE	N ... S		rock								
CASTRES	W ... E, Agout		porous rock								
CHARLIEU	W ... E		clay								
CLERMONT-FERRAND	N ... S	I, II, III, IV									
CORDES	W ... E		rock								
COSNE sur LOIRE	W ... E, Loire		alluvium								
DONZÈRE	NE ... SW, Rhône										

FIGURE 14.13
Underneath 20 French towns: a "Michelin Guide" (Carver 1983b).

them, and all at much the same time – the early Middle Ages. Among them are Dublin, Perth, York, Bergen, Trondheim and Ribe (see page 11). Within such varieties of deposit from town to town, it is possible to compile a kind of "Michelin Guide", offering in this case not quality restaurants, but something equally juicy – gourmet deposits awaiting researchers of different periods of history (FIG 14.13).

Resource modelling is an expanding and productive area of archaeology, valuable for research and resource management alike. Under the latest legislation in the USA and Europe, every new building project requires an archaeological evaluation, or something very like it. This normally proceeds in stages. A rapid "desktop assessment" of a site, using existing information, may be enough to make a decision about whether it is worth saving. Usually, we won't know enough, and a full evaluation will be required with field survey – non-destructive if possible. The information will be fed into the project design; the resource model, the research agenda and the social context forming the essential components (see also the procedures outlined in FIG 14.2).

Contents of a Project Design

Evaluation provides the input for Project Design (the PD). Together, the three factors – what is left of the archaeology, what we can know from it and the social context of the work – assign a current value to the site, and provide the point of departure for the design study. The output of the design process consists of two proposed programmes of work. The *research programme* is aimed at new knowledge, and divides into programmes of fieldwork, analysis and publication. The *resource management programme* is aimed at protecting the resource, and divides into programmes for conservation and for presenting what will remain to the public.

TABLE 14.1 is an attempt at offering a general list of contents for a project design: rather optimistic since the range of such documents naturally varies enormously. A published project design for a major research project may run to a hundred pages with illustrations. A project design for a watching brief on the car park of the village pub might be half a page. Thus the table is more of a checklist of the sort of studies that might be included. In the real world of academic and commercial archaeology, there are particular formats that are preferred by research sponsors or planning authorities to conform with their own regulations. Projects coming out of the academic sector, and following the "research cycle" will naturally have a different emphasis to those commissioned from the commercial sector and following the "heritage cycle". We will visit these cycles in Chapter 15. Meanwhile let's look at the generic content of the PD, and how it may be successfully implemented.

A project design should have five components. First comes an *introduction,* which explains where the project is to be located, how it came about and its aims and objectives. Next is a summary of the *evaluation,* under its headings of the resource model, the research agenda and the current social context. And then the meat of the

TABLE 14.1 Contents of a Project Design (author)

Introduction

0.1 Circumstances which have led to the present project being designed.
0.2 Context of the project, its location, its itinerary through the planning process.
0.3 Discovery. The archaeology concerned; previous work.
0.4 Scoping. The current expected work programme and its anticipated outcome.
0.5 Objectives. The reasons for preparing a project design.

Evaluation

1.1 Background: the political and geographical characteristics of the area where the research is to be carried out.
1.2. Description of site/area.
1.3. Summary of previous work and current land use.
1.4. Resource model.
1.5. Research agenda.
1.6. Current threats to the resource.
1.7. Ethical considerations: known concerns of the local and the descendant communities.

Research options

2.1. Research objectives, selected from the agenda.
2.2. Theory: matching the objectives to the resource available.
2.3. Method: how the objectives will be achieved – area to be investigated, sample units, recovery levels, data to be recorded, analyses proposed, outcome anticipated, publication envisaged.
2.4. Research options: what fieldwork is proposed.

Conservation options

3.1. The conservation value (significance/importance) of the building, site or landscape (new or existing Conservation Plan).
3.2. The impact of the proposed research programme.
3.3. The impact of proposed development.
3.4. Mitigation options: preservation by record.
3.5. Conservation options available.
3.6. Display options and implications for conservation.

Recommended integrated programme

4.0 The zero option: no further action because there is nothing of significance there or because the site should be left alone.
4.1. Research programme.
    *Programme of fieldwork and timetable
    *Recording system to be employed
    *Results anticipated
    *Provisional programme of analysis
    *Provisional programme for archive and publication
4.2. Conservation programme.
    *Destiny of the site or area after fieldwork
    *Measures for conservation
    *Measures for public presentation or access
    *Measures for public benefit
4.3 Proposals for display and storage (in partner museum).
4.4 Proposals for public communication.

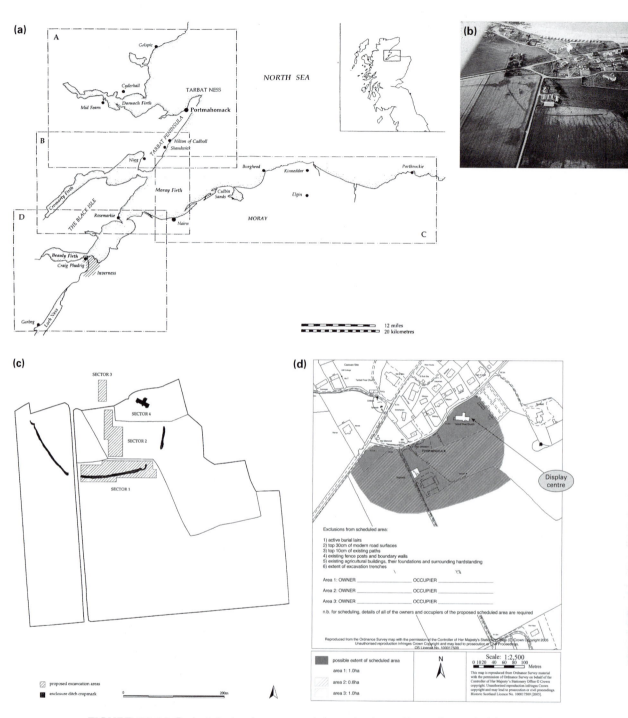

FIGURE 14.14 Project design for a research investigation at Portmahomack: (a) research area; (b) AP locating site; (c) areas for excavation; and (d) areas for conservation author).

document: a *research programme*, detailing the proposed fieldwork, and giving provisional programmes for analysis and publication, as so far anticipated from the evaluation; and a *conservation programme*, detailing the measures to be taken for conserving the deposit during and after the investigation, and for conserving the finds and records in a museum (in agreed partnership). Finally an *integrated programme* summarises all the recommended actions.

A largely academic project will tend to privilege component 3, the research programme, but since it concerns the expenditure of some of the archaeological resource, it will also need to present a conservation plan before it begins (FIG 14.14). By contrast, conservation normally lies at the heart of a commercial project: typical commercial tasks are the preparation of *Conservation Plans* for the long term protection of a site, or *Mitigation Strategies*, to reduce and compensate for the damage to deposits due to development, either through the design of special foundations (which minimise damage) or through recording of the strata in advance ("preservation by record") (FIG 14.15). In these cases, the research that is possible, or the *research dividend*, maybe be rather small. On the other hand it may turn out highly productive. Which is only to say that measures taken under the heading "Conservation" may also have research value.

(b)

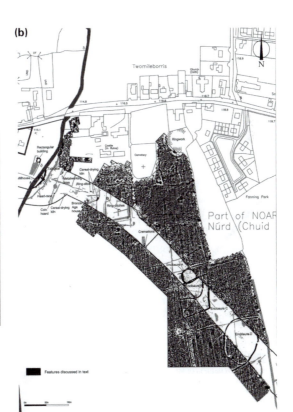

(a)

FIGURE 14.15
Project design for a commercial project. Investigation of the corridor of the N75 link road, by geophysical survey and excavation (Ó'Droma 2008).

There may also be some uncertainty about where to put "display", since on the one hand researchers will always regard it as part of their publication programme, while on the other, site display must always be integrated with the site conservation plans. But checklists are checklists; they are meant only as a general aide-memoire, a summary of duties. The structure of a PD will be influenced by local practice and by the underlying objective. But as a generality, and it is a generality on which this book insists, every archaeological project needs a design, and every design should pay attention to both the research and the conservation outcome.

The proposals of a PD may be directed towards good research or good preservation. In the countryside, a road might be diverted from the interesting sites found by evaluation, leaving archaeology to tidy up the scraps. In the town, the developer might be asked to redesign his building, e.g. put it on a concrete raft or piles to soften its impact on the archaeological deposits, rather than pay for a full excavation.

Research projects have been slower to adopt the package, but now it is becoming more common and may soon be mandatory, as planners realise that excavation in the name of research should be subject to the same controls as any other change in the use of a piece of land.

Implementation

It is axiomatic that a project design should be produced before, rather than after, major fieldwork begins, just as in architecture the blueprint comes before the building. In the commercial sector, the design will be hammered out at series of meetings that can feature the landowner, the developer, the planning authority, the planning authority's curator, the local authority's archaeologist, and the developer's archaeologist (FIG 14.16).

Archaeology, like architecture, is a socially embedded venture, so it is also axiomatic that the design should be exposed to comment. There are three traditional ways of doing this. First, pre-select a targeted group of interested parties and invite them to respond. This may include consultation with a funding committee, a research committee, special research seminars, representatives of local peoples, representatives of special interest groups and so on. Second, the project design may be placed in the public domain for those sufficiently interested to consult it. This is the system practised by the British planning authorities: the proposal is placed in the town hall and a certain number of days is allowed for objections to be registered. The third method of exposing a project design is to *publish it* – for example, online – meaning that it will get much more exposure than simply to those who have been invited or those who might have an objection. This is the more correct procedure for research projects since the interested parties may be globally dispersed.

Modern authors have rightly emphasised the idea of multi-vocality, but of course this means much more than asking the opinion of colleagues, locals and participants, an

FIGURE 14.16 Site meeting in Norwich, England (author).

in-depth consultation exercise. In general, all projects are routinely subject to consultation, but that is not the same thing as exposure to the public. Commercial projects are announced through the planning system, but the archaeological proposals may not be detailed. And research projects may not be announced to the public at all. From the principles already advanced it would seem logical to say that while circulating a draft project design for consultation is essential, a commercial design for an archaeology project should actually be tabled with the planning application, so that anyone, and in particular any archaeologist, can see what archaeological response is intended to a development. In an era of falling standards, such a measure seems to me obligatory if we are to have any chance of applying quality control and paying for archaeology at a proper rate.

Major research projects, I believe, should also have their project designs published. Clearly it is right that local people and participants in the scheme should have an input, but they are only a small fraction of the interested parties. Among the most affected are the other academics who are not involved and not on the site, but are nevertheless stakeholders in every sense. A modern major research project may cost millions of pounds and involve a great deal of excavation; it will change the available history, and indeed this is its intention, so that a wide research community and its future teaching will be implicated. Publication of the design is the only reliable way to reach this community (see in Chapter 2 for more on this).

Note that having official permission to do fieldwork does not of itself mean that the support of all sectors has been obtained (see Chapter 2, page 37). At Portmahomack, visitors to the graveyard objected to excavations in the strongest terms, in spite of the fact that the archaeologists had permission from government, local government and the elders of the church of Scotland. Only when the proposals had been published and announced on local radio, could it be said that the project could proceed in a true spirit of multi-vocality.

From what has been said, it is clear that a project design must be publicly exposed in advance, and that the project concerned should not expect to continue for longer than it has academic validity and public support. How long is that? Academic progress is rapid, or to put it another way, academic opinion is volatile; as we have seen in the last two decades the emphasis of research, and its agenda, have changed radically. Similarly, in many parts of the world, the population is highly mobile; both local and descendant interests may be reconstituted or re-emphasised. These interests and their expression are not entirely unconnected with global politics, which tends to change direction every few years as presidents and prime ministers are well aware. In the modern world the maximum viable timescale for an intellectually sound archae-ological project is therefore about six years. Proposals to excavate for longer than this must attract the suspicion that the project is disregarding the social context and has motivations which are not actually academic or archaeological.

As advanced in an earlier chapter (Chapter 2, page 34), once a Project Design arrives at the point of consensus, it takes the character of a *social contract*. It represents not only what is intended, but the consent that was achieved at the time of its consultation and publication. This is true multi-vocality. By the same token, it is not legitimate to depart from the programme as soon as the public's back is turned. Once a project is underway, the project design continues to provide a valuable point of reference, and acts as its own built-in monitoring device. We stick to a PD programme for ethical reasons, because we said we would; only this agreed part of the resource was to be destroyed, only this amount of money was to be expended. When you hear of an archaeologist "having a free hand", you can be sure that something has gone seriously wrong with the design process.

Is this too constraining, too reductive, too oppressive of the creative spirit? Not at all; the greatest creative spirits in the arts and sciences work and have always worked in exactly the same way. A sculptor who wants a personal vision immortalised in bronze in a public place must first present a maquette for broad consultation. Sculptors do not expect to get paid for producing something different and to take as long as they feel like. If a scientist investigating TB persuades you that they have a potential breakthrough, he/she does not expect to spend the money on developing an electric scooter. Archaeologists too are people who break new ground on behalf of the public. They are not there to serve their own profession but the wider world, by bringing into public ownership new knowledge of the human experience.

Conclusion

Design is the backbone of archaeological investigation. All archaeological theory and method are subsumed in the design process; neither theory nor method, nor even research objectives nor social pressures alone determine the outcome of archaeological investigation. It is the reasoning and balancing of design, explicit or not, that produces our results.

For the field archaeologist the most crucial factor is the deposit; it is the one thing that varies most from place to place, and the one that you cannot change. It will be a major component in the evaluation that feeds design. But the research agenda and the social context are determinant too. The input of project design is the evaluation, and its output is the research programme and the resource management programme: giving the site its meaning and its future are ways of realising its current value (FIG 14.17).

Project design is pivotal to the whole process of archaeological investigation from the exploration of the ground to the dissemination of knowledge and the creation of heritage. This process is expressed diagrammatically in FIG 14.18. It can be seen that design splits the forces of archaeological investigation into two: one emphasising the values of research; the other the values of conservation. This split is reflected in other ways: research and conservation are paid for by different kinds of sponsorship, and have therefore created two different branches in the profession to serve them – one

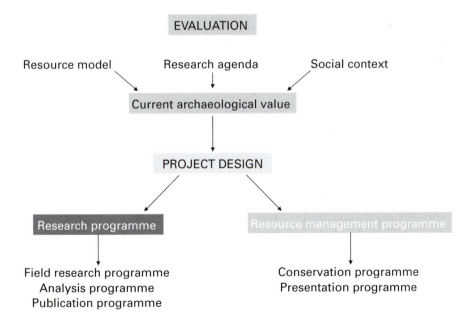

FIGURE 14.17 Evaluation and project design, summary.

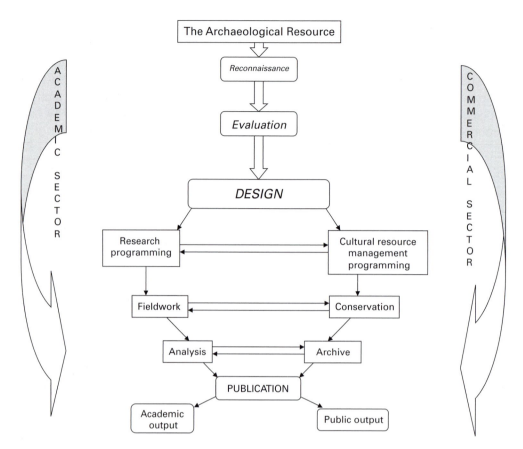

FIGURE 14.18 Archaeological investigation – the process (author).

mainly academic, the other mainly governmental and commercial. If these are two mainlines leading from and to the same destination, there are plenty of potential crossing points between them. A professional archaeologist can work in the academic and commercial sectors at various stages in one career, and in theory the mobility should be easy and seamless. In practice, the politics and economics of a country can make obstacles and lower horizons; but it need not be so. Let's turn to this in our next chapter.

Briefing

Design stages: King 2000; Neumann and Sanford 2001a and b (the section 106 process), Andrews and Thomas 1995 (MAP 2) and for MORPHE, see www.english-heritage.org.uk/upload/pdf/MoRPHE-Project-Managers-Guide.pdf; **significance:** Lipe 1984; Butler 1987; Rhoads 1992, Schaafsma 1989. **Evaluation:** Rich 1816;

M. Carver 1978, Shott 1987, M. Carver, 1996 2003; Association of County Archaeological Officers 1993, Institute of Field Archaeologists 1994 (UK), Hardesty et al 2000 (USA); **research frameworks:** Darvill 2005 was a fine research framework for the Stonehenge area, a kind of generalised advanced blueprint with plenty of consultation; but it did not constitute a project design, since a project had yet to be proposed; **social context:** M. Carver 2003 (pp. 7–23) for Wood Quay, Broadway. **Resource modelling: rural:** M. Carver 1986 (Sutton Hoo), Stein 1991 (use of coring), Howard et al 2008 (Trent valley); **urban:** CNAU 1990, M. Carver 1983, 1993, 2003 (111–46); **environmental evaluation and design:** Association for Environmental Archaeology 1995.

Research programmes: both the academic and commercial communities are remarkably reticent about publishing their research programmes in advance and one usually has to winkle them out retrospectively from the final publications. The Irish National Roads Authority is making a special effort to get the maximum research dividends out of Irish roads schemes: see papers in O'Sullivan and Stanley 2008; some other projects well worth a visit are Kvamme and Ahler 2007 (integrated survey and excavation); O'Neill 1993 (excavation size); Geib 1996 (Glen Canyon); Talon 1994 (investigations in advance of a TGV railway); Bonnet 1993 (Geneva cathedral); Burnouf et al 1991 (multi-disciplinary investigations in Lyon).

Conservation plans: Kate Clark (ed.) 1999; English Heritage 1997; 2000a, Kerr 1996, 2000; Nixon 2004 (preservation in situ); Brereton 1991 (repair of buildings); Arup 1991, Carver 2003 (appendix) for piling options developed at York. Carver and Lelong 2004 assess the role of cultural landscapes and "wilderness", particularly in Scotland; **implementation and monitoring:** Andrews and Thomas 1995; Bleed 1983; **project management:** Cooper 1995.

15 OUR PROFESSION AND ITS CONTEXT

What sort of a state are you in?

Archaeology is a lot of fun – especially in the field. Why should anyone get paid to do it? The same could be said about football, singing and cooking – which all have professional and amateur branches and often find it hard to keep the balance between them. At the moment, amateur archaeology is having a hard time, either because it is regarded as unskilled, and thus a threat to the resource, or because the frameworks for including volunteer help have not been properly developed. But we can say one thing with confidence: if there is no clear route into a profession for volunteers, no support for an activity beyond legal obligation, then its standing and standards will eventually suffer. Perhaps it is especially important for archaeology, a subject that promotes universal "human values", to stay close friends with its amateur following.

Professional archaeologists have been at work in government institutions and universities since the 18th century, augmented by wealthy amateurs. The government departments – Ministries of Culture and Academies of Science – have expanded as the range of archaeological activity has expanded: from an initial brief to care for ancient monuments, to a need to count them, an interest in understanding them and to making them available to a wider public. The early legislation of most countries reflects this point of departure: archaeological remains are cultural property, and it is the government's job to look after them on behalf of future generations. As government heritage institutions and universities have completed more research, as they have understood more about their own lands, the repertoire of sites, monuments and objects that deserves to be considered as cultural property has enlarged year on year. At first only buildings were cherished, and then pieces of land; and among objects it was gold and silver that attracted government care, then flint implements, then pottery, and eventually ancient animal bones, plant remains, insect husks and even soil samples came to be seen as part of our *heritage*. It is not easy to keep up with the administrative and financial implications of this ever-increasing repertoire, and it is not surprising that most archaeologists consider the protective legislation of their

own countries to be lagging behind the corpus of what they have gradually learnt to value.

An explosion of concern for cultural remains can be noted world wide from the 1970s, perhaps not unconnected with the first views of our planet from space. Archaeological interest was extended from the monuments we could see to the remains that still lay hidden, and these were increasingly viewed less as *national property*, and more as an *international resource*. Everyday, somewhere in the world this resource was being damaged to make room for some new facility for the living human family. Legislation now had to be extended to include the assessment and rescue of what was destined to disappear.

In addition to the new determination to do what we could to save the past from the present, a number of communities began to feel that their own past was slipping away from them. Rather than just being "rescued", they preferred specific cultural resources to come under their control. At first this was applied in particular to human remains; but it is being extended to cover all artefacts that relate to the affiliations of a given "descendant community". Similarly the range of "heritage" can be extended, from those buildings and monuments that have been designated by central government and its scholarly advisors, to those sites that local or descendant communities consider of value to them. The social context thus encourages modern authorities to define the heritage by political as well as academic criteria, and involve local as well as national and international interests.

We have met these values in earlier chapters. But in the modern world we do not yet meet them equally in all the world's countries: legislation tends to be enacted only when it is needed. As social pressure increases, the basic legal provision, a scheme for designating and protecting specific monuments, is broadened into a more general protection of heritage assets, and then into protocols that allow or demand a response when damage to such assets is anticipated.

As an example, the US 1906 *Antiquities Act* gave federal officials the task of protecting specific archaeological sites as public resources and provided measures for combating vandalism and looting there. The need for more comprehensive legislation became apparent with large-scale development schemes – mainly dam-building – in the 1930s and 1940s. The *Works Program Administration* (WPA) which operated from 1935 to 1943 as part of the New Deal was a major effort to save archaeological data from the many sites that were to be drowned as a result of dam construction. This programme made use of unemployed labour during the Depression of the late 1930s. Many of the excavations were reported in a standardised manner because they were done under the supervision of one archaeologist, William Webb, so making the information comparable and usable by other archaeologists. The (Missouri) *River Basin program* that followed (1945–69) included a series of reservoirs constructed under the jurisdiction of the *US Army Corps of Engineers*. The archaeology programme, administered by the *National Parks Service*, was tailored to record "historical and archaeological data which might otherwise be lost as the result of the construction of a dam". These projects set the scene for a formal response to the widespread destruction of archaeological sites by development. They also laid the foundations for the influential role of the US Army Corps of Engineers and the National Parks Service in North American archaeology.

After World War II, as a result of economic and population growth, there was much inadvertent damage to sites in the wake of construction – of offices, factories, houses, shopping malls, and associated infrastructure – and additional losses were caused by an increase in "pot hunting", the looting of sites for saleable antiquities. Archaeologists and the public began to exert pressure through the political process, with the ultimate passage of a series of laws that afforded some protection to archaeological and historic sites, now to be called "cultural resources". The first of these, the 1966 *National Historic Preservation Act* (NHPA), established a *National Register of Historic Places* (administered by the Secretary of the Interior through the National Park Service), a list of sites that came under the protection of the federal authorities. The register was served by an *Advisory Council on Historic Preservation* (ACHP) and in each state by a *State Historic Preservation Office* (SHPO – colloquially "shippo"), which had the task of resolving conflicts over the historic status of individual properties. *Section 106* of this act provided for the conservation or recording of any new site that was eligible to be included in the National Register, at the expense of the firm or agency developing or changing the use of the site. "Section 106" thus gave the basis for a CRM profession and gave its name to a whole procedure (see Chapter 14).

The process of monitoring and mitigating damage to archaeological sites developed with the *National Environmental Policy Act* (NEPA) of 1969, which provided for an evaluation of the impact on the environment of a development proposal (called an *Environmental Impact Statement*, or EIS). Archaeological and historic resources (including architectural structures) could be included as analogous to environmental resources such as endangered species of plants and animals, in the sense that they too were rare and finite, and in addition, non-renewable. The *Archaeological and Historic Preservation Act* (AHPA) of 1974 authorised federal funding for the recovery of data that would be lost by a project in which the federal government was involved. With the *Archaeological Resources Protection Act* (ARPA) of 1979 (amended 1988), even the *intention* to loot became a felony. The act also required federal agencies to make surveys of resources and develop public education programs.

Subsequent legislation has broadened the range of what is valuable and to whom. The *Native American Graves Protection and Repatriation Act* of 1990 (NAGPRA) recognised the right of descendant communities to reclaim and dispose of human remains in their ancestral territories. When human remains are encountered, the field archaeologist makes contact with the Native American authority to negotiate access and ask for a period of study. Where the identity of the descendant community is

uncertain, the discovery of the assemblage is officially announced and time allowed for it to be claimed. Bones may usually be studied with permission and then are returned ("repatriated") for reburial. Now that the interests of descendant communities are officially encoded, a new era of co-operation can begin. For example between 1975 and 1994 archaeologists and Zuni leaders have provided an integrated program of CRM within Zuni property, using Federal regulations and Zuni initiatives working together to produce conservation plans, a research programme and a museum.

The states of Australia have taken these ideas further, introducing legislation and principles for the adoption and conservation of monuments chosen on the basis of their value to aborigine and other communities (the Burra Charter, 1979). These can include valued natural places, as well as the more conventional archaeological sites. It could be said that much (but not all) of the world has now embraced the principles of a heritage which is valued beyond national boundaries: the Malta (or Valetta) Convention of 1992 was signed by countries willing to subscribe to the idea of a "world heritage" and they vowed to value and protect archaeological deposits in the event of their imminent destruction.

It is important to know about these legal provisions, not just because they tell us where ethical thinking is going, but because of their impact on the world of work: as public concern and legislation expand the range of heritage, the archaeology profession expands with it. It is the obligations undertaken by governments that ultimately create the work for archaeologists in the official and commercial sectors. However, much depends on how any one country decides to shoulder the responsibilities implicit in the care and exploitation of the heritage, or to use the current term, in "managing" it.

Purely as a notional convenience, we could see three types of regime in the world, with three approaches to heritage management, each creating different kinds of opportunity for the field archaeologist (FIG 15.1). In an *unregulated* country, heritage is not valued or, if it is, is regarded as a private or academic interest, not a public concern. Legislation is minimal, finance for research is raised from personal wealth, charities and trusts, and archaeological work in the field is carried out by academics, students and volunteers. Archaeological remains are deemed the property of landowners, who have the right to dig up their land, and to sell any artefacts unearthed. In this regime, teaching in universities constitutes the only paid work in archaeological investigation. There is no quality control in the field, beyond the endemic desire of academics to criticise each other. This is effectively an 18th to 19th century system, and no countries of the modern world are likely to subscribe to it – or at least to admit to it if they do.

In countries with a *regulated* heritage control, we can expect all matters relating to archaeology to be in the hands of the state. Legislation is here rigorous and all-embracing: the heritage is for all citizens, alive and yet unborn. Its protection is

Type of regime	Unregulated	Regulated	Deregulated
Source of finance	Trusts, charities	State	Developer
Method of procurement	Ad hoc	State programme Media pressure	Planning system Planning consultants Curators' specs
Who does the fieldwork?	Volunteers, students, directed by individual researcher	Labourers, directed by Inspector	Archaeological Contractor Professional excavators
Research output	Peer pressure Depends on the Individual	Depends on Government priorities	(Not part of contract)
Quality control	Peer group	Inspectors Licences	Consultants (?)

FIGURE 15.1 What sort of state are you in?

paramount. Researchers require the state's permission to excavate, and the state exercises quality control through reporting and inspection. All ancient artefacts belong to the state, so that none may enter the marketplace, and treasure-hunting is illegal. Any archaeological site that is due for development is first thoroughly recorded by excavation, survey and library research at government expense. Professional archaeologists are found in universities but the majority are employed directly by the state, either as researchers (in Academies of Science) or as administrators in offices of Heritage Management or Cultural Resources. Ultimately all the finance supporting archaeology comes from taxation.

The *deregulated* approach combines some aspects of both the unregulated and fully regulated systems. It acknowledges the state's responsibility to protect monuments for the future, but these monuments are selected and listed in advance (*scheduled monuments* or *monuments in care*). The landowner is the legitimate inheritor of all artefacts except certain valuable types (for example gold and silver). Treasure hunting is legal if the landowner allows it. Archaeological investigation too is largely a matter for the landowner, although there may be attempts at quality control through the licensing of excavators (as in Ireland), or encouraging them to belong to self-regulating institutes (as in the UK and USA). Finance for research projects comes from research councils, charities and the private sector, and is mainly undertaken by university staff. Investigation in advance of development is governed by environmental impact

legislation and paid for by the developer (the principle of "polluter pays"). It is undertaken for these "clients" by the private sector operating in archaeological firms or companies.

These days no one country will recognise itself as belonging exclusively to any one of these three prescriptions. But it would be fair to say that in the past Europe and the former Eastern Bloc have generally aspired to the regulated type of regime and to some extent still do. Deregulated regimes may be noted in the USA and UK, which try to balance strict control of archaeological resources with market principles and academic and personal freedom. There is continual skirmishing at the margins – for example over the sale of antiquities, treasure hunting, admissions charges for museums and public access to privately owned sites. The political desire to increase wealth means increasing development opportunities and cutting red tape. Although the redevelopment of archaeological sites is regulated through the planning system, the commissioning of evaluation and investigations in advance of building is effectively in the developers' hands. Finance for rescue archaeology therefore does not depend on taxation, but on the developer, who in the interest of shareholders will prefer to pay as little as possible.

Of itself this has created a work force, a commercial sector, which in the USA and UK greatly outnumbers all other forms of archaeological employment. The market principle operates here: the developer has a wide choice of contractors and is entitled to choose the cheapest. So although it has created a big and busy profession, the pricing tends to drive down the quality of work, and idealistic archaeologists find themselves being paid primarily to get archaeological evidence out of the way in short order, rather than study it with research questions in mind.

No-one knows the future of global practice, but one can at present note a general political trend towards more deregulated systems in modern Europe. For this reason, and also because the deregulated system incorporates aspects of the other two, I chose to use it in what follows. The idea is to show how field archaeologists are used by the world of work. Rather than a litany of job titles, I propose to connect the various areas of employment to the axis provided by Field Research Procedure – with which we are already familiar. This means that everyone employed in archaeology may be seen as contributing to some part of the journey of investigation – which, as readers will know by now, constitutes, in my view, the substance of what we do.

The stages of Field Research Procedure were recalled in the last chapter and summarised in its FIG 14.18, taking us from a site at the top (the archaeological resource) to its destiny as a protected or published monument. It is a feature of the deregulated system that the academic sector, paid to research, operates at arm's length from the commercial sector, paid to manage the heritage and rescue it where necessary. These primary concerns are reflected in this model of the profession, which shows the archaeological process embraced by the two sectors at left and right. As the diagram tries to indicate, there is, in theory, considerable cross-over between them; but in practice not as much as we would like. The controlling factor is money, for the money determines the form and purpose of employment. Since the money for research and the money for heritage management comes from separate sources (at least in the UK which provides my examples here), it will be convenient to treat each as its own system, and see what kinds of employment result from following the cycles: one for research and one for heritage management.

The research cycle

In the deregulated system those paid to do research are found predominately in universities, as opposed to Academies of Science, government service or museums. University research staff tend to be recruited from students who undertake a PhD – which constitutes the principal research training course. They may be appointed as *lecturers*, who also teach, or *fellows*, who mainly research. Universities get most of their money from the state via research councils, which like to monitor and grade the research they do; but increasingly, in archaeology as in science, money for research also comes from the private sector. University archaeologists often find that they need more money, especially for large-scale excavation, than the research councils can find; they therefore try to gather funds in a mixed portfolio, from research councils, from local government, from industry or from the state lottery.

A new project begins with a research question, and a place on the ground to address it. In most cases the researcher is the principal driver of funding and has to resource every stage of the investigation, punctuated by continuous redesigns and resubmissions to grant-giving bodies (FIG 15.2). The reconnaissance stage may be conducted in libraries and archives, without cost. If reconnaissance is required in the field, it can be carried out with relatively small sums provided by the university ("priming funds") used to pay for aerial survey, or a term off to be spent in the archives, for example. But the university teacher's main resource is students, who can be willingly deployed for field-walking and for excavation in the form of field schools. This is how most of us get started.

A major research project requires an evaluation and project design, and these can sometimes also be prepared using priming funds. Once the project design exists, the business of proper fundraising can begin, since no serious sponsor would contemplate supporting an archaeological project without one. Incredibly some still do, and we are presented with the sorry spectacle of academics who drag an unplanned project forward season by season, not finishing for a decade, a quarter of a century or perhaps never. These projects have done great damage to the academic sector in the eyes of commercial archaeologists – who have to work in a much more disciplined environment (see below).

Assuming that realistic funds have been raised, the university archaeologist will perform the fieldwork in summer seasons, hopefully to a high standard, and then

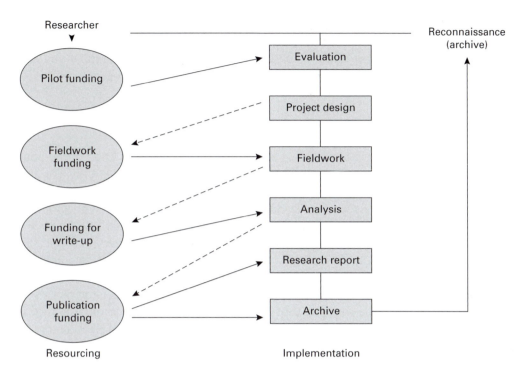

FIGURE 15.2 The research cycle.

undertake the analysis and the preparation of an archive. Although they will hope to achieve much of this by using their own time and that of their colleagues and students, in a modern project some specialist analysis will be bought in from the commercial sector. *Specialists* have set up private businesses for the analysis of pottery, textiles, metallurgy, animal bone, human bone, pollen, soils and for radiocarbon and dendrochronology. They charge by the hour, and follow the basic FRP in miniature – they look at the collection, evaluate it, cost the work, do it and produce a report. Some work from home, combining the job with bringing up a family, while others may hold a post in a laboratory that encourages external contracts.

Academics are assessed as professionals in terms of their published output, and this in turn is graded by peer review (i.e. other academics). In this process, the criterion of excellence is not quantity or even quality, but impact, a subjective, if expert view of academic influence. Nevertheless, it encourages research output, and the ideal end of the research cycle is an article in a journal, a book, an exhibition or a displayed site and often all of these. Field research projects are the stuff of archaeological research, but they are onerous to administer, usually without permanent staff, in amongst all the other demands of university life. As for impact, they tend to be slow burners – they are read intermittently over long spans of time rather than making an immediate (brief) explosion. For this reason, some academics have tended to move away from excavation and into survey, which is easier to run, can make use of unskilled student labour, is fast to write up, has fewer conservation responsibilities and wins quicker credits. This may change of course but, as it stands, if you like digging, you will get a great deal more of it in the commercial sector.

The heritage cycle

The mission of heritage is to conserve and to mobilise the appreciation of the past for the present and for the future. The emphasis is on management – managing the curation of sites and finds, managing the destruction of the evidence due to development, managing public access. The responsibility is divided between the government sector, the local government sector and the commercial sector, and the tasks are numerous. Government and local government archaeologists are very active in the reconnaissance and evaluation stages. In the UK the archaeological resource, its sites, monuments and historic buildings, is now known collectively as the *historic environment*, which aligns it in government circles with the natural environment (see Chapter 14). Legislation requires that the historic environment is recorded (in a National Monuments Record, now the Historic Environment Record, HER) and continually monitored and audited. At the level of *national government* this management task is delegated to a ministry or an agency which serves the requirements of a particular piece of heritage legislation (English Heritage and Historic Scotland are examples in the UK). Archaeological employees may be civil servants or employed on a similar basis. They maintain a central register or "schedule" of pre-selected sites and monuments protected by legislation. They implement legislation and advice for local government, and they have their own state properties ("properties in care") to maintain and display to the public. Particular sites or landscapes deemed as needing special attention become the subject of *Conservation Plans*, which set out their historical, prehistorical and environmental assets, why these may be in danger, and how they might be cared for. Such plans may be prepared in-house, or commissioned from the commercial sector. Government employees these days rarely dig or research themselves, but they get to visit lots of sites and to mount exhibitions and displays.

At *local government level* in the UK county archaeologists have the care of the existing resource and manage its release for research and mitigation when threatened by new development; in this role they are sometimes termed "curators", i.e. curators of the underground resource. They maintain a *register* or *record* of all sites and finds which come to light in their region (constituting the local SMR, Sites and Monuments Record, now HER). A new code of practice allows metal-detectorists to seek and keep metal artefacts, but encourages them to declare them so they can be recorded in the local HER. This has given employment to a new group of archaeologists working for the *Portable Antiquities Scheme* (see Chapter 4). Usually attached to museums, they see (briefly) all the finds that come in and cause them to be recorded before returning them to the owner or finder.

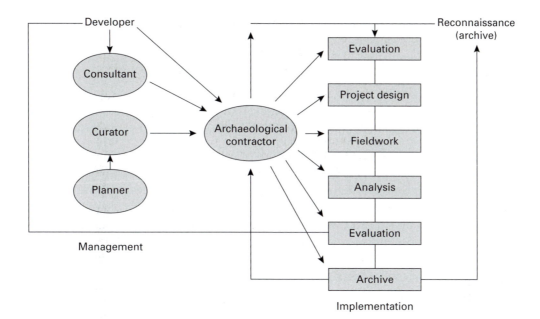

FIGURE 15.3 The heritage cycle. The "curator" in this diagram is the local government archaeologist in the UK or SHIPPO (State Historic Preservation Office) in the USA.

Local government archaeologists also manage the consequences of new development in their region, a process generally known as *mitigation*, in recognition that the damage being done to the resource is not averted, but compensated through the making of a record (FIG 15.3). In the UK this branch of curation is supported by advice from central government in the form of planning guidance notes – Planning Policy Guidance note 15 for historic buildings and 16 for archaeological deposits. PPG15 and PPG16 do not give legal protection to archaeological resources and do not oblige developers to pay for research; but they give moral authority to planners to ask developers to pay for evaluation and, depending on the result, to either alter their construction plans or pay for archaeological excavation as a condition of planning permission.

A preliminary or *desktop* assessment of every site is now routine before permission for construction can be given, and the local curator will usually demand additional information in the form of a field evaluation. The main task of local government archaeologists is to monitor the damage to the Historic Environment caused by new development and to require compensation as far as possible. For this reason they may find themselves in a planning department (while others are in "education and leisure", with museums). Acting as "curator of the resource" the local government archaeologist will draft the specification or scope of work that is required of an evaluation, to ensure (as far as possible) that these are not being done on the cheap. The specification usually focuses on the deposit model and the research potential, and more rarely, the social context. Armed with this specification, the developer will then purchase the evaluation from a private contractor (an *archaeological company*, i.e. firm). The company follows the specification and produces an evaluation report for the developer, who will then normally ask for a project design (mitigation strategy) for the investigation that should be carried out before development can begin. This project design will be attached to the application for planning permission, and its execution becomes a condition under which planning permission is granted.

Developers are supplied by the local authority with a list of suitable archaeological companies, who are invited to bid for work on the basis of competitive tender. Some developers are obliged to ask for tenders by law and to select the cheapest bid. This does not encourage good quality archaeology: it drives down the price, and thus the time and care dedicated to the investigation. Under such economic pressure this investigation can become more and more of a peremptory recording exercise and less what it is intended to be, a study offering a research dividend. The archaeological company has a mixed motive for wanting to raise the price of its contracts. On the one hand they want to make more of the research opportunity, and on the other they have employees to pay and need to win the tender. The local government and central government offices may well wish to raise the price too, but the legislative framework does not generally give them the power to interfere with the market.

In the UK, developers have responded to pressure to commission expensive archae-ological investigations by employing a go-between, the *archaeological consultant*, someone who arranges and manages the archaeological work on their behalf. Theoretically, the role of the consultant is to match the proposed development to the local archaeological specification and encourage the production of a design which will best serve the interests of the developer and the archaeology. This can work where the consultant has enough archaeological knowledge, but it is the developer that pays consultants' fees, and so there is little doubt where their first loyalty lies. In FIG 15.3, the main route shown is the dialogue that runs between the developer, to the planner, the consultant and the archaeological contractor. In this event, the archaeological contractor is at the end of the food chain, and their aspirations to be good researchers are being squeezed by the consultants' mission to give the developer a good service and keep the price down. Elsewhere however, as in the USA, the consultant is not (yet) a player, and the client route runs directly between the developer and the archae-ological contractor.

Inside an archaeological company we find *directors* or *partners*, who bid for new work from planners and developers, *project managers* who carry out evaluations, surveys and excavations, *supervisors* responsible for delegated areas or assemblages and specialist *buildings archaeologists* who record buildings and compose conservation plans. These personalities have featured extensively in the pictures of this book and a little gallery will be seen in Colour Plate 16. Increasingly, archaeological companies also require a *digital expert* to design data bases and programmes for the rapid production of plans and drawings via interfaces with new technology: TST, GPS, geo-physics, GIS. Staff are usually recruited direct from universities, which equip them with knowledge of the research agenda and something of field method, but not for many of the vital skills of the commercial sector: the management of people, the arts of negotiation with other professionals and the handling of large financial accounts. This still tends to be learnt on the job.

Companies also bid for contracts to write up their work, that is, to do analyses and prepare a field report, in the first place in the form of a Client Report (see Chapter 13, page 318). Funding comparative research and the publication of a research report can be more of a problem; the government guidelines only allow for "preservation by record"; the developers are not obliged to pay for research publication, and so they don't. This has the effect of removing the staff of archaeological companies into the wings of the research theatre, causing them understandable frustration. However, Sweden now requires developers to allow for research time on mitigation projects, and it is to be hoped that other countries will follow suit. Apart from this, the work is very varied, outdoors and in, and developers may occasionally commission a pamphlet or exhibition which places new discoveries before the public.

All the material discovered in the course of the heritage cycle (and it is now a vast amount) finds its way into a *museum* for permanent storage, together with the records. The museum is the local home of heritage, where everyone from the youngest school child to the oldest pensioner takes their inquiries. If you like communication, the best job is probably in a museum, where interaction with the public of all ages is continuous. Since archaeology is rarely taught in schools, this is also a good place of employment for those who like teaching and working with children. Museums have the responsibility of archiving most of the material from research and commercial operations, and together with *display designers*, museum staff get to create new exhibitions. Like members of archaeological companies, the museum archaeologist has to be a jack of all trades – but that has attractions of its own.

The deregulated system of archaeological procurement appears to have many more players than the state service, and the world of work seems quite complex. I say "appears" because those working inside a state archaeological service may tell you that theirs is even more complex, with just as many players and ever more tortuous procedures separating the archaeologist from the archaeology. But at least state services have control and believe that they can keep the standards high and serve the unborn to the best effect. In a deregulated community, the archaeologist is expected to ride the market and to maintain standards while competing with others on the basis of price. The building industry, moreover, is no safe source of work, especially in times of financial downturn.

This is the big paradox, since when all is said and done, a lower price is the enemy of quality. As with builders and others, the archaeologists operating outside the state are largely expected to regulate themselves, and have formed societies, like the

Society for Professional Archaeologists, SOPA, in the USA or institutes like the Institute for Archaeologists, IFA, in the UK. Although initially all-embracing, these bodies naturally became increasingly geared to the needs of the commercial archaeologists who relied on them. Thus SOPA was replaced by the RPA, a register of professional archaeologists, designed to protect the public from poor products, while the business end of the association, its lobby, emerged as the American Cultural Resources Association (ACRA).

ACRA, a likely sign of the future, is the highly successful representative body of a multi-million dollar industry. It describes itself as "a trade association" and was established in March 1995 to serve the needs of the cultural resources industry in the USA: "Covering the fields of historic preservation, history, archaeology, architectural history, historical architecture, and landscape architecture, the aim is to promote professional, ethical, and business practices for the benefit of the resources, the public, and the members of the association." ACRA lists its responsibilities to the public, to its clients, to its employees and to its colleagues, and does so openly on the internet. ACRA notes that it is a primary obligation of an ACRA member to serve the public interest. Members shall put conservation first, shall strive to respect the concerns of people whose histories and/or resources are the subject of cultural resources investigation and shall not make exaggerated, misleading, or unwarranted statements about their work. They are "obligated to provide diligent, creative, honest, and competent services and professional advice to their clients". They undertake to exercise independent professional judgment on behalf of their clients, but at the same time they undertake to respect their confidentiality, and will accept the decisions of a client concerning the objectives and nature of the professional services, "unless the decisions involve conduct that is illegal or inconsistent with the ACRA member's obligations to the public interest". This might seem like quite a balancing act, given that the client is a developer and primarily interested in building a new road or putting up a new building, rather than adding another few footnotes to history. But a declared list of mutually supported obligations of this kind makes it harder for clients to get work done on the cheap.

In Europe, some countries, notably France, have kept the procurement of archaeology largely within the embrace of government. Its executive arm is INRAP (Institut National de Recherches Archéologiques Préventives) which is financed by a tax rendered on every square metre of ground that is to be developed. This model has several advantages – the main one in the context of this chapter being that it offers the field archaeologists reasonably secure employment within a college of researchers.

Archaeologists in other European countries remark that the tendering system works, but only at the expense of the employee. In other words, the net loss of trying to keep up archaeological standards in an arena of competitive pricing is borne by the diggers' paypacket. This has much to do with a country's current level of investment and fiscal

optimism as well as the esteem in which the archaeological profession is held. The miracle is that in less than thirty years, the jobbing archaeologist has changed from a passionate amateur, feeding off condescending scraps, to a fully fledged professional with a seat at the table when any major development is planned. Naturally where archaeologists can match strong flexible procedures with a creative hunger for the public benefits of their subject, confidence among clients, planners and public that this is a job worth doing, and worth doing well, should only increase. And with it will increase the satisfaction and security of private sector employment.

The creative spirit

There is archaeological work in every country that has a past, builds a motorway, welcomes a tourist or teaches a student (FIG 15.4). The economic climate will freeze some corners of our profession and warm up others, but it is hard to imagine now a day when no one will need or heed the business of archaeological investigation. There is still a great deal to do to make this profession solid and viable: the recognition that new knowledge is the hard currency of the cultural resource and the historic environment, the disengagement of value from price, the creation of clearer career structures and the avoidance of volunteer and wage poverty. We need a better match between a country's income and its cultural assets and a more international approach to definitions of archaeological value, procedures of investigation and quality control. These things will come as confidence in the professional ethos increases.

INSPECTOR	Civil servant (or equivalent)	Ensures that legislation is respected, sites are cared for and presented to the public
CURATOR	Local government official	Works for protection and recording of sites
MUSEUM KEEPER	Local government official	Administers and researches collections, devises exhibitions and educates children and public
UNIVERSITY TEACHER	University employee	Teaches and researches
FIELD ARCHAEOLOGIST	Company employee or self-employed	Executes and reports CRM projects
CONSULTANT	Company employee or self-employed	Designs and manages archaeological projects
COMMUNICATOR	Self-employed	Publishes books, designs exhibitions, broadcasts

FIGURE 15.4 What jobs are there? (tinker, tailor for archaeologists).

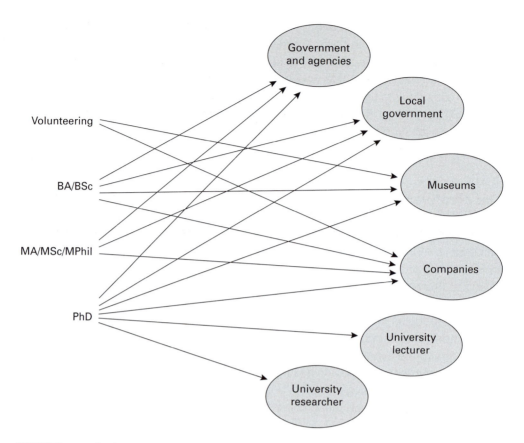

FIGURE 15.5 Professional archaeology: the way in.

This is a profession on the rise and worth joining, and getting in has several routes, conventional and unconventional (FIG 15.5). There are now plenty of degree courses, not only to meet the subject face to face in the classroom and the field, but to make the contacts which (as in showbusiness) will keep you going when the going gets tough. Those that are migrants from other industries or subject areas are especially welcome since archaeology benefits from every kind of prior experience. Entry here is most usefully achieved by a one year MA course. And in spite of the professional aura there are still points of entry for the volunteer. Some companies take volunteers – and all should. And to enter the museum profession, starting as a volunteer is mandatory.

For those that love archaeology, what it finds, how it finds it, its team work and its passion for the dead people who never had a history (or even, in some cases, much of a life), the opportunities to work as a professional are huge and varied. Archaeology is about everything and everyone who ever lived, so it cannot be boring. Public output and academic output lie at the end of our two cycles and they have been served to some extent by academic reports, archives, museum exhibitions and site interpretations. However the public is hungrier than that, and archaeologists driven by a creative urge will find themselves attracted to writing books and making films and TV programmes for adults and children. There is of course a whole media profession already, and full time professional authors and presenters often imagine that they can communicate the excitement and significance of archaeology without knowing anything about it. But we are by no means the only media victims, and the answer is not to moan about it, but for archaeologists themselves to get in on the act. Our subject needs knowledgeable writers, illustrators, artists and TV presenters – and if you do not see yourself flourishing in academic, government or commercial circles, why not dare to be an artist and release the creative spirit on archaeology's behalf? Who – if not us – can convey the real excitement of the smell of fresh earth, the glint of metal, the gradual emergence of the damp patches left by the vanished posts of a great timber hall?

For the person who tells the story best is the one who has lived it – the digger with trowel and shovel, the walker over miles of hills studded with derelict dwellings, the pattern-seeker poring over an oversize diagram, the lover of potsherds and flints, the field archaeologist, the reader of this book.

Briefing

Ethics and values: Smith and Wobst's *Indigenous Archaeologies* (2005) gives an inspiring overview of the present tensions and future prospects of research inclusivity. L. Smith 2004, 2006 for a reasoned positioning of the cultural heritage in global society. See also Lipe 1984 (on values), Lynott and Wylie 1995 (ethics), ICOMOS 1994 (Nara), ICOMOS 2004 (Burra); Carver 1996 (on archaeological value as knowledge rather than cultural property); Olivier and Clark 2001 define "Historic Environment" as the more all-embracing successor to archaeological heritage.

Resource management, worldwide: Cleere (ed.) 1984, Cleere 1989, B. Coles, 1995 (wetland), M. Carver 2001 (field archaeology); **UK:** English Heritage 2006 (principles), HLC and management of historic landscapes (UK) Rippon 2004; English Heritage 2000a (lithic scatters); Hunter and Ralston (eds) 1993; **Europe:** Council of Europe 1992, 2005, Ullén 2004 (deterioration of bronzes); Wilkinson et al 2006 (threat from cultivation); **USA:** Advasio and Carlisle 1988; Neumann and Sanford 2001a and b; McManamon and Hatton (eds) (2000); **Australia:** NSW State Agency Heritage Guide 2005; (**Japan**) Agency for Cultural Affairs 1994; **China:** Republic of, 1993, Qian, Fengqi 2007.

Heritage Cycle: USA: Neumann and Sanford 2001a and b; US Department of the Interior, National Park Service 1999 (preparing National Landmark nominations); Dorochoff 2007 on how to negotiate with stakeholders; **NAGPRA:** Dincauze 1986; Garratt-Frost 1992; Schneider, A.L. 1996; Zuni research collaboration: Anyon and

Ferguson 1995; **UK: planning guidance:** Department of the Environment (UK) 1990 (PPG16, sites); Department of the Environment (UK) 1994 (PPG 15, buildings); Andrews and Thomas 1995 (MAP2); see also MoRPHE www.english-heritage. org.uk/upload/pdf/MoRPHE-Project-Managers-Guide.pdf, and Chapter 14; Cumberpatch and Blinkhorn 2001 (players), Collcutt 1993 (archaeological consultants), Blockley 1995 (commercial archaeology), Davis et al 2004 (mitigation of construction), Clarke 1998 (conservation plans); **France:** Lombardo 1994 (autoroute); **Holland:** Willems and Brandt 2004; for **ACRA:** http://ethics. iit.edu/ codes/coe/amer.cultur.reso.assoc.html.

Integrating research and CRM: M. Carver 2001 (field archaeology and the initiative from **Sweden**), Willems 2001, and other papers in Kobyliñski, 2001; Goodyear 1978 (research design in CRM); University College Dublin 2006 (CRM and research).

GLOSSARY, ACRONYMS AND ABBREVIATIONS

ACRA: American Cultural Resources Association (www.acra-crm.org) ACRA Executive Secretary, PO Box 4020, Ithaca NY 14852 (607) 257–2126 2

ADS: Archaeology Data Service (York, UK) (www.ahds.ads.ac.uk)

Anaerobic deposit: strata preserved by being deprived of air.

Analysis: study of records from fieldwork. *Analytical destiny*: the intended analysis for a record. *Analytical itinerary*: the logical steps of an analytical argument. Stage 5 of Field Research Procedure.

Appraisal (UK): preliminary archaeological review of terrain, using existing documentation, before a *planning application* is submitted. Equivalent to Desk-based Assessment.

Archive: general unspecific term to denote unpublished archaeological records. See Field Records, Field Report.

Artefact (US artifact)**:** an object or part of an object made by humans; also waste products from making an object.

Assemblage: the finds (artefacts and biota) collected from a context, a feature, a scatter, a site, etc. Commonly, that part of the contexts removed from the site for further study (also *finds*).

Balk (US), baulk (UK): the edge of an excavation; in a quadrant or box excavation, the bar of soil between excavated areas.

Biota, biological material: items or fragments deriving from animal, vegetable or mineral objects, whether collected by humans (anthropogenic) or naturally, and whether macroscopic (visible to the naked eye, like a cow femur) or microscopic (only visible with a microscope, like pollen).

BIA: Bureau of Indian Affairs

BMP BitMap: a file extension containing a graphics file.

Brief: outline of work for an archaeological intervention. Issued by a curator or a client to an archaeological contractor. See Scope of Work.

CAD: Computer-aided design.

CD-ROM (Compact Disk Read only memory): a disk used to store and transfer digital data.

Client: the person or agency paying for archaeological intervention.

Compliance archaeology: CRM mitigation projects.

Conservation: (1) a programme or policy of protection for an archaeological site or landscape; (2) laboratory measures for the protection of an artefact from decay.

Consultant: archaeologist hired by a client or curator to give advice on the discovery and protection of, or mitigation of damage to, archaeological sites.

Context: any part of a deposit that we observe or define or interpret as belonging together. A context has shape (layer, heap) and content (soil, sand, stones). All the material in a deposit is assignable to a context, including the fills of pits or the bricks or timbers in a wall. A context can be defined in any way the archaeologist feels to be useful, including as a boundary or the infinitely thin interface between contexts. Contexts are not always deposited, but may form in situ (for example the B horizon of a soil, see Chapter 1).

Contour, contour survey: map showing the heights above sea level in the form of thick continuous lines over ground of the same height.

Contractor: archaeological contractors are firms or companies paid to make archaeological records in advance of construction or other site operations by development contractors.

Cultural resource: any archaeological artefact, feature, site or landscape.

CRM (Cultural Resource Management): The exercise of conservation and investigation of archaeological sites and buildings in accordance with a country's laws of heritage protection.

Culture, material culture: a group of objects and/or practices that frequently occurred together in the past. This general term coined by Gordon Childe is used vaguely these days, when it is less accepted that culture equates to people. Some archaeologists have begun to use "material culture" to mean cultural material, i.e. objects.

Cumulative section: a section assembled from strips drawn one at a time each vertically above the other. Also known as a *running section*.

Curator: has two different archaeological meanings: (1) a person or agency responsible for the exercise of laws protecting archaeological sites and landscapes; (2) a person employed by a museum to manage artefact collections.

Data: the entities in which an archaeological deposit is defined. Some archaeologists prefer to use a single "stratigraphic unit" or "context"; others prefer a hierarchy of units ("component", "context", "feature", "structure").

Data Structure Report (DSR): preliminary report on the findings of an excavation and their significance. The agency Historic Scotland requires a DSR at the conclusion of each season as a condition of grant.

Decay trajectory: the process whereby a deposit alters its character through time by means of natural and human agencies.

Deposit: any part of the ground that is the object of archaeological investigation, including the naturally deposited soils and subsoils. Once all or part of a deposit is recorded it becomes a *context* (qv). An excavated archaeological deposit may be defined as *an artefact that is only seen once and never seen whole.*

Desk-based assessment: UK equivalent to appraisal.

Destructive methods: those which destroy the strata.

DTM (Digital Terrain Model): computer generated topographical plan.

EDM: (1) Electronic Distance Measurer; (2) Electronic Document Management.

EH: English Heritage; the governing archaeological agency for England.

EPA: Environmental Protection Agency.

Ecofact: alternative term for *biota* (qv).

Evaluation: the assignment of value to an archaeological site or landscape; the process of arriving at such a value, specifically, a field investigation designed to determine current value. Stage 2 of Field Research Procedure.

Feature: a feature is an interpretation imposed on a set of *contexts*. Typical interpretations include things made by people like a floor, a wall, a pit, a path or a midden heap and events or activities marked by a hiatus in the strata or a distribution of objects; thus a feature can be seen as an artefact that cannot be recovered (Sharer and Ashmore 1979). The whole of a deposit is always divided into contexts; but these may or may not be grouped into features. Conceptually, features are higher-order stratigraphic units, additional but not alternative to contexts.

Field walking: UK equivalent to surface collection.

Field Records: the primary records, written, drawn, digital and photographic made in the field.

Framework: (usually) intellectual or regulatory terms of reference – for example, for Planning, Conservation or Research.

Geoplot: a commercially available program used to download process and display geophysical survey data.

GIS (Geographical Information System): A computer program featuring files of digital plans and the applications designed to manipulate them. GIS stores spatial information in layers, which can be combined or overlaid to search for patterns.

GPS (Global Positioning by Satellite): A device for locating the user with the aid of electromagnetic transmissions to and from satellites. GPS accuracy varies from handheld (nearest 5m) to base stations which can provide locations to the nearest millimetre.

HABS: Historic American Building Survey.

Hachure: method of signalling a break of slope in a topographical survey, using narrow triangles (hachures).

Historic Building Record/Survey: Field Record of the plan and fabric of a building.

HER (Historic Environment Record): inventory of all sites and finds from a specific area.

Horizon: horizontal slice through an archaeological deposit.

HTML: Hyper Text Markup Language.

Implementation: the execution of a programme. Stage 4 of Field Research Procedure.

Interpretation: in preparation of reports: real-life ideas suggested by data from excavation or survey; in the display of sites: guidance to visitors (in the form of panels or pamphlets) on the meaning or range of meanings of what they can see.

Intervention: any field action by an archaeological investigator that involves examining a deposit, i.e intervenes in the decay trajectory. Interventions may be excavations or surveys and nearly every archaeological investigation in the field constitutes an intervention of some kind, whether destructive, non-destructive, invasive or non-invasive (qv).

Invasive methods: those that penetrate the ground.

JPEG: (Joint Photographic Expert Group): a standard image compression algorithm, designed for full colour or grey scale digital images of photographs.

Lab Reports: the primary report describing what was done in the field and lab, the analyses and their significance (also known as Field Reports).

MAP, MAP2 (Management of Archaeological Projects): a staged project management procedure promoted by English Heritage (see Chapter 14).

Matrix: a word with four commonly used meanings in archaeology: (1) dirt/earth which contains artefacts and other objects (e.g. Sharer and Ashmore 1976; Neumann and Sanford 2001b, 177). Here we use the terms *deposit* (unspecific) or *context* (when defined). (2) mineral mixture containing a metal, *ore*; (3) the mathematician's array of numbers, as used in statistics; (4) a diagram showing a sequence of excavated contexts (e.g. Harris 1989, Harris et al 1993). Here we use *sequence diagram* (see Chapter 11).

Mitigation: Measures taken to compensate society for losses to cultural resources. These measures frequently include archaeological investigation, evaluation, buildings recording and field research.

Mitigation strategy: project design for a mitigation project.

Munsell colour chart: a book of colours used to describe and characterise colours of soils.

MORPHE (Management of Research Projects for the Historic Environment)**:** a management procedure for archaelogical projects supported by English Heritage (see Chapter 14).

MSC (Manpower Services Commission)**:** in the UK a body that hired archaeologists to undertake investigations in the 1970s to alleviate unemployment (cf WPA).

NPS (USA)**:** National Park Service; US government agency responsible for designated open spaces and conservation practice www.cr.nps.gov/ncptt/irg/welcome

Occupation: site or deposit which contains evidence for human activity.

PDF (Portable Document Format)**:** digital form of an illustrated document.

PPG (Planning Policy Guidance)**:** PPG 16 governs mitigation in CRM archaeology in the UK.

Planning: has three commonly used meanings in archaeology: (1) In the UK by law the Planning Process provides for a Planning Application to be submitted to obtain Planning Permission required for any construction that alters the use of land. Planning Policy Guidance Note 16 (PPG16) governs mitigation in CRM archaeology in the UK; (2) The act of recording site geometry as a 2-D scale drawing (drawing a plan); (3) The process of designing a programme of work for a project (making a plan).

Profile: a sideways view of a building, feature or archaeological deposit; a drawing of the same showing the top and bottom of the area viewed. Compare *section*.

Project Design: a detailed statement of the objectives, methods and programme of an archaeological investigation. Stage 3 of Field Research Procedure.

Project outline: equivalent to Scope of Work.

Publication: communication of the results of fieldwork. Stage 5 of Field Research Procedure.

Reconnaissance: projects designed to locate sites. Stage 1 of Field Research Procedure.

Record: the documentation drawn from an archaeological deposit; the records are written, drawn, and photographic records and samples (including finds)

Remote Mapping: (1) making a map of features discovered by remote sensing; (2) On excavation, mapping from a number of digital points.

Remote Sensing: method of exploring archaeological features, sites and landscapes without physical contact; includes aerial, geophysical, chemical and other methods.

Rescue archaeology: recording sites before their destruction. (See also Compliance, CRM, Mitigation, Section 106.)

Research Agenda: a current list of questions about the past that archaeologists would like answered.

Research Design: the objectives and methods of a research programme.

Research Dividend: the research benefits drawn from an opportunity to investigate – especially during a mitigation exercise.

Research Framework: an appreciation of how the questions in a research agenda might be addressed.

Research Objectives: the list of investigations in a research programme.

Research Priorities: the research objectives currently deemed most important.

Research Programme: the investigations to be carried out, in order.

Research Strategy: the overall research intentions in a project design.

Resource: (1) The archaeological resource, potential evidence for the past buried under the ground or incorporated in a building; (2) material and financial support for a project

Resource management: The conservation and presentation of an archaeological landscape, site or historic building.

Resource Model: Three-dimensional descriptive model of buried archaeological strata.

Sampling has four common meanings in archaeology: (1) In regional reconnaissance, evaluation and investigation, the choice of areas in which to look for and record surface material (Chapter 4); (2) In site studies, the choice of area to excavate (Chapter 6); (3) In excavation, taking of packets of soil for further analysis (Chapter 6) (4) In excavation or survey, the selection of part of a macroscopic assemblage to represent the whole (e.g. brick samples from builder's rubble), the rest being discarded (thrown away) (Chapter 6).

RPA: Register of Professional Archaeologists (USA). (www.rpanet.org)

Scope of Work: outline programme of work for an archaeological intervention. Issued by a curator or a client to an archaeological contractor. Equivalent to Project Outline and Brief.

Section: vertical slice through an archaeological deposit; an annotated drawn record of the same.

Section 106 archaeology: regulation enabling and governing CRM projects in the USA.

Sequence diagram: a diagram representing the deposition sequence of archaeological strata. The "Harris matrix" is an example of a sequence diagram using contexts.

Seriation: a method of placing strata or artefacts in their most likely order by date. It is based on the idea that contexts (or objects) nearest to each other in date are also similar in their content.

SHIPPO: State Historic Preservation Office. The office responsible for ensuring compliance with CRM regulations on the historic environment in the USA.

Shovel-scraping: cleaning the surface of a deposit by skimming with a shovel, with the blade held flat.

Shovel-testing: digging an array of small shovel-sized pits to expose buried strata and artefacts. Used for the survey of opaque terrain.

Site: (1) a place where archaeologists are at work, especially when excavating; (2) a place once occupied by humans as a settlement, cemetery, hunting area, etc. It is not always clear in the literature which of these meanings is intended. Thus "the site was owned by Messrs Smith and Jones" refers to a piece of land of archaeological interest in the present day; "the site was defined by a scatter of flint flakes" refers to an area of ancient use; "the site measured 40×40m" means an excavation area; "the site stretched from the river to the crest of the ridge" means the ancient occupation area. In this book "site" mostly means an area subjected to archaeological investigation.

Specification: detailed programme of work, as proposed by client, curator, consultant or archaeological contractor.

Strata: (1) in geology, naturally deposited layers lying in sequence; (2) in Field Archaeology, most commonly, material deposited in an archaeological site. Here we use the term *context*; (3) in survey projects, areas to be surveyed; here we use *zones*.

Stratification: (1) the relationship of finds, contexts, features, structures in the ground; (2) also used to denote the division into areas for reconnaissance, evaluation, or survey (here we use *zonation*).

Stratigraphy: the reading of the *stratification* and its presentation in the form of a graphical model (such as a *section* or a *sequence diagram*).

Strip: to remove the turf or topsoil; strip and map: to strip and then clean and map the exposed surface; strip, map and wrap: to strip and map and then rebury the exposed surface having covered it with a protective sheet.

Structure: a structure is an interpretation imposed on a set of *features*. Examples of structures are a set of walls in use together (a building), a set of posts in a row (a fence), a grave covered with earth (a burial mound).

Surface collection: area survey, mapping the position (and maybe picking up) artefacts lying on the ground surface.

Survey: investigation of a building, site or landscape from the air or surface.

Tableau: used for the layout of a burial as excavated.

Template: the layout of survey or excavation sample areas.

Test-pit, test transect: square (e.g. 1×1m) or linear (e.g. 1×100m) excavation designed to discover depth and character of archaeological strata.

Topographic survey: measured three-dimensional map of ground surface.

Terrain: the natural character and properties of the land in which a *deposit* is located. Terrain will describe the subsoil, topsoil, topography and current vegetation or land use (see Chapter 3).

TIFF (Tagged Interchange File Format)**:** an industry-standard raster data format. Supports black-and-white, grey scale, pseudocolour and true colour images, all of which can be stored in compressed or uncompressed format. Commonly used in desktop publishing.

URL (Uniform Resource Locator)**:** the address by which a website is found.

Viewshed analysis: a GIS application which shows up parts of landscape inter-visible with a given point.

Vista analysis: construction of lines of sight between monuments, settlements and other types of site.

Watching brief (also archaeological monitoring)**:** programme of observation and recording carried out by an archaeologist attendant on site during development works.

WPA (Works Progress Administration)**:** US scheme whereby archaeologists and their workforce were hired to undertake investigations over large areas.

Zonation: the division of a piece of land into zones on the basis of its surface character for purposes of reconnaissance, evaluation or investigation, using area sampling.

ABBREVIATIONS

(see also Glossary)

Am.Ant.	American Antiquity (USA)
Ant.J.	Antiquaries Journal
Arch.J.	The Archaeological Journal (London)
BAR	British Archaeological Reports (*Tempus Reparatum*, Oxford)
CBA	Council for British Archaeology (York)
CRM	Cultural Resource Management (USA)
CUP	Cambridge University Press (Cambridge UK)
EUP	Edinburgh University Press (UK)
HMSO	Her Majesty's Stationery Office (UK government publisher)
J.Arch.Sci.	The Journal of Archaeological Science (UK)
JFA	Journal of Field Archaeology (USA)
Med.Arch.	Medieval Archaeology (UK)
OUP	Oxford University Press (Oxford UK)
PSAS	Proceedings of the Society of Antiquaries of Scotland
RCAHMS	Royal Commission on the Ancient and Historical Monuments of Scotland

BIBLIOGRAPHY

*This bibliography lists the works referred to in '**Briefings**' at the end of each chapter. Note that many of the articles in journals can be assessed online, including the numerous citations from Antiquity (see http: //antiquity.ac.uk).*

Adams, R.Mc. 1981 *Heartland of Cities: surveys of ancient settlement and land use on the central floodplain of the Euphrates* (Chicago: University of Chicago Press).

ADS (Archaeology Data Service) 1999 *Archiving Aerial Photography and Remote Sensing Data* by Robert Bewley, Danny Donoghue, Vince Gaffney, Martijn van Leusen and Alicia Wise (Oxford: Oxbow).

Advasio, J. and R. Carlisle 1988 'Some thoughts on cultural resource management in the United States', *Antiquity* 62: 72–87.

Agency for Cultural Affairs (Japan) 1994 *An Overview of Japan's Policies on the Protection of Cultural Properties.*

Aitken, M.J. 1990 *Science-based dating in Archaeology* (Longman: London and New York).

Aitken, M.J. 1991 'Thermoluminescence dating', in Goeksu, Oberhofer and Regulla, 121–40; 'Sediment and optical dating', ibid. 141–54.

Aitken, M. and R. Milligan 1992 'Ground-probing RADAR in archaeology: practicalities and problems', *The Field Archaeologist* 16: 288–91.

Aitken, M., G. Webster and A. Rees 1958 'Magnetic prospecting', *Antiquity* 32: 270–1.

Alcock, N.W. et al 1996 *Recording Timber-Framed Buildings: a glossary* (2nd edn. Council for British Archaeology).

Alcock, S.E., J.F. Cherry and J.L. Davis 1994 'Intensive survey, agricultural practice and the Classical landscape of Greece', in I. Morris (ed.) *Classical Greece: Ancient Histories and New Archaeologies* (CUP): 137–70.

Alcock, Susan and John Cherry 1996 'Survey at any price?', *Antiquity* 70: 207–11.

Alizadeh, K. and J.A. Ur 2007 'Formation and destruction of pastoral and irrigation landscapes on the Mughan Steppe, north-western Iran', *Antiquity* 81: 148–60.

Allan, Sarah (ed.) 2005 *The Formation of Chinese Civilization. An archaeological perspective* (Yale University Press).

Allen, K.M., S.W. Green and E.B.W. Zubrow (eds) 1990 *Interpreting Space: GIS and archaeology* (London: Taylor & Francis).

Allen, J. and A. Holt 1997 *Health and Safety in Field Archaeology, SCAUM* British and Irish Archaeological Bibliography, Vol. 1 no. 2, Council for British Archaeology.

Ambrose, W.R. 2001 'Obsidian hydration dating', in Brothwell and Pollard, 81–92.

Amendolea, B. (acd) 1995 *I Siti Archeologici. Un Problema di Musealizzazione all'Aperto* (provincia di Roma).

Ammerman, A.J. 1981 'Surveys and archaeological research', *Annual Review of Anthropology* 10: 63–88.

Ammerman, A.J. 1985 'Plow-zone experiments in Calabria, Italy', *JFA* 12(1): 33–40.

Andrews, Gill and Roger Thomas 1995 'The management of archaeological projects: theory and practice in the UK' in Malcolm Cooper, Anthony Firth, John Carman and David Wheatley (eds) *Managing Archaeology* (London: Routledge): 189–207.

Arnold, Jeanne E., Elizabeth L. Ambos and Daniel O. Larson 1997 'Geophysical surveys of stratigraphically complex Island California sites: new implications for household archaeology', *Antiquity* 71: 157–68.

Anyon, Roger and T.J. Ferguson 1995 'Cultural resources management at the Pueblo of Zuni, New Mexico, USA', *Antiquity* 69: 913–30.

Arthur, Paul and S. Sindbaek 2007 'Trade and Exchange', in J. Graham-Campbell (ed.) *The Archaeology of Medieval Europe* Vol. I (Aarhus: University Press): 289–315.

Artz, Joe Alan, Shesh Mathur and John F. Doershuk 1998 'Past landscapes, Future roads. GIS, Archeology and Highway Planning in Iowa' *CRM* 21.5: 21–2.

Arup, Ove and partners and University of York 1991 *York Development and Archaeology Study* (English Heritage and York City Council).

Ashmore, W. and B. Knapp (eds) 1999 *Archaeologies of Landscape* (Oxford: Blackwell).

Aspinall, A. 1992 'New developments in geophysical prospection', in A. Pollard (ed.) *New Developments in Archaeological Science* (OUP): 233–44.

Association for Environmental Archaeology 1995 *Environmental archaeology and archaeological evaluations*.

Association of County Archaeological Officers 1993 *Model Briefs and Specifications for Archaeological Assessments and Field Evaluations*.

Aston, M.A., M.H. Martin and A.W. Jackson 1998 'The potential for heavy soil analysis on low status archaeological sites at Shapwick, Somerset', *Antiquity* 72: 838–47.

Aston, Michael and Christopher Gerrard 1999 '"Unique, traditional and charming": the Shapwick Project, Somerset', *Ant.J.* 79: 1–58.

Atkinson, J.A. 1995 *The House, Granton-on-Spey* (GUARD, Glasgow).

Atkinson, R.J.C. 1946 *Field Archaeology* (London: Methuen).

Atkinson, R.J.C. 1957 'Worms and weathering', *Antiquity* 31: 219–33.

Atkinson, R.J.C. 1985 'Worms, charcoal and post-holes', *Antiquity* 59: 47–8.

Backmann, H. 1982 *The identification of slags from archaeological sites* (Inst. of Arch. London Occ. Paper 6).

Bahn, P. and C. Renfrew 2008 *Archaeology: theories, methods and practice* (5th edn. London and New York: Thames and Hudson).

Bailey, G. and G. Thomas 1987 'The use of percussion drilling to obtain core samples from rock shelter deposits', *Antiquity* 61: 433–9.

Bailey, Geoff (ed.) 1997 *Klithi: Paleolithic settlement and Quarternary landscapes in northwest Greece. Vol 1: Excavation and intra-site analysis at Klithi* (Cambridge: McDonald Institute Monographs).

Bailey, Richard N., Eric Cambridge and Denis H. Briggs 1988 *Dowsing and Church Archaeology* (Intercept, Wimborne).

Baillie, M.G.L. 1995 *A slice through time* (London: Batsford).

Baillie, M.G.L. 1991 'Dendrochronology', in Goeksu, Oberhofer and Regulla: 195–216.

Ball, J. and R. Kelsay 1992 'Prehistoric intrasettlement land use and residual soil phosphate levels in the Upper Belize Valley, Central America', in T. Killion (ed.) *Gardens of Prehistory: The archaeology of settlement agriculture in greater Meso-America* (Alabama: University of Alabama Press) 234–62.

Banerjee, Rowena 2008 'Experimental geochemistry: a multi-elemental characterisation of known activity areas', *Antiquity* 82: ProjGall 318.

Banning, E.B. 2002 *Archaeological Survey* (Plenum).

Barham, A.J. and R.I. Macphail (eds) 1995 *Archaeological Sediments and Soils. Analysis, interpretation and management* (London: University College).

Barker, Graeme 1991 'Approaches to area survey' in G. Barker and J. Lloyd (eds) *Roman Landscapes: Archaeological Survey in the Mediterranean Region* (British School at Rome Archaeological Monograph 2): 1–10.

Barker, Graeme 1995 'The Biferno Valley survey: methodologies', in G. Barker (ed.) *A Mediterranean Valley. Landscape archaeology and Annales history in the Biferno Valley* (London: Leicester University Press): 40–61.

Barker, Graeme (ed.) 1999 *The Companion Encyclopaedia of Archaeology* (London and New York: Routledge).

Barker, H. 1958 'Radiocarbon dating: its scope and limitations', *Antiquity* 32: 253–63.

Barker, P.A. 1969 'Some aspects of the excavation of timber buildings', *World Archaeology* 1: 220–30.

Barker, P.A. 1977 *Techniques of Archaeological Excavation* (London: Batsford).

Barker, P.A. 1993 *Techniques of Archaeological Excavation* (3rd edn. London: Batsford).

Barker, P.A. and R. Higham 1982 *Hen Domen Montgomery. A Timber Castle on the English–Welsh border* (Royal Archaeological Institute).

Bartram, Lawrence E., Ellen M. Kroll and Henry T. Bunn 1991 'Variability in Camp Structure and Bone Food Refuse Patterning at Kua San Hunter-Gatherer Camps', in Ellen M. Kroll and T. Douglas Price (eds) *The Interpretation of Archaeological Spatial Patterning* (New York): 77–148.

Bass G.F. and F.H. Van Doorninck jnr 1982 *Yassi Ada. A seventh century Byzantine shipwreck* (Texas A&M: University Press).

Bass, G. (ed.) 2005 *Beneath Seven Seas* (London: Thames and Hudson).

Batey, R. 1987 'Subsurface interface RADAR at Sepphoris, Israel, 1985', *JFA* 14: 1–8.

Baxter, M.J. 1994 *Exploratory Multivariate Analysis in Archaeology* (EUP).

Bayliss, Alex, Fachtna McAvoy and Alasdair Whittle 2007 'The world recreated: redating Silbury Hill in its monumental landscape', *Antiquity* 81: 26–53.

Bänteli, Kurt 1993 'Die Entwicklung des Gerberhauses am Beispiel des Hauses "Zur Gerbe"', in Schaffhausen in anon. (ed.) *Stadtluft, Hirsebrei und Bettelmönch. Die Stadt um 1300* (Landesdenkmalamt Baden-Württemberg und der Stadt Zürich): 420–4.

Beaudry, Mary C. (ed.) 1988 *Documentary Archaeology in the New World* (CUP).

Beck, A., G. Philip, M. Abdulkarim and D. Donaghue 2007 'Evaluation of Corona and Ikonos high resolution satellite imagery for *Archaeological Prospection* in western Syria', *Antiquity* 81: 161–75.

Becker, H. 1995 'From nanoTesla to picoTesla – a new window for magnetic prospecting in archaeology', *Archaeological Prospection* 2: 217–28.

Bell, M. and J. Boardman (eds) 1992 *Past and present soil erosion: archaeological and geological perspectives* (Oxford: Oxbow).

Bell, M., P.J. Fowler and S.W. Hillson 1996 *The experimental earthwork project 1960–1992* (CBA Research Report 100).

Bentley, R. Alexander, Hallie R. Buckley, Matthew Spriggs, Stuart Bedford, Chris J. Ottley, Geoff M. Nowell, Colin G. Macpherson and D. Graham Pearson 2007 'Lapita migrants in the Pacific's oldest cemetery: isotopic analysis at Teouma, Vanuatu', *Am.Ant.* 72.4: 645–56.

Berstan, R., A.W. Stott, S. Minnit, C. Bronk Ramsey, R.E.M. Hedges and R.P. Evershed 2008 'Direct dating of pottery from its organic residues: new precision using compound-specific carbon isotopes', *Antiquity* 82: 702–13.

Besteman, J.C., J.M. Bos, D.A. Gerrets, H.A. Heidinga and J. De Konig 1999 *The Excavations at Wijnaldum. Reports on Frisia in Roman and Medieval Times* Vol. 1 (A.A. Balkema/Rotterdam/Brookfield).

Bewley, R.H. 1993 'Aerial photography for archaeologists', in Hunter and Ralston, 197–204.

Bewley, R.H., S.P. Crutchley and C.A. Shell 2005 'New light on an ancient landscape: lidar survey in the Stonehenge World Heritage Site', *Antiquity* 79: 636–47.

Bibby, David I. 1993 'Building stratigraphic sequences in excavations: an example from Konstanz, Germany', in Harris et al: 104–21.

Biddle, M. and B. Kjølbye-Biddle 1969 'Metres, areas and robbing', *World Archaeology* 1: 208–19.

Billman, Brian R. and Gary M. Feinman (eds) 1999 *Settlement Pattern Studies in the Americas. Fifty Years since Virú* (Smithsonian Institution Press: Washington DC).

Binford, L.R. 1972 *An Archaeological Perspective* (New York; Seminar) reprinting 'A Consideration of Archaeological Research Design' (1964) 135–63 and 'Archaeological Perspectives' (1968) 78–113.

Binford, L.R. 1983 *In Pursuit of the Past* (London and New York: Thames and Hudson).

Binford, L.R. 1989 *Debating Archaeology* (New York: Academic Press).

Binks, G., J. Dyke and P. Dagnall 1988 *Visitors Welcome: A Manual on the Presentation and Interpretation of Archaeological Excavations* (Centre for Environmental Interpretation, Manchester Polytechnic/English Heritage).

Bintliff, J., B. Davis, C. Gaffney, A. Snodgrass and A. Waters 1992 'Trace metal accumulation in soils on and around ancient settlement in Greece', in P. Spoerry (ed.) *Geoprospection in the Archaeological Landscape* (Oxford: Oxbow): 9–24.

Bintliff, John and Anthony Snodgrass 1988a 'Off-site pottery distributions: a regional and inter-regional perspective', *Current Anthropology* 29(3): 506–13.

Bintliff, John and Anthony Snodgrass 1988b: 'Mediterranean survey and the city', *Antiquity* 62: 57–71.

Bjelajaā, V., E. Luby and R. Ray 1996 'A validation test of a field-based phosphate analysis technique', *J.Arch.Sci.* 23(2): 243–8.

Bland, Roger 2005 'A pragmatic approach to the problem of portable antiquities: the experience of England and Wales', *Antiquity* 79: 440–9.

Blankholm, Hans Peter 1991 *Intra-site Spatial Analysis in Theory and Practice* (Aarhus University Press).

Blanton, R.E., S. Kowaleski, G. Feinmann and J. Appel 1982 *Monte Alban's hinterland Part I The prehispanic settlement patterns of the central and southern parts of the valley of Oaxaca, Mexico* (Ann Arbor).

Bleed, P. 1983 'Management techniques and archaeological fieldwork', *JFA* 10: 494–8.

Blockley, Marion 1995 'Archaeologists in the marketplace', in Cooper et al: 101–18.

Bloemker, J. and C. Oakley 1999 'The firebreak plow and subsurface site discovery', *JFA* 26: 75–82.

Boddington, A., A.N. Garland and R. Janaway (eds) 1987 *Death, decay and reconstruction: approaches to archaeology and forensic science* (Manchester University Press).

Boismier, W.A. 1997 *Modelling the effects of tillage processes on artefact distribution in the ploughzone: a simulation study of tillage-induced pattern formation* (BAR 259).

Bollong, C. 1994 'Analysis of site stratigraphy and formation processes using patterns of pottery sherd distribution', *JFA* 21: 15–28.

Bonnet, C. 1993 *Les Fouilles de l'ancien groupe episcopal de Geneve (1976–1993)* (Cahiers d'archéologie genevoise 1).

Bonnichsen, R. 1973 'Millie's Camp: an experiment in archaeology', *World Archaeology* 4: 277–91.

Bonsall, C. and C. Tolan-Smith (eds) 1997 *The Human Use of Caves* (BAR Int 667).

Borg, K., U. Nasman and E. Wegraus (eds) 1976 *Eketorp. Fortification and settlement on Oland, Sweden* Vol. 1 *The Monument* (Stockholm).

Bostyn, Françoise c.2004 *Néolithique ancien en Normandie: Le village Villeneuve–Saint-Germain de Poses 'Sur la Mare' et les sites de la boucle du Vaudreuil* (La Société Préhistorique Française/INRAP).

Bowman, S. 1990 *Radiocarbon dating* (British Museum).

Brandt, Roel, Bert J. Groenewoudt and Kenneth L. Kvamme 1992 'An experiment in archaeological site location: modelling in the Netherlands using GIS techniques', *World Archaeology* 24.2: 268–82.

Brereton, Christopher 1991 *The Repair of Historic Buildings: Advice on Principles and Methods* (English Heritage).

British Museum 2008 *Annual Treasure Report 2005/6* (British Museum).

Brogiolo, Gian Pietro 1988 *Archeologia dell'Edilizia Storica* (Como: Edizioni New Press).

Brogiolo, G.-P. and L. Castelletti (eds) 1991 *Archeologia a Monte Barro I. Il Grande edificio e le torri* (Lecco).

Brogiolo, G.-P. and L. Castelletti (eds) 2001 *Archeologia a Monte Barro II. Gli Scavi 1990–97 e le ricerche al S. Martin di Lecco* (Consorzio Parco Monte Barro).

Bronk Ramsey, C. 1995 'Radiocarbon calibration and analysis of stratigraphy: the program Oxcal', *Radiocarbon* 37(2): 425–30.

Bronk Ramsey, C. 1998 'Probability and dating', *Radiocarbon* 40.1: 461–74

Bronk Ramsey, Christopher C., E. Buck, W.W. Manning, P. Reimer. and H. Van der Plicht 2006 'Developments in radiocarbon calibration for archaeology', *Antiquity* 80: 783–9.

Brothwell, D. 1982 *Digging up Bones* (London: BM. NH).

Brothwell, D.R. and A.M. Pollard (eds) 2001 *Handbook of Archaeological Sciences* (John Wiley: Chichester).

Brown, A.E. (ed.) 1991 *Garden Archaeology* (London: CBA Research Report 78).

Brown, J.A. 1975 'Deep site excavation strategy as a sampling problem'. in Mueller: 155–69.

Brown, S. 1997 *A practical guide to measuring and drawing a timber-framed building*, Chelmsford: Essex Historic Buildings Group.

Brown, T.A. 2001 'Ancient DNA', in Brothwell and Pollard: 301–12.

Brusasco, Paolo 2004 'Theory and practice in the study of Mesopotamian domestic space', *Antiquity* 78: 142–57.

Buck, C.E. 2001 'Applications of the Bayesian statistical paradigm', in Brothwell and Pollard: 695–702.

Buck, C.E., J.B. Kenworthy, C.D. Litton, and A.F.M. Smith, 1991 'Combining archaeological and radiocarbon information. A Bayesian approach to calibration', *Antiquity* 65: 808–21.

Budd, P., Andrew Millard, Carolyn Chenery, Sam Lucy, Charlotte Roberts 2004 'Investigating population movement by stable isotope analysis: a report from Britain', *Antiquity* 78: 127–41.

Bull, I.D., I.A. Simson, P.F. Van Bergen and R.P. Evershed 1999 'Muck 'n' molecules: organic geochemical methods for detecting ancient manuring', *Antiquity* 73: 83–96.

Bunting, Scott and Geoffrey D. Summers 2002 'Modelling terrain: the Global Positioning System (GPS) survey', *Antiquity* 76: 639–40.

Burnouf, Joelle, Jean-Oliver Guilhot, Marie-Odile Mandy, and Christian Orcel, 1991 *Le Pont de la Guilotière. Franchir le Rhône a Lyon* (Circonscriptions des Antiquités Historiques, Lyon).

Butler, William B. 1979 'The no-collection strategy' in archaeology *Am.Ant.* 44: 795–9.

—— 1987 'Significance and other frustrations in Cultural Resource Management' *Am.Ant.* 52.4: 820–29.

Calaway, M.J. 2005 'Ice cores, sediments and civilisation collapse: a cautionary tale from Lake Titicaca', *Antiquity* 79: 778–90.

Cameron, A.D. 1986 *Go listen to the crofters* (Acair Ltd: Isle of Lewis).

Cameron, C.M. and S.A. Tomkin (eds) 1993 *Abandonment of Settlements and Regions. Ethnoarchaeological and archaeological approaches* (CUP).

Canti, M.G. 1998 'The micromorphological identification of faecal spherulites from archaeological and modern materials', *J.Arch.Sci.* 25: 435–44.

Carlin, Neil, Linda Clarke and Fintan Walsh 2008 *The archaeology of life and death in the Boyne floodplain: the linear landscape of the M4, Kinnegad–Enfield–Kilcock motorway* (Dublin: NRA Scheme Monographs 2).

Carter, Tristan, Stéphan Dubernet, Rachel King, François-Xavier Le Bourdonnec, Marina Milič, Gérard Poupeau and Steven Shackley 2008 'Eastern Anatolian obsidians at Çatalhöyük and the reconfiguration of regional interaction in the Early Ceramic Neolithic', *Antiquity* 82: 900–9.

Carver, Emma and Lelong, Olivia (eds) 2004 *Modern views – ancient lands. New work and thought on cultural landscapes* (BAR 377).

Carver, Jay 2009 'Recent publications in roads archaeology', *Antiquity* 83: 219–22.

Carver, Martin 1978 'Early Shrewsbury: an archaeological definition', in 1975 *Transactions of the Shropshire Archaeological Society* 59 (1973/4 iss. 1978) 225–63.

Carver, Martin 1979a 'Three Saxo-Norman tenements in Durham City', *Med.Arch.* 23: 1–80.

Carver, Martin 1979b 'Notes on some general principles for the analysis of excavated data', *Science and Archaeology* 21: 1–14.

Carver, Martin 1980 'The excavation of three medieval craftsmen's tenements at Sidbury, Worcester', in M.O.H. Carver (ed.) *Medieval Worcester – an archaeological framework* (Worcester: Trans. Worcestershire Archaeological Society 7): 155–219.

Carver, Martin 1983a 'Valutazione, strategia ed analisi nei siti pluristratificati', *Archeologia Medievale* 10: 49–71.

Carver, Martin 1983b 'Forty French Towns: an essay on archaeological site evaluation and historical aims', in *Oxford Journal of Archaeology* 2.3: 339–78.

Carver, Martin (ed.) 1983c *Two Town Houses in Medieval Shrewsbury* (trans. Shropshire Archaeological Society, 49).

Carver, Martin 1985 'Theory and practice in urban pottery seriation', *J.Arch.Sci.* 12: 353–66.

Carver, Martin 1986 (Evaluation and Project Design) *Bulletin of the Sutton Hoo Research Committee* 4.

Carver, Martin 1987 *Underneath English Towns* (London: Batsford).

Carver, Martin 1989 'Digging for ideas', *Antiquity* 63: 666–74.

Carver, Martin 1990 'Digging for data: archaeological approaches to data definition, acquisition and analysis', in R. Francovich and D. Manacorda (acd) *Lo Scavo Archeologico: Dalla Diagnosi all'Edizione* (Firenze): 45–120.

Carver, Martin 1993 *Arguments in Stone: Archaeological Research and the European Town in the First Millennium AD* (Oxford: Oxbow).

Carver, Martin 1995 'On and off the Edda', in O. Olsen, J.S. Madsen and F. Riek (eds) *Ship-shape Essays for Ole Crumlin-Pedersen* (Copenhagen: Vikingesskibshallen I Roskilde): 305–12.

Carver, Martin 1996 'On archaeological value', *Antiquity* 70: 45–56.

Carver, Martin 1998 *Sutton Hoo. Burial Ground of Kings?* (London: British Museum Press).

Carver, Martin 1999a 'Field Archaeology', in G. Barker (ed.) *Companion Encyclopaedia to Archaeology* (Routledge): 128–81.

Carver, Martin 2001 'The Future of Field Archaeology', in Z. Kobyliński (ed.) *Whither Archaeology in the 21st century* (European Science Foundation,Warsaw): 118–32.

Carver, Martin 2002 'Marriages of true minds: archaeology with texts', in B. Cunliffe, W. Davis and C. Renfrew (eds) *Archaeology: The Widening Debate* (OUP): 465–96.

Carver, Martin 2003 *Archaeological value and evaluation* (Societá Archeologica Padana, Mantova).

Carver, Martin 2005 *Sutton Hoo. A seventh century princely burial ground and its context* (London: British Museum Press).

Carver, Martin 2007a 'The Future of Antiquity', in M. Rundqvist (ed.) *Scholarly Journals between the Past and the Future* (Kungl.Vitterhets Historie och Antikvitets Akademien Konferenser 65): 30–49.

Carver, Martin 2007b 'Archaeological journals, academics and open access', *European Journal of Archaeology* 10.3: 135–48.

Carver, Martin 2008 *Portmahomack: Monastery of the Picts* (Edinburgh University Press).

Carver, Martin and Djemal Soudi 1996 'Archaeological Reconnaissance and Evaluation in the Achir Basin (Algeria)', *Archéologie Islamique* 6: 7–44.

Carver, Martin and Cecily Spall 2004 'Excavating a *parchmenerie*: archaeological correlates of making parchment at the Pictish monastery at Portmahomack, Easter Ross', PSAS 134: 183–200.

Carver, Martin, Catherine Hills and Jonathan Scheschkewitz 2009 *Wasperton. A Roman, British and Anglo-Saxon Community in Central England* (Woodbridge: Boydell Press).

Casana, Jesse and Jackson Cothren 2008 'Stereo analysis, DEM extraction and orthor-tectification of CORONA satellite imagery: archaeological applications from the Near East', *Antiquity* 82: 732–49.

Cattaneo, C., P. Gelsthorpe, R.J. Sokol and D. Smillie 1991 'Identification of ancient blood and tissue – ELISA and DNA analysis', *Antiquity* 65: 878–81.

Cessford, Craig 2005 'Heavy residue analysis', in Hodder: 45–64.

Chadwick, A. 1997 'Archaeology at the edge of chaos. Further towards reflexive excavation methodology', *Assemblage* 3 (www.shef.ac.uk).

Challis, Keith, Ziga Kokalj, Mark Kincey, Derek Moscrop and Andy J. Howard 2008 'Airborne lidar and historic environment records', *Antiquity* 82: 1055–64.

Chapman, Henry 2006 *Landscape archaeology and GIS* (Stroud: Tempus).

Charles, F.W.B. 1997 *The Great Barn of Bredon. Its fire and rebuilding* (Oxford: Oxbow).

Cherry, J.F., C. Gamble and S. Shennan (eds) 1978 *Sampling in contemporary British archaeology* (BAR).

China, Republic of, 1993 *The Laws of the People's Republic of China on the Protection of Cultural Relics* (Forbidden City Publishing House).

China, State Administration of Cultural Heritage 2007 *Major Archaeological Discoveries in China (in 2006)* (Beijing: Cultural Relics Press).

Claassen, C. 1998 *Shells* (CUP).

Clark, A. 1975 'Geophysical surveying in archaeology', *Antiquity* 49: 298–9.

Clark, A.J. 1990 *Seeing beneath the soil: prospecting methods in archaeology* (London: Batsford).

Clark, Kate (ed.) 1999 *Conservation Plans in Action. Proceedings of the Oxford Conference* (English Heritage).

Clark, Kate 2001 *Informed conservation: understanding historic buildings and their landscapes for conservation* (London: English Heritage).

Clarke, David L. 1968 *Analytical Archaeology* (London: Methuen).

Clay, R. Berle 2001 'Complementary geophysical survey techniques: why two ways are always better than one', *South-eastern Archaeology* 20(1): 31–43.

Cleere, H. (ed.) 1984 *Approaches to the Archaeological Heritage: A Comparative Study of World Cultural Resource Management Systems* (CUP).

Cleere, H. (ed.) 1989 *Archaeological Heritage Management in the Modern World* (London).

CNAU 1990 *Documents d'évaluation du Patrimoine Archéologique des Villes de France* (Douai, Angers, etc from 1990; Centre National d'Archéologie Urbaine, Ministère de la Culture).

Colardelle, M. and Verdele, E. 1993 *Les habitats du lac de Paladru (Isère) dans leur environnement* (Paris: Editions de la Maison des Sciences de l'Homme).

Cole, M.D. and A. Watchman 2005 'AMS dating of rock art in the Laura Region, Cape York Peninsula, Australia – protocols and results of recent research', *Antiquity* 79: 661–78.

Cole, Mark, A. Andrew, E.U. David, Neil T. Linford, Paul K. Linford and Andrew W. Payne 1997 'Non-destructive techniques in English gardens: geophysical techniques', in Jacques, 26–39.

Coles, B., J. Coles and M.S. Jørgensen (eds) 1999 *Bog bodies, sacred sites and wetland archaeology* (WARP: Exeter).

Coles, B. (ed.) 1992 *The Wetland Revolution in Prehistory* (London: Thames and Hudson).

Coles, B.1995 *Wetland Management. A Survey for English Heritage* (Exeter: Wetland Archaeological Research Paper 9).

Coles, B. and J. 1996 *Enlarging the past: the contribution of wetland archaeology* (Edinburgh: Society of Antiquaries of Scotland).

Collcutt, S. 1993 'The archaeologist as consultant', in Hunter and Ralston: 158–68.

Collins, James M. and Brian Leigh Molyneaux 2003 *Archaeological Survey* (Walnut Creek CA: AltaMira Press).

Condron, Frances, Julian Richards, Damian Robinson and Alicia Wise 1999 *Strategies for Digital Data* (Archaeology Data Service, University of York).

Coningham, R., P. Gunawardhana, M. Manuel, G. Adikari, M. Katugampola, R. Young, A. Schmidt, K. Krishnana, I. Simpson, G. McDonnell and C. Batt 2007 'The state of theocracy: defining an early medieval hinterland in Sri Lanka', *Antiquity* 81: 699–719.

Connah, G. (ed.) 1983 *Australian Field Archaeology. A Guide to Techniques* (Australian Institute of Aboriginal Studies, Canberra).

Conway, J.S. 1983 'An investigation of soil phosphorus distribution within occupation deposits from a Romano-British hut group', *J.Arch.Sci.* 10: 117– 28.

Conyers, Lawrence B. and Dean Goodman 1997 *Ground-penetrating Radar. An introduction for archaeologists* (Walnut Creek CA: AltaMira Press).

Cooney, G. 2006 'New Grange – a view from the platform', *Antiquity* 80: 697–708.

Cooper, Malcolm 1995 'The archaeological manager: applying management models to archaeology', in Cooper et al, 71–88.

Cooper, Malcolm, Anthony Firth, John Carman and David Wheatley (eds) 1995 *Managing Archaeology* (London and New York: Routledge).

Copley, M.S., R. Berstan, S.N. Dudd, A. Aillaud, A.J Mukherjee, V. Straker, S. Payne, and R.P. Evershed 2005 'Processing of milk products in pottery vessels through British pre-history', *Antiquity* 79: 895–908.

Council of Europe 1992 *European convention on the protection of the archaeological heritage (revised) Valletta 1992* (European Treaty Series 143; Strasbourg).

Council of Europe 2000 *European Landscape Convention.* Florence: Council of Europe (European Treaty Series No. 176). http://conventions.coe.int/Treaty/en/Treaties/Html/176.htm.

Council of Europe 2005 *Framework convention on the Values of Cultural Heritage for Society* (Faro: CoE, CETS 199).

Courty, M.-A., P. Goldberg and R. Macphail 1990 *Soils and micromorphology in archaeology* (Cambridge: University Press).

Cowgill, G.L. 1990 'Towards refining concepts of full-coverage survey', in S.K. Fish and S. Kowalewski (eds) *The Archaeology of Regions: a case study for full-coverage survey* (Washington DC: Smithsonian University Press): 249–59.

Cowgill, G.L., J.H. Altschuhl and R.S. Sload 1984 'Spatial analysis at Teotihuacan' in Hietala: 154–95.

Cox, C. 1992 'Satellite imagery, aerial photography and wetland archaeology', *World Archaeology* 24(2): 249–67.

Cox, M. and S. Mays 2000 *Human Osteology in Archaeology and Forensic Science* (London: Greenwich Medical Media).

Craddock, P., D. Gurney, F. Pryor and M. Hughes 1985 'The application of phosphate analysis to the location and interpretation of archaeological sites', *Arch.J.* 142: 361–76.

Craig, O.E., J. Chapman, C. Heron, L.H. Willis, L. Bartosiewicz, G. Taylor, A. Whittle and M. Collins 2005 'Did the first farmers of central and eastern Europe produce dairy foods?', *Antiquity* 79: 882–94.

Crawford, O.G.S. 1929 *Air-photography for archaeologists* (HMSO).

Crawford, O.G.S. 1933 'New technique', *Antiquity* 7: 468–71.

Crawford, O.G.S.1951 Editorial', *Antiquity* 25: 1–3.

Crawford, O.G.S. 1953 *Archaeology in the Field* (London: J.M. Dent).

Cronyn, J.M. 1990 *The Elements of Archaeological Conservation* (London and New York: Routledge).

Cruise, Gill and Richard Macphail, 2000 'Microstratigraphic signatures of experimental rural occupation deposits and archaeological sites', in Roskams: 183–92.

Cumberpatch, C.G. and P.W. Blinkhorn 2001 'Clients, contractors, curators and archaeology. Who owns the past?', in M. Pluciennik (ed.) *The Responsibilities of Archaeologists* (BAR Int S981): 39–46.

Cunliffe, Barry 1971 *Fishbourne. A Roman Palace and its Garden* (London and New York: Thames and Hudson).

Cunliffe, Barry 1987 *Hengistbury Head Dorset. Vol. I The Prehistoric and Roman Settlement, 3500BC–AD500* (Oxford: Oxford University Committee for Archaeology, Monograph 13).

Currie, C.K. and M. Locock 1991 'An evaluation of archaeological techniques used at Castle Bromwich Hall 1989–90', *Garden History* 19/1: 77–99.

Dalland, M. 1984 'A procedure for use in stratigraphical analysis', *Scottish Archaeological Review* 3.2: 116–27.

Darvill, T. (ed.) 2005 *Stonehenge World Heritage Site: an archaeological research framework* (English Heritage).

Darwin, C. 1888 *The formation of vegetable mould through the action of worms, with other observations on their habits* (London: John Murray).

David, A. 2001 'The role and practice of archaeological prospection', in Brothwell and Pollard: 521–28.

David, Andrew, Mark Cole, Tim Horsley, Neil Linford, Paul Linford and Louise Martin 2004 'A rival to Stonehenge? Geophysical survey at Stanton Drew, England', *Antiquity* 78: 341–58.

David, Nicholas and Carol Kramer 2001 *Ethnoarchaeology in Action* (CUP).

Davidson, D.A. and I.A. Simpson 2001 'Archaeology and soil micromorphology', in Brothwell and Pollard: 167–78.

Davidson, D., S. Carter and T. Quine 1992 'An evaluation of micromorphology as an aid to archaeological interpretation', *Geoarchaeology* 7.1: 55–65.

Davies, Martin 1993 'The application of the Harris Matrix to the recording of standing structures', in Harris et al: 167–80.

Davies, O. 1959 'Termites and soil-stratification in equatorial Africa', *Antiquity* 33: 290–1.

Davis, M.J., K.L.A. Gdaniec, M. Brice and L. White 2004 *Mitigation of construction impact on archaeological remains* (with contributions by C.A.I. French and R. Thorne; English Heritage).

Deetz, James 1967 *Invitation to Archaeology* (Natural History Press).

Department of the Environment (UK) 1973 *Safety in Construction Work: Demolitions* (London).

Department of the Environment (UK) 1974 *Safety in Construction Work: Excavations* (London).

Department of the Environment (UK) 1975 *Safety in Construction Work: Basic Rules for Safety and Health at Work* (London).

Department of the Environment (UK) 1990 *Archaeology and Planning* (Planning Policy Guidance 16).

Department of the Environment (UK) 1994 *Planning and the Historic Environment* (Planning Policy Guidance 15).

Dever, W.G. and H.D. Lance 1982 *A Manual of Field Excavation* (Hebrew University College–Jewish Institute of Religion. Nelson Glueck School of Biblical Archaeology).

Devereux, B.J., G.S. Amable, P. Crow and A.D. Cliff 2005 'The potential of airborne lidar for detection of archaeological features under woodland canopies', *Antiquity* 79: 648–60.

Dillon, B.D. 1989 *Practical Archaeology. Field and Laboratory Techniques and Archaeological Logistics* (Institute of Archaeology, UCLA).

Dincauze, D. 1986 'Public Archaeology Forum: report to the Society for American Archaeology on the Conference on Reburial Issues', *JFA* 13: 116–18.

—— 2000 *Integrating Environmental Archaeology: Principles and Practice* (Cambridge and New York: CUP).

Donaghue, D.N.M. 2001 'Remote Sensing', in Brothwell and Pollard: 555–64.

Doneus, Michael, Alois Eder-Hinterleitner and Wolfgang Neubauer (eds) 2001 *Archaeological Prospection* 4th International Conference on Archaeological Prospection (Austrian Academy of Sciences).

Doran, G. 1992 'Problems and potential of wet sites in North America: the example of Windover', in B. Coles: 125–34.

Doran, G. 2002 *Windover: multidisciplinary investigations of an Early Archaic Florida cemetery* (Gainsville: University Press of Florida).

Dorochoff, Nicholas 2007 *Negotiation basics for cultural resource managers* (Walnut Creek: Left Coast Press).

Dunnell, R.C. 1990 'Artefact size and lateral displacement under tillage – comments of the Odell and Cowan experiment', *Am.Ant.* 55: 292–94.

Dunnell, R.C. 1992 'The notion site', in J. Rossignol and L. Wandsnider (eds) *Space, Time and Archaeological Landscapes* (New York: Plenum Press): 21–41.

Durham, B. 1977 'Archaeological investigations at St Aldates, Oxford', *Oxoniensia* 42: 82–203.

Edis, J., D. Macleod and R.H. Bewley 1989 'An archaeological guide to the classification of cropmarks and soil marks', *Antiquity* 63: 112–26.

Edmonds, Mark R. 1995 *Stone tools and society: working stone in Neolithic and Bronze Age Britain* (London: Batsford).

Edmonds, Mark R. 2001 'Lithic exploitation and use', in Brothwell and Pollard: 461–70.

Edmonds, M. and G. McElearney 1999 'Inhabitation and access. Landscape and the Internet at Gardom's Edge', *Internet Arch.* 6 (intarch.ac.uk).

Eidt, R. 1984 *Advances in abandoned settlement analysis: application to prehistoric anthrosols in Columbia, South America* (Milwaukee: University of Wisconsin).

English Heritage (David, Andrew) 1995 *Geophysical survey in archaeological field evaluation* (English Heritage).

English Heritage 1997 *Conservation Plans: a brief introduction* (English Heritage).

English Heritage 2000a *Managing Lithic Scatters. Archaeological Guidance for planning authorities and developers* (English Heritage).

English Heritage 2000b *Metric survey specifications for English Heritage* (English Heritage).

English Heritage 2006 *Conservation Principles* (English Heritage).

English Heritage n.d. *Historic Environment Local Management* (Swindon).

Evans, J. and O'Connor, T. 1999 *Environmental Archaeology. Principles and Methods* (Stroud: Sutton Publishing).

Evans, J.G. 1972 *Land Snails in Archaeology* (London and New York: Seminar Press).

Evans, J.G. and S. Limbrey 1974 'The experimental earthwork at Morden Bog, Wareham, Dorset, England', *Proceedings of the Prehistoric Society* 40: 170–202.

Evans, C., and I. Hodder 2006 *A Woodland Archaeology. The Haddenham Project Vol. I* (McDonald Institute Monograph, Cambridge).

Evershed, R.P., S.N. Dudd, M.J. Lockheart and S. Jim 2001 'Lipids in archaeology', in Brothwell and Pollard: 331–50.

Fagan, B. (ed.) 1996 *Eyewitness to Discovery* (OUP).

Fanning, Patricia C. and Simon J. Holdaway 2004 'Artifact Visibility at Open Sites in Western New South Wales, Australia', *JFA* 29 (2003/2004) 255–71.

Faustmann, Antje and Rog Palmer 2005 'Wings over Armenia: use of a paramotor for archaeological aerial survey', *Antiquity* 79: 402–10.

Fenton, Alexander 1999 *Scottish Country Life* (rev. edn. Phantassie: Tuckwell Press).

Fenwick, Helen 2004 'Ancient roads and GPS survey: modelling the Amarna Plain', *Antiquity* 78: 880–5.

Fieller, N.R.J., D.D. Gilbertson and N.G.A. Ralph (eds) 1985 *Paleoenvironmental investigation: research design, methods and data analysis* (BAR Int 258).

Fiorato, Veronica, Anthea Boylston and Christopher Knüssel (eds) 2007 *Blood Red Roses. The archaeology of a mass grave from the battle of Towton* (2nd edn. Oxford: Oxbow).

Fish, S.K. and S. Kowalewski (eds) 1990 *The Archaeology of Regions: a Case Study for Full-Coverage Survey* (Washington, DC: Smithsonian University Press).

Fitts, William R. 2005 'Precision GPS Surveying at Medieval Cottam, East Yorkshire England', *JFA* 30: 181–90.

Flannery, Kent V. (ed.) 1976 *The Early Mesoamerican Village* (New York: Academic Press).

Fleming, Andrew 2008 *The Dartmoor Reaves* (2nd edn. Oxford: Windgather).

Fleming, Andrew and Louise Barker 2008 'Monks and local communities: the Late-Medieval landscape of Troed y Rhiw, Caron Uwch Clawdd, Ceredigion', *Med.Arch.* 52: 261–90.

Flemming, N. (ed.) 2004 *Submarine Prehistoric Archaeology of the North Sea: Research Priorities and Collaboration with Industry* (London: CBA Research Report 141).

Foard, Glenn 2001 'The archaeology of attack: battles and sieges of the English Civil War', in Freeman and Pollard: 87–104.

Foster, Sally 1989 'Analysis of spatial patterns in buildings (access analysis) as an insight into social structure: examples from the Scottish Iron Age', *Antiquity* 63: 40–50.

Fox, Richard A. 1993 *Archaeology, history and Custer's Lost Battle. The Little Big Horn reexamined* (Norman and London: University of Oklahoma Press).

Framework Archaeology 2006 *Landscape Evolution in the Middle Thames Valley* (Framework Archaeology Monograph 1).

Framework Archaeology 2008 *From hunter gatherers to huntsmen. A history of the Stansted landscape* (Framework Archaeology Monograph 2).

Francovich, R. and H. Patterson (eds) 2000 *Extracting meaning from ploughsoil assemblages* (The Archaeology of Mediterranean Landscapes 5; Oxford: Oxbow).

Frankel, D. and J.M. Webb 2006 'Neighbours: Negotiating space in a prehistoric village', *Antiquity* 80: 287–302.

Franken, H.J. 1965 'Taking the baulks home', *Antiquity* 39: 140–42.

Freeman, Philip 1998 '"And the rest is history. And archaeology": The potential of battlefield archaeology', *Antiquity* 72: 948–50.

Freeman, Philip and A. Pollard (eds) 2001 *Fields of conflict: progress and prospect in Battlefield Archaeology* (BAR Int 958).

Freestone, I.C. and D. Gaimster (eds) 1997 *Pottery in the making* (London: British Museum Press).

French, C.A.I. 2003 *Geoarchaeology in Action. Studies in soil micromorphology and landscape evolution* (London: Routledge).

Freter, A. 1993 'Obsidian-hydration dating: its past, present and future application in Mesoamerica', *Ancient Mesoamerica* 4: 285–303.

Gaffney, C. and J. Gater 1993 'Practice and method in the application of geophysical techniques in archaeology', in Hunter and Ralston: 205–14.

Gaffney, C., J. Gater, P. Linford, V. Gaffney and R. White 2000 'Large scale systematic fluxgate gradiometry at the Roman City of Wroxeter', *Archaeological Prospection* 7: 81–99.

Gaffney, V.L., J. Bintliff and B. Slapsak 1991 'Site formation processes and the Hvar Survey Project, Yugoslavia', in Scholfield: 59–77.

Gaffney, V. and J. Gater 2003 *Revealing the buried past. Geophysics for archaeologists* (Tempus).

Gaffney, V., K. Thomson, S. Fitch (eds) 2007 *Mapping Doggerland: the Mesolithic Landscapes of the Southern North Sea* (Oxford: Archaeopress).

Galiberti, Attilio (ed.) 2005 *Defensola. Una miniera di selce di 7000 anni fa* (Siena: Protagon Editori Toscani).

Garfinkel, Y., A. Vered and O. Bar-Yosef 2006 'The domestication of water; the Neolithic well at Sha'ar Hagolan, Jordan Valley, Israel', *Antiquity* 80: 686–96.

Gardin, J.-C. 2000 'Surface archaeology under time constraint: theory and practice in central Asia', in A. Buko and P. Urbanczyk (eds) *Archeologia w teorii i w praktyce* (Warsawa): 295–305.

Garratt-Frost, S. 1992 *The Law and Burial Archaeology* (Birmingham: IFA Tech Paper 11).

GBG (Geotechnics Ltd.) 2001 *Non-destructive investigation of standing structures* (Edinburgh: Historic Scotland).

Geib, Phil R. 1996 *Glen Canyon Revisited* (University of Utah Press Anthropological Paper 119).

Gelling, M. 1988 *Signposts to the Past* (Chichester: Phillimore).

Gersbach, E. 1989 *Ausgrabungung heute. Methoden und Techniken der Feldgrabung* (Wissenschaftliche Buchgesellschaft Darmstadt).

Gheyle, W., Raf Trommelmans, Jean Bourgeois, Rudi Goossens, Ignace Bourgeois, Alain De Wulf and Tom Willems 2004 'Evaluating CORONA: A case study in the Altai Republic (South Siberia)', *Antiquity* 78: 391–403.

Gibson, Alex 1999 *The Walton Basin, Powys, Wales. Survey at the Hindwell Neolithic Enclosure* (Clwyd-Powys Archaeological Trust, Welshpool).

Gibson, A. and A. Wood 1997 *Prehistoric pottery for the archaeologist* (Leicester: Leicester University Press).

Gilbert, B.M., L.D. Martin, and H.G. Savage 1985 *Avian Osteology* (Arizona: Flagstaff).

Gilbertson, D.D., M. Kent and J. Grattan (eds) 1996 *The Outer Hebrides: the last 14,000 years* (Sheffield: Sheffield Academic Press).

Gillings, M. 2001 'Spatial information and archaeology', in Brothwell and Pollard: 671–84.

Given, M. and B. Knapp 2003 *The Sydney Cyprus Survey Project: Social approaches to regional archaeological survey* (Los Angeles: UCLA).

Godden, Mackay 1999 *The Cumberland/Gloucester Streets sites, The Rocks. Archaeological Investigation Report* (Sydney: Godden Mackay Logan).

Goeksu, H.Y., M. Oberhofer and D. Regulla (eds) 1991 *Scientific Dating Methods* (Dordrecht: Kluwer Academic Publishers).

Goldberg, Paul and Richard I. Macphail 2006 *Practical and Theoretical Geoarchaeology* (Oxford: Blackwell).

Goodman, D. and Y. Nishimura 1993 'A ground-radar view of Japanese burial mounds', *Antiquity* 67: 349–54.

Goodman, D. and Y. Nishimura 2000 'Ground penetrating radar survey at Wroxeter', *Archaeological Prospection* 7: 101–105.

Goodman D., Y. Nishimura and J.D. Rogers 1995 'GPR. Time slices in archaeological prospection', *Archaeological Prospection* 2: 85–90.

Goodyear, A.C., M.L. Raeb and T.C. Klinger 1978 'The status of archaeological research design in Cultural Resource Management', *Am.Ant.* 43: 150–73.

Gould, R. 1995a 'Archaeological survey by air: an update for the 1990s', *JFA* 22: 257– 61.

Gould, R. 1995b 'Developing rectification programs for small computers', *Archaeological Prospection* 7: 1–16.

Gowland, R.L. and A.T. Chamberlain 2005 'Detecting plague: palaeo-demographic characterisation of a catastrophic death assemblage', *Antiquity* 79: 146–57.

Grauer, Anne L. (ed.) 1995 *Bodies of Evidence. Reconstructing history through skeletal analysis* (New York: Wiley).

Gray, J. and K. Walford 1999 'One good site deserves another: electronic publishing in field archaeology', *Internet Archaeology* 7 (http: //intarch.ac.uk/journal/issue 7).

Greenacre, Michael 1983 *Theory and Applications of Correspondence Analysis* (London: Academic Press).

Gregory, D. 2000 'Underwater reconnaissance', *Maritime Archaeology Newsletter* from Roskilde, Denmark 14: 20–2

Gresham, C.A. 1961 'Earthworms and archaeology', *Antiquity* 35: 235–6.

Griffin, R.C., H. Moody, K.E.H. Penkman and M.J. Collins 2008 'The application of amino acid racemization in the acid-soluble fraction of enamel to the estimation of the age of human teeth', *Forensic Science International* 175: 11–16.

Grimes, W.F. 1968 *The Excavation of Roman and Medieval London* (London: Routledge & Kegan Paul).

Grün, R. 2001 'Trapped Charge Dating (ESR, TL, OSL)', in Brothwell and Pollard: 47–62.

Haglund, William D. and Marcella H. Sorg (eds) 2002 *Advances in Forensic Taphonomy. Method, Theory and Archaeological Perspectives* (London: CRC Press).

Haigh, J. 1991 'The AERIAL Program, version 4. 1', *Aerial Archaeology Group News* 3: 28–30.

Haigh, J., and S. Ipson 1994 'Economical possibilities for the rectification of digital images', *Archaeological Computing Newsletter* 38: 8–13.

Hall, A.R. 2002 'Weaving a thread or spinning a yarn? Towards an archaeological indicator package for textile working', in Willy Groeman-van Waateringe, Ben van Beek and Willy Meetz (eds) *Het Instituut Viftig Jaar* (Amsterdam: Instituut voor Prae und Protohistorie): 37–44.

Hall, A.R., A.K.G. Jones and H.K. Kenward 1983 'Cereal bran and human faecal remains from archaeological deposits – some preliminary observations', in B. Proudfoot (ed.) *Site, environment and economy. Symposia of the Association for Environmental Archaeology* 3 (BAR Int 173): 85–104.

Hall, A. and H. Kenward 2003 'Can we identify biological indicator groups for craft, industry and other activities?', in P. Murphy and P.E.J. Wiltshire (eds) *The Environmental Archaeology of Industry. Symposia of the Association for Environmental Archaeology* 20 (Oxford: Oxbow): 114–30.

Hall, R.A. 1984 *The Viking Dig* (London: Bodley Head).

Hamerow, Helena 1993 *Excavations at Mucking Volume 2: The Anglo-Saxon Settlement* (London: English Heritage).

Hammond, Norman 1991b 'Matrices and Maya archaeology', *JFA* 18: 29–42.

Hammond, Norman (ed.) 1991a Cuello. *An Early Maya Community in Belize* (CUP).

Hardesty, D.L., B.J. Little and D. Fowler 2000 *Assessing Site Significance: A Guide for Archaeologists and Historians* (Walnut Creek CA: AltaMira Press).

Harding, A. 1999 'Establishing archaeological chronologies', in G. Barker (ed.) *The Companion Encyclopaedia of Archaeology* (London and New York: Routledge): 182–221.

Harris, E.C. 1975 'The stratigraphic sequence: a question of time', *World Archaeology* 7. 1: 109–21.

Harris, E.C. 1977 'Units of archaeological stratification', *Norwegian Archaeological Review* 10. 1: 84–106.

Harris, E.C. 1989 *Principles of Archaeological Stratigraphy* (2nd edn. London and New York: Academic Press).

Harris, E.C., M.R. Brown III, and G.J. Brown (eds) 1993 *Practices of Archaeological Stratigraphy* (Academic Press).

Haselgrove, C., M. Millett and I. Smith (eds) 1985 *Archaeology from the ploughsoil: studies in the collection and interpretation of field survey data* (Sheffield University).

Hassan, F. 1997 'Beyond the surface: comments on Hodder's "reflexive excavation methodology"', *Antiquity* 71: 1020–5.

Hatt, G. 1938 *Jernsalders Bopladser i Himmerland* (Aaborger for Nordisk Oldkyndighed og Historie, Copenhagen).

Hedges, R.E.M. 2001 'Overview – Dating in Archaeology; past, present and future', in Brothwell and Pollard: 3–8.

Heffernan, Thomas Farel 1988 *Wood Quay. The clash over Dublin's past* (Austin: University of Texas Press).

Henderson, J. 1987 'Factors determining the state of preservation of human remains', in A. Boddington, A.N. Garland and R. Janaway (eds) *Death, decay and reconstruction: approaches to archaeology and forensic science* (Manchester: Manchester University Press): 43–54.

Henderson, J. 2000 *The science and archaeology of materials* (London: Routledge).

Henderson, J. 2001 'Glass and glazes', in Brothwell and Pollard: 471–82.

Henshilwood, C.S., J.C. Sealy, R.J. Yates, K. Cruz-Uribe, P. Goldberg, F.E. Grine, R.G. Klein, C. Poggenpoel, K.L. Wan Niekerk, I. Watts 2001 'Blombos Cave, southern Cape, South Africa: Preliminary report on the 1992–1999 excavations of the Middle Stone Age levels', *J.Arch.Sci.* 28(5): 421–8.

Heron, C. and R.P. Evershed 1993 'The analysis of organic residues and the study of pottery use', *Archaeological Method and Theory* 5: 247–84.

Heron, C. and R.P. Evershed 2001 'Geochemical prospecting', in Brothwell and Pollard: 565–574.

Herring, Peter 1998 *Cornwall's Historic Landscape. Presenting a method of historic landscape character assessment* (Cornwall County Council).

Herring, Peter, Adam Sharpe, John R. Smith and Colum Giles 2008 *Bodmin Moor. An archaeological survey. Volume 2: the industrial and post-medieval landscapes* (English Heritage).

Hesse, B. and P. Wapnish 1985 *Animal bone archaeology from objectives to analysis* (Washington: Taraxacum Press).

Hester, T.R., H.J. Shafer and K.L. Feder 1997 *Field Methods in Archaeology* (7th edn. Mayfield Publishing, California, London, Toronto).

Hietala, H.-J. (ed.) 1984 *Intrasite spatial analysis in archaeology* (CUP).

Hill, J.D. 1995 *Ritual and rubbish in the Iron Age of Wessex* (BAR).

Hillier, W. and J. Hanson 1984 *The social logic of space* (CUP).

Hillman, G. 1981 'Reconstructing crop husbandry practices from charred remains of crops', in R. Mercer (ed.) *Farming practice in British prehistory* (EUP) 123–62.

Hillson, S. 1986 *Teeth* (CUP).

Historic Scotland 2001 *External lime coatings on traditional buildings* (Edinburgh: Historic Scotland).

Historic Scotland 2002 *Conservation of plasterwork* (Edinburgh: Historic Scotland).

Historic Scotland 2003 *Preparation and use of lime mortars* (Edinburgh: Historic Scotland).

Hodder, I. and C. Orton 1976 *Spatial analysis in archaeology* (CUP).

Hodder, I. 1986 *The Present Past* (London: Batsford).

Hodder, I. 1991 *Reading the Past* (2nd edn. CUP).

Hodder, I. 1992 *Theory and Practice in Archaeology* (London: Routledge).

Hodder, I. (ed.) 1996 *On the Surface: Çatalhöyük 1993–1995* (British Institute at Ankara: McDonald Institute Monograph Cambridge).

Hodder, I. 1997 '"Always momentary, fluid and flexible": towards a reflexive excavation methodology', *Antiquity* 71: 691–700.

Hodder, I. 1999 *The Archaeological Process. An Introduction* (Oxford: Blackwell).

Hodder, I. (ed.) 2000 *Towards reflexive method in archaeology: the example at Çatalhöyük* (British Institute of Archaeology at Ankara: McDonald Institute Monograph).

Hodder, I. (ed.) 2005 *Inhabiting Çatalhöyük reports from the 1995–99 seasons* (British Institute of Archaeology at Ankara and McDonald Institute monographs 38).

Hodder, I. *Çatalhöyük: The Leopard's Tale: revealing the mysteries of Turkey's ancient 'town'* (London: Thames and Hudson).

Hodges, R. 1993 *San Vincenzo al Volturno I* (British School at Rome, 7).

Hodges, Henry 1989 *Artifacts* (London: Duckworth).

Hogg, Alan G., Thomas F.G. Higham, David J. Lowe, Jonathan G. Palmer, Paula J. Reimer and Rewi M. Newnham 2003 'A wiggle-match date for Polynesian settlement of New Zealand', *Antiquity* 77: 116–25.

Hope-Taylor, B. 1977 *Yeavering: an Anglo-British centre of early Northumbria* (HMSO).

Hoskins, W.G. 1967 *Fieldwork in Local History* (Faber).

Howard, A.J., A.G. Brown, C.J. Carey, K. Challis, L.P. Cooper, M. Kincey and P. Toms 2008 'Archaeological resource modelling in temperate river valleys: a case study from the Trent Valley, UK', *Antiquity* 81: 1040–54.

Howard, Phil 2007 *Archaeological surveying and mapping. Recording and depicting the landscape* (London: Routledge).

Howe, John Allen 2001 *The geology of building stones*, reprint edition of original 1910 publication, with an introduction by David Jefferson (Shaftesbury: Donhead).

Howell, T.V. 1993 'Evaluating the utility of auger testing as a predictor of subsurface artifact densities', *JFA* 20(4): 475–84.

Hritz, C. and T.J. Wilkinson 2006 'Using Shuttle Radar Topography to map ancient water channels in Mesopotamia', *Antiquity* 80: 415–24.

HSE (Health and Safety Executive) 1997 *Approved Practice for Scientific and Archaeological Diving Projects* (Diving Work Regulations: HMSO).

Hunter, J. and I. Ralston (eds) 1993 *Archaeological Resource Management in the UK: an introduction* (Institute of Field Archaeologists, Birmingham).

Hummler, Madeleine 2005 'Before Sutton Hoo: The prehistoric settlement (c. 3000BC to AD550)', in Carver: 391–458.

Hurman, B. and M. Steiner (eds) 1995 *The Survey and Recording of Historic Buildings*, (Association of Archaeological Illustrators and Surveyors Technical Paper No 12).

Hyland, D.C., J.M. Tersak, J.M. Adovasio, and M.I. Siegel 1990 'Identification of the species of origin of residual blood on lithic materials', *Am.Ant.* 55: 104–112.

ICOMOS 1994 *The Nara Document on Authenticity*.

ICOMOS 2004 *The Illustrated Burra Charter*.

Imai, T., T. Sakayama, and T. Kanemori 1987 'Use of ground-probing radar and resistivity surveys for archaeological investigations', *Geophysics* 52(2): 137–50.

Institute of Field Archaeologists 1994 *Standard and Guidance for Archaeological Field Evaluation*.

Jacques, David (ed.) 1997 'The techniques and uses of garden archaeology', *Journal of Garden History* 17.1.

James, N. 1998 'Comparative studies in the presentation of archaeological sites', *Antiquity* 72: 412–13.

James, S.R. 1997 'Methodological issues concerning screen size recovery rates and their effects on archaeological interpretations', *J.Arch.Sci.* 24: 385–97.

Jiang, Leping and Liu, Li 2006 'New evidence for the origins of sedentism and rice domestication in the Lower Yangzi River, China', *Antiquity* 80: 355–61.

Johnson, Matthew 1999 *Archaeological Theory: an introduction* (Oxford: Blackwell).

Johnson, Nicholas and Peter Rose 1994 *Bodmin Moor. An archaeological survey. Vol. I The human landscape to c.1800* (English Heritage Archaeological Report no. 24).

Jones, A.K.G and T.P. O'Connor 2001 'Vertebrate resources', in Brothwell and Pollard: 415–26.

Jones, Martin K. 2002 *The Molecule Hunt: Archaeology and the Search for Ancient DNA* (New York: Arcade Publishing).

Joukovsky, M. 1980 *A Complete Manual of Field Archaeology. Tools and Techniques of Fieldwork for Archaeologists* (Engelwood Cliffs: Prentice-Hall).

Julyan, Robert 1996 *The Placenames of New Mexico* (Univ. of New Mexico Press, Albuquerque).

Kenward, H.K. 1978 'The analysis of archaeological insect assemblages: a new approach', *The Archaeology of York* 19/1 (York).

Kenward, H.K. and A.R. Hall 1995 'Enhancing bioarchaeological interpretation using indicator groups: stable manure as a paradigm', *J.Arch.Sci.* 24: 663–73.

Kenward, H.K. and A.R. Hall 2000 'Decay of delicate organic remains in shallow urban deposits: are we at a watershed?', *Antiquity* 74: 519–25.

Kerr, J.S. 1996 *The Conservation Plan: a guide to the preparation of Conservation Plans for places of European cultural significance* (4th edn. The National Trust of Australia (NSW), Sydney).

Kerr, J.S. 2000 *The Conservation Plan* (Sydney: National Trust of New South Wales).

Kidd, Dorothy I., 1996 *To see oursels. Rural Scotland in old photographs* (Edinburgh: National Museums of Scotland).

Kidder, A.V. 1962 *An Introductory Study of Southwestern Archaeology, with a preliminary account of the excavation at Pecos* (Yale University Press; appeared 1924).

King, Thomas F. 2000 *Federal Planning and Historic Places. The Section 106 Process* (Walnut Creek CA: AltaMira Press).

Knappett, Karl, Tim Evans and Ray Rivers 2008 'Modelling maritime interaction in the Aegean Bronze Age', *Antiquity* 81: 1009–24.

Kobyliński, Zbigniew (ed.) 2001a *Quo vadis archaeologia? Whither European Archaeology in the 21st century?* (Proceedings of the European Science Foundation Exploratory Workshop, 12–13 October, Warsaw 2001.)

Kobyliński, Zbigniew 2001b 'Archaeological heritage and archaeological sources: new vision of the subject of archaeology', in Kobyliński 2001a: 76–82.

Koldewey, R. 1914 *The Excavations at Babylon* (London: Macmillan).

Kowaleski, S., G. Feinman, R. Blanton, L. Finstein and L. Nicholas 1989 *Monte Albán's hinterland, Part II: The Prehispanic settlement patterns in Tlacolula, Etla, and Ocotlan, the Valley of Oaxaca, Mexico* (Ann Arbor (MI), University of Michigan. Memoirs of the Museum of Anthropology 23).

Krakker, J.J., M.J. Shott and P.D. Welch 1983 'Design and evaluation of shovel-test sampling in regional archaeological survey', *JFA* 10(4): 469–80.

Kroll, Ellen M. and T. Douglas Price (eds) 1991 *The Interpretation of Archaeological Spatial Patterning* (New York).

Kubiena, W.L. 1953 *The Soils of Europe* (Murphy: London).

Kuna, M. 1998 'Method of surface artifacts survey', in E. Neustupny (ed.) *Space in Prehistoric Bohemia* (Czech Academy of Sciences): 77–83.

Kuniholm, P.I. 2001 'Dendrochronology and other applications of tree-ring studies in archaeology', in Brothwell and Pollard: 35–47.

Kvamme, K.L. 1989 'Geographic Information Systems in Regional Archaeological Research and in Data Management', Archaeological Method and Theory 1: 139–203.

Kvamme, Kenneth and Stanley A. Ahler 2007 'Integrated remote sensing and excavation at a double ditch State Historic Site, North Dakota', *Am.Ant.* 72.3: 539–61.

Larsson, L. 2007 'The Iron Age ritual building at Uppåkra, southern Sweden', *Antiquity* 81: 11–25.

Latham, A.G. 2001 'Uranium series dating', in Brothwell and Pollard: 63–72.

Lawson, Andrew J. (ed.) 1983 *The archaeology of Witton, near North Walsham* (Gressenhall: East Anglian Archaeology 18).

Layard, A.H. 1854 *Nineveh and its Remains*, 2 vols (London: John Murray).

Layton, R. and Ucko, P. (eds) 1999 *Archaeology and Anthropology of Landscape* (London: Routledge).

Leach, Peter 1994 *The Surveying of Archaeological Sites* (London: Archetype Publications).

Legrand, Sophie 2006 'The emergence of the Karasuk culture', *Antiquity* 80: 843–79.

Lelong, Olivia and Gavin MacGregor 2007 *The lands of ancient Lothian. Interpreting the archaeology of the A1* (Edinburgh: Society of Antiquaries of Scotland).

Lhomme, Vincent 2007 'Tools, space and behaviour in the Lower Palaeolithic: discoveries at Soucy in the Paris basin', *Antiquity* 81: 536–54.

Lipe, W. 1984 'Value and meaning in cultural resources', in H. Cleere (ed.) *Approaches to the Archaeological Heritage* (CUP): 1–11.

Lippi, R. 1988 'Paleotopography and phosphate analysis of a buried jungle site in Ecuador', *JFA* 15: 85–97.

Lock, G. and Z. Stanãiã (eds) *Archaeology and geographical information systems: a European perspective* (London: Taylor & Francis).

Locock, M. 1995 'The effectiveness of dowsing as a method of determining the nature and location of buried features on historic garden sites', *Archaeological Prospection* 2: 15–18.

Lombardo, Jean-Luc 1994 'L'accessibilité aux terrains: l'exemple de l'autoroute A16', *Nouvelles d'Archéologie* 58: 11–15.

Lohrum, Burghard 1993 Fachwerkbau in anon. (ed.) *Stadtluft, Hirsebrei und Bettelmönch. Die Stadt um 1300* (Landesdenkmalamt Baden-Württemberg und der Stadt Zürich): 248–66.

Lowe, Christopher 1998 *Coastal erosion and the archaeological assessment of an eroding shoreline at St Boniface Church, Papa Westray, Orkney* (Sutton Publishing: Historic Scotland).

Loy, T.H. and E.J. Dixon 1998 'Blood residues on fluted points from eastern Beringia', *Am.Ant.* 63. 1: 21–46.

Lucas, G. 2001 *Critical approaches to fieldwork* (London: Routledge).

Lyall, J. and D. Powlesland 1996 'High Resolution Fluxgate Gradiometry (West Heslerton)', *Internet Archaeology* 1.

Lyell, C. 1830–3 *Principles of Geology* (London: Murray).

Lynott, M.J. and A. Wylie (eds) 1995 *Ethics in American Archaeology* (Washington D.C.: Society for American Archaeology).

MacGregor, A. 1985 *Bone, antler, ivory and horn* (London: Croom Helm).

MacManamon, F.P. 1984 'Discovering sites unseen', *Advances in Archaeological Method and Theory* 7: 223–92.

MacManamon, F. and A. Hatton (eds) (2000) *Cultural Resource Management in Contemporary Society: perspectives on managing and presenting the past* (London: Routledge).

Macphail, R.I. 1994 'The reworking of urban stratigraphy by human and natural processes', in A.R. Hall and H.K. Kenward (eds) *Urban-rural connexions: perspectives for environmental archaeology* (Oxford: Oxbow): 13–43.

Macphail, Richard I., Henri Galinié and Frans Verhaeghe 2003 'A future for Dark Earth?', *Antiquity* 77: 349–58.

Manacorda, D., 1982 *Archeologia Urbana A Roma: Il Progetto Della Crypta Balbi* (Biblioteca di Archeologia Medievale).

Mannoni, T. and A. Molinari (eds) 1990 *Scienze in Archeologia* (All'Insegna del Giglio: Firenze.)

Marcus, Joyce and Kent V. Flannery 1996 *Zapotec Civilization: How Urban Society Evolved in Mexico's Oaxaca Valley* (London: Thames and Hudson).

Marquardt, William H., and Patty Jo Watson (eds) 2005 *Archaeology of the Middle Green River Region, Kentucky* (Gainesville: University of Florida).

Masterson, Barry 1999 'Archaeological applications of modern survey techniques', *Discovery Programme Reports* 5: 131–46.

Matiskainen, H. and P. Alhonen 1984 'Diatoms as indicators of provenance in Finnish sub-Neolithic pottery', *J.Arch.Sci.* 11: 147–58.

Matthews, Roger (ed.) 1999 *Excavations at Tell Brak. Vol 4: Exploring an Upper Mesopotamian regional centre, 1994–1996* (British School of Archaeology in Iraq).

Matthews, W. 1995 'Micromorphological characterization and interpretation of occupation deposits and microstratigraphic sequences at Abu Salbikh, Southern Iraq', in A.J. Barham and R.I. Macphail (eds) *Archaeological Sediments and Soils* (London: Institute of Archaeology): 41–74.

Matthews, W., C.A.I. French, T. Lawrence and D. Cutler 1996 'Multiple surfaces: the micromorphology', in I. Hodder (ed.) *On the surface* (McDonald Institute and British Institute of Archaeology, Ankara): 301–42.

Matthews, W., C.A.I. French, T. Lawrence, D.F. Cutler and M.K. Jones 1997 'Microstratigraphic traces of site formation processes and human activities', *World Archaeology* 29.2: 281–308.

Matthews, W., J.N. Postgate, S. Payne, M.P.O. Charles and K. Dobney 1994 'The imprint of living in an early Mesopotamian city: questions and answers' in R. Luff and P. Rowley-Conwy (eds) *Whither Environmental Archaeology?* (Oxford: Oxbow Monograph 38): 171–212.

Matthews, Wendy 2005 'Traces of use and concepts of space', in I. Hodder (ed.) 2005b: 355–98.

McAlester, Virginia and Lee McAlester 1984 *A Field Guide to American Houses* (New York: Knopf).

McCullagh, R.P.J. and R. Tipping (eds) 1998 *The Lairg Project 1988–1996. The evolution of an archaeological landscape in Northern Scotland* (Edinburgh STAR).

McKinley, J.I. and J.M. Bond 2001 'Cremated bone', in Brothwell and Pollard: 281–92.

McKinley, Jacqueline I. and Charlotte Roberts 1993 *Excavation and post-excavation treatment of cremated and inhumed human remains* (IFA Technical Paper 13).

McMinn, R.M.H., R.T. Hutchings and B.M. Logan 1987 *The human skeleton: a photographic manual* (London: Wolfe Medical Publications).

Middleton, A. and I. Freestone (eds) 1991 *Recent Developments in Ceramic Petrology* (British Museum).

Middleton, R. and D. Winstanley 1993 'GIS in a landscape archaeology context', in J. Andresen, T. Madsen and I. Scollar (eds) *Computing the Past: Computer Applications and Quantitative Methods in Archaeology CAA92* (Aarhus: Aarhus University Press): 151–8.

Middleton, William D., T. Douglas Price and David C. Meiggs 2005 'Chemical analysis of Floor sediments for the identification of anthropogenic activity residues', in I. Hodder 2005b: 399–412.

Millard, A. 2001 'The deterioration of bone', in Brothwell and Pollard: 637–48.

Miller, N.F. and K.L. Gleason 1994 *The archaeology of garden and field* (Philadelphia: University of Pennsylvania Press).

Miller, Pat and Tom Wilson with Chiz Harward 2005 *Saxon, Medieval and post-Medieval settlement at Sol Central, Marefair, Northampton. Archaeological Excavations 1998–2000* (Museum of London: MoLAS Monograph 27).

Mithen, S. (ed.) 2000 *Hunter-gatherer landscape archaeology: the Southern Hebrides Mesolithic Project, 1988–1998* (Cambridge: McDonald Institute for Archaeological Research).

MoLAS 1994 *Museum of London Archaeology Service Archaeological Site Manual* (London).

Moore, P.D., J.A. Webb, and D. Collinson 1991 *An illustrated guide to pollen analysis* (London: Hodder and Stoughton).

Muckleroy, K. 1978 *Maritime Archaeology* (CUP).

Mueller, J.W. (ed.) 1975 *Sampling in Archaeology* (Tucson: University of Arizona Press).

Mukherjee, Anna, Elisa Rossberger, Matthew A. James, Peter Pfälzner, Catherine L. Higgitt, Raymond White, David A. Peggie, Dany Azar and R.P. Evershed 2008 'The Qatna Lion: scientific confirmation of Baltic amber in late Bronze Age Syria', *Antiquity* 82: 49–59.

Müller-Wille, Michael (ed.) 1991 *Starigrad/Oldenburg. Ein slawischer Herrschersitz des frühen Mittelalters in Ostholstein* (Neumünster: Karl Wachholtz Verlag).

Mulligan, Connie J. 2006 'Anthropological applications of Ancient DNA: problems and prospects', *Am.Ant.* 71.2: 365–80.

Munch, Gerd Stamsø, Olav Sverre Johansen, and Else Roesdahl (eds) 2003 *Borg in Lofoten. A chieftain's farm in North Norway* (Trondheim: Tapir Academic Press).

Myhre, B. 1987 'Chieftain's graves and chiefdom territories in south Norway in the migration period', *Studien zur Sachsenforschung* 6: 169–87.

Mytum, Harold 2000 *Recording and Analyzing Graveyards* (York: Council for British Archaeology, Practical Handbook 15).

Mytum, Harold 2004 *Mortuary Monuments and Burial Grounds of the Historic Period* (New York: Kluwer Academic/Plenum Publishers).

Nance, J. and B. Ball 1986 'No surprises? The reliability and validity of test-pit sampling', *Am.Ant.* 51 457–83.

NAS 1992 *Archaeology underwater: The NAS guide to principles and practice* (London: Nautical Archaeology Society).

Neumann, Thomas W. and Robert M. 2001a *Cultural Resources Archaeology. An Introduction* (Walnut Creek CA: AltaMira Press).

Neumann, Thomas W. and Robert M. 2001b *Practicing Archaeology. A Training Manual for Cultural Resources Archaeology* (Walnut Creek CA: AltaMira Press).

Newman, Conor 1997 *Tara. An archaeological survey* (Discovery Programme Monograph 2).

Nicholson, R.A. 2001 'Taphonomic Investigations', in Brothwell and Pollard: 179–90.

Niquette, C. 1997 'Hard hat archaeology', *Society for American Archaeology* 15.3: 15–16.

Nixon, Taryn (ed.) 2004 *Preserving archaeological remains in situ?* (Proceedings of the 2nd conference 12–14 September 2001, MOLAS).

Northedge, Alastair 2005 'Remarks on Samarra and the archaeology of large cities', *Antiquity* 79: 119–29.

NRA (National Roads Authority, Ireland) 2005 *The M3 Clonee to North of Kells Motorway. Archaeology Information Series* (NRA and Meath County Council).

NSW Heritage 2002a *Guidelines for Photographic Recording of Heritage Sites, Buildings and Structures*, June 1994 (updated 2002).

NSW Heritage 2002b *How to Prepare Archival Records of Heritage Items, June 1998* (updated 2002).

NSW State Agency Heritage Guide 2005 *Management of Heritage Assets by NSW Government Agencies* (Part 1: State-owned Heritage Management Principles; Part 2: Heritage Asset Management Guidelines) (www.heritage.nsw.gov.au).

O'Connor, T.P. 2000. *The Archaeology of Animal Bones* (Stroud: Sutton Publishing).

O'Connor, T.P. (ed.) 2005 *Biosphere to lithosphere. New studies in vertebrate taphonomy* (Oxford: Oxbow).

Ó Droma, Mícheál 2008 'Archaeological investigations at Twomileborris, Co Tipperary', in Jerry O'Sullivan and Michael Stanley (eds) *Roads, Rediscovery and Research. Proceedings of a public seminar on archaeological discoveries on national road schemes* (Dublin: National Roads Authority): 45–58.

O'Neill, D. 1993 'Excavation sample size: a cautionary tale', *Am.Ant.* 58: 523–9.

O'Sullivan, Ann and John Sheehan 1996 *The Iveragh Peninsula. An archaeological survey of South Kerry* (Cork: Cork University Press).

O'Sullivan, Jerry and Michael Stanley 2008 *Roads, Rediscovery and Research. Proceedings of a public seminar on archaeological discoveries on national road schemes* (Dublin: National Roads Authority).

Oates, David, Joan Oates and Helen McDonald (eds) 1998 *Excavations at Tell Brak 1: The Mitanni and Old Babylonian periods* (McDonald Institute Monograph).

Oates, David, Joan Oates and Helen McDonald 2001 *Excavations at Tell Brak 2: Nagar in the 3rd Millennium BC* (McDonald Institute for Archaeological Research/British School of Archaeology in Iraq).

Oates, Joan, Augusta MacMahon, Philip Karsgaard, Salam Al Quntar and Jason Ur 2007 'Early Mesopotamian urbanism: a new view from the north', *Antiquity* 81: 585–600.

Odell, G.H. and F. Cowan 1987 'Estimating tillage effects on artifact distributions', *Am.Ant.* 52: 456–84.

Ogleby, C. 1994 'Geographic Information systems in archaeology and anthropology: a case study from the Arawe Islands, Papua New Guinea', in I. Johnson (ed.) *Methods in the Mountains. Proceedings of the UISPP Commission IV Meeting. Mount Victoria, Australia, August 1993* (Sydney: Sydney University Archaeological Methods Series 2): 99–113.

Olivier, A. and Kate Clark 2001 'Changing approaches to the historic environment', in Kobyliński: 92–105 (with discussion).

Olivier, L. and J. Kovaãik 2006 'The "Briquetage de la Seille" (Lorraine, France): protoindustrial salt production in the European Iron Age', *Antiquity* 80: 558–66.

Orton, C. 1980 *Mathematics in Archaeology* (London: Collins).

Orton, C. 1993 'How many pots make five? An historical review of pottery quantification', *Archaeometry* 35: 169–84.

Orton, C. 2000 *Sampling in Archaeology* (CUP).

Paice, P. 1991 'Extensions to the Harris matrix system to illustrate stratigraphic discussion of an archaeological site', *JFA* 18: 17–28.

Palmer, R. 1984 *Danebury, an Iron Age hillfort in Hampshire: an aerial photographic interpretation of its environs* (London: Royal Commission on Historical Monuments).

Palmer, R. and C. Cox 1993 *Uses of Aerial Photography in Archaeological Evaluation* (IFA Tech Paper 12).

Papadopoulos, John K., Lorenc Bejko and Sarah P. Morris 2008 'Reconstructing the prehistoric burial tumulus of Lofkënd in Albania', *Antiquity* 82: 686–701.

Pasquinucci, Marinella and Frédéric Trément (eds) 2000 *Non-destructive techniques applied to landscape survey* (Oxford: Oxbow).

Payne, S. 1972 'Partial recovery and sample bias: the results of some sieving experiments', in E.S. Higgs (ed.) *Papers in Economic Prehistory* (CUP): 49–64.

Payton, Robert (ed.) 1992 *Retrieval of objects from archaeological sites* (Denbigh: Archtype).

Peacock, D.P.S. 1969 'Neolithic pottery production in Cornwall', *Antiquity* 43: 145–8.

Penn, Kenneth and Birte Brugmann 2007 *Aspects of Anglo-Saxon Inhumation Burial: Morningthorpe, Spong Hill, Bergh Apton and Westgarth Gardens* (Gressinghall: East Anglian Archaeology 119).

Petrie, W.F. 1904 *Methods and Aims in Archaeology* (London: Macmillan & Co).

Philip, G., D. Donoghue, A. Beck and N. Galiatsatos 2002 'CORONA satellite photography: an archaeological application from the Middle East', *Antiquity* 76: 109–18.

Phillips, Derek and Brenda Heywood 1995 *Excavations at York Minster Vol 1. From Roman fortress to Norman cathedral* (HMSO).

Pitt Rivers, A.L.F. 1886–90 *Excavations in Cranborne Chase* (4 vols; privately printed).

Platt, Colin and Richard Coleman-Smith 1975 *Excavations in Medieval Southampton, 1953–1969* (Leicester: Leicester University Press).

Plenderleith, H.J. and A.E.A. Werner 1971 *The Conservation of Antiquities and Works of Art. Treatment, Repair, Restoration* (2nd edn. OUP).

Plog, Stephen, Fred Plog and Walter Wait 1982 'Decision making in modern surveys, repr', in Schiffer: 607–45.

Poirier, D.A. and K.L. Feder 2001 *Dangerous Places: Health, Safety and Archaeology* (Bergin and Garvey, Westport, Connecticut).

Poulter, Andrew 1995 *Nicopolis ad Istrum: A Roman, Late Roman and Early Byzantine City. Excavations 1985–1992* (Society for the Promotion of Roman Studies. Journal of Roman Studies Monograph 8).

Poulter, Andrew 1998 'Field Survey at Louloudies: a new late Roman fortification in Pieria', *Annual of the British School at Athens* 93: 463–511.

Powlesland, D., J. Lyall and D.N.M. Donoghue 1997 'Enhancing the Record through Remote Sensing. The application and integration of multi-sensor, non-invasive remote sensing techniques for the enhancement of the Sites and Monuments Record. Heslerton Parish Project, N. Yorkshire, England', *Internet Archaeology* 2 (http: //intarch.ac.uk).

Purdy, B.A. (ed.) 1988 *Wet Site Archaeology* (Caldwell, New Jersey: Telford Press).

Qian, Fengqi 2007 'China's Burra Charter: The Formation and Implementation of the China Principles', *International Journal of Heritage Studies*, 13(3): 255–64.

Rackham, J. 1994 *Animal Bones* (London: British Museum).

Ramqvist, P.H. 1992 *Högom. The excavations 1949–1984* (Umeå).

Rapp jnr, Rip and Christopher Hill, 1998 *Geoarchaeology. The earth science approach to archaeological interpretation* (Yale University Press).

RCAHMS 1993 *Strath of Kildonan. An archaeological survey* (Edinburgh).

RCAHMS 2007 *In the Shadow of Bennachie. A Field Archaeology of Donside, Aberdeen* (Edinburgh: Society of Antiquaries on Scotland and RCAHMS).

Read, Dwight W. 2007 *Artifact Classification. A Conceptual and Methodological Approach* (Walnut Creek: Left Coast Press).

Redman, C. 1973 'Multi-stage fieldwork and analytical techniques', *Am.Ant.* 38: 61–79.

Redman, C. 1986 *Qsar es-Seghir. An archaeological view of Medieval life* (London and New York: Academic Press).

Redman, C. 1987 'Surface collection, sampling and research design: a retrospective', *Am.Ant.* 52(2): 249–65.

Redman C. and P.J. Watson 1970 'Systematic intensive surface collection', *Am.Ant.* 35: 279–91.

Reitz, E.J. and E.S. Wing 1999 *Zooarchaeology* (CUP).

Renfrew, J. 1973 *Paleoethnobotany* (London and New York: Academic Press).

Retallack, Gregory J. 2001 *Soils of the Past. An introduction to Paleopedology* (2nd edn. Oxford: Blackwell).

Reynolds, Andrew 1999 *Later Anglo-Saxon England. Life and landscape* (Stroud: Tempus).

Rhoads, James W. 1992 'Significant sites and non-site archaeology: a case study from Southeast Australia', *World Archaeology* 24.2: 198–217.

Rice, P.M. 1987 *Pottery analysis: a sourcebook* (Chicago: University of Chicago Press).

Rich, C.J. 1816 *Memoir on the Ruins of Babylon* (2nd edn. London: Longman).

Richards, Julian D. 1997 'Preservation and re-use of digital data: the role of the Archaeology Data Service', *Antiquity* 71: 1057–59.

Richards, Julian D. 2006 'Archaeology, e-publication and the semantic web', *Antiquity* 80: 970–79.

Richards, Julian D. and N.S. Ryan 1985 *Data processing in archaeology* (CUP).

Rick, J.W. 1976 'Downslope movement and archaeological intra-site spatial analysis', *Am.Ant.* 41: 133–44.

Rink, W.J. and J. Bartoll 2005 'Dating the geometric Nasca lines in the Peruvian desert', *Antiquity* 79, 390–401.

Rippon, S. 2004 *Historic landscape analysis: deciphering the countryside* (York: Council for British Archaeologists).

Robertson, Elizabeth C., Jeffery D. Seibert, Deepika C. Fernandez, Marc U. Zender 2006 *Space and Spatial Analysis in Archaeology* (Mexico: University of New Mexico Press).

Robinson, M. 2001 'Insects as palaeoenvironmental indicators', in Brothwell and Pollard: 121–34.

Rogers, Alan and Trevor Rowley (eds) 1974 *Landscapes and Documents* (London: National Council of Social Service).

Rosen, A.M. 1986 *Cities of Clay: the Geoarchaeology of Tells* (Chicago: University of Chicago Press).

Roskams, S. (ed.) 2000 *Interpreting Stratigraphy. Site evaluation, recording procedures and stratigraphic analysis. Papers presented to the Interpreting Stratigraphy Conferences 1993–1997* (BAR Int 910).

Roskams, S. 2001 *Excavation* (Cambridge: Cambridge Manuals in Archaeology).

Rothschild, Nan, Barbara Mills, J.T. Ferguson, Susan Dublin, 1993 'Abandonment at Zuni farming villages', in Cameron and Tomkin 124–34.

Rowsome, Peter 2000 *Heart of the City. Roman, Medieval and Modern London revealed by Archaeology at No. 1 Poultry* (English Heritage/MOLAS).

Samson, Ross (ed.) 1990 *The Social Archaeology of Houses* (Edinburgh: Edinburgh University Press).

Schaafsma, C.F. 1989 'Significant until proven otherwise: problems versus representative samples', in Cleere: Chapter 3.

Schiffer, Michael B. 1976 *Behavioral Archaeology* (New York: Academic Press).

Schiffer, Michael B. 1987 *Formation Processes of the Archaeological Record* (Albuquerque: University of New Mexico Press).

Schliemann, H. 1880 *Ilios: the city and country of the Trojans* (London: J.M. Murray).

Schmidt, E. 1972 *Atlas of Animal Bones* (Elsevier Science Ltd).

Schneider, Alan L. 1996 *NAGPRA and Federal Land Management* (course handbook prepared by the author, 1437 SW Columbia, Suite 200, Portland OR. 97201 USA).

Schneider, J.E. 1993 Zürich in anon. (ed.) *Stadtluft, Hirsebrei und Bettelmönch. Die Stadt um 1300* (Landesdenkmalamt Baden-Württemberg und der Stadt Zürich): 69–92.

Scholfield, A.J. (ed.) 1991 *Interpreting artefact scatters: contributions to ploughzone archaeology* (Oxford: Oxbow).

Schuchardt, C. 1891 *Schliemann's Excavations at Troy* (London).

Schwein, Jean-Jacques 1992 *Strasbourg. Document d'évaluation du patrimoine archéologique urbain* (Tours: Centre National d'Archéologie Urbaine).

Seymour, Deni J. 2009 'Nineteenth-century Apache wickiups: historically documented models for the archaeological signatures of the dwellings of mobile people', *Antiquity* 83: 157–64.

Shaffer B.S., J.P. Dering, J. Labadie, T.B. Pearl and A.M. Huebner, 1997 'Bioturbation of submerged sites by the Asiatic clam: a case study from Armistad Reservoir, SW Texas', *JFA* 24.1: 135–8.

Sharer, Robert J. and Wendy Ashmore 1979 *Fundamentals of Archaeology* (London: Benjamin/Cummings).

Sheets, Payson D. (ed.) 2002 *Before the volcano erupted: the ancient Cerén village in Central America* (Austin: University of Texas Press).

Sherratt, A. 2004 'Spotting tells from space', *Antiquity* 78: ProjGall 301.

Shillito, Lisa-Marie, Wendy Matthews and Matthew Arnold 2008 'Investigating midden formation processes and cultural activities at Neolithic Çatalhöyük, Turkey', *Antiquity* 82: ProjGall 317.

Shopland, Norena 2006 *A Finds Manual. Excavating, processing and storing* (Stroud: Tempus).

Shott, M. 1985 'Shovel-test sampling as a site discovery technique: a case study from Michigan', *JFA* 12: 457–68.

Shott, M. 1987 'Feature discovery and the sampling requirements of archaeological evaluations', *JFA* 14: 359–71.

Shott, M. 1989 'Shovel-test sampling in archaeological survey: comments on Nance and Ball,and Lightfoot', *Am.Ant.* 54: 396–404

Shott, M. 1995 'Reliability of archaeological records on cultivated surfaces: a Michigan case study', *JFA* 22: 475–90.

Sindbaek, S.M. 2007 'Networks and nodal points: the emergence of towns in early Viking Age Scandinavia', *Antiquity* 81: 119–32.

Sjösvärd, Lars, Maria Vretemark and Helmer Gustavson 1983 'A Vendel warrior from Vallentuna', in J.P. Lamm and H.-Å. Nordström (eds) *Vendel Period Studies* (Stockholm: Statens Historiska Museum): 133–50.

Smith, Claire and H. Martin Wobst (eds) 2005 *Indigenous Archaeologies: decolonizing theory and practice* (Routledge: One World Archaeology 47).

Smith, Laurajane 2004 *Archaeological Theory and the Politics of Cultural Heritage* (London and New York: Routledge).

Smith, Laurajane 2006 *Uses of Heritage* (London: Routledge).

Snodgrass, Anthony 1990 'Survey archaeology and the rural landscape of the Greek City', in Oswyn Murray and Simon Price (eds) *The Greek City From Homer to Alexander* (Oxford: Clarendon): 113–36.

Steensberg, A. 1940 'Review of Hatt 1938', *Antiquity* 14: 218–21.

Stein, J.K. 1991 '"Coring", in *CRM* and archaeology: a reminder', *Am.Ant.* 56. 1: 1348–142.

Steinberg, John M. 1996 'Ploughzone sampling in Denmark: isolating and interpreting site signatures from disturbed contexts', *Antiquity* 70: 368–92.

Sternberg, R.S. 2001 'Magnetic properties and archaeomagnetism', in Brothwell and Pollard: 73–80.

Stevenson, Marc G. 1991 'Beyond the Formation of Hearth-Associated Artifact Assemblages', in Ellen M. Kroll and T. Douglas Price (eds) *The Interpretation of Archaeological Spatial Patterning* (New York: Plenum Press): 269–300.

Stjernquist, Berta 1993 *Gårdlösa 2, An Iron Age Community in its Natural and Social Setting* (Almqvist & Wiksell International, Stockholm).

Swallow, P., R. Dallas, S. Jackson and D. Watt 2004 *Measurement and recording of historic buildings* (2nd edn. Shaftesbury: Donhead).

Swan, Lorraine M. 2007 'Economic and ideological roles of copper ingots in prehistoric Zimbabwe', *Antiquity* 81: 999–1012.

Talon, Marc 1994 'Prospection et évaluation sur le tracé du TGV Nord et de l'interconnexion', Nouvelles d'Archéologie 58: 25–9.

Taylor, R.E. 2001 'Radiocarbon dating', in Brothwell and Pollard: 23–34.

Taylor, R.E. and M.J. Aitken 1997 *Chronometric dating in archaeology* (London and New York: Plenum Press).

Taylor, Christopher 1974 *Fieldwork in Medieval Archaeology* (London: Batsford).

Taylor, Christopher 1983 *The Archaeology of Gardens* (Aylesbury: Shire Archaeology).

Terranato, N. and A. Ammerman 1996 'Visibility and site recovery in the Cecina Valley Italy', *JFA* 23: 91–109.

Thomas, David Hurst 1998 *Archaeology* (3rd edn. Fort Worth: Harcourt Brace College Publishers).

Thompson, S.K. 1996 *Adaptive Sampling* (New York: John Wiley).

Thunell, R.C., E. Tappa, D.M. Anderson 1995 'Sediment fluxes and varve formation in Santa Barbara Basin, offshore California', *Geology* 23(12): 1083–6.

Tilley, Christopher 1994 *A Phenomenology of Landscape* (Oxford: Berg).

Trigger, Bruce 1978 *Time and Traditions. Essays in Archaeological Interpretation* (Edinburgh: Edinburgh University Press).

Trigger, Bruce 2007 *A History of Archaeological Thought* (2nd edn. CUP).

Turner, Sam 2006 *Making a Christian Landscape* (Exeter: University of Exeter Press).

Tylecote, R.F. 1986 *The Prehistory of Metallurgy in the British Isles* (London: Institute of Metals).

Ullén, I., A.G. Nord, M. Fjaestad, E. Mattsson, G. Ch. Borg and K. Tronner 2004 'The degradation of archaeological bronzes underground: the evidence of museum collections', *Antiquity* 78: 380–90.

Underhill, A.P., G.M. Feinman, L. Nicholas, G. Bennett, Fengshu Cai, Haiguang Yu, Fengshi Luan and Hui Fang 2002 'Regional survey and the development of complex societies in south-eastern Shandong, China', *Antiquity* 76: 745–55.

University College Dublin 2006 *Archaeology 2020: Repositioning Irish Archaeology in the Knowledge Society. A realistically achievable perspective* (University College Dublin and The Heritage Council; www.ucd.ie/archaeology).

Ur, Jason 2003 'CORONA satellite photography and ancient roads networks: a northern Mesopotamian case study', *Antiquity* 77: 102–15.

US Army Corps of Engineers 1996 *Safety and Health Requirements Manual*. EM. 385-1-1 (US Government Printing Office, Washington DC).

US Department of the Interior, National Park Service 1999 *How to Prepare National Historic Landmark Nominations*.

Vita-Finzi, C. 1978 *Archaeological Sites in their Setting* (London and New York: Thames and Hudson).

Volpe, Giuliano (ed.) 1998 *San Giusto La villa, le ecclesiae. Primi resultati dagli scavi nel sito rurale San Giusto (Lucera) 1995–1997* (Bari: Edipuglia).

Walker, K. 1990 *Guidelines for the preparation of excavation archives for long-term storage* (London: UKIC. Archaeology Section).

Warren, John 1999 *Conservation of earth structures* (Oxford: Butterworth-Heinemann).

Watkinson, David, and Virginia Neal 1998 *First Aid for Finds* (3rd edn. London: UK Institute for Conservation).

Watt, D. and P. Swallow 1996 *Surveying Historic Buildings* (Shaftesbury: Donhead Publishing).

Weaver, M. 1997 *Conserving buildings: manual of techniques and material* (Chichester: Wiley).

Wessex Archaeology 2004 *Lydiard Park, Swindon. Report on the Archaeological Investigations* (Client Report 55380.02).

Weymouth, J. 1995 *Geophysical evaluation of two Hopewell sites in Ross County, Ohio* (Midwest Archaeological Center, NPS, Lincoln NE).

Weymouth, J. 1986 'Geophysical methods of archaeological site surveying' *Advances in Archaeological Method and Theory* 9: 311–95.

Wheeler, A. and A. Jones 1989 *Fishes* (CUP).

Wheeler, R.E.M. 1954 *Archaeology from the Earth* (Oxford: Clarendon Press).

Whitbread, I.K. 2001 'Ceramic petrology, clay geochemistry and ceramic production – from technology to the mind of the potter', in Brothwell and Pollard: 449–60.

Whitmer, Ann, Ann Ramenofsky, Jacob Thomas, Louis Thibodeaux, Stephen Field and Bob Miller 1989 'Stability or instability. The role of diffusion in trace element studies', *Archaeological Method and Theory* 1: 205–73.

Wilkinson, K., A. Tyler, D. Davidson and I. Grieve 2006 'Quantifying the threat to archaeological sites from the erosion of cultivated soil', *Antiquity* 80: 658–70.

Wilkinson, T.J. 2001 'Surface collection techniques in field archaeology: theory and practice', in Brothwell and Pollard: 529–42.

Willems, W.J.H. 2001 'Archaeological heritage management and research', in Kobyliñski: 83–91.

Willems, W.J.H. and R.W. Brandt 2004 *Dutch Archaeology Quality Standard* (Den Haag: Rijksinpectie voor de Archeologie).

Willey, G.R. (ed.) 1953 *Prehistoric Settlement Patterns in the Virú Valley, Peru* (Bureau of American Ethnology Bulletin 155; Washington DC: Smithsonian Institute).

Willey, Gordon R. 1999 'The Virú Valley Projects and Settlement Archaeology: Some Reminiscences and Contemporary Comments', in Billman and Feinman: 9–11.

Willey, G.R. and J.A. Sabloff 1974 *A History of American Archaeology* (London: Thames and Hudson).

Williams, D. 1990 'The study of ancient ceramics: the contribution of the petrographic method', in Mannoni and Molinari: 43–64.

Wilson, D.R. 1982 *Air Photo Interpretation for Archaeologists* (London: Batsford).

Wood, Jason (ed.) 1994 *Buildings Archaeology. Applications in practice* (Oxford: Oxbow).

Wood, W. Raymond and Donald Lee Johnson 1982 'A survey of disturbance processes in archaeological site formation', in Schiffer: 539–607.

Woodward, Ann and Peter Leach 1993 *The Uley Shrines: Excavation of a ritual complex on West Hill, Uley 1977–79* (London: English Heritage).

Yorston R., V.L. Gaffney and P.R. Reynolds 1990 'Simulation of artifact movement due to cultivation', *J.Arch.Sci.* 17: 67–83.

Yvorra, P. 2003 'The management of space in a Palaeolithic rock shelter: defining activity areas by spatial analysis', *Antiquity* 77: 336–44.

INDEX

recovery levels, **CP 4B, 5A**, 55, 124–38, **125**, 217; Level A, **124**; Level B, **127**; Level C, **128**; Level D, 128, **130**; Level E, 131–4, 248; Level F, 134–8

Redman, Charles, 119

re-enactment, **328**

refitting, 247, **248**

reflexive approach, 27, 31–2, 34, 312

register of significant sites (USA), 340

remote mapping, **43**, 90, 106, 171, 176, 344, 383; underwater, 191

remote sensing, 111, 383

rescue archaeology (*see also* commercial, compliance, Section 106, mitigation), 27, 33, 113–48, 159–60, 171–3, 319, 335–61

research: agenda, 43, 340–1, **342**, 384; cycle, 368–70; design, 335–61; 384; dividend, 319, 341, 355, 372, 384; excavation, 113–48; framework, **46**, 384; landscape survey, 78–85; objectives, 384; programme, 34, 352, 384; reports, 319–25; strategy, 384; site survey, 106–9

residual objects, 274–5, 288, 291

residues in pots, 218, 237

resource, archaeological, the, 160, 175, 225, 312, 318, 335–40, 355, 358, 363, definition, 384

resource model, 111, 343–52; *see also* deposit model; 384

resource management programme, 352, 359–75; *see also* conservation, CRM

Retallack, Gregory, 65

Rickeby, Sweden, 248, **249**

ROV (Remote Operating Vehicle), 191

RPA (Register of Professional Archaeologists, USA), 374

St. Agnes, Cornwall, England, **77**

San Giusto, Puglia, Italy, **CP 7**, 171, **172**, 173

Samarra, Iraq, **70**

sampling, definition of terms as used in archaeology, 384

sampling (areas); adaptive, 75; in excavation areas, 117–19, **120**, 148, 155; in survey, 28–9, 74, **76;** random,

29, 32, 74, 119, **120;** a shell mound, 155; systematic, 74, **76;** templates, 76

sampling (assemblages): **CP 10**, 217, 221–2; types of sample taken on site, 135, **223**; grab, 221; monolith, **CP 10**

sandbags, 147, 148, 180

satellite survey, 72, **73**

Schaffhausen, Switzerland, **CP 11a**

Schliemann, H., 26

scope of work, 384

screening, *see* sieving

section (excavation record) **CP 1b**, 30, 117, 123, 130–1, **143–4**, **156**, 158, **211**; running section, 133; definition of, 384

section 106 archaeology (US), 384

Seiler, Michael, 109

Selinunte, Sicily, temples at **3**

Selling, Dagmar, 135

sensitivity template, 345, **346**

sequence diagrams, for strata, 208, **212**, 275–95; rectified, 288; for buildings, **179, 279**; for structures, **CP 12, 294**; definition, 384; *and see* seriation

seriation, of artefacts, 201, 203, 267, 268, 280; of assemblages, 280–1, 287–92; 384

services, underground, 90, 347

scheduled monuments (UK), 366

Schiffer, Michael, 7–8, 119

Schnitt method, 117, **118**, 121, 158

Shapwick, England, 106

Sha'ar Hagolan, Israel, **144**

Sheets, Payson, 98

sherd-yard, 167

SHIPPO (State Historic Preservation Office, USA), 385, 364

shovels, types of, 127

shovel-scraping, 385

shovel-testing, 69, 385

Shrewsbury, England, 176, **177, 178**

sieving, 138, 153, 163, 169, 188, 217, 220–1, **222**, 223, 231

'signatures' of materials, 15

significance, 340

silicon rubber moulding, 135

Syria, satellite survey in, **73**
system, archaeology as, 28
systemic context 8
Szymanski, John, 98

tableau (in burials), 173–4, 238
TAQ (terminus ante quem), 272–5
Tarbat, Scotland, 202; *see also*
    Portmahomack
team, *see* workforce
Tel el-Amarna, Egypt, **93**
tells, *see* sites
Tell Brak, Syria, **73**, 165, **166**, 167
template (in design), 386
tephrachronology, 271
Teotihuacan, Mexico, 252, **254**
terps, *see* sites
terrain, 3–24, 31–2, 35, 59, 69, 74–5, 82,
    91, 97, 103, 105, 117, 119–21, 129,
    147–9, 151–93, 344; definition of the
    term, 386
test-trenches, **159**, 160, 189–90, **344**
test-pits, 100, 101, **102**, 105, 111, 119,
    153, 155, 163, 344, **345**, 347, 386; *see
    also* sampling
textiles, 185, 219
Thiessen polygons, **260**
Throckmorton, Peter, 188
timeline, 300, **301**
time slices, 98
Tipasa, Algeria, **327**
Tipping, Richard, 105
TL (thermoluminescence), 267, 270–2
topographic survey, **68**, **91**
total excavation, 27, 49, 167
tower, use of, *see* hi-view
Towton, battle of, 108
TPQ (terminus post quem), 272–5
TST (total station theodolite), 64, 67, 91,
    129
trace archaeology, **21**, 94, 132, 135, 164,
    169, 240–1; *see* horizons,
microassemblage, microstratigraphy
transect, 28, 49, 50, 63–4, 74, 80, 82, 105,
    167, 386
transforms (formation processes), 8
treasure hunting, 47

tree-pits, 52
trend mapping, 260
Troodos mountains, Cyprus, 82, 84
trowels, types of, 128
Troy, 26
TV, field archaeology on, 51, 57, 245,
    315–16, 325–6, 330, 377

Uist, Scotland, 100
Uley, England, 252, **253, 300**
underwater, archaeology, 184–91
universities, as archaeological practitioners,
    368–70
Ur, Iraq, 261, **264**
uranium series dating, 270–2
urban archaeology, *see* sites, urban
US Army Corps of Engineers, 363–4

Valletta Convention, 365
value, as guiding principle, value-led
    archaeological investigation, 33–6, 39,
    59, 75–6, 82, 84–6, 152, 174, 294, 299,
    319, 324, 335–41, 343, 352, 355, 359,
    362–3, 365, 375, **339**; human, 362;
    see also evaluation
varves, 271
vegetation mapping, 42, 93, **95**
viewshed analysis, 386
Viking ship, experimental, **307**
Virú valley, Peru, **79**
visitors, to excavations, **51–3**, 57, 115,
    146, 315, 318, 325–30, **358**
vista analysis, 386
volcano, sites buried by, 4

Wade, Keith, 82
wall foundation, **21**
Wasperton, England, 283–7
water, use of on site, for spraying, 54, 55,
    129, 141, 147, 158
water curtain, 186–7
Watson, Patty Jo, 155
Webb, William, 363
well, **21, 144**
Wessex Archaeology, 109
West Stow, England, **328**
wetland archaeology, 184–91